Kingfisher Illustrated Encyclopedia of Animals

Kingfisher Books, Grisewood & Dempsey Ltd.
Elsley House, 24–30 Great Titchfield Street
London W1P 7AD

This revised edition published in 1992 by Kingfisher
Books.
Originally published in 1984 as the Dictionary of
Animals by Kingfisher Books.
Text © Grisewood & Dempsey Ltd., 1984, 1992
Illustrations © Grisewood & Dempsey Ltd., 1984, 1992

BRITISH LIBRARY CATALOGUING IN PUBLICATION DATA
A catalogue record for this book is available from the
British Library.

ISBN 0 86272 826 6

Phototypeset by Southern Positives and Negatives
(SPAN), Lingfield, Surrey.
Printed in Italy.

Kingfisher
Illustrated
Encyclopedia
of Animals

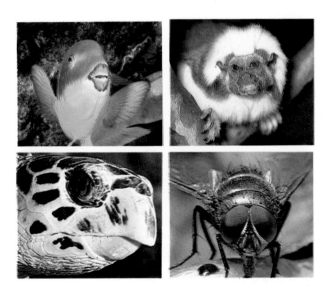

Consultant Editor: Michael Chinery

Kingfisher Books

INTRODUCTION

More than a million kinds of animal have been discovered on the Earth so far, and many more will undoubtedly be discovered as people continue to explore the forests and seas and the many other habitats on our planet.

The animals form one of the two great kingdoms of the living world; the other is the plants. Because of the immense variety of animal life – ranging from minute protozoans visible only through a microscope to the huge blue whale, 30 metres long and over 100 tonnes in weight – it is not easy to define an animal. But there are a number of features which, taken together, separate most animals from most plants.

The biggest difference is in the method of feeding, or obtaining energy. Unlike green plants, animals cannot make their own food, and they have to take in ready-made food in the form of other animal or plant matter. Such food has to be found, and most animals are therefore able to move about freely. They also have nervous systems to control their movements, and sense organs to help them to find suitable food.

Taken together, these features readily distinguish all the larger animals from the plants, but there are still a number of microscopic organisms which defy a firm classification. These include free-swimming creatures with sensitive eye-spots, which sometimes feed like plants – by taking in water and carbon dioxide and combining them to form sugars – and sometimes take in food like animals. Zoologists claim these creatures as animals, botanists treat them as algae, while a few biologists actually put them into a separate kingdom known as the Protista. However we classify these "difficult" organisms, we can be fairly sure that it was through creatures like this that both the animal and plant kingdoms arose some 2000 million years ago.

Classifying Animals

Zoologists have divided the animal kingdom into about 30 major groups called *phyla*. The members of each phylum share the same basic structure and organization, although they may look very different. Fishes, birds, and humans, for example, all belong to one phylum – the Chordata – because all have backbones, but their external appearances are totally different.

The phyla are divided up into a number of *classes*, whose members have much more in common. All the birds, for example, are warm-blooded, feathered, egg-laying creatures and all are placed in the class Aves.

Classes are divided into *orders*, and the members of an order have even more in common with each other. The Falconiformes, for example, contains the hawks and eagles and their relatives – all day-flying birds of prey with sharp talons and hooked beaks.

Within each order, there are usually a number of *families*, each of which contains very closely related kinds of animals. In the animal kingdom, a family name always ends in -idae.

Within each family, there are one or more *genera* (singular: genus), whose members are even more closely related and often very similar. For example, the buzzard and the rough-legged buzzard are much alike, and both are members of the genus *Buteo*. Each distinct kind, or species of animal has a scientific name made up of the name of its genus and a specific name. For example, the rough-legged buzzard is known as *Buteo lagopus*, while the buzzard is *Buteo buteo*. These scientific names, which are usually printed in italics, are understood by zoologists all over the world.

The members of each animal species contain the "blueprint" for that species in the cells of their bodies and, because they usually mate only with their own kind, they automatically produce more of the same kind when they breed. Animals are not normally attracted to other species for mating because they don't give the right signals, and mating between different species is often physically impossible even if they meet. Closely related species do occasionally mate in captivity, however, and the offspring of such pairings are called hybrids. The best-known example is the mule, resulting from the mating of a male ass or donkey and a female horse. Hybrids are generally sterile, however, and cannot produce further offspring, and so the species do not become mixed up.

With or Without Backbones

One commonly used method of splitting up the animal kingdom is to divide it into animals with backbones (vertebrates) and animals without backbones (invertebrates). This is quite a useful division, especially for study and teaching purposes, but it is a very unequal division. There are invertebrate animals in all the phyla, but the vertebrates belong to just one part of one phylum – the Chordata. The vertebrates include the largest animals and most of the familiar ones, such as cats, dogs, horses, cows and birds. They also include all the fishes, amphibians and reptiles. The invertebrates include the worms, slugs, snails, insects, spiders and many others. But it must not be thought that all the vertebrates are large and all the invertebrates small. The largest invertebrates – the giant squids of the genus *Architeuthis* – have bodies that are about 5 metres long, with tentacles three times this length. They weigh up to 2 tonnes. Compare these figures with those for the smallest vertebrate: the dwarf goby. This minute fish from the Philippines is 13 mm long. The smallest mammal, which is the Etruscan shrew, has a body that is only 5 cm long. It is a good deal smaller than many insects.

The **arrow-poison frog** secretes a powerful poison from its skin.

A

The **aardvark** escapes from its enemies by burrowing at lightning speed with its formidable digging claws.

Aardvark

The aardvark gets its name from the Afrikaans word meaning "earth pig". It is an African burrowing mammal with a stumpy, thick-set body, a large snout, donkey-like ears and a tough grey skin sparsely covered with coarse hair. The animal stands about 60 cm high at the shoulder, and its tail, which tapers at the end, is about 60 cm long. The feet have very strong digging claws – four on the front feet and five on the hind.

The aardvark is nocturnal and a TERMITE eater. With its powerful claws it can rip through the walls of termite nests that are difficult for a man to break down with a pick. Having made a hole in the nest, the animal inserts its long slender tongue and laps the insects up.

The mouth contains 26 teeth, which are unusual in having no enamel and no roots, and they continue to grow throughout the animal's life.

ORDER: Tubulidentata;
FAMILY: Orycteropidae;
SPECIES: *Orycteropus afer.*

Aardwolf

The aardwolf is a member of the HYENA family, but has larger ears and weaker jaws than true hyenas. Its name is Afrikaans for "earth wolf". The aardwolf ranges through southern and eastern Africa, living mainly in sandy plains or bushy country. It spends the day in rock crevices, or in a sleeping chamber at the end of a long burrow.

Aardwolves feed at night on insects which they sweep up with a long, tacky tongue. One aardwolf stomach was found to contain 40,000 termites. When insects are in short supply, mice, small birds and eggs are eaten.

Aardwolves breed once a year. Each litter contains two to four young, born blind. The animal's enemies are PYTHONS, LIONS and LEOPARDS. It defends itself by emitting a stinking fluid from the anal glands.

ORDER: Carnivora;
FAMILY: Hyaenidae;
SPECIES: *Proteles cristatus.*

Abalone

Abalones are sea snails related to the LIMPETS. They live in many coastal areas, especially in warmer regions. The body is little more than a muscular foot with a head at one end. The head carries a pair of eyes and sensory tentacles, and a frill of tentacles surrounds the body. Water is drawn in beneath the shell and the oxygen is extracted as it passes over the gills. The water is then expelled through a line of holes which run across the top of the shell.

Abalones avoid the light and come out at night to find food. They are vegetarians, crawling over rock faces and browsing on seaweeds. An abalone scrapes up its food with its *radula*, a tongue made up of large numbers of small horny teeth.

ORDER: Archaeogastropoda;
FAMILY: Haliotidae;
GENUS: *Haliotis.*

Accentor

Accentors are small, sparrow-like birds found throughout Europe and Asia. Unlike SPARROWS, they have slender, finely pointed bills

and they are, in fact, more closely related to THRUSHES or WARBLERS. The two species found in Europe are the dunnock, or hedge-sparrow, and the alpine accentor, which is found from Spain to Japan. The latter is a larger, more brightly coloured bird than the sombre grey and brown dunnock, and has a whitish bib spotted with black.

Accentors usually live in mountainous regions, often well above the tree line. The alpine accentor is no exception, one race breeding at altitudes of up to 5486 metres. Most accentors breed at lower levels, however, in scrub-type vegetation. The dunnock is particularly common in woods, hedgerows and gardens. In summer, accentors feed on insects; in winter, they live almost entirely on seeds and berries.

ORDER: Passeriformes;
FAMILY: Prunellidae;
GENUS: *Prunella*.

Acorn Worm

There are about 70 species of acorn worms, ranging from about 50 to 190 cm in length. The body has three main parts, the front one of which is acorn-shaped and known as the *proboscis*. A short, fleshy collar lies just behind the proboscis, and the rest of the body is known as the trunk.

Acorn worms live on the sea bed, from the shore line down to depths of 3050 metres. Each

Left: The **Alpine accentor** lives on rocky mountain slopes. Above: the **dunnock** resembles a house sparrow except for its slender beak.

animal normally digs itself a U-shaped burrow and lives there with the proboscis sticking out of one opening. Water and debris is drawn in through the mouth, which is at the junction of the proboscis and the collar. The water then flows out through the gill slits, but food particles are passed further down the digestive tract. The sexes are separate. Eggs and sperm are merely shed into the water and fertilisation occurs by chance. Most eggs are very small and they produce small *larvae* which swim freely in the plankton for a short while before settling on the sea bed.

PHYLUM: Hemichordata;
CLASS: Enteropneusta.

Addax

The addax, also known as the screwhorn antelope, is closely related to the ORYX. The addax's graceful, spiralling horns were prized by hunters. At one time the addax was common across the Sahara, but hunting and the

The **addax** is a large antelope with a rather cattle-like appearance.

destruction of its habitat have made it rare. Now, probably only about 6000 live in the wild, but some have recently been bred in zoos. One young is born at a time, usually in winter or early spring. Adult males reach 102 cm at the shoulder and weigh around 113 kg. In winter, the body is greyish-brown, but it turns sandy or almost white in summer. The short, splayed hooves are adapted to journeys over desert sands. The addax can go for long periods without drinking water; it gets water from the plants it eats and from dew.

ORDER: Artiodactyla;
FAMILY: Bovidae;
SPECIES: *Addax nasomaculatus*.

Adder

The adder belongs to the viper family. It has a rather short, fat body and a short tail. The record length is 81 cm. Its colour is generally a shade of brown, olive, grey or cream with a dark zig-zag line running down its back. The females can often be distinguished from the males because their colour is more reddish with darker red or brown markings.

Adders live in most of Europe and across Asia, and are the only snakes that live north of the Arctic Circle. They often bask in the sunshine on moors or hedgebanks and also live in marshy fields. They feed on LIZARDS, MICE, VOLES and SHREWS. The young are born in August or September, and during the winter they *hibernate*. In northern Europe, hibernation lasts up to 275 days: in the south the winter sleep may take up as little as 105 days. Adder bites are poisonous to small animals but seldom fatal to human beings.
ORDER: Squamata;
FAMILY: Viperidae;
SPECIES: *Vipera berus*.

The **adder**, or common viper of Europe, is easily recognized by its diamond-patterned back.

Aestivation

Shortage of water during hot, dry seasons causes some animals to hide away and go to sleep. This "summer sleep" is called aestivation. Desert animals, including frogs and toads and some small rodents, avoid the heat and drought this way. So, too, do some reptiles. The African LUNG-FISH burrows in the mud on the bed of its dried up river and waits until the water starts to flow again.

The **agouti**, a South American rodent, looks rat-like, but it is more closely related to the guinea pig.

Agouti

Agoutis are rodents that look rather like long-legged GUINEA PIGS. Several species are found in Central and South America. They are mainly vegetarian, and like many other rodents, hoard food in small stores buried near landmarks. The agouti has many enemies. Although it makes its home in a shallow burrow, it prefers to escape by running away, often heading for the nearest river as it is a good swimmer. The agouti's slender build gives it great agility, and it can leap about 6 metres from a standing start. The agouti has become well adapted for running with its long legs and hoof-like claws.
ORDER: Rodentia;
FAMILY: Dasyproctidae;
GENUS: *Dasyprocta*.

Albatross

Albatrosses are large seabirds related to petrels. They have powerful hooked bills, stout bodies and long slender wings. The plumage of these birds is white with black parts or, in some species, brown. Albatrosses spend most of the time at sea, coming inland only to breed. They are expert gliders and can remain airborne for long periods. There are 13 species, 9 of which are only found in the southern hemi-sphere. They breed mainly in the Antarctic and oceanic islands. Another three species are found in the North Pacific, while the waved albatross breeds on the Galapagos Islands. The largest and best known is the wandering albatross. It has a wing span of over 3.7 metres.

All species of albatross feed on marine life from the sea's surface, such as fish, squid and crustaceans. They may live for 70 years. They do not breed until they are at least seven years old. Breeding grounds are usually on cliff tops, where the birds can take off easily. The albatross became well known through Coleridge's "Rhyme of the Ancient Mariner" as the bird of ill omen.
ORDER: Procellariiformes;
FAMILY: Diomedeidae;
GENUS: *Diomedea*.

An **albatross** in flight. The bird spends most of its life soaring effortlessly over the vast oceans.

Alderfly

There are many species of alderflies. They are compact, dark-bodied and dark-winged relatives of the LACEWINGS. They fly poorly and are rarely found far from the still or slow moving water in which they spend their early lives. The *larvae* live in mud and silt and feed on other small animals. They have a feathery appearance, due to numerous external gills on the abdomen. They spend about a year in the water, and then pupate in debris at the water's edge. The adults may take nectar from flowers, but are most often seen just sitting on waterside plants. The females lay large clusters of eggs on leaves which hang over the water.

ORDER: Neuroptera;
FAMILY: Sialidae.

The **alderfly** is a poor flier.

Alewife

The alewife is a food fish of North America. It spawns in lakes and rivers from the St Lawrence Seaway southwards. As an ocean fish it is about 30 cm long when fully grown. In appearance, the alewife resembles its relatives the HERRING and the SHAD. When good catches are made, large quantities of the fish may be ground up to make fertilizer.

ORDER: Clupeiformes;
FAMILY: Clupeidae;
SPECIES: *Pomobolus pseudoharengus*.

Alligator

Alligators are large scaly reptiles that live on the banks of rivers and in the water. There are two species: the American alligator and the Chinese alligator. The American alligator is the larger of the two, the record length being 5.84 metres. American alligators live in the south-eastern United States. Chinese alligators are found only in the Yangtze River basin. Alligators eat fish, small mammals and birds. Each adult female lays 15 to 80 eggs in a nest mound she has made from mud and rotting vegetation. The heat produced by this decaying process helps to hatch the eggs two to three months later. Meanwhile the female stays close by. Then she removes the vegetation to help her hatchlings out.

Alligators are similar to CROCODILES. The main difference between the crocodiles and alligators

The **American alligator** can be as large and as dangerous as a crocodile.

is in the teeth. When an alligator's mouth is shut, the upper teeth lie outside the lower teeth with its fourth lower tooth hidden in a pit in the upper jaw. With crocodiles, the teeth in the upper and lower jaws are in line and the fourth lower tooth is visible when the jaws are closed. An alligator also has a broader, shorter head and a blunter snout than a crocodile.

ORDER: Crocodilia;
FAMILY: Alligatoridae;
SPECIES: American: *Alligator mississippiensis*; Chinese: *Alligator sinensis*.

Alpaca

The alpaca lives in the mountains of Peru, Bolivia and Chile at altitudes between 2400 and 3600 metres above sea-level. It is closely related to the LLAMA, which it resembles, but is smaller, being less than 122 cm at the shoulder.

The alpaca's fleece, which may be black, white or brown, grows between 20 and 41 cm long. It is finer and straighter than that of any other animal and alpacas are reared for this fine wool.

ORDER: Artiodactyla;
FAMILY: Camelidae;
SPECIES: *Lama pacos*.

Amoeba

The amoebae are minute single-cell animals. The majority of species are less than 0.5 mm across, although some reach 3 mm in diameter. The animals have no fixed shape and they continually push out "arms" in various directions. The protoplasm which makes up the bulk of the cell flows into one of the "arms". The whole animal thus moves forward.

Most species live in water, but some occur in damp soil and some live as parasites inside other animals. The typical amoeba feeds by engulfing other small organisms with its arms and digesting them. Amoebae normally reproduce simply by splitting into two halves, but when the water be-

comes cold or begins to dry up an amoeba can form a tough wall around itself and go into a dormant state. When favourable conditions return, the wall breaks down and out come not one but scores of tiny amoebae to repopulate the pond.

PHYLUM: Protozoa;
CLASS: Sarcodina.

Amphibians

The Class Amphibia is represented by about 2500 species of *carnivorous* animals arranged in three distinct groups. These are the frogs and toads, the newts and salamanders, and the caecilians.

The amphibians evolved from some kind of lobe-finned fish about 400 million years ago, and today's amphibians are very different from the ancestral forms. They have not really broken away from the water, however, for they lack waterproof skins and they can survive only in moist conditions. Most of them have to return to the water to breed. But some species spend all their lives in the water, and some have become fully land-living by giving birth to miniature adults instead of laying eggs in the water.

Amphipod

The name given to more than 4500 species of small crustaceans ranging in size from more than 25 mm to less than 1 mm in length. Their bodies are compressed from side to side, and the backs are curved in an arc when at rest. They have many pairs of legs. Those on the front part of the body are used for walking and those on the rear part for swimming. Most amphipods live in the sea, but some are found in fresh water or on land. They are scavengers, feeding on any kind of

The **alpaca's** handsome brown coat keeps it warm in the cold air of the Andes Mountains.

Left: An **amphipod** – the freshwater shrimp Gammarus, enlarged 5 times.

dead plant or animal matter. The so-called freshwater shrimp and a number of sea species belong to the genus *Gammarus*. The males are often seen carrying the females under their bodies.
ORDER: Amphipoda.

Amphisbaena

Amphisbaenids, or worm lizards, are a strange family of reptiles which spend most of their lives underground, coming to the surface only at night or after heavy rain. Their bodies are well adapted for burrowing, most species having lost all trace of limbs, and their eyes are small. Their bodies are covered with scales arranged in rings, so at first glance they look like earthworms. The head and tail are often blunt and hard to tell apart. This helped to give the animals their name, which means "coming both ways". People used to think that each end of an amphisbaena had a head. Amphisbaenids live mainly in tropical lands, and feed on ANTS and other insects.
ORDER: Squamata;
FAMILY: Amphisbaenidae.

The **anaconda** is one of the world's largest and heaviest snakes. It can swallow whole animals over a metre long.

Anaconda

This name usually describes the water boa, one of the world's largest snakes. It lives in much of tropical South America east of the Andes. It is said to grow longer than 9 metres, and only the reticulated PYTHON rivals it for size.

Anacondas are olive green with large, round, black spots along the body. They seldom wander far from water, by day resting in pools or sluggish streams, or sunbathing on low branches over water. There they lie in wait for DEER, PECCARIES, fish and other animals. Anacondas kill either by drowning their prey or by constricting it with their long coils until the victim suffocates.

Like other boas, anacondas give birth to live young instead of laying eggs. One female will produce 20 to 40, even as many as 100, young at a time. Each young is up to a metre long.
ORDER: Squamata;
FAMILY: Boidae;
SPECIES: *Eunectes murinus*.

The **anchovy** feeds on surface plankton.

Anchovy

The name given to about 100 species of small food fishes related to the HERRING. These live in vast shoals in tropical and temperate seas and are also common in bays and estuaries. Besides being an important source of human food, anchovies are a favourite prey of the great TUNAS and of seabirds. Their maximum size is about 20 cm.
ORDER: Clupeiformes;
FAMILY: Clupeidae.

Angelfish

Freshwater fishes, common in tropical aquaria. Marine angelfishes are very similar, narrow-bodied bony fishes having equally

Angelfish

Angelfish are favourites in the aquarium. The angel fish above is the original natural silver fish. The black and gold fish is a small Pacific variety. The imperial fish can be 40 cm long.

Black and gold angelfish

Imperial angelfish

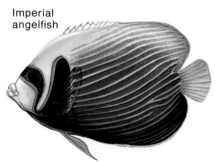

brilliant colours. Both types get the name angelfish from their delicate bodies and winglike or flaplike *pectoral fins*. Angelfishes can be observed in aquaria displaying their colours, advertising their territorial rights and telling other members of their species to keep away.

Angelfishes range in length from 5 to 60 cm. They feed on small water animals, picking these up

with a small mouth which contains many crushing teeth. Some have slender snouts for winkling out prey from crevices.
ORDER: Perciformes;
FAMILIES: Chaetodontidae and Pomocanthidae (marine); Cichlidae (freshwater).

Anglerfish

Anyone of 350 or more species of strange-looking fishes, all of which catch their prey by angling with a rod and line. This rod is really an extension of a spine or ray of the *dorsal fin*. The squat, ugly bodies of anglerfishes are explained by their sedentary way of life. Because they remain quite still, ang-

ling, for most of the time, they have no need for the streamlining which goes with fast swimming.

Anglerfishes fall into two groups. One group is drab in colour and the bodies of the anglers are often covered with flaps of skin, very like the seaweed in which the fishes are to be found. The other group, the deep-sea anglers, are generally black in colour, which conceals their bodies in the dark mid-deeps in which they live. However, their fishing line is often luminous, to attract unwary prey.

The **angwantibo** was unknown to Europeans until 1860, when it was discovered in the Cameroons.

In four species of these fishes the much smaller male fish attaches himself to the female's body with his jaws and his body eventually fuses with hers to share the same blood system. This attachment of the male ensures fertilization of the female anglerfish, who might otherwise have to wait a very long time, in the inky vastness, before meeting another male.
ORDER: Lophiiformes;

Angwantibo

The angwantibo is a rare animal which looks like a cross between a kitten and a BUSHBABY. The name probably comes from a West African word, "angwan", which means cat. One sub-species has soft, thick fur which is yellowish-brown or fawn with whitish under-parts. The other sub-species is generally golden-red, with greyish under-parts. The angwantibo lives in Africa, between the lower Niger and Zaire rivers. This agile animal lives in tall trees. It is active at night and little is known of its habits.
ORDER: Primates;
FAMILY: Lorisidae;
SPECIES: *Arctocebus calabarensis.*

Ani

The ani are a sub-family of the cuckoos, though they do not lay their eggs in the nests of other birds as many cuckoos do. Anis are about 38 cm long, and range from the southern borders of the United States to Argentina. They live in flocks and often follow other animals to feed on the insects driven out by their approach. Each flock numbers from 7 to 15 birds, often mostly males. The flock occupies a territory that it defends against neighbouring flocks of anis. The territory contains separate areas for roosting and nesting, and for feeding.
ORDER: Cuculiformes;
FAMILY: Cuculidae;
SPECIES: *Crotophaga.*

Animal Language

Animals use sounds and gestures to communicate, just as people do. But they also use the sense of touch and the sense of smell, senses that are developed only partly in man. Animal language is limited in what it can convey. The principal messages concern danger, the location of food, the ownership of territory and the urge to mate. Other signals help to keep families and groups together.

Bird song is one of the most familiar sounds in the animal world. A bird's song in the spring may convey either or both of two messages – "This is my territory, keep off" or "I want a mate". Birds that flock together, such as rooks or starlings, often "chatter" in a companionable way. Birds have certain calls that they use for keeping in touch. For example, mother birds and their young call to each other. Such call sounds are apparently instinctive. So are many of the warning notes such as the alarm call of the blackbird. But birds learn some songs only by imitating their parents.

Mammals use sound a great deal, too. A domestic cat purrs to show that it is pleased and snarls and spits when it is afraid or angry. Cats have learned to miaow when they want to be let out or be fed. Here, cats are using language to communicate with humans. This use of language between different species is unusual. In the wild, wolves howl to signal to each other. There is also a pack howl which is a kind of get-together signal. During a pack howl the wolves wag their tails and appear friendly and excited towards one another. When hunting they communicate with short sharp barks.

Fish also communicate by sounds. The grunting noises made by catfish apparently serve as call signals to keep a shoal together in darkness. Other fish appear to make sounds that help them to find mates. Mammals that live in the sea, such as whales and dolphins (which are among the most intelligent animals), also make a variety of noises. Scientists do not yet know exactly what these signals convey.

Gestures and action play a great part in the language of animals. Male fiddler crabs wave their giant claws to attract females in a gesture that is just like our beckoning. Rabbits signal the approach of danger by thumping on the ground with their long hind legs. Ants communicate by touching their antennae.

Possibly the most elaborate system of communication by gestures is that made by honeybees. A worker bee that has found a source of nectar or pollen performs a kind of dance in front of her fellow workers to let them know where the source is. If it is near the hive she does a round dance; if it is farther away she performs a figure of eight, wagging her tail. The speed of the dance conveys very accurately the distance of the food. The direction of part of the dance indicates the direction from the hive.

Animals use scent for communicating much more than people do. A dog, for example, leaves it own scent on trees and other objects in order to mark out its territory. Fish and other animals release some chemical substances when they are hurt or frightened. Other animals of the same species scent danger and keep away. Fish such as minnows that are hunted by pike can smell their enemies at a distance. In the insect world smells are very important. Ants leave a chemical trail behind them which other ants can follow. Scent also plays a great part in courtship. Male and female fish are guided to each other by it, and tests have shown that the scent of a female moth will lure males from considerable distances.

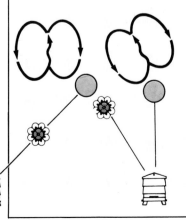

When a bee finds nectar, it dances to tell the other bees where the nectar is. The direction of the dance shows where the source is in relation to the sun.

The greylag goose communicates different emotions by standing in different positions. The top bird is about to attack, the other is on the defence.

Annelids

This animal phylum contains the segmented worms – long animals whose bodies are clearly organized in rings, or segments. There are about 9000 species, and they include earthworms, leeches, and the numerous forms of BRISTLE-WORMS that swim in the sea and burrow in the sea bed. These animals fall into three distinct classes.

Earthworms look quite smooth, but nearly every segment actually bears four pairs of small bristles on its lower surface, and these bristles give the animal a good grip on the sides of its tunnels. Earth-worms are *hermaphrodite*, meaning that each individual has both male and female organs, but they have to pair up before they can lay their eggs.

Leeches have no bristles, but there is a powerful sucker at each end of the body. Most leeches live in fresh water and they are hermaphrodite.

Bristleworms have numerous bristles on lobes extending from nearly every segment. Apart from a few river species, they all live in the sea, but they are very variable in shapes and habits. Unlike the other annelids, the bristle-worms usually have separate sexes.

Leafcutter ants cut pieces of leaves and carry them to their nests. They feed on mould which they grow on pulped leaves.

Wood ant   Black ant

A **wood ants' nest** cut open to show different rooms. The ants obtain honey dew from aphids by stroking them with their antennae.

Anoa

Two species of small, wild cattle found only in Sulawesi (Celebes) in Indonesia, They are also called dwarf buffalo. The mountain anoa is the smaller of the two species, standing 60 to 90 cm at the shoulder. The lowland anoa is nearly 107 cm high. Anoa have straight, conical, backward-pointing horns up to 30 cm long. These brown or black animals have always been treated as two species, but some experts now think that they may be varieties of the same species. Because of hunting, the cutting down of mountain forests and the draining of lowland swamps, the numbers of anoa have been much reduced. There is a danger that they may become extinct.
ORDER: Artiodactyla;
FAMILY: Bovidae;
SPECIES: Mountain: *Anoa anoa*; lowland: *Anoa depressicornis*.

Ant

The ants are an immense family of insects, with about 15,000 species, belonging to the same order as the bees and wasps. They vary a great deal in size, but can always be recognized by their elbowed an-tennae and the slender waist which bears one or two distinct bulges. The females of many species can defend themselves with stings, and those that lack stings can often fire acid at their attackers. As in bees and wasps, the males do not have a sting.

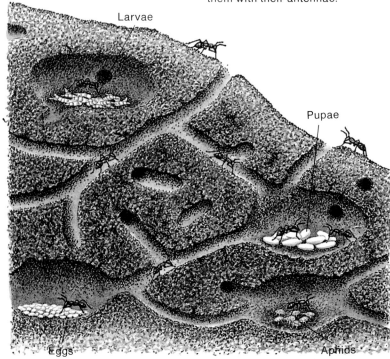

Larvae

Pupae

Eggs

Aphids

All ant species are social, living in colonies containing anything from a few dozen to several million individuals. Each colony is ruled by one or more queens, but the great bulk of the population consists of workers. These are sterile females which never grow wings. Some workers may be larger than others and have much bigger jaws. These are called soldiers, and their job is to defend the colony, but not all ant species have soldiers.

The queens of most species have

Ants bring cocoons to a spot where the Sun's warmth can speed up development.

wings when they first mature, and many fly out in great mating swarms, but they break off their wings before re-joining the colony or starting a new one. Male ants, also winged, only appear at certain times of the year – just in time for the mating flights. The males are produced from unfertilized eggs laid by the queens. New queens

and workers develop from fertilized eggs, but grubs destined to be queens receive more food and thus grow much bigger.

The ARMY ANTS have no settled home, but other ant species all have some kind of nest. Species with small colonies may nest in hollow plant stems, while WEAVER ANTS nest in pouches formed by fixing several leaves together. Many tropical ants build nests in the trees, using soil and chewed wood mixed with saliva as their

Left: **Weaver ants** glue leaves together to make nests. Below: Ants gathering honeydew from bugs on a eucalyptus tree.

needs and they overcome this problem by taking slaves. They raid the nests of other ants and steal pupae. The ants emerging from these pupae become workers in the nests of their captors.

The army ants and some other species are pure carnivores, eating nothing but the flesh of other animals. We can call these species hunting ants. There are also a number of harvesting ants, which feed mainly on seeds. These ants inhabit relatively dry areas and can be seen dragging seeds into their nests from all directions. The leaf-cutter ants of tropical Ameria actually grow their own food. They cut pieces of leaves from the plants and carry them to their nests where they chew them to pulp. The pulp is then spread out in the chambers and moulds grow on it. The ants eat nothing but these moulds. Most ants, however, are omnivorous, eating fruit and various small animals. Honeydew from APHIDS is another favourite food, and some ants actually herd the aphids as people herd cows. They use their jaws and stings to protect the aphids from various enemies, and even carry aphids into their nests and install them on roots passing through the chambers.

ORDER: Hymenoptera;
FAMILY: Formicidae.

building material. The most common types of nest, however, are in the ground. Soil is dug out to form underground chambers, and the ants usually make use of the mounds of excavated soil as well.

Ant nests have none of the elaborate cell architecture found in the nests of the social wasps and the honey bee, but the larger nests are efficiently organized. Each of the numerous chambers has a particular use and may be a nursery, a larder, a garden, or even a cemetery. In the centre of the nest, there is a royal chamber in which the queen lays her eggs. She is constantly tended by workers, and as long as she remains in good health the colony runs very smoothly. Workers take the eggs to hatchery chambers, and may move the larvae again when they hatch. The larvae are fed by the workers, and when fully grown they spin silken cocoons around themselves. These cocoons, which are often sold as "ant eggs" in pet shops, are usually taken to a chamber near the surface of the nest. There the Sun's warmth can speed up the development of the adults.

After mating, a queen may enter an existing colony – often her original home – or she may start a new one. In starting a new colony, the queen generally secretes herself in the ground, lays a few eggs, and rears a few small workers by feeding them on further eggs. These workers then set about building the nest.

There is another method of starting a colony. In this, the new queen enters the nest of another species. She lays eggs there, and the hosts rear her young. After a while she displaces the original queen, and the colony gradually becomes populated entirely with the invading queen's offspring.

A number of species are unable to rear enough workers for their

Antbird

A family of 221 species of birds found in Central and northern South America, and also on Trinidad and Tobago. They live in lowland thickets and forests and on mountain ranges, but never in open country. All are fairly small, ranging in size from around 9 to 36 cm in length. Their beaks are usually hooked and their plumage is generally dull, with patches of black and white. In many species there is a marked difference be-

tween the sexes. Most feed on insects and small snails, and not especially on ants.
ORDER: Passeriformes;
FAMILY: Formicariidae.

Anteater

Anteaters are found in Central and South America. They eat many kinds of insects, but generally feed on ANTS and TERMITES. An anteater uses the sharp claws of its forefeet to tear a hole in the wall of a termite nest, pushes its muzzle inside and laps up the inhabitants by means of a sticky saliva on its 20 to 25 cm tongue.

There are three South American species. The giant anteater is of a startling appearance. Its long, cylindrical snout is balanced by an untidily bushy tail. Its front feet face one another, the formidable claws folded inwards so that the animal walks on its knuckles The hind feet, however, stand flat on the ground. From nose to rump, the giant anteater is 90 to 122 cm long. Its tail adds another 60 to 90 cm. Its hair is coarse and stiff, grey-brown on the head and body, becoming darker on the hind-quarters and tail. Across the shoulders, wedge-shaped black stripes bordered with white effectively camouflage the animal by breaking up its outline.

The giant anteater lives in the swamps, grasslands and open forests from Belize and Guatemala to northern Argentina. It spends most of its life in a search for food, shuffling about with its nose to the ground.

Female giant anteaters have single offspring. The young are probably born in spring after a gestation period of 190 days. The baby stays with its mother until she is pregnant again, travelling easily by clinging to her back.

The silky or two-toed anteater and the tamandua have shorter snouts and lack the giant ant-eater's plume of hair on their tails. All of the anteater's manage to eat without teeth. The silky anteater is

named for the soft texture of its coat. It is squirrel-sized with a long *prehensile* tail. The tamandua, too, has a prehensile tail, but naked along its length. The fur is usually tan with a black "wasitcoat".
ORDER: Edentata;
FAMILY: Myrmecophagidae;
SPECIES: Giant: *Myrmecophaga tridactyla*; silky (two-toed): *Cyclopes didactylus*; tamandua: *Tamandua tetradactyla*.

The **giant anteater's** front feet are turned inwards so that the animal walks on its knuckles.

Antelope

Antelopes belong to the same family as CATTLE, GOATS and SHEEP. They are mostly delicate and timid creatures, capable of running at great speed on their slender legs when threatened by

A large male waterbuck. These **antelopes** are native to most parts of Africa south of the Sahara.

predators. A few species live in Asia, including the SAIGA of Central Asia, various GAZELLES in the deserts of south-western Asia, and the BLACKBUCK and NILGAI of India. There are no true antelopes in the Americas, although one North American animal is called the PRONGHORN antelope. But this animal belongs to a different, ancient family that arose and developed in North America.

Africa has the greatest number of species and the largest populations of antelopes, many of which can be seen in huge herds, particularly in some of the magnificent national parks. There are 72 African species in all, and they occur throughout the continent, as they are adapted to many kinds of habitats. For example, the rare ADDAX is adapted to the life in deserts, and some antelopes, like the BONGO, live in forests. Others live on mountainsides and a few, such as the WATERBUCK, prefer marshes. Some species, such as the lechwe, may spend all day submerged in water up to their necks in flooded grassland. However, most antelopes are found on the *savanna* of eastern and southern Africa. Antelopes vary in size from the tiny DIK-DIK, DUIKER, SUNI, and royal antelope to the massive giant ELAND, the largest of all antelopes. The difference in size is caused by adaptation to environment, as is the varying diet of antelopes. Because of special adaptations, various antelopes and other aimals can live side by side without competition over the same food. They graze and browse on a very wide range of plants, and where two species feed on one type of plant they usually eat different parts of it.

Nearly all antelopes have horns. Females may be horned, but their

Kudu and springbok antelopes drinking at a Namibian waterhole.

horns are mostly smaller than those of the males. Horns may be short and straight or long and elaborately curved, sometimes in an elegant spiral, but they are never forked like the antlers of DEER. The horns are sometimes interlocked in combats between males at the mating season or in the defence of territory. The fight then becomes a pushing contest. But sharp, pointed horns may be used as weapons. The ORYX have speared lions with their horns and BUSHBUCK have been known to kill men. The coats of antelopes are mostly smooth. Many colours and patterns occur, although brown and grey are the most common colours.

Because of their attractive horns, their edible meat and useful skins, several species of antelope have been over-hunted and are threatened with extinction. Only a few hundred of the magnificent giant SABLE ANTELOPE of Angola have survived. But they are now being protected.

ORDER: Artiodactyla;
FAMILY: Bovidae.

Ant-lion

Adult ant-lions are mostly rather large insects related to the LACE-WINGS. They could be confused with DRAGONFLIES at first sight, but they fly much more slowly and have much larger, clubbed antennae. These insects are found mainly in the tropics, although some species live in Europe – especially in southern areas. Several species occur in the United States.

Ant-lions get their name from the habits of the larvae, which feed on ants and other small insects. Some larvae live freely on the ground, but the best known make little pits in sandy soil. These larvae bury themselves at the bottom of their pits, with just their great jaws above the sand, and wait for their prey to tumble in. The larvae are often called doodle-bugs in the United States.

ORDER: Neuroptera;
FAMILY: Myrmeleontidae.

Aphid

The aphids are also known as plant-lice. They are small, sap-sucking bugs that do great harm to many crops and other plants. Familiar examples include the blackfly, which attacks beans and spinach, and various species of

The **ant-lion larva** has fearsome jaws with which it grabs its prey.

greenfly which infest roses. The insects have pear-shaped bodies, with or without wings, and small heads with a slender beak which pierces the plant tissues. The hind end of the body usually has a pair of horns, called *cornicles*, which give off waxy and rather pungent secretions. These horns protect the

Apes

Apes are the monkey-like animals that are nearest to Man in structure and development. For this reason they are called anthropoid – "Man-like". It was once thought that Man was descended from the apes, but it now seems certain that apes and men as we know them today had a common ancestor.

Two of the four kinds of apes – the orang utan and the gibbon – live in Asia. The other two – the chimpanzee and the gorilla – live in Africa. Remains of the earliest Hominids – the group that includes both apes and human beings have been found in these two continents.

The apes resemble Man in having no tail, and in walking upright some of the time. Their brains are much better developed than those of other primates. Most of the bones, muscles, nerves and other internal organs of apes are very similar to those of Man. But apes have shorter legs and longer arms than human beings, and their big toes are more thumb-like.

Skeletons of man and **ape**. The ape's arms are longer than its legs and the pelvic girdle (stippled) has developed to suit the different postures.

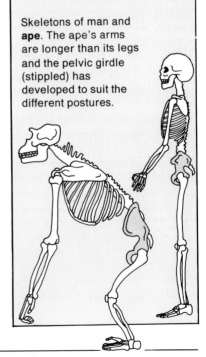

aphids from some of their enemies, although they do not deter the LADYBIRDS and LACEWINGS. Aphids are rarely more than about 3 mm long. They live on roots, stems and leaves, and, as well as merely removing sap from the plants, also carry serious viral diseases. Large aphid populations may cause leaves to curl up, and some species cause the formation of growths called *galls*.

Many aphids have complicated life histories, and this is particularly true of those living in cool climates. The blackfly, for example, passes the winter in the egg stage on various shrubs. The eggs hatch in spring and the resulting insects are all wingless females. These reproduce without mating – a phenomenon known as *parthenogenesis* – and bring forth active young at the rate of several each day. These youngsters, again all female, are soon reproducing themselves, and winged individuals begin to appear. These fly to the beans and other host plants and continue to reproduce at a rapid rate. Great populations of winged and wingless aphids thus develop on the plants. The winged forms can move about and spread the infestation over a wide area. Male aphids appear later in the summer. They mate with certain females, which then lay the winter eggs on the shrubs.

The sap on which the aphids feed is very rich in sugar, but contains little protein. In order to get enough protein, the aphids have to take in far too much sugar, but they simply pass the excess sugar out again at the hind end in the form of a sweet liquid called honeydew. The leaves of many trees become sticky with honeydew in the summer. Ants are very fond of sweet things and they regularly stroke the aphids to make them give out honeydew. Some ants actually guard the aphid colonies, and may even take aphids into their nests to protect them.
ORDER: Hemiptera-Homoptera.

Green aphids cluster on a rose shoot to drink its sap through their long, piercing beaks.

Apollo butterfly

The beautiful apollo butterfly, which is related to the SWALLOWTAIL, flies in the mountainous parts of Europe and Asia. Throughout the summer it can be seen floating elegantly from flower to flower or sunning itself on the ground. Its dark, hairy body helps to absorb heat in the cool climate. The caterpillar feeds on saxifrage and other alpine plants and, unlike most butterfly *larvae*, spins a *cocoon* in which to pupate. The butterfly is not found above about 1800 metres, but related species occur higher up in the Alps and in other mountain ranges in Asia and North America.
ORDER: Lepidoptera;
FAMILY: Papilionidae;
SPECIES: *Parnassius apollo*.

Apollo butterflies are found in many parts of the world, usually in high places.

Arachnids

The Class Arachnida contains the SPIDERS, SCORPIONS, MITES, TICKS, and a few other groups on land and in the sea. There are usually four pairs of walking legs, and the animals lack *antennae* and wings. Some mites suck plant sap, and the ticks are blood-suckers, but most arachnids are *carnivores*, despite the fact that they have no real jaws.

The garden spider is one of the most often-seen **arachnids**.

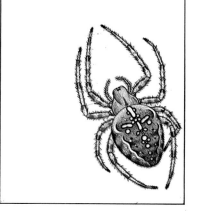

Small Apollo
male

Clouded Apollo
male

Apollo
male

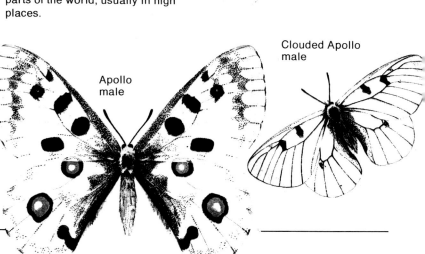

Arapaima

One of the largest of all freshwater fishes, the arapaima grows up to 4.6 metres in length and 200 kg in weight. It lives in shallow waters of rivers of northern South America. It has an ancestry going back 100 million years without much change, and can be regarded as a living fossil.

Among the primitive features of the arapaima is the way it uses its *swim bladder* as a lung, rising to the surface every now and then to take a gulp of air. This feature is most probably an adaptation towards survival in drought conditions, similar to the adaptations of the LUNGFISHES.

Arapaimas eat anything from worms, snails and weeds, to fishes of medium size.
ORDER: Osteoglossiformes;
FAMILY: Osteoglossidae;
SPECIES: *Arapaima gigas.*

Archerfish

A group of freshwater or slightly salty water fishes which shoot down their insect prey with well-aimed drops of water. There are five species, living in rivers and mangrove swamps from India through South-East Asia to the northern shore of Australia.

Archerfishes mainly feed on small water creatures swimming or floating near the surface. But from time to time they rise to the surface and spit a trail of water droplets which can bring down insects. These insects can be crawling on leaves or stems, as far away as 2 metres. At the moment of shooting the tip of the snout just breaks the water but the fish's eyes remain submerged. A sudden, powerful movement of the archerfish's gill-

covers pumps water through the gills into the mouth. At the same time the fish raises its tongue to convert a groove in the roof of its mouth into a narrow tube, through which the water is driven at high speed. Archerfishes begin to shoot at prey in this manner when they are still very young and small in size. As they grow, their range and accuracy increase.
ORDER: Perciformes;
FAMILY: Toxotidae.

Arctic fox

The Arctic fox is similar to the red fox, but is smaller, with smaller ears which help to retain heat. It lives in the *tundra* regions of Europe Asia, North America and Greenland. In winter its thick

Archerfish capture insects by shooting out jets of water. The tongue and roof of the fish's mouth form the equivalent of a gun barrel.

Arctic foxes change colour with the seasons.

white coat provides it with insulation and camouflage in the snow. In summer its coat is greyish-yellow with white under-parts. Hairs on the soles of its feet give the fox a good grip on snow and ice.

Arctic foxes live in small groups and eat a wide variety of food. In winter, food is difficult to find and they follow POLAR BEARS to take advantage of any uneaten seal meat. In summer, however, food is more plentiful. They catch birds, such as gulls and ducks, and mammals, such as voles and hares. In Europe, LEMMINGS are the main source of food and the population of foxes rises and falls with the explosive rise and fall of lemming populations.

Breeding begins in April and 5 to 8 cubs are born in May or June, However, when lemmings are abundant, as many as 20 cubs may be born in the same litter. A second litter is born in July or August.
ORDER: Carnivora;
FAMILY: Canidae;
SPECIES: *Alopex lagopus.*

Armadillo

The name, armadillo, means "little armoured thing" in Spanish which refers to the animal's *carapace*, or body armour. The carapace is unusual in that it is made up of

small plates of bone rather than of compressed hair or *keratin*. This gives this fast-moving animal a formidable defence. The three-banded armadillo or apara is additionally protected by its ability to roll into a ball. When forced to swim, the weight of its carapace would be a disadvantage except that the armadillo has developed an inflatable intestine which gives it added bouyancy.

Armadillos, of which there are 20 species, are found only in the Americas. The largest is the giant armadillo of the rain forest of eastern South America. The giant's 90 cm body can weigh up to 59 kg. It has up to 100 small teeth, more than double the number found in most other mammals. The smallest species is only 15 cm long.

Most armadillos are nocturnal and live in burrows one metre beneath the surface. They are omnivorous, living on insects, snakes and lizards as well as plants. The armadillo uses its sickle-like claws to dig into ant and termite runs, extracting the insects with its long, extensible tongue.
ORDER: Edentata;
FAMILY: Dasypodidae.

Armoured catfish

The name given to any one of 30 species of South American cat-fishes, with *barbels* or whiskers which give them their name. All

The **three-banded armadillo** has bony plates that give the animal a formidable defence. It can also protect itself by curling into a ball.

these small stream-dwellers are remarkable for the bony armour which clothes their bodies. They are for the most part bottom dwellers, feeding on small animals and fallen carrion found in the mud. Their armour is protective against attack by other fishes. One species, the talking catfish, is the most heavily armoured of all fishes, being covered with bony plates and spines.
ORDER: Siluriformes;
FAMILY: Doradidae (thorny cat-fishes), Callichthyidae (mailed cat-fishes).

Army ant

The army ants, also called driver or legionary ants, are ants that have no permanent homes, although, like all ants, they live in colonies. Some colonies contain millions of individuals. There are several different species, scattered through most of the tropical regions. They are all fiercely carni-vorous and they eat almost any kind of animal that cannot escape from their marching columns. Even a horse will be killed and stripped to a skeleton by some of the African species if it is tethered in their path, but the usual prey are insects and other small animals.

At night, the worker ants cluster together to form a dense mass, sometimes as much as a metre across. Their legs are intertwined, and their bodies form a living nest for the queen and youngsters in the centre. This temporary home is called a bivouac. At daybreak, the workers stream out to forage, and their columns look like ropes snaking over the ground. The large-jawed soldiers march along on the outside of the columns to protect them. The columns usually fan out after a while and cover a wide area. Prey is torn to pieces when caught, and stored along the route. The ants collect it as they return to the bivouac later in the day.

Towards dusk, they stream out again carrying the larvae. The queen moves with them on this occasion and they settle into a new bivouac perhaps 100 metres away, ready to hunt over a new area the next day. The queen has distinct periods of egg-laying, and when she is ready to lay, the colony becomes more settled. A bivouac may then last for three weeks or more, and the ants go out from the same place each day. But as soon as the eggs hatch the ants become nomadic again, because they need extra food for the larvae and would soon exhaust one area. The queens are very much larger than the workers, and wingless. Males are also very large – up to 5 cm long – and they have wings. They are sometimes known as sausage flies because of their shape.
ORDER: Hymenoptera;
FAMILY: Formicidae.

Arrow-poison frog

Arrow-poison frogs secrete a powerful poison which can cause instant death. The frogs are found only in Central and South America, where Indians have long extracted the poison from their bodies to use on arrowheads.

The **arrow-poison frog** secretes a powerful poison from its skin.

Many species are brilliantly coloured. The strawberry arrow-poison frog is red and black. Another kind is yellow with stripes of black running lengthwise down the head and body and around the limbs. A Cuban member of the family, is the smallest frog in the world, measuring less than 1.3 cm.
ORDER: Salientia;
FAMILY: Dendrobatidae.

Arrow worm

This name applies to 65 species of tiny, transparent animals that form part of the PLANKTON. Arrow worms vary from 2 to 10 cm in length. Their bodies are divided into three sections; a short head, a long trunk, and a short tail. They are very difficult to see, except for their black eyes and any food they may have swallowed. They eat other small animals and larvae in the plankton. Each individual contains both male and female organs.
PHYLUM: Chaetognatha.

Asp

The asp is a snake in the same family as the ADDER. Their colours are rather similar, but the asp's back is often marked with dark slanting bars, and a streak down the middle. Also, the asp's snout is

Arthropods

This is the largest of all the animal phyla. It contains more species than all the other phyla put together. There are very nearly a million known species. The name of the phylum means "jointed foot" and refers to the clearly jointed appearance of the limbs. The body is also clearly segmented in most arthropods, and it seems certain that the arthropods evolved from some kind of ANNELID ancestor that developed legs. All arthropods have a tough, and often very hard coat, or *exoskeleton*. This does not grow with the animal and all arthropods must *moult* at intervals. The old coat is shed and a new coat is formed underneath.

The arthropods include CENTIPEDES, MILLIPEDES, SHRIMPS, CRABS, all the INSECTS, SPIDERS and SCORPIONS.

Great diving beetle

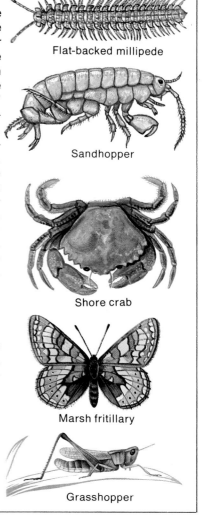

Flat-backed millipede

Sandhopper

Shore crab

Marsh fritillary

Grasshopper

turned up, unlike the adder's.

The asp is common in many parts of Europe, usually farther south than the adder. Asps like waste-land, hedges and scrub. Some have been found high up in the Alps. They are slow moving but aggressive and more dangerous to people than adders; their bites can be fatal.
ORDER: Squamata;
FAMILY: Viperidae;
SPECIES: *Vipera aspis*.

The **asp** is more aggressive and dangerous than its close relative, the adder.

Ass

There are two species of wild asses. The North African ass probably gave rise to the domestic DONKEY. Asses stand 0.9 to 1.4 metres high at the shoulder and have a grey or brownish coat. The legs are often striped and the ears long. Mules are the offspring of female horses and male asses. The parents of the rarer hinny are a female ass and a male horse. Both *hybrids* are sterile. Wild asses live in desert or semi-desert areas, sometimes on plains, but more often in hilly regions. These wary animals live in troops of 10 to 12, consisting of a stallion, several females and some young. Courtship takes place in the spring or early summer and the foals are born 11 to 12 months later. Man is the wild ass's main enemy, and WOLVES attack solitary animals.
ORDER: Perissodactyla;
FAMILY: Equidae;
SPECIES: North African: *Equus asinus*; Central Asian: *Equus hemionus*.

Assassin Bug

The assassin bugs, of which there are more than 3000 species, are predatory bugs that feed mainly on other insects. Reaching lengths of 4 cm or more, they are generally stoutly built, but some are very slender. Assassin bugs often resemble the insects on which they feed. They usually grasp prey in their front legs, and then plunge their long, curved beaks in to suck the juices.
ORDER: Hemiptera-Heteroptera;
FAMILY: Reduviidae.

Atlas moth

With a wing-span reaching 25 cm, the atlas moth is one of the world's largest moths. It lives in India and other parts of South-East Asia, where its caterpillar feeds on various shrubs. It is related to the giant peacock moth, and also to the tussore silk moths which pro-

A **wild ass** from North Africa. This animal probably gave rise to the donkey. The legs are often striped like a zebra's.

duce some of our commercial silk.
ORDER: Lepidoptera;
FAMILY: Saturniidae;
SPECIES: *Attacus atlas*.

Avadavat

A strikingly-coloured bird, the avadavat is the size of a WREN. There are three races: the Indian avadavat, the Javan avadavat and the golden-bellied avadavat of Burma. Males are coppery to bright red with black underparts, and a reddish-brown crown. The back, rump, wings and belly are spotted with white. The females are more sombre. Avadavats preen each other.
ORDER: Passeriformes;
FAMILY: Estrildidae;
SPECIES: *Estrilda amandava*.

Avocet

Avocets are wading birds which can be identified by their long, upward-curving beaks. There are four species. Three are shore birds, while the Chilean avocet lives in the high Andes mountains.

The Old World avocet has a distinctive and striking plumage, patterned in black and white. This pattern helps to break up the bird's body outline and thus conceal it on the ground. Such patterning is known as disruptive coloration. The American avocet and the Australian avocet have a different plumage.

Avocets live on small crustaceans, fish, molluscs and plant material. Their curved beaks sweep the water just below the surface as they wade through the shallows. They often feed in groups, sometimes composed of as many as 300 birds.

ORDER: Charadriiformes;
FAMILY: Recurvirostridae.

Axis deer

Two species of axis deer live in India, the more common being the spotted deer. This is the most abundant deer in India and it is popularly known by its Hindustani name of chital. It is one of the most beautiful deer, with a bright reddish-brown coat decorated with lines of white spots and set off by conspicuous white under-parts. The deer stands up to 90 cm at the shoulder and lives in large herds. The males drop their slender antlers at any time of the year, and breeding also occurs at all seasons. Chital can be found throughout India and Sri Lanka, in both plains and forests. The hog deer, found on the plains between northern India and Indo-China, is another axis deer, although quite unlike the chital. It is a squat, pig-like animal with short legs, and it runs rather than bounds. It does not live in large herds. Its coat is yellowish to reddish brown and slightly speckled, but the young are heavily spotted. The two species readily interbreed where their ranges meet.

ORDER: Artiodactyla;
FAMILY: Cervidae;
SPECIES: Spotted: *Axis axis*; hog: *Axis porcinus*.

Axolotl

The axolotl is a newt-like creature with a surprising way of life. It always lives in water and lays eggs while still in its aquatic larval stage. This is as though a frog laid eggs while still a tadpole.

Axolotls are 10 to 18 cm long. They are usually black, or dark brown with black spots, but albinos are quite common. The legs and feet are small and weak,

The delicate-beaked **avocet** is a common wader of mud flats.

but an axolotl has a long, deep tail that helps it to swim. It breathes through feathery gills behind its head.

Axolotls live in certain lakes in Mexico. They keep to the water if possible, because their bodies might dry up on the barren land around. If the lakes dry up, axolotls become adult salamanders, able to breathe air and walk on land, but they still need to find a damp shady place to survive.

ORDER: Caudata;
FAMILY: Ambystomidae;
SPECIES: *Siredon mexicanum*.

Aye-aye

The extremely rare aye-aye lives deep in the forests of Madagascar. When it was first found in 1780, it was thought to be a species of squirrel. Only later, when its anatomy was studied, was it seen to be a primate.

The aye-aye is the size of a cat, with a bushy tail as long as its body. The thick coat is dark brown or black, while the fur

around the face is yellowish-white. The face is rounded, with large eyes and naked, erect ears. Its feet and hands are unusual, especially the long, narrow middle finger of each hand, which is used for grooming, scratching and picking the teeth as well as for probing for insects in crevices. A nocturnal animal, the aye-aye spends the day in a hollow tree or among branches. It eats insect grubs and fruit. It is named after the grating sound which it sometimes makes.

ORDER: Primates;
FAMILY: Daubentonidae;
SPECIES: *Daubentonia madagascariensis*.

The **axolotl** is a strange amphibian that lives in the wild only in certain lakes around Mexico City.

B

Baboon

Baboons are monkeys that have forsaken a life in trees for a life on the ground, although they sleep in trees at night. Found in most parts of Africa, baboons live in close family groups, called troops. A troop may contain some old males, juveniles, females and babies. In a small troop, there may be only one male. Their chief enemies are lions and leopards. When threatened, baboons make for the trees or rocks. When they are safe, they bark defiance and throw stones, and old males may even turn on a predator and force it to retreat. Baboons breed all the year round. They eat plant and animal foods and can be serious pests when raiding crops.

Baboons are smaller than chimpanzees. They have long dog-like muzzles with large teeth, and long tails There are six species. The chacma baboon lives in eastern and southern Africa. The yellow baboon lives in central Africa. The doguera baboon ranges from Ethiopia to Kenya. The Guinea baboon is found in west-central Africa. The hamadryas or sacred baboon occurs in north-eastern Africa and Arabia. The gelada baboon is confined to Ethiopia.
ORDER: Primates;
FAMILY: Cercopithecidae.

Badger

Badgers are bear-like animals that belong to the same family as STOATS and WEASELS. They have stocky bodies about 1 metre long, short tails, and short but powerful legs armed with strong claws on the front feet. Like other members of the family, they have *musk* glands at the base of the tail and leave five-toed footprints.

The European badger is found all over Europe and Asia. It is rarely seen, however, because it is nocturnal and very wary. At a distance, the European badger's coat looks grey, but the individual hairs are actually black and white. The belly and legs of the animal are black. The most striking part of the European badger, however, is the head. This is white with two broad, black stripes running from behind the ears almost to the tip of the muzzle. The purpose of these

The European **badger** is a wary creature.

markings is uncertain. It is unlikely that they are warning colours, as badgers have no serious enemies other than human beings. It is probable, therefore, that these markings help individuals to recognize each other in the dark.

The hog badger is found in China and neighbouring parts of South-East Asia and can be distinguished from the European badger by its naked, pig-like snout. The American badger is smaller than the European badger and is widespread in North America.

Badgers live in holes, or sets, excavated in the ground and filled with bracken and other vegetation for bedding. They emerge at night to feed mainly on earthworms, but also on small rodents, insects, snails, grass, nuts and berries.

Badgers probably pair for life. Breeding begins in July or August, but the cubs are not born until the following February or March. After 6 to 8 weeks they emerge from the set, but remain with their parents for about another six months.
ORDER: Carnivora;
FAMILY: Mustelidae;
SPECIES: European: *Meles meles*;
American: *Taxidea taxus*.

Baboons spend most of their life on the ground but are still quite at home in trees.

Balance of Nature

Unless disturbed by Man, any one part of the countryside will always tend to support the same animals and plants. This ability of nature to remain unchanged is called the balance of Nature. For example, if a stretch of grassland is able to provide food for a dozen rabbits, then a dozen rabbits will generally be found there. If too many rabbits move in, then there will not be enough food for them all. Some will either die or migrate, and the balance will be restored. Similarly, if the grassland becomes overgrown, more animals will arrive to feed on it. The same area of grassland may provide enough rabbits to feed one fox. If the fox eats all the rabbits, it too will have to move on while the population recovers.

Over long periods there are, of course, changes. Some are cyclic, occurring every few years. For example, every four years the numbers of snowy owls in the Arctic rise to a peak level, then drop back. Over much longer periods, of thousands of years, permanent changes occur – generally due to changes of climate. For example, the lion, a warm-climate animal, was once plentiful in Europe, where the climate has now become too cold for it to survive.

Bald eagle

The bald eagle is one of the sea eagles and is famous as the national emblem of the United States. Until about seven years old, the bald eagle looks very like the golden eagle, for it has not yet developed the distinctive white feathers on the tail and head, which give the bird its popular name. Once common throughout North America, the bald eagle has become rare owing to hunting, loss of habitat and the harmful effects of pesticides. It is now found only in Florida and Alaska. Bald eagles nest in trees or on cliffs, feeding on fish, rabbits, waterfowl, and even young deer.

ORDER: Falconiformes;
FAMILY: Accipitridae;
SPECIES: *Haliaeetus leucocephalus*.

Bandicoot

Bandicoots are *marsupials* that look like rats. The 19 species of bandicoot range over parts of Australia, Tasmania and Papua New Guinea. Bandicoots are nocturnal. Some species eat only bulbs, roots and seeds, but others are wholly carnivorous, eating earthworms, small lizards, mice, slugs and snails. Two species of rabbit bandicoot, sometimes called bilbies, dig burrows 90 to 183 cm long in which they shelter during the hot desert days. Pig-footed bandicoots are now almost extinct. The name comes from the

The **barbary ape** is the only monkey living in Europe.

The **bald eagle** is badly named. Its white head is well feathered.

front feet which are cloven-hoofed, like those of a pig. But, to make this animal even stranger, the hind feet are more like those of a horse.

ORDER: Marsupialia;
FAMILY: Paramelidae.

Barbary ape

The Barbary ape is the only *primate* (apart from man) which lives in Europe, in a small colony in Gibraltar. It also occurs in parts of Algeria and Morocco. Barbary apes are monkeys of the MACAQUE family, but were called apes because they have a very small tail, which can be seen only when the animal is handled. Barbary apes are about 60 cm long and weigh 4 to 9 kg. The coat is thick, coarse and brown. They roam in large bands and are good tree climbers and balancers. Babies may be born at any time of the year.

ORDER: Primates;
FAMILY: Cercopithecidae;
SPECIES: *Macaca sylvanus*.

Barbary sheep

The Barbary sheep is the only African wild sheep. It lives in dry, hilly regions in North Africa and feeds on the scattered shrubs and grasses. It stands a maximum of 109 cm at the shoulder and weighs up to 115 kg. It has a short, fawn-coloured coat, with a fringe of long hair that hangs down from the chest over the front legs, and a longish tail. A gland beneath the tail gives the sheep a goat-like odour. Males have smooth, thick, backward-sweeping horns. The sheep live in small herds, but the rams are often solitary, except during the mating season. Young males form bachelor herds.

ORDER: Artiodactyla;
FAMILY: Bovidae;
SPECIES: *Ammotragus lervia.*

Barbel

The barbel is a freshwater fish of the CARP family that lives in European rivers. In the Danube, the barbel when fully grown can weigh as much as 23 kg. Even larger is its close relative of Indian rivers, the mahseer, a food fish weighing up to 45 kg. These fishes have four barbels or feelers around the mouth, which are studded with taste buds for the detection of small prey in the bottom mud.

ORDER: Cypriniformes;
FAMILY: Cyprinidae;
SPECIES: Barbus barbus.

The **barbel** is a large river-fish.

Barber fish

Barber fish is a name applied to many fishes belonging to several different orders and families. These fishes all have in common the habit of barbering, or cleaning, other fishes, to free them from patches of dead skin and skin

Above: **Barbary sheep**, father and son. Only adult males have large, backward-sweeping horns.

Below: A tiny **barber fish** (or cleaner fish) removes parasites from the mouth of a larger fish.

parasites. In this way the barber fishes get their food.

Barber fishes often live in a rock crevice close to a brilliantly coloured sea anemone or sponge which advertises their presence. Customer fishes have been observed to queue up at the "sign", waiting their turn to be cleaned. A customer fish will allow the much smaller barber fish to enter its gill chambers and its mouth to make a thorough job of the cleaning. Large sharks, with their batteries of razor-sharp teeth, are often cleaned in this way without any harm coming to the little barber fishes.

Bark beetle

The bark beetles are small insects related to the WEEVILS. Their larvae live just under the bark of various trees, and produce intricate patterns of tunnels as they chew their way through the nutritious tissues between the bark and the hard wood. Each species produces its own characteristic pattern, based on the original arrangement of the eggs laid under the bark by the female. Heavy infestations can reduce timber production, and the most destructive species is the elm bark beetle, which carries Dutch elm disease. This disease has killed millions of elm trees. The adult beetles, which are brown and bullet-shaped, chew tender leaves and buds on the twigs.

ORDER: Coleoptera;
FAMILY: Scolytidae.

When the tide is in, the **barnacle** opens its bony plates and puts out feathery limbs to catch food.

Barnacle

The 800 species of barnacle are crustaceans, the adult forms of which encrust rocks, the piles of piers and the bottoms of ships. The animal has been aptly described as "standing on its head and kicking food into its mouth". The barnacle's head is cemented firmly to rock or other underwater objects. The shell is made up of several plates, which are open while the animal is submerged, but closed if it is exposed to air by the receding tide. While submerged, the barnacle moves its feathery

Elm wood from which the bark has been removed shows the tunnels made by the **bark beetle** (inset).

legs in and out of the shell to comb food from the water.

There are two basic types of barnacle. Acorn barnacles are the most numerous animals on shore, and up to 30,000 have been found on one square yard. Most acorn barnacles are small, but one American species has a diameter of nearly 30 cm. The second type, the goose barnacles, hang from a tough stalk that is formed from the front part of the head. The larvae of both types float freely in the sea until they settle and become adults.

ORDER: Thoracica.

Barnacle goose

The barnacle goose is similar to, but smaller than, the CANADA GOOSE. Its plumage is grey with black stripes, the neck is black and

The **barnacle goose** gets its name from an ancient belief that the birds hatch from goose barnacles.

A **barn owl** flies silently. Its fluffy flight feathers muffle the noise of its wingbeats.

the head is white. It breeds in the Arctic and migrates south to parts of northern Europe for the winter. The common name dates from the Middle Ages. Before the breeding sites of barnacle geese were known, people thought that they hatched from goose barnacles because they looked something like them. They feed on a variety of plants, and on a few small animals. Unlike other geese, they build down-filled nests on the rocky ledges of cliffs.
ORDER: Anseriformes;
FAMILY: Anatidae;
SPECIES: *Branta leucopsis*.

Barn owl

The barn owl is the most widely spread land bird in the world. Varieties are found in every continent except Antarctica. Seen flying soundlessly at dusk, the barn owl looks ghostly white. Its upper parts are actually orange-brown, speckled with grey. The under-parts and heart-shaped face are pure white. Its appearance and strange shriek have made the barn owl a favourite with story-tellers as a bird of ill omen. But it is in fact a most useful bird, for its prey consists largely of mice, voles and other pests.

Barn owls often nest in old farm buildings. The female begins to incubate each egg as soon as it is laid, so the young hatch at different times. This makes the parents' task of gathering food less of a strain. Like other owls, the barn owl cannot digest fur and bones. It ejects this waste matter as pellets.
ORDER: Strigiformes;
FAMILY: Tytonidae;
SPECIES: *Tyto alba*.

Barracuda

The barracuda is a fierce and voracious fish. It has a torpedo-shaped body, a jutting lower jaw and a wicked set of fangs. It is a shoal fish when young but the largest barracudas, up to 2.7 metres in length, are solitary fishes.

Barracudas charge through shoals of prey fishes with snapping bites. They may round up the rest of a shoal and herd it until the time comes for the barracudas' next meal. Divers often fear barracudas more than they fear SHARKS, because a barracuda hunts by

sight and will attack any flashing metallic object such as a fishing spear.
ORDER: Perciformes;
FAMILY: Sphyraenidae.

Basilisk

There are several species of basilisks, all living in tropical America. They are iguana lizards and are named after the fabled basilisk, whose glance was said to kill. But basilisks are harmless except to the birds and rodents that they catch and eat. They also eat some vegetable food.

Basilisks grow about 60 cm long. They have a long tapering tail, and males have a crest of skin that runs down the head, back and tail. If an enemy comes near, a basilisk runs away on its long hind legs that end in long toes fringed with scales. This lizard can even run on water for a short distance without sinking.
ORDER: Squamata;
FAMILY: Iguanidae;
SPECIES: *Basiliscus basiliscus*.

Basilisks are related to the iguanas. The male has a large crest.

Basking Shark

The basking shark is a huge but inoffensive shark, often more than 13 metres long. After the equally harmless whale shark, it is the largest of all sharks. These giant fishes both feed on the smallest of sea creatures. They swim slowly forward with their mouths open, straining out from the sea-water great quantities of the floating bodies of the tiny animals and plants of the plankton.

The basking shark lives in temperate seas throughout the world but is most common in the North Atlantic. A second species of basking shark is believed to live in seas off the coast of Australia. Basking sharks enter coastal waters in summer, either singly, or in groups and shoals of up to 60 fishes. They are fished chiefly for their great livers, which provide much of the world's "cod liver oil".

ORDER: Lamniformes;
FAMILY: Cetorhinidae;
SPECIES: Cetorhinus maximus.

The **bass** is found chiefly along ocean coasts.

Bass

The common bass is a popular marine sport fish having the general appearance and size of a SALMON (to which, however, it is unrelated). Certain freshwater fishes having spiny fins similar to those of the common bass are also known as bass. This name, then, is applied to several fishes belonging to different genera, or even to different families, of fishes.

The common bass and its marine relatives feed largely on PRAWNS, SHRIMPS, CRABS and small fishes. One near relative, the stone bass, or wreckfish, gets the latter name from its peculiar habit of swimming close by floating wreck-

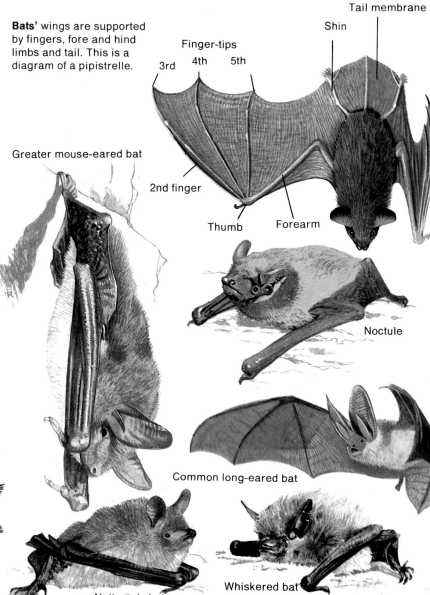

Bats' wings are supported by fingers, fore and hind limbs and tail. This is a diagram of a pipistrelle.

Tail membrane
Shin
Finger-tips
3rd 4th 5th
2nd finger
Thumb Forearm

Greater mouse-eared bat

Noctule

Common long-eared bat

Natterer's bat

Whiskered bat

age. Many other relatives of the common bass are *hermaphrodite*, with both male and female sex organs, while others are *inter-sexes*, changing from male to female or vice versa.

ORDER: Perciformes;
FAMILY: Serranidae.

Bat

Of all the world's mammals, bats are the only ones that can really fly. Most of the 18 families and 180 genera of bats live in the tropics, but they are widely distributed throughout warm and temperate climates in both hemispheres.

They do not inhabit polar or high mountain regions.

Bats are acrobatic fliers. Their wings are extensions of the skin of their bellies and back. The skin is stretched between the "fingers" of the forelimbs, the sides of the body, and the hind limbs. Their flying action has been likened to swimming in air. The animal operates its wings by co-ordinated movements of arms and legs similar to a swimmer doing the breast stroke. Many species have a further membrane joining the hind legs. The tail is generally completely enclosed in this membrane.

Like other mammals, bats

suckle their young. They are warm-blooded and furry. Females usually bear only one offspring each season. Hibernating species of bats generally mate in the autumn. The male's sperm is held in the female's reproductive tract until winter is past. Then she releases the sperm to fertilize her *ovum* in spring. This delay in the fertilization of the egg ensures that birth will occur at a suitable season. The young bats of some species stay with their mothers even in flight, clinging to the mother's fur with their milk teeth. Although slow to breed, bats keep up their numbers because they live a long time: more than 20 years in the wild.

Many bats that live in temperate regions hibernate in cold weather. They hang upside down, hooking their feet into a crevice in the roof of a cave or in a hollow tree. Their body heat falls, and all body processes slow down. Their intake of oxygen drops to a hundredth of its normal level. Even when sleeping during the day at an active time of year, bats may become torpid, but quickly recover normal temperature when they wake for the night's food gathering.

Contrary to what many people think, bats see quite well, but most species find their food at night when they must use means other than sight. They have a good sense of smell, but depend principally on echo-location. They utter high-pitched sounds extremely rapidly, between 100 and 200 times a second. These sound waves hit objects in the bats' flight path and are echoed back to the bats' ears. The echoes of these pulsing cries tell a bat what is in its path even in total darkness. If it is pursuing an insect, a bat locates it by echo, then makes a "lap" of its wings to guide the creature into its jaws. Bats eat a wide variety of foods. These include insects, fish, blood, fruit and nectar.

Bat species vary greatly in size. The smallest is the bumble-bee bat

The fruit-eating **bat** has a face that strongly resembles that of a fox. It is often called a flying fox.

which is just over 2.5 cm long with a wingspan of about 15 cm. The largest is one of the FLYING FOXES, with a wingspan of about 1.8 metres and body length of 40 cm.
ORDER: Chiroptera.

The **grizzly bear** is at home in water. This one is probably hunting for salmon or trout.

Bat-eared fox

The bat-eared or big-eared fox has a narrow face, long ears, a limp brush and a yellowish coat. It resembles a JACKAL. With a length of 46 to 58 cm it is much the same size as a RED FOX, but at 3 to 4.5 kg, it is barely half the weight.

Bat-eared foxes are found in open sandy ground in most parts of Africa, where their main enemies are man and leopards. They are nocturnal, but the animals' strong curiosity brings them out in daylight, usually in pairs. Their diet consists mainly of termites and other insects which they crush with their pointed teeth. But they will also eat small rodents, carrion, nestlings and eggs. The animal's hearing is very sensitive. Their young are born in litters of 2 to 5, usually in the rainy season.
ORDER: Carnivora;
FAMILY: Canidae;
SPECIES: *Octocyon megalotis*.

Bear

Bears are large mammals with powerful limbs, strong claws and short tails. Like BADGERS, they differ from other carnivores in that they eat plants as well as flesh. They are mainly slow-moving

ground-dwellers but they can walk on their hind legs and climb trees.

The northern members of the family are the American BLACK BEAR, the BROWN BEAR and the POLAR BEAR. Other species include the moon bear, or Himalayan black bear, the SLOTH BEAR, or Indian bear, the Malayan SUN BEAR and the SPECTACLED BEAR of South America.
ORDER: Carnivora;
FAMILY: Ursidae.

The **beaver** fells a tree by cutting chips from the trunk with its large front teeth. It is a skilled dam and lodge builder (right).

Beaver

There are two species of beaver. The European beaver is now found only in Scandinavia, along rivers in European Russia, and in the Elbe and Rhone valleys. The North American beaver has been reduced in numbers by fur trapping and the loss of its habitat. It survives in Canada and the northern United States.

Among the rodents, only the CAPYBARA is larger than the beaver. Stout-bodied with dark brown fur, the beaver is about 1 metre long, with a broad flat tail, powerful limbs and a blunt muzzle. It has five toes on each foot. Those on the front feet are strongly clawed, and are used for digging, handling food and carrying sticks and mud. The hind feet are webbed for swimming, with special split claws which the beaver uses for grooming its dense fur and heavy outer coat, and for spreading oil to act as a water-proofing insulation. The tail is used as a rudder when the beaver is swimming, and as a support when the animal stands up on dry land to gnaw at trees. Underwater, the beaver's nostrils and ears close automatically, and it can stay submerged for up to 15 minutes.

Beavers, probably the best-known of nature's "engineers", live in small family groups. They are skilled at felling trees and building dams in order to provide themselves with a safe home and a guaranteed food supply. Their home may be a burrow in a bank

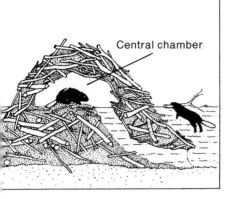

Central chamber

or a "lodge" in a pond made by damming a river. To fell trees, the beaver uses its large cutting *incisor* teeth as chisels to chew chips out of the trunks. It feeds on bark and sapwood, using larger branches as building material for the dam and lodge. The upper half of the lodge projects above water; inside is a dry central chamber, with one or more escape tunnels leading to underwater exits.

Beavers have been hunted for their furs and for their *musk*. Their natural enemies include the WOLVERINE, COYOTE, WOLF, LYNX, PUMA and BEAR. When alarmed, the beaver warns of danger by smacking its broad tail onto the water.

ORDER: Rodentia;
FAMILY: Castoridae;
SPECIES: North American: *Castor canadiensis*; European: *Castor fiber*.

Bee

The bees belong to the same group of insects as the WASP and ANTS. They all have four wings, but the hind ones are small and linked to the front wings by rows of tiny hooks. The insects are mostly brown or black and, unlike wasps, they are generally rather furry. The female nearly always carries a sting, although there are some stingless species. The sting is used for defence. Bees have both sucking and biting mouth-parts and they feed on nectar and pollen which they collect from the

A queen **bee** lays one egg in each of the cells made by the workers. The workers surround the queen to clean and feed her.

flowers. They play a vital role in the pollination of many plants, including many important fruit crops. Nectar is collected with the tongue, while pollen is picked up on the body hairs. Much of the food is taken back to the nest to be stored or fed to the grubs, although the nectar is converted to honey before it is stored.

The HONEY BEE and the BUMBLE BEE, together with a few other kinds of bees, are social insects. They live in colonies of anything from a few dozen to several thousand individuals. All the members work for the good of the colony as a whole. Most bees, however, are solitary insects and, after mating, each female provides

just for herself and her own offspring. Each female excavates a small nest burrow in the ground or in dead wood, or even in loose mortar in buildings, and stocks it with pollen and nectar. Eggs are laid, usually one to each chamber of the nest, and the female then closes up the entrance and flies away. She does not normally have any further contact with her eggs or grubs, which feed happily on the stored food and emerge as adults a few months later. There are a few species, however, in which the female stays around her nest and brings further food supplies as the grubs get bigger.

Cuckoo bees, as their name suggests, do not make their own nests. Some lay their eggs in bumble bee nests and rely on the bumble bees to feed the grubs. Others lay their eggs in the nests of

solitary bees, and their grubs live off the food stored for the rightful occupants. The cuckoo bees do not possess pollen baskets or other equipment for gathering and collecting pollen because they never need to stock any nests.
ORDER: Hymenoptera;
FAMILY: Apidae.

Bee-eater

Bee-eaters make up a family of brilliantly coloured birds. They vary in length from 15 to 36 cm, and are related to KINGFISHERS and ROLLERS, which are also noted for their bright colours. They live in tropical regions of Asia and Africa, although a few species extend into milder temperate areas. Bee-eaters nest in burrows dug with the bill and feet in sandy banks, though in Africa they sometimes use the burrows of AARDVARKS. They get their name from their habit of catching bees and wasps, which they can do without being stung. They also eat dragonflies, beetles and flies, seizing the insects in flight.
ORDER: Coraciiformes;
FAMILY: Meropidae;

A **carmine bee-eater**, one of the most colourful of all African birds.

Beetle

The beetles form the largest of the insect orders, with more than 350,000 known species. They include the bulkiest of all insects – the fist-sized Goliath beetles, which may weigh about 100 grams – and also some of the smallest, with lengths of less than 0.5 mm. There are normally two pairs of wings, but the front ones are hard and horny and conceal the delicate hind wings for most of the time. The front wings are called *elytra*, and they meet in a straight line down the middle of the insect's back. In most beetles, they cover the whole of the abdomen, but some groups, notably the ROVE BEETLES, have very short elytra and a naked abdomen. Some beetles have no hind wings, and some, such as the female GLOW-WORM, have no wings at all.

Beetles live just about everywhere on earth. Many live in fresh water, usually carrying their air supplies around with them under their elytra. All beetles have biting jaws and can eat most kinds of solid food. Some also manage to lap up nectar and other liquid foods. LADYBIRDS, GROUND BEETLES and the fast-running tiger beetles are predatory creatures, feeding largely on other insects.

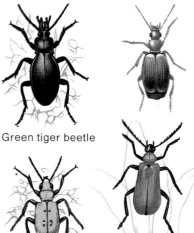

Violet ground beetle   Bombardier beetle

Green tiger beetle

Cardinal beetle

Four of the vast group of **beetles**. The **violet ground beetle** is flightless. The **bombardier beetle** can fire a puff of corrosive liquid when disturbed.

Glow-worms and many other terrestrial species are also predators, and so are most of the WATER BEETLES. The latter often attack fishes and other creatures much larger than themselves. Thousands of beetles are vegetarians, feeding on all parts of plants including hard, dry seeds and the wood of tree trunks. Many

The **oil beetle** can discharge an oily liquid when alarmed.

of these plant-eating species are serious pests, causing huge losses of grain and other foodstuffs in the fields and also in warehouses. Wood-boring beetles, such as the DEATHWATCH BEETLE and the FURNITURE BEETLE, cause severe damage to buildings and to furniture. There are also hordes of scavenging beetles, which feed on dung and carrion or make a living from the debris that accumulates in the nests of birds and other animals. Several of these debris-feeding species find their way into houses, where they feed on carpets and other fabrics.

Beetle larvae vary even more in form than the adults, although they usually inhabit the same places and feed on similar foods. They also have biting jaws like those of the adults. Ground beetle larvae are active runners with strong legs on which to chase their prey, but the larvae of most leaf-feeding beetles are sluggish creatures with soft, fat bodies and short legs. DUNG BEETLE larvae and those living in timber are surrounded by food and do not have to move much. They generally have fat bodies, often curved in a C-shape, and short legs. WEEVIL larvae, which are also usually surrounded by food, have no legs at all.

All beetles pass through a *pupa* stage between the larval and adult stages. Adults can be found at all times of year, even in cold climates. Some fly readily, but others are reluctant to fly even when disturbed, and the wingless ones, of course, are unable to fly.
ORDER: Coleoptera.

Bellbird

The name given to several species of unrelated birds whose song has a metallic ring. There are four species related to the COTINGAS, which live in the forests of South and Central America. One of these, the three-wattled bellbird, has an odd appearance with its three grey-black, turkey-like

A **bighorn** ewe feeding on sparse winter grass.

wattles dangling from the base of its bill. The crested bellbird of Australia is a colourful bird, reddish-brown above and white below. It is related to the FLY-CATCHERS and feeds on grubs, insects and seeds.
ORDER: Passeriformes.

Beluga

The beluga or white whale is a relative of the DOLPHIN. It grows to about 6 metres in length, and lives in Arctic waters, often swimming up rivers.

Under water the beluga "talks" in a series of whistles, earning it the whalers' nickname of "sea canary". One of the toothed whales, the beluga feeds on fish, shrimps, cuttlefish and crabs.

Belugas were once seen in enormous schools of as many as 10,000 individuals, but whaling has greatly reduced their numbers. Normally they move in groups of about a dozen. Their chief enemy is the killer whale.
ORDER: Cetacea;
FAMILY: Monodontidae;
SPECIES: *Delphinapterus leucas*.

Bichir

The bichir is a fish of the River Nile, with many extraordinary

and primitive features. Like other fishes it has gills, but it uses its *swim-bladder* to breathe air, and if held under water it will drown. Also, the bichir's swim-bladder is paired like the lungs of a land animal, whereas in most other fishes it is single.

The bichir has been described as a missing link between the two great groups of fishes – the cartilaginous fishes, or sharks, and the bony, or true, fishes.

The bichir has peculiar front fins, shaped like legs, on which it stalks its prey on the river bed, rather as a cat stalks a mouse. It finds its prey in the mud with the aid of tube-shaped nostrils, yet another strange feature of this most unusual fish.
ORDER: Polypteriformes;
FAMILY: Polypteridae;
SPECIES: *Polypterus bichir*.

Bighorn

The bighorn is a wild sheep which lives in western North America in dry upland country or above the tree-line. Males have huge horns that curve around the back of the head. In old animals, the horns come forward to the level of the eyes. Females have small, slightly curving horns. These powerful animals have little to fear except man. Mating occurs in winter and the young are born six and a half months later. Bighorn sheep, both male and female, sometimes charge at each other and crash head on. Such bone-jarring combats may last for hours.

ORDER: Artiodactyla;
FAMILY: Bovidae;
SPECIES: *Ovis canadensis.*

Bird-eating spider

The bird-eating spiders are among the largest living spiders, having a leg span of up to 20 cm. They live in the Amazon forests of South America, where they hunt small mammals and drag hummingbirds from their nests. They do not spin a web. These spiders are not particularly dangerous to humans; the venom is about as painful as a bee sting, but the body is covered with fine hairs which can irritate the skin of anyone who handles it. The bird-eating spiders are sometimes referred to as tarantulas, but the true TARANTULA is a wolf spider found in southern Europe.

ORDER: Araneae;
FAMILY: Aviculariidae.

A **bird-eating spider** has seized a locust and plunged in its great fangs.

A great **bird of paradise**. These beautiful birds are confined to New Guinea and Australia.

Bird of paradise

The name given to the 43 species of the most colourful and ornate bird family. All live in the forests of New Guinea and neighbouring small islands, apart from four species which live in the mountain forests of north-eastern Australia. Most birds of paradise have long, lacy plumes extending well beyond the tail when they are at rest. When displaying, the plumes form a fan over the back. Courtship displays are often long, elaborate and acrobatic. Some species have rather dull plumage, and the males and females are alike, but in the majority, the sexes differ markedly. The females are dull but the males have brightly coloured plumage. The numbers of many species were severely reduced by local use of the feathers in headdresses and by their export overseas for the fashion industry. Restrictions imposed in the 1920s have helped some species to recover.

ORDER: Passeriformes;
FAMILY: Paradisaeidae.

Birdwing butterfly

The birdwings include some of the largest and most beautiful of all butterflies. They live in the forests of South-East Asia and New Guinea, and some of the females exceed 25 cm in wing-span. The males are a little smaller, but much more colourful, with velvety black wings marked with beautiful iridescent colours. Males sometimes congregate in their hundreds to drink from muddy river banks.

ORDER: Lepidoptera;
FAMILY: Papilionidae.

Bishop bird

Bishop birds make up a group of birds within the family of WEAVER-BIRDS, which also includes the SPARROWS. They are small birds, about 13 cm long, and are found in tropical and sub-tropical regions of Africa, often in open grassland or clearings in forests. Outside the breeding season, bishop birds are dull-coloured, like sparrows, but at breeding time, the males don bright colours; the fire-crowned bishop bird becomes bright red and black for example. Bishop

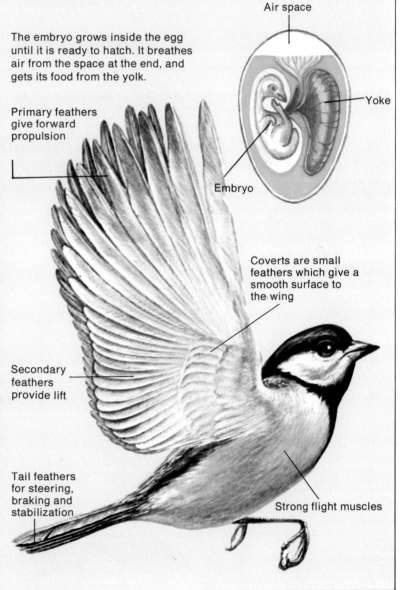

Birds

Birds belong to the animal Class Aves and are distinguished from all other animals by their feathers. The front limbs have been turned into wings, although not all birds can actually fly. Birds are warm-blooded, which means that they can keep their bodies at a constant high temperature regardless of the surrounding temperatures, and thus work more efficiently.

Modern birds have no teeth, but their horny beaks serve the same purpose. The beaks vary in shape according to the diet. All bird species lay eggs, and there is often a long period of parental care before the young birds are able to fend for themselves.

There are 27 orders of living birds. Just over 5000 of the 8600 species belong to just one order – the Passeriformes, or perching birds. These are also known as song birds, and they include all the small birds of the forest and countryside as well as a few larger ones such as the CROWS.

A **great tit** in flight.

The embryo grows inside the egg until it is ready to hatch. It breathes air from the space at the end, and gets its food from the yolk.

Air space

Yoke

Embryo

Primary feathers give forward propulsion

Coverts are small feathers which give a smooth surface to the wing

Secondary feathers provide lift

Tail feathers for steering, braking and stabilization

Strong flight muscles

birds are renowned for their polygamy, which is unusual among birds, each male mating with up to six females.

ORDER: Passeriformes;
FAMILY: Ploceidae.

Bison

There are two species of bison: the American bison, often incorrectly called the buffalo; and the European bison or wisent. These massive, ox-like animals weigh up to 1360 kg. The largest stand 183 cm at the shoulder, which is raised in a hump. The hair on the head, neck, shoulders and forelegs is long and shaggy. The forehead is broad and both sexes have two short, curving horns. The American bison has a longer coat than the wisent, the horns are smaller and less curved and the hindquarters are smaller. There are two varieties of American bison. The plains bison is smaller and lighter in colour than the wood bison of Canada, but it has a heavier head and hump.

Bison live in herds, which once numbered thousands of animals. North America once had 50 million bison but by 1889 only 540 were left. The American Indians killed bison for food, but it was the Europeans who massacred the herds. They killed bison for their meat and skins and also for sport. European bison also nearly became extinct, as their forest habitat was destroyed. The last truly wild bison, in the Bialowieza forest of Poland, were killed during World War I. But European bison were bred in zoos and, in 1959, a herd was re-established in Bialowieza. The American plains bison now number several thousands and Canadian wood bison are protected in a reserve in Alberta. Bison mate between July and September, and gestation takes about nine months.

ORDER: Artiodactyla;
FAMILY: Bovidae;
SPECIES: American: *Bison bison*; European: *Bison bonasus*.

The male red **bishop bird**.

Bitterling

This small, freshwater fish of European rivers is notable for its remarkable breeding behaviour. This involves a freshwater mussel, which is both the breeding ground of the fish and also a kind of partner.

During the breeding season the female bitterling develops a long tube through which she lays her eggs in the gills of the mussel. The male bitterling then exudes his milt, or sperms, also into the

The **bitterling** is about 9 cm long.

mussel, but through its *siphon*. Fertilization of the eggs and early development of the fish take place entirely inside the mussel, the little fishes, or fry, only leaving after about a month. But at the time of egg-laying, the mussel also produces its larvae, which attach themselves to the female bitterling's skin. There, they feed and develop for three months, before dropping from the fish as small but perfectly formed mussels.

ORDER: Cypriniformes;
FAMILY: Cyprinidae;
SPECIES: *Rhodeus sericens*.

Bittern

Bitterns are a sub-family of the HERONS. Like herons, bitterns have long, pointed bills but the neck is shorter and thicker than that of the common heron and the body is rather smaller. The plumage is brown, mottled with black, with a white chin and black cap. The feathers down the front of the neck are long, forming a kind of ruff. The most familiar species in Europe is known for its booming call, like the bellow of a bull. The American bittern differs from the European species in that it has a black patch on either side of the neck, the plumage is more streaked, and it does not have a black cap. Bitterns feed on animals living in reed beds, where they also nest.

ORDER: Ciconiiformes;
FAMILY: Ardeidae.

Bird with a booming call – the **bittern**.

Black bear

There are five species of black bear, all of them smaller than the brown bear. The best-known species is the American Black bear, which is up to 1.5 metres long and weighs up to 230 kg. The fur is not always black; it may be chocolate brown, cinnamon brown or blue-black. However, the black bear can be distinguished from the brown bear by its shorter fur and claws. The Himalayan black bear is similar to the American but is distinguished by a pale V-shaped mark on its chest.

Black bears originally roamed in all the wooded areas of North America. They have since been eliminated from much of their former range, but are increasing in national parks where they have become used to humans and are harmless unless provoked or allowed to become over-friendly.

Black bears breed in June and gestation takes 100 to 210 days. However, black bears sleep through the winter (but do not hibernate in the true sense) and when the cubs are born in January the mother only rouses herself sufficiently to bite through the *umbilical cords* before continuing her sleep for another two months. Meanwhile, the cubs, blind and weighing only 280 grams at birth, alternately drink her milk and sleep. They remain with their mother for six months.

The black bear is the original Teddy Bear. In 1902 Theodore (Teddy) Roosevelt, then President of the United States, caught a black bear and took it home as a pet. Morris Michton, a New York toymaker, then had the idea of manufacturing the small fur-covered Teddy Bears that have since become so popular all over the world.

ORDER: Carnivora;
FAMILY: Ursidae.

Blackbird

The European blackbird is a member of the THRUSH family, with races in Asia and North Africa. A bird of hedgerows and thickets, it is also common in gardens and on farms. The male is

Male

Female

The male **blackbird** is all black, with a bright yellow beak. The female is dark brown all over and is sometimes confused with the thrush. Some blackbirds are albinos that have white patches, or may even be entirely white.

Below: A cock **blackbird** brings a beakful of insects for its ravenous brood.

25 cm long, has a yellow bill and a glossy black plumage. The female is browner, with a brown bill and a speckled breast, and is sometimes confused with a thrush. The blackbird has a rich song, but it is perhaps best known for its rattle-like alarm note which also serves as a warning to other birds that a predator is about. Blackbirds feed especially on berries and soft fruits, but also eat worms, grubs, seeds and small snails. They usually nest in bushes. The cup-shaped nest is generally built by the female, and 3 to 5 eggs are laid.

The New World blackbirds belong to an entirely different family from the European species. The red-winged blackbird is found throughout most of North America, and is so named for the red and yellow tipped shoulders of the male. They live in swamps and marshes, nesting among the reeds. Their diet consists mostly of insects and seed.

ORDER: Passeriformes;
FAMILIES: Turdidae (European); Icteridae (New World).

Blackbuck

The blackbuck or Indian antelope is one of the fastest land animals, being credited with speeds of 80 km/h when alarmed. It can leap about 1.8 metres into the air and can cover up to 7 metres in one bound. The blackbuck is found on the open plains of Pakistan and southern and central India, where it lives in herds ruled by a dominant male. It is just under 122 cm long and weighs up to 36 kg. The adult male is a different colour from the female. The upper parts of the buck are a dark brown, while those of the doe and the young are yellowish-fawn. Only the buck has horns.

ORDER: Artiodactyla;
FAMILY: Bovidae;
SPECIES: *Antilope cervicapra*.

Black-headed Gull

The black-headed gull is one of the smaller gulls. It is distinguished from other gulls by the chocolate-brown "hood" on its head. In winter, the hood disappears, except for small patches on the sides of the head and in front of the eyes. The body is white, with a grey back and wings. The wing tips are black and the bill and legs red. Black-headed gulls are found over most of Europe and Asia, not only around shores but also inland, where they may follow ploughs or search for scraps in towns.

ORDER: Charadriiformes;
FAMILY: Laridae;
SPECIES: *Larus ridibundus*.

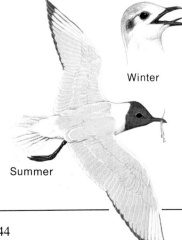

Winter

Summer

Black widow spider

This species of spider is found all over the warmer parts of the world. The North American species is feared for its powerful venom, but although its attack is painful it is rarely fatal unless its victims are very young, old or unwell. The venom seems to be strongest in the sub-species which lives in the southern United States. The black widow spins an irregular web, which often includes a short funnel of silk; the male's web is smaller. The spider inhabits cool, dark places, such as cellars and outbuildings. It appears that most human victims are attacked in primitive latrines. Death, when it does result, is probably caused by shock.

People believe that the black widow gets her name because she eats her mate. Although this is sometimes the case, males in captivity have been known to mate with several females.

ORDER: Araneae;
FAMILY: Theridiidae;
SPECIES: *Latrodectus mactans*.

Blenny

The common name of a very large assemblage of fishes belonging to 20 or so different families. Mostly, these fishes are small inhabitants of shallow areas of temperate and

An African **black widow spider** spinning its web. The red spot may have an hour-glass shape.

tropical seas. Many live near the shore line and can often be found lurking under stones or in seaweed. They are also commonly found in rock pools after the retreat of the tide.

A common feature of these species of fishes is a long *dorsal fin* that extends from the back of the head along the back, either nearly reaching the tail or completely fusing with it. Most blennies seem to eat a wide variety of foods. In their inshore waters, they are easy prey for sharp-eyed gulls or scavenging rats, but they get some protection from camouflage. They are able to change the mottled patterns of their bodies to match their stony background.

ORDER: Perciformes;
FAMILY: Blenniidae and others.

Blister beetle

The many species of blister beetles are soft-bodied insects with soft *elytra*. They get their name because they contain a substance

Male Montague's **blennies** are blue-spotted.

called cantharidin, which causes blistering of the skin. Merely touching one of these insects, especially on the elytra, can cause a burning sensation and painful blisters. Most species possess bright warning colours. They live mainly in dry climates, but the Spanish fly, a handsome metallic green insect, is widespread in the southern half of Europe. The adult feeds on various trees and shrubs, but the larva lives as a parasite in the nests of solitary bees. Most other blister beetle grubs live in this way, although some attack grasshopper eggs.
ORDER: Coleoptera;
FAMILY: Meloidae.

Blow-fly

This name is given to several species of stout flies whose maggots develop in rotting flesh. Best known are the bluebottles and greenbottles which are beautifully coloured with metallic sheens, but have rather unpleasant habits. Bluebottles regularly enter houses in their search for meat or fish in which to lay their eggs, and their noisy flight can be most annoying. Greenbottles are less inclined to come inside, but can often be seen resting on sunny walls. They lay their eggs in various sorts of carrion, and often

Right: The **greenbottle** and **bluebottle** with maggot. Below: a greenbottle sucking up its food.

on living animals, especially sheep. The resulting maggots feed on the living flesh, causing serious sores.
ORDER: Diptera;
FAMILY: Calliphoridae.

Bluefish

The bluefish is a fast-swimming and fierce ocean fish, about 40 cm long, with a bluish or greenish body. It lives in large schools. Bluefish schools roam tropical and subtropical waters, and the trail of such a school is often marked by widespread blood and fragments of fish, showing the damage it has inflicted on other shoals of fishes. Bluefish occur in quite incredible numbers. The population of the western Atlantic in summer has been estimated at a thousand million. Moreover, each bluefish is likely to kill 10 other fishes each day! Man takes his revenge on the bluefish by catching 18 million kg each year for food.
ORDER: Perciformes;
FAMILY: Pomatomidae;
SPECIES: *Pomatomus saltatrix*.

Blue butterfly

The blue butterflies, of which there are several hundred species, are small insects related to the COPPER and HAIRSTREAK butterflies. They get their name because the males of most of the species are bright blue on the upper side. The females are usually brown, with a greater or lesser scattering of blue

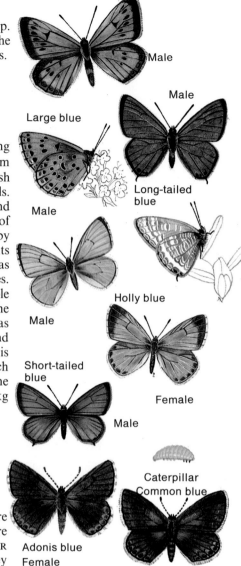

Male
Large blue
Male
Male
Long-tailed blue
Male
Holly blue
Male
Short-tailed blue
Female
Male
Caterpillar Common blue
Adonis blue Female
Female

Below: The male **common blue**, one of the commonest butterflies.

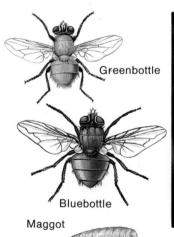

Greenbottle

Bluebottle

Maggot

scales around the wing bases. The under-sides of both sexes are usually decorated with black and white eye-spots and often bear orange spots around the margins. The hind wings often carry small "tails", but in some tropical species, popularly known as "back-to-front" butterflies, these projections are very long and look like additional antennae. Black spots at the hind margin of the wing resemble eyes, and the whole effect is to produce a false head at the hind end when the butterfly is at rest. This arrangement deceives many birds, which attack the hind end instead of the true head. The butterfly can then fly away, for it is not harmed if small parts of its wings are torn. Most blues of the temperate regions inhabit grasslands, where their larvae feed on vetches and related plants. The caterpillars of the North American harvester and its Asian relatives prey on aphids. The European large blue has a truly amazing life history, during which the caterpillars are collected by ants and taken into their nest. The caterpillars are fed with young ants, and in return they give out a sugary substance which the ants lap up eagerly. Many tropical blues live in the forests.

ORDER: Lepidoptera;
FAMILY: Lycaenidae.

Blue whale

The blue whale is the largest animal that has ever lived. It can reach a length of 30 metres and a weight of 135 tonnes. Sadly, its great size has made it a target for

The largest **blue whale** ever caught was over 33 metres in length.

the whaler's harpoon. Over-hunting in the Arctic and Antarctic oceans, by whaling fleets eager for the vast quantities of blubber in the blue whale, has so reduced its numbers that the species is now on the brink of extinction.

Blue whales are baleen whales (see WHALE). They swallow enormous amounts of food to supply energy to their huge bodies, and a blue whale's stomach has been found to contain 2 tonnes of krill. They usually swim alone or in small groups. Apart from man, their only enemy is the killer whale, which will attack young blue whales. When danger threatens, other whales will come to the aid of their fellow, and a male never deserts a harpooned female – thereby sealing his own fate.

ORDER: Cetacea;
FAMILY: Balaenopteridae;
SPECIES: *Balaenoptera musculus.*

Boa

Boas are part of the Boidae family, which also includes pythons. The most well-known species, but by no means the largest, is the boa constrictor. Averaging 3 to 4 metres and weighing around 60 kg, this ground-dwelling snake lives among forest flora in the warmest parts of the Americas, from Mexico to northern Argentina.

As its name suggests, the boa constrictor kills its prey by squeezing or constricting. Death is by suffocation rather than crushing – the victim's ribcage is squeezed so tightly it cannot fill its lungs. Large lizards, birds and small mammals are common prey, but tales of boas constricting human victims to death are far-fetched. In fact, boa constrictors have been

kept as pets on Brazilian farms, to control rats and mice.

Other boas include the ANACONDA, the largest reptile in the world, and less well-known species like the sand boas and tree boas. Most boas prefer habitats with an abundance of plant life and water, but sand boas have adapted to life in dry regions. Living just beneath the surface, their bodies can withstand extremes of heat. Tree boas have also adapted their bodies to fit their surroundings. Beautiful green colouration and flattened bodies, which allow them to press close to tree branches, are ideal camouflage for forest life.

ORDER: Squamata;
FAMILY: Boidae;
SPECIES: *Constrictor constrictor* (boa constrictor).

Bobcat

The bobcat is the North American equivalent of the European WILD CAT. Bobcats weigh up to 9 kg and measure up to 90 cm including the very short tail. The ears are tipped with pointed tufts, rather like those of the closely related LYNX. Experiments suggest that the tufts somehow help the ears collect sounds. Most bobcats are brown, spotted with grey or white. Their range stretches from Canada to Mexico, including habitats from deserts to forests.

These solitary creatures hunt at night. The size of each animal's range may be 8 to 80 km across according to the food supply the range holds. Bobcats mainly hunt rabbits and rodents, but will tackle many other kinds of prey, even killing deer and domestic livestock. Most females give birth to two kits, usually at the end of

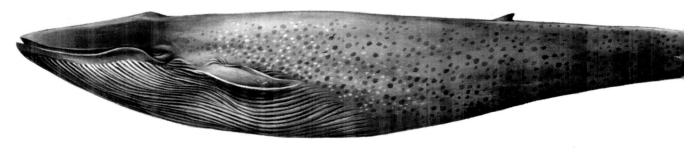

winter. The young are prey to foxes and horned owls. Adult bobcats are killed by pumas and they are widely persecuted by man.

ORDER: Carnivora;
FAMILY: Felidae;
SPECIES: *Lynx rufus*.

Bollworm

This name is given to the caterpillars of several kinds of moths that feed in the seed capsules, or bolls, of cotton. The most serious of these pests is the cotton bollworm which also attacks maize and many other crops. The adult moth is pale brown and about 3.5 cm across the wings. The female lays her eggs on the leaves and flowers, and the caterpillars nibble any part of the plant at first. They eventually make their way into the bolls and eat the seeds, so that the cotton fibres fail to develop.

ORDER: Lepidoptera;
FAMILY: Noctuidae.

Bonito

The name given to a number of large relatives of MACKERELS. All are important food fishes, living mainly in tropical and subtropical parts of the Atlantic and more sparingly in temperate parts of this ocean. These lively, streamlined fishes are also caught for sport.

Bonito are hunting fishes, swimming in shoals when young but becoming more solitary with age. Sailors on sailing ships knew the large bonito well because they were likely to appear whenever the ship had flushed a shoal of flying fish, which are the bonitos' favourite food. Bonito are not among the fastest swimmers of the mackerel family, their fastest recorded swimming speed being a mere 16 km/h, far less than that of their great relatives the tunas.

ORDER: Perciformes;
FAMILY: Scombridae.

Bontebok

The bontebok was nearly wiped out by hunters in the 1800s. It was saved by a farmer in Cape Province, South Africa, who enclosed some of these fast-running antelopes on his land and established a breeding herd. Today, bontebok can be seen only on private farms and in national parks. The bontebok stands about 122 cm at the shoulder and weighs up to 90 kg. The horns are 38 to 41 cm long. The name bontebok means "painted buck" and this glossy reddish-brown animal has a white blaze on the face, a white rump and white on the insides of the legs.

ORDER: Artiodactyla;
FAMILY: Bovidae;
SPECIES: *Damaliscus pygargus*.

Booby

Six species of the GANNET family which live in tropical regions are known as boobies. The name

A pair of **boobies** perform the first steps of their ritual courtship dance which will end with the female touching the male's bill or neck. The female builds a cup-shaped nest.

comes from the Spanish word "bobo", meaning "dunce". Boobies are so called because they are clumsy on land and do not fear human beings. They are goose-sized birds, with thick necks and large heads, and long, powerful wings.

All boobies nest in colonies, the birds usually crowded together, but nesting sites vary. Pairs are slow to form, but once formed, a pair stays together for life. The nest is built of seaweed, feathers, fish bones and droppings which the male collects and deposits in front of the female as she builds up a cup-shaped nest. Two eggs are laid but rarely more than one is reared.

ORDER: Pelecaniformes;
FAMILY: Sulidae.

Booklouse

Booklice, also called dustlice, are very small, flattened, wingless insects that are usually found indoors in dusty corners and among piles of books and papers. They feed on debris and on the tiny moulds associated with it. There are numerous species, and they belong to a group called psocids. This group also includes many winged insects that live on tree trunks. These are called barklice because they chew the algae on the bark.

ORDER: Psocoptera.

Boomslang

The boomslang is one of the few rearfanged snakes which are dangerous to man. Boomslang bites are usually fatal, unless very quickly treated. The venom runs down grooves in some of the teeth in the back part of the upper jaw. This slender, bright green snake lives in Africa. It slides gracefully among branches well above the ground where it hunts for birds, tree lizards and small mammals. It often snatches eggs and fledglings from their nests. The female lays her eggs in a warm, moist hollow, often in a sandy bank, but sometimes in a woodpecker's nest hole in a tree.

ORDER: Squamata;
FAMILY: Colubridae;
SPECIES: *Dispholidus typus*.

A cock **satin bower-bird** sits in the bower of twigs it has built.

Bower-bird

The name given to a number of species of birds that build "bowers" from twigs, grass, leaves and other plant material. The bower is used by the male bower-bird as a centre point for the elaborate courtship displays with which he attracts a mate. After mating, the female builds a simple nest away from the bower.

Bower-birds live in Australia and New Guinea. The bower may vary in complexity from a simple clearing on the ground to a tall tower with a tepee-like roof. Some have many compartments. They are nearly always decorated with brightly-coloured and glittering objects – snail shells, seeds, pebbles, dead insects and feathers, for example. Man-made objects are also used, such as bottle tops. Three species actually mix pigments and paint the walls of their bowers.

ORDER: Passeriformes;
FAMILY: Ptilonorhynchidae.

Bowfin

The bowfin is a primitive fish that lives in lakes and rivers of North America. It is like a PIKE in shape and size, with powerful jaws that show it is a predator. Like LUNG-FISHES, the bowfin lives in sluggish

The **brambling** can be recognized by its orange breast.

Female

Male
(summer)

Male
(winter)

waters containing little dissolved oxygen, and, like them, it uses its *swim-bladder* to breathe air. The male fish makes a nest and guards the eggs and young.

ORDER: Amiiformes;
FAMILY: Amiidae;
SPECIES: *Amia calva*.

Brambling

The brambling looks like a CHAF-FINCH, but differs in having a white rump and less white on the wings. It also has a bold orange shoulder patch and breast, and the male has a black (not blue) head and mantle in spring and summer. This attractive bird breeds in the far north of Europe and Asia, nesting among the birch woods and willow thickets and feeding on buds, seeds, fruits and insects. Bramblings migrate southward for the winter, which they spend in the southern half of Europe and the Middle East. Birds nesting in Siberia fly to Japan for the winter.

ORDER: Passeriformes;
FAMILY: Fringillidae;
SPECIES: *Fringilla montifringilla*.

Bream

Sea bream include several fishes more properly called WRASSES, but the name bream usually refers to a freshwater fish belonging to the CARP family. Freshwater bream are stocky, narrow-bodied fishes living in slow-moving rivers and lakes throughout northern and eastern Europe. They generally grow to about 60 cm in length, but because they are so deep-bodied they can weigh up to 8 kg.

Bream are sluggish moving fishes that feed on small creatures in the mud but occasionally snap up small fishes. They have a mouth which can be pushed out like a tube for feeding. They provide good sport for fishermen only in the breeding season, when they leap and roll at the surface before spawning.

ORDER: Cypriniformes;
FAMILY: Cyprinidae.

Brine shrimp

The brine shrimp is a small crustacean, closely related to the FAIRY SHRIMP. It lives in salty lakes and pools, generally in water that is twice as salty as sea-water. Although less than 1 cm long, these shrimps are often so abundant that the water appears red. The brine shrimp has two pairs of antennae, two compound eyes on stalks, and a third eye in the middle of its head. It has 11 pairs of limbs.

ORDER: Anostraca;
SPECIES: *Artemia salina*.

Bristlemouth

A type of small, deep-sea fish which, although not widely known, is probably the commonest of all ocean fishes. The reason for the obscurity of bristlemouth fishes is that when they are fished out of the ocean depths, their flimsy bodies are so broken up by the net as to be almost unrecognizable.

Bristlemouths are small fishes usually not more than 5 cm long. Owing to their skimpy skeletons and poorly developed muscles, they weigh very little. Bristlemouths, like many other deep-sea creatures, have rows of light organs on their bodies. These fishes get their name from their wide gape and bristle-like teeth.

ORDER: Salmoniformes;
FAMILY: Gonostomatidae.

The **bream** is a deep-bodied fish with a high back.

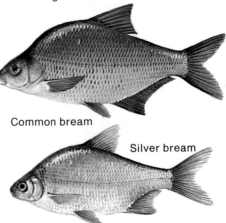

Common bream

Silver bream

Bristletail

The bristletails are primitive, wingless insects. There are two distinct groups – those with two "tails" and those with three. Two-tailed bristletails are very slender, soil-living insects. Their tails are usually slender, but in some species they are stouter and sometimes resemble little pincers. Most feed on decaying plant material. Some of the three-tailed species live under stones on the seashore, but the best-known are the domestic SILVERFISH and firebrat.

ORDERS: Diplura (two-tailed); Thysanura (three-tailed).

Bristleworm

The bristleworms form one of the main groups into which the segmented worms, or ANNELIDS, are divided. With few exceptions, the bristleworms are sea creatures. Most have cylindrical bodies, along which are a number of limb-

Three kinds of **bristleworm**. The peacock worm and *Serpula vermicularis* live in tubes.

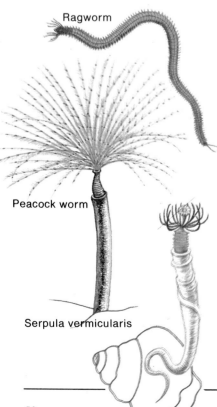

Ragworm

Peacock worm

Serpula vermicularis

Although the **brown bear** is a carnivore, it eats berries and other plant material.

like projections called *parapodia*. Each parapodium carries bunches of bristles. There are more than 5000 species of bristleworms, ranging in length from a fraction of a centimetre to more than 6 metres. Colours range from dull brown to pink, red and green.

Some bristleworms live in tubes in the sea-bed, while others move about, swimming or crawling under shells and rocks. Bristleworms feed on particles of plant and animal matter which they filter from the water or mud, though some are active carnivores.

A few are parasites of other marine creatures. Familiar bristleworms include the LUGWORMS and ragworms used as bait by fishermen, and the sea-mice, which are not really worm-like in shape and have a felt-like covering of short bristles over their backs.

CLASS: Polychaeta.

Brittlestar

These ECHINODERMS look like slender STARFISHES, with five snake-like arms joined to a central disc, or body. These arms break off easily, but the animal can regrow them. They are covered with rows of hard plates and spines. On the under-side of each arm are tube feet, which are used for feeding. Brittlestars feed on small particles of animal and plant life, and also on larger animals. They normally move about by "rowing" through the sea-bed mud with their arms.

CLASS: Ophiuroidea;
ORDER: Ophiurida.

Brown bear

There is uncertainty as to whether there are many species of brown bear or only one. However, most zoologists now believe that there is only one species, of which there are several races of sub-species.

The European brown bear once roamed all over Europe and Asia, but its European range is now confined to parts of the Pyrenees, Swiss Alps, Carpathians, Balkans, Norway, Sweden and Finland. It is 1.5 to 2.4 metres long and weighs 91 to 349 kg.

The grizzly bear is the North American race of brown bear, and is larger than the European race. Like other bears, it was once widely distributed, but is now mostly confined to northern Canada. It is said to have poor eyesight, but its sense of smell is acute. The Kodiak bear is the largest of the brown bears, being about 3 metres long and weighing 700 to 800 kg. It is found mainly on Kodiak Island, off the coast of Alaska.

Brown bears live in wild, mountainous country, wandering about singly or in family groups. Their home ranges have an average radius of 30 km or more. They are not normally aggressive, but can be very dangerous if aroused. Most attacks are mac oy injured bears or females separated from their cubs. Grizzly bears have the greatest reputation for fierceness, but the enormous and powerful Kodiak bear is truly terrifying when angry. It is said to be able to kill a horse or an ox with one blow of its forepaw.

Like other bears, brown bears eat a wide variety of both plant and animal food. Among other things they are highly skilled at fishing – standing patiently in shallow water and scooping up fish as they swim by. They are particularly partial to salmon.

Their breeding habits are similar to those of BLACK BEARS. They mate in June and the cubs, weighing 0.5 to 0.7 kg, are born in January, during the winter sleep.
ORDER: Carnivora;
FAMILY: Ursidae;
SPECIES: *Ursus arctos.*

Brown butterfly

The browns are a large group of butterflies. They are called this because most of the several hundred species are mostly brown. The most obvious feature, however, is the possession of a number of prominent eye-spots around the edges of the wings. These eye-spots are simply patterns, each consisting of a light ring with a dark centre, and they act as decoys. Birds see the spots and peck at them instead of attacking the butterfly's body. The insect is not harmed and is able to fly away with no more than a small piece cut out of its wing. There are some very large members in the family, but most of the browns are medium-sized butterflies, with the females often larger and paler than the males. They are found mainly on grassland and heathland or in light woodland. Quite a number of species have also made their homes on mountain-tops, especially in the Alps and Pyrenees. The caterpillars feed almost exclusively on grasses. Familiar European species include the meadow brown, the ringlet and the wall brown. The family also includes the marbled white. This is white,

with black or brown marbling, but it still has the characteristic eye-spots of the browns. In North America, the brown butterflies are variously known as nymphs and satyrs. Two common species are the common wood nymph and the pearly eye.
ORDER: Lepidoptera;
FAMILY: Satyridae.

Budgerigar

The budgerigar is an Australian member of the parrot family. It lives in the desert parts of Australia, travelling in large flocks from one feeding ground to another

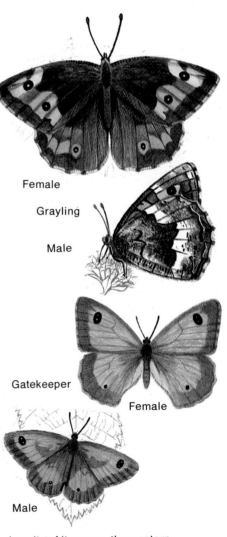

Female

Grayling

Male

Gatekeeper

Female

Male

In spite of its name, the western **marbled white** (left) is a brown butterfly. The **grayling** (above) is common in many parts.

except in the breeding season. Budgerigars eat seeds and fruit, and are a threat to grain crops. They nest in trees, carving out nest holes in rotten wood.

Wild budgerigars are grass-green with bright yellow on the head and long tapering blue tails. The upper parts are barred and scalloped with black and yellow, and there is a blue patch on each cheek and three black spots on each side of the throat. The base of the bill is blue in males and brownish in females.

Budgerigars are popular as cage birds, and selective breeding has produced many colour varieties, including darker shades of green, blue, yellow, grey and olive. The birds readily mimic other sounds in captivity, including human speech.

ORDER: Psittaciformes;
FAMILY: Psittacidae;
SPECIES: *Melopsittacus undulatus.*

Bugs

The bugs are an immense group of insects ranging from tiny APHIDS and SCALE INSECTS to large CICADAS and giant WATER BUGS 10 cm long. Their habits are equally wide-ranging, but they all possess needle-like mouth parts which they plunge into plants or other animals to suck their juices. There are two distinct sections within the group – the Heteroptera and the Homoptera. Some experts consider these to be separate orders, while others put them into a single order known as the Hemiptera. Heteropteran bugs may be winged or wingless, but when wings are present there is a tough, horny base part and a membranous tip to each front wing. The hind wings are completely membrane. The wings are folded flat over the body at rest and, unlike beetle *elytra*, they overlap each other. Heteropteran bugs include both sap-sucking and carnivorous species, and many live in the water.

Homopteran bugs are all sap-feeders and they live on land. The front wings may be tough, or they may be membranous, but they are always of a uniform texture. They are usually held roof-like over the body at rest. The antennae are usually very small and bristle-like, although they are quite long in the aphids. Many of the homopteran bugs can jump, and are known as hoppers.

All the bugs grow up through nymphal stages which resemble the adults, and there is no chrysalis stage. There are well over 50,000 species.

ORDER: Hemiptera.

A red-whiskered **bulbul**. Bulbuls often form large, noisy flocks.

Bulbul

The name given to members of a family of 119 species of small birds that live in the warmer parts of Europe, Asia and Africa. They have also been introduced to other countries such as New Zealand and the United States. They range from the size of a house sparrow to the size of a blackbird. Generally dull in colour, the sexes are usually similar. Some species have bright patches of red, yellow or white.

Out of the breeding season bulbuls live in noisy flocks. They are mostly forest dwellers.

ORDER: Passeriformes;
FAMILY: Pycnonotidae.

Bullfinch

A brightly-coloured FINCH found across Europe and Asia from the British Isles to Japan. It generally inhabits woodlands. Bullfinches feed on buds and seeds, causing enormous damage to fruit trees as they work their way along the branches from the tips, stripping the buds as they go. They do this after their supply of seeds has been

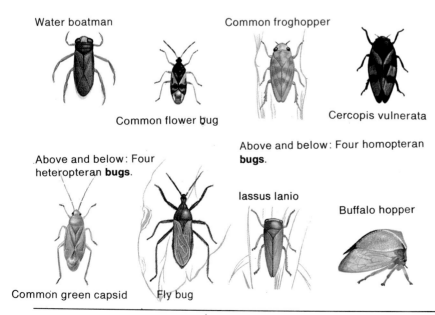

Water boatman

Common flower bug

Above and below: Four heteropteran **bugs**.

Common green capsid   Fly bug

Common froghopper

Cercopis vulnerata

Above and below: Four homopteran **bugs**.

Iassus lanio

Buffalo hopper

A cock **bullfinch** displays his splendid breast.

exhausted. Their nests are made of fine twigs with moss and lichen and are built in hedgerows. There may be three clutches of 4 to 5 eggs.
ORDER: Passeriformes;
FAMILY: Fringillidae;
SPECIES: *Pyrrhula pyrrhula*.

Bullfrog

This large North American frog can grow up to 20 cm in length. Bullfrogs seldom leave water except in very wet weather. They lie along the water's edge, and pounce on passing worms or insects. But bullfrogs take much larger prey as well. A big bullfrog can gobble up baby terrapins, small snakes, mice and ducklings. Even swallows flying by may be snatched from the air.
ORDER: Salientia
FAMILY: Ranidae;
SPECIES: *Rana catesbiana*.

Bullhead

The bullhead is a freshwater fish living in European rivers. How-

ever, the name bullhead is also given to a number of other small freshwater and marine fishes living in various parts of the world.

In North America, relatives of the bullhead are known as SCULPINS, and the term bullhead is applied to the CATFISHES. In the southern United States a marine fish of the Sciaenidae family is also called bullhead.

The European bullhead is 7 to 15 cm long with a broad, flat head that is rounded in front, and a body stout in the head region and tapering to the tail. Its colour is normally greenish-yellow with dark bars and blotches, but the bullhead can change its colour patterns to match those of the stony river bed on which it is lying. Also it may change colour as a result of fear or rage.

The bullhead is a highly aggressive little fish which will nip any unwary finger and for this reason it has been a source of sport to children. It seeks the cover of stones and when disturbed darts away to fresh cover with such speed as to be practically invisible. Bullheads feed mostly at night, mainly on insects but also on anything else that comes along, including fishes as big as or even bigger than itself. The sharp spines on its gill covers give it protection against all but the largest predators. A HERON can manage a bullhead easily, but a GREBE, which does not have the trick of turning the fish to swallow it head-first, may well choke on a bullhead's gill-cover spines.
ORDER: Scorpaeniformes;
FAMILY: Cottidae.

White-tailed bumblebee (queen)

Bumble bee

These large, hairy, black and yellow bees are found in most temperate regions, buzzing around flowers in summer. Like the HONEY BEES they are social insects, although their colonies are generally smaller and less complex – between 50 and several hundred members. Unlike honey bees, only the queen lives through the winter, and bumble bees do not die when they sting.

A bumble bee colony begins in spring when the queen emerges from hibernation. She builds a nest with moss and grass on, or under, the ground (old mouse holes are popular) and stocks it with pollen and nectar from nearby flowers. This is mixed to form "bee bread". Wax secreted from the queen's *abdomen* is used to make individual chambers or cells in which she lays her eggs and stores the food supply. The eggs develop into larvae, then pupate within a week or two. Young bumble bees, called workers, emerge. Some leave the nest to help the queen collect further supplies of pollen and nectar, while others build more wax cells to enlarge the colony. Later the colony rears drones and queens.

Bumble bees are farmers' best friends because they pollinate, or help to fertilize, many plants such as clover which are important as

Below: A **bumble bee** sips nectar. Bumble bees form colonies, but these are smaller than those of honeybees.

food for livestock. They have developed long tongues for sipping the sweet liquid nectar found deep within flowers. As they do this, tiny grains of pollen stick to their hairy legs and bodies. When they visit other flowers, some of the pollen brushes off and fertilizes the flowers. The rest of the pollen is carried back to the nest with the nectar, which is regurgitated and mixed with enzymes to change it into honey. Unlike honey bees, they do not produce enough honey to be collected by humans.
ORDER: Hymenoptera;
FAMILY: Apidae.

Bunting

A name used in the Old World for a group of finchlike birds which live mostly in open country. Members of the same group are known as "sparrows" or "finches" in America and the name, bunting, is used for the colourful members of a closely related group that includes CARDINALS. Old World buntings occur throughout Europe, most of Asia and large parts of Africa. Examples are the yellowhammer, reed bunting and the corn bunting.

A **burnet moth** displays narrow wings brightly patched with colour.

Corn bunting

Male (summer)

Female

male (winter)

Reed bunting

Many buntings are migratory, moving south in the autumn and returning to their northern breeding grounds in the spring. Outside the breeding season many buntings form flocks. They feed on seeds, especially those of grasses, and on insects and their larvae.
ORDER: Passeriformes;
FAMILY: Emberizidae.

Burnet moth

The burnets are brightly coloured, day-flying moths found mainly in grassy places. Black and red are the main colours, but close examination reveals that the front wings of many species are a deep metallic green, especially when the insects are freshly emerged from their pupae. The bold colours warn birds and other predators that the burnets are unpleasant to eat; in fact, they contain a form of cyanide in their bodies. The antennae are markedly thicker at the tips, but there is no risk of confusing these insects with butterflies because of their very narrow front wings. Although they beat their wings rapidly, they fly slowly and appear to drift from flower to flower. The larvae feed on various low-growing plants and pupate in papery cocoons on grass stems.
ORDER: Lepidoptera;
FAMILY: Zygaenidae.

Burrowing owl

The little burrowing owl was once common on the prairies of North

America, but the spread of agriculture has reduced its numbers. Only 23 cm high, it is unusual among owls in that it hunts by day as well as by night, pouncing on small rodents and insects. It nests in a burrow, usually taking over a hole made by some other animal, although it can dig by scraping with its talons. The eggs are laid at the end of the burrow and guarded by the parents. Burrowing owls used to breed in colonies, but most of these have disappeared.

ORDER: Strigiformes;
FAMILY: Strigidae;
SPECIES: *Speotyto cunicularia*.

Burying beetle

The burying beetles, also called sexton beetles, feed on, and breed in, the dead bodies of small animals. Males and females usually work in pairs, and they bury the carrion by scraping the soil away from underneath it. If the soil is too hard where the beetles find the carcase, they may drag it to a more convenient place. Some are jet black, but the most familiar species carry bright orange bands on their *elytra*. Having buried a carcase, the female lays her eggs beside it. The grubs that hatch out feed partly on the decaying meat, and partly on the fly larvae and other scavengers that feed there.

ORDER: Coleoptera;
FAMILY: Silphidae.

Burying beetles

Bushbaby

The bushbaby, also called the galago, is an agile, nocturnal animal. It leaps easily from branch to branch and a standing jump of 225 cm has been recorded. There are five species, all of which occur in Africa south of the Sahara. The most widespread, the Senegal bushbaby, is 41 cm long, including the tail. It has a round head, with large eyes and a short muzzle. The ears are large and the fur ranges from yellowish-grey to brown. The hind legs are longer than the front legs. The ends of a bushbaby's fingers and toes are flattened with pads of thick skin on the underside that help it get a grip on the smooth bark of the trees from which it gets its food – insects, especially locusts, fruit and birds' eggs, as well as flowers, pollen and honey.

Unusually for a large animal, the bushbaby pollinates plants. Thicktailed bushbabies feed on the newly opened flowers of the baobab tree, eating only the outer parts of the flowers, so that no damage is caused to seed or fruit production. As they feed they pick up the pollen on their snouts which they then transfer to the next flower, so pollinating it.

ORDER: Primates;
FAMILY: Lorisidae.

Bushbuck

The bushbuck is an antelope, closely related to the NYALA and KUDU, which inhabits the forests and bush of Africa south of the Sahara. It stands up to 76 cm at the shoulder and weighs between

Dark bush cricket

Speckled bush cricket

The **bushbuck** is a small antelope that lives in the forest and bush of southern Africa.

45 and 77 kg. The colour of the back and flanks ranges from a light tawny in females to a dark brown in the larger males, with white spots and stripes. The sharp horns of the male may reach 56 cm. Females may also have horns but are generally hornless. The horns are used to fight off predators. Bushbuck have been known to kill leopards, wild dogs and, when wounded, even men.

ORDER: Artiodactyla;
FAMILY: Bovidae;
SPECIES: *Tragelaphus scriptus*.

Bush-cricket

Bush-crickets are often confused with GRASSHOPPERS, but they can be distinguished very easily by their long *antennae*, often much longer than the body. Female bush-crickets are also easily identifed by their curved, sabre-like *ovipositor*. Bush-crickets are much more nocturnal than grasshoppers

Great green bush cricket

The great green **bush cricket** above sings loudly in long bursts.

and, as the name suggests, prefer shrubs and hedgerows. Some, such as the great green bush-cricket, are fully winged and fly well, while others are quite flightless. The tizi, from southern Europe, is a well-known flightless species. Some American species, known as katydids, are noted for their loud songs. The insects seem to be calling "Katy-did, Katy-did", hence their name. Katydids can be heard most often in late summer and the autumn. Male bush-crickets sing by rubbing their wing bases together, and even the flightless species have enough wing to produce their calls. These are often much higher-pitched than grasshoppers calls. Bush-crickets eat both plant and animal matter, but small insects are their main food. There are thousands of species and they are especially numerous in the tropics.
ORDER: Orthoptera;
FAMILY: Tettigoniidae.

Bushmaster

The bushmaster is the largest poisonous snake found in the Americas. It can be up to 3.7 metres long and is the only American PIT VIPER to lay eggs. Another unusual feature is the small, silent "rattle" at the end of the tail. This earns the snake its name *muta*, meaning "silent".

This snake occurs in northern South America and Central America. Its pale brown body marked with dark brown blotches conceals it in its forest habitat. Its bite is deadly, but is seldom used on people.
ORDER: Squamata;
FAMILY: Crotalidae;
SPECIES: *Lachesis muta*.

Bushpig

The bushpig lives in mostly broken country in Africa south of the Sahara and in Madagascar. The bushpig can run fast, swim well and shows spirited defence against intruders, such as its main preda-

tor, the leopard. Although it is a sensitive, shy animal, it is a menace to farmers because of the damage it does to crops. The bushpig is stout-bodied, with a large head, and a coat of short bristles. Young adults are reddish, but older animals become reddish-brown or black. The height at the shoulder averages 76 cm and the pig can weigh up to 136 kg. There are two pairs of tusks which are more apparent when the mouth is open. The upper tusk is 8 cm long and the lower one is 19 cm long.
ORDER: Artiodactyla;
FAMILY: Suidae.
SPECIES: *Potamochoerus porcus*.

Bustard

A group of large birds 36 to 132 cm in length. Bustards are birds of open country, such as plains, downs and deserts, where their mottled grey or brown plumage camouflages them and they can run freely on their powerful legs. There are 22 species of bustard, spread across the Old World from the Canary Islands to Australia, although most species live in Africa. Many of them now have a reduced range because of over-hunting.

Bustards are noted for their striking courtship displays. The male great bustard undergoes a remarkable transformation when it displays. From being a rather dull grey and brown bird, it sud-

Little **bustards**.

Male

Female

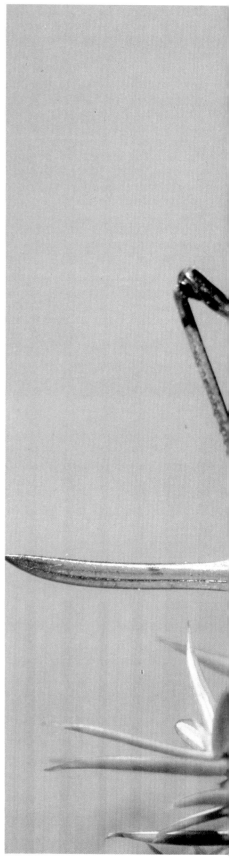

Right: A female **bush cricket**. Note the sabre-like ovipositor

denly becomes a billowing mass of white feathers. The feathers on the back are turned over, and the tail is turned up and over the back, to display the white undersides. The nest is merely some trampled grass or a depression in the ground.
ORDER: Gruiformes;
FAMILY: Otididae.

Butcherbird

The name butcherbird is given to six species of birds from Australia and New Guinea which impale their prey on thorns, or even barbed wire. They belong to the same family as the currawongs and bell-magpies, and bear some resemblance to CROWS and SHRIKES. They have large heads and hooked, shrike-like bills. Shrikes are also sometimes referred to as butcherbirds. Butcherbirds stay paired throughout the year. They are shy birds but are noted for their song.
ORDER: Passeriformes;
FAMILY: Cracticidae.

Butterflies and Moths

With over 150,000 known species, the butterflies and moths form one of the largest of the insect orders. They range from huge ATLAS MOTHS and BIRDWING BUTTER-FLIES, with wing-spans exceeding 25 cm, to ones barely 3 mm across the wings. Apart from a few wingless female moths, the insects all have four wings which are clothed with tiny scales. These give the wings their colours and patterns, but they rub off quite easily and older insects often lose much of their colour. The insects feed almost entirely on nectar, although some butterflies also enjoy the juices of ripe fruit and even those of rotting meat. The liquids are sucked up through a long tongue, or *proboscis*, which acts like a drinking straw. The tongues of some moths are several centimetres long, so the insects can reach the nectar in deep-throated flowers – often while hovering in

An elegant North American **moon moth**. Note the feathery antennae.

front of the flowers. When not in use, the proboscis is coiled up like a watch spring under the head. A number of moths have no proboscis and do not feed in the adult state. One small group actually has functional jaws and feeds by chewing pollen. No more than 13 mm across their metallic wings, these little insects are quite common on sedges and buttercups in the spring.

The division of the order into butterflies and moths is a very unequal one, and also a very artificial one. The butterflies account for roughly 20,000 species, arranged in no more than a dozen families, and there is the same degree of difference between a butterfly and a HAWKMOTH as there is between that same hawk-moth and a CLOTHES MOTH. The division was used by the early naturalists, who called brightly coloured, day-flying species butterflies, and the duller, nocturnal species moths, but this distinction is not valid in every case. The BURNET MOTHS, for example, are brilliantly coloured, day-flying insects. There is no one difference between all the moths and all the butterflies, although most of the temperate species can be distinguished without much difficulty. Most butterflies have clubbed *antennae*, but few of the moths show this feature; their

A butterfly's lifecycle.

Adult

Eggs

Caterpillar

Pupa

Peacock

Peacock caterpillar

Camberwell beauty

Above: A narrow-bordered bee hawkmoth, showing its striking resemblance to a bumble bee.

Broad-bordered
bee hawkmoth

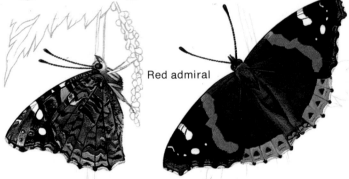

Red admiral

Left: A magnified photograph of a section of a butterfly's wing.

wings are held together by a large overlap.

Males and females find each other by sight or by scent, and often by a combination of the two. The scent may be emitted by the female, as in many SILK MOTHS and EMPEROR MOTHS, or by the male, as in many butterflies. The males of the emperor and silk moths are so sensitive to the female scent that they can find females from well over a kilometre away. After mating, the female lays her eggs, usually placing them in batches on the correct food plant for the resulting *larvae*, or caterpillars. She uses her feet to "taste" the plant first and make sure that it is suitable. Most caterpillars are fussy about their food and are restricted to just one food plant or a group of closely related plants. Most feed freely on leaves, but some tunnel into stems and fruits, and some eat roots. Larvae of the pigmy moths are so small that they can spend their lives tunnelling between the upper and lower surfaces of leaves. The larvae of the CLOTHES MOTHS are unusual in that they eat wool and other animal material.

All caterpillars have biting mouths, quite unlike the *probosci* of the adults. They have three pairs of true legs at the front, and two to five pairs of fleshy *prolegs* farther back. Most species moult four times, and then they are ready to pupate. It is during the pupal

antennae are usually thread-like or feathery. The burnets have clubbed antennae, but to distinguish these from butterflies it is only necessary to look under the wings. Springing from the "shoulder" of the hind wing there is a stout bristle called the *frenulum*. It sticks forward and latches into a little clip on the front wing. Its purpose is to hold the two wings together in flight. Most moths have a frenulum, but butterflies do not. Their

stage that the caterpillar's body is converted into that of the adult. Most moth larvae pupate in underground chambers or spin silken cocoons among the vegetation or the debris on the ground. SKIPPER BUTTERFLIES make flimsy *cocoons*, but most other butterflies have naked pupae, or *chrysalises*. These may hang upside down from the food plants, or they may be attached in an upright position to suitable stems or fences and held in place by a silken girdle. The caterpillar produces the silken supports before changing into the chrysalis. The chrysalis stage may last several weeks, or throughout the winter. When the adult is ready to emerge, its wing patterns can be seen through the chrysalis wall. The wings are soft and crumpled at first, but they soon expand and harden and the insect can fly away. ORDER: Lepidoptera.

Butterfly fish

Butterfly fish is the name given to many different kinds of salt-water fishes, but it is most descriptive of the one species of freshwater butterfly fish, which lives in West African rivers. Measuring only 10 cm long, this fish has several characteristics which can be com-

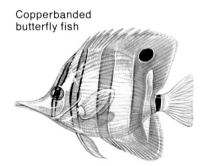

Copperbanded butterfly fish

pared with a butterfly's, most particularly its large, delicate *pectoral fins* which are spread like wings and which allow the butterfly fish to fly or glide over the surface of the water. Its other fins, which may act as stabilizers in flight, are also large and wing-like or rudder-like.

The butterfly fish is a surface-swimmer, with a boat-shaped body flattened at the top, and a mouth that faces upwards. Its colour is grey-green to silver brown and its body is marked with spots and streaks. It is a rather unlikely relative of the giant ARAPAIMA of South American rivers.
ORDER: Osteoglossiformes;
FAMILY: Pantodontidae.

The freshwater **butterfly fish** (left) lives in West African rivers. It is a surface-dweller with large pectoral fins resembling outspread butterfly wings. The copperbanded butterfly fish is one of many marine fish of this name.

Buzzards (left and above) are well known for their effortless, gliding flight.

Buzzard

The common buzzard of Europe is one of a number of large HAWKS bearing this name. Buzzards resemble EAGLES in their soaring flight. All are large birds, with wing spans of up to 1.5 metres. In flight, buzzards spiral effortlessly with their broad wings outstretched, rising in the thermals (warm air currents) for great distances. They can thus fly long distances without wasting energy flapping their wings, and buzzards migrate using this technique. In America, the term buzzard is applied more commonly to vultures, whereas members of the genus *Buteo* are called hawks.

Buzzards hunt by pouncing on animals on the ground. They sit motionless on a favourite perch, scanning the ground with their keen eyes, or hover in mid-air. They feed mainly on rabbits, voles, mice and lizards. After courtship, during which the male and female indulge in graceful aerobatics, a large bowl-shaped nest is made in a tree or on a rock ledge. Normally two eggs are laid, but up to six have been recorded.
ORDER: Falconiformes;
FAMILY: Accipitridae;
SPECIES: *Buteo buteo*.

C

Cabbage white butterfly

The cabbage white, also known as the large white, is a serious pest of cabbages and related plants in many parts of the world. The adult is an attractive white insect with black markings, and the female lays batches of yellow eggs on the food plants in spring and summer. The black and yellow caterpillars eat the leaves and then pupate on convenient walls and fences. Relatively few become adult butterflies, however, because a little ICHNEUMON fly attacks many of the caterpillars. Shrivelled caterpillar skins are very common in late summer, with clusters of yellow ichneumon cocoons around them. The closely related small white is an even worse pest, as it is found almost all over the world. In the New World, the small white is known as the European cabbage butterfly.

ORDER: Lepidoptera;
FAMILY: Pieridae;
SPECIES: *Pieris brassicae* (cabbage white); *Pieris rapae* (small white).

The **large white** and **small white butterflies** are serious pests. The caterpillars eat vast quantities of food plants.

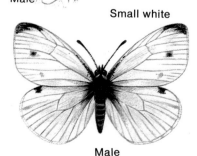

Male

Small white

Female

Caterpillar

Male

Cacomistle

A relative of the RACCOON, the cacomistle is a slender animal. It is up to 76 cm long, of which 43 cm is a bushy tail ringed black and white, and weighs only about 1 kg. The coat is greyish buff, darker along the back, with white underparts. It is found in the southern and western parts of the United States and in Mexico,

The cacomistle is a shy, nocturnal animal. It sleeps by day in a den among rocks and emerges at night to feed on small rodents, birds, lizards and insects. It is an agile tree-climber.

ORDER: Carnivora;
FAMILY: Procyonidae;
SPECIES: *Bassariscus astutus*.

Caddis fly

The caddis flies are mostly small or medium sized moth-like insects, whose wings are clothed with fine hairs. Most are black or brown in colour, and they usually rest with the wings held roof-like over the

Continued on page 64

Camouflage

Unless they have special means of defence or escape, animals must conceal themselves from their enemies. One way is to merge with the colour of their surroundings. Where such resemblance is useful, natural selection has produced beautifully adapted animals. The mainly brown grazing animals merge with the plains where they feed – especially when one remembers that their enemies – lions and the like – see only in shades of grey. This general colour resemblance, however, is only part of the answer. A solid body will tend to stand out in relief against the background of shading effects.

A great many animals have darker colours on the top surface than underneath. This is called counter-shading. In Nature, the light usually comes from above and there is shadow below. This effect is countered by the coloration of the body and the result is that all shadows disappear and the animal merges as a flat shape into the background. Counter-shading is prominent among the grazing mammals where it is produced by gradation of colour or by patterns that change lower down the body. The zebra's stripes and the giraffe's pattern, for instance, produce counter-shading when seen at a distance. These patterns are also disruptive.

Disruptive colouring is another very important feature of animal life. Contrasting colours and patterns break up the outline of the body and draw attention away from the whole shape. Although an animal with disruptive colouring may look obvious close to, or out of its natural surroundings, against a natural background it may completely disappear. Fishes, snakes and many ground-nesting birds make use of this type of coloration.

The CHAMELEON employs a different method of colour camouflage. If a dark coloured chameleon is put on a leafy branch, it will seem to disappear from sight in about 15 minutes. It is one of a number of animals that gain protection by changing their colours to blend in with the background. The colour change is a natural process involving redistribution of *pigments* in the skin.

Most of the animals that can change their colours have the pigments in special colour cells called chromatophores.

In the centre of the picture a **lappet moth** is perfectly **camouflaged** as a dead leaf.

This **bush cricket** has the colour, shape and texture of the leaf on which it perches.

Chromatophores respond to light and, in a lesser degree, to temperature. Although in some animals, the actual colour cells expand and contract, it is more common for the pigment to be withdrawn into the centre of the cell or spread out along the branches.

There are two types of colour cell response. One, known as direct or primary response, is caused by light falling on the cells themselves. Strong light causes the pigment to contract and the overall colour of the animal becomes pale.

The other type of response – indirect or secondary – is via the eyes and the brain. When the eyes detect a dark background, messages arrive at the colour cells causing them to expand and produce a darker coloration. A light background similarly produces a contraction of the pigments. The messages to the colour cells may be in the form of direct nerve impulses from the brain. Alternatively, the brain may cause the release of *hormones* that act on the colour cells. In many animals, both nerve and hormone messages are concerned with the control of the colour cells.

Flatfishes such as the plaice are well-known for their colour-changing ability. They contain black pigment together with others ranging from yellow to red. Combinations of these are enough to produce a likeness to the majority of natural backgrounds. Flatfish can even produce a reasonable copy of a chess-board pattern if the colours are available in its skin.

A different form of camouflage involves the resemblance of an animal to its surroundings. Some of the best examples are to be found among the insects. Many butterflies, although they may be brightly coloured on the upper side, resemble leaves when at rest. Stick-insects and leaf-insects are other well-known examples. Several species of tree-hopper are almost indistinguishable from thorns when sitting on the appropriate twigs, and various caterpillars resemble twigs themselves. Some seahorses are disguised so well that they completely disappear against a background of seaweed.

Mimicry is the name given to the cases where an animal benefits from resembling another animal rather than its surroundings. Among so many species of insect, it happens that a number of them look alike. If one species is protected – by evil smell, sting or warning colours – other similar-looking ones will also derive benefit. The resemblance will then be continued and improved by natural selection over many generations.

Nature designed this caterpillar to look like twigs.

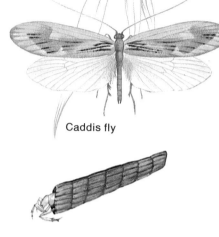

Caddis fly

Left: A **caddis fly** in its typical resting position, with antennae pointing to the front.

body and the *antennae* held straight out in front. There are nearly 6000 known species, and with few exceptions they spend their early lives in the water. Some larvae live freely in the ponds and streams, catching and eating an assortment of small animals. Some species that live in running water actually spin silken fishing nets among the plants to trap plant debris and small animals for food. Caddis *larvae* are best known, however, for the portable cases that most of them build to protect their soft bodies. Sand grains, small snail shells, pieces of stick and leaf fragments are all used to build these tubular cases on frame-works of silk. Each species has its own special design. Some actually fix their cases to large stones. Case-building larvae are generally plant-eaters or scavengers. The larvae pupate in the cases, and the pupae can actually swim to the surface to allow the adults to escape. Most adults remain close to the water and rarely feed.
ORDER: Trichoptera.

Caiman

Caimans are closely related to ALLIGATORS. One difference is that some caimans have belly skin that is reinforced with bony plates. All five caiman species live in north-ern South America, and one occurs as far north as southern Mexico. The smallest species is the dwarf caiman, up to 1.2 metres long. The largest is the black caiman, up to 4.6 metres long.
ORDER: Crocodilia;
FAMILY: Alligatoridae.

Camel

Camels are invaluable animals to the desert people of Asia and Africa. They provide the chief means of transportation and are

Arabian **camels** taking in water. The hump contains fat as a reserve of energy.

an important source of food, clothing and shelter.

There are two species: the one-humped or Arabian camel and the Bactrian or two-humped camel. Bactrian camels have shorter legs and are heavier than Arabian camels. Arabian camels, most of which live in Africa, are not generally wild, although there are herds which have descended from escaped domestic animals. But Bactrian camels, which are confined to Asia, have survived in the wild in the Gobi desert in Central Asia. Gobi camels are active by day and are extremely shy. They live in groups consisting of one male and about five females.

Camels have long legs, a long neck, coarse hair and tufted tails. Their feet have two toes, united by a tough web, with nails and tough, padded soles. A camel stands up to 1.8 metres at the shoulder and weighs up to 500 kg. The hump may weigh 45 kg. It contains fat and is a reserve of energy.

The camel is well adapted to life in deserts. Its long eyelashes protect the eyes from windblown sand and its nostrils are easily closed. The feet are broad and enable the camel to walk easily over soft sand. The form of its body, with long neck and legs, provide a large surface area relative to the body's volume, which allows for easy loss of heat. But its best known adaptation is the ability to go for long periods with very little food and drink. The camel sweats little and this helps it retain water. It gets water by eating desert plants, but it can go on a totally dry diet for several weeks, although it will steadily lose water. It is able to lose up to one quarter of its body weight in water without showing signs of distress. Thirsty camels have been known to drink 100 litres of water or more in 10 minutes. The water passes from the stomach into the body tissues and, after such a drink the body appears swollen. Camels can live up to 50 years.
ORDER: Artiodactyla;
FAMILY: Camelidae;
SPECIES: *Camelus dromedarius* (Arabian); *Camelus bactrianus* (Bactrian).

Canada goose

The Canada goose is the most widespread and best known goose in North America. It is a large, grey-brown goose with a black head, neck and tail and a white patch on the chin. Canada geese live in Alaska, Canada and the northern USA. In winter they migrate as far south as the Gulf of Mexico. They prefer inland waters, although they are also found in estuaries and on coasts. Outside the breeding season they may form groups of 200 to 300.

Canada geese are mainly vegetarian. On land they graze grass, rushes and sedges. In the sea they eat algae and eelgrass. They have favourite feeding grounds and generally congregate in areas

The **Canada goose** is a North American bird that has been introduced to Europe.

where food is abundant at a particular time of year. During the breeding season they eat small water animals as well as plants. They mate for life and the eggs are incubated in nests on the ground.
ORDER: Anseriformes;
FAMILY: Anatidae;
SPECIES: *Branta canadensis*.

Canary

The canary is a member of the FINCH family, native to the Canary Islands, the Azores and Madeira. It was imported into Europe in the 16th century and has since been bred to produce a number of colour varieties, from yellow, through orange to those streaked with brown or black. Canaries live in bushes and clumps of trees, readily coming into gardens. Very popular as caged birds, canaries are noted for their song. In the wild, their main food is small seeds but they also eat leaf and fruit buds.

ORDER: Passeriformes;
FAMILY: Fringillidae;
SPECIES: *Serinus canaria*.

Cape buffalo

By repute, the Cape buffalo is the most dangerous of African big game animals because it tends to charge whenever it is disturbed, and a charging buffalo is not easily stopped. Its only natural enemy is the lion, which it often kills in combat. The bulky, ox-like buffalo stands 122 to 152 cm at the shoulder and the powerful adult bulls weigh nearly a tonne. The head and shoulders are heavily built and the large horns spring from broad bases, sometimes meeting in the middle of the forehead and curving first down and then up, and finishing in a point. The longest horns recorded span 142 cm. The coat is brownish-black, and is thick in young buffaloes and sparse in older ones. The Cape buffalo was once common throughout Africa south of the Sahara, but hunting and cattle disease have greatly reduced numbers in many places. Herds of 1000 to 2000 can still be seen in such places as Kruger National Park, South Africa.

ORDER: Artiodactyla;
FAMILY: Bovidae;
SPECIES: *Syncerus caffer*.

Cape hunting dog

The cape hunting dog, or African wild dog, is a ferocious animal only distantly related to other members of the dog family. Unlike the others, it has only four toes on each foot – the dew claw is missing. It stands about 60 cm at the shoulder and measures up to 120 cm from its nose to the tip of its bushy tail. Its coat is mottled black, yellow and white.

Cape hunting dogs are found in the savanna of Africa, south of the Sahara desert. They live in packs of 4 to 60 individuals and a pack usually remains in one area as long as food is abundant. Their prey consists of antelopes and other grazing animals – even large wildebeest. The pack hunts together in an organized manner. They can run long distances and will chase their prey until it collapses with exhaustion. Often, they begin tearing it to pieces before it is dead.

ORDER: Carnivora;
FAMILY: Canidae;
SPECIES: *Lycaon pictus*.

Cape buffalo at a wallow.

Capercaillie

A large game bird of which there are two species. One lives in Scandinavia, Russia and Central Europe, with isolated populations in the Pyrenees and Scotland. The second species lives in eastern Sibera. The male capercaillie is dark grey and nearly a metre long. It has a spectacular courtship display in which it raises its neck and fans out its tail. The female is smaller and brown, resembling a large GROUSE. Capercaillies live in coniferous forests, and are able to survive the winter mainly by eating pine needles.
ORDER: Galliformes;
FAMILY: Tetraonidae;
SPECIES: *Tetrao urogallus* (European); *Tetrao parvirostris* (Siberian).

The male **capercaillie** fans its tail when courting the female.

Male

Female

Capuchin

The capuchin is the once-familiar monkey of the organ-grinder. It is an intelligent animal and popular in zoos and as a pet. Although there is still some dispute, most authorities now say that there are four species, belonging to the genus *Cebus*, and 33 sub-species. They live in troops in the forests of tropical South and Central America and fruit is their main

The **cardinal** is a familiar songbird of North America. The male's plumage is a brighter red.

food. Capuchins are small monkeys, measuring 30 to 38 cm long. Their tails, which may be 60 cm long, are used to grasp objects out of reach of the hands.
ORDER: Primates;
FAMILY: Cebidae.

Capybara

The capybara is the largest living rodent. It looks rather pig-like, with hoof-like claws, a large short-eared head and coarse brown hair. It may be over a metre long and weigh up to 54 kg. A native of South America, it is always found near water. Capybaras swim and dive well, using their slightly webbed feet as paddles. Their stored layers of fat give them natural buoyancy in the water. Capybaras eat water plants and grass, browsing in water or on grassland. If alarmed, the inoffensive capybara gallops for the safety of the nearest water.
ORDER: Rodentia;
FAMILY: Hydrochoeridae;
SPECIES: *Hydrochoerus hydrochoeris.*

Caracal

This medium-sized cat has a short reddish coat, long legs, and long black ear tufts. Some zoologists consider it to be a true LYNX, while others see it as akin to the SERVAL. Caracals live in savanna and semi-desert throughout Africa and in parts of southern Asia as far east as India. They are becoming very scarce, and are extremely rare in Asia. They feed on a variety of animals, sometimes the prey being as large as a small antelope. Caracals are good jumpers, and will strike down birds that are already airborne by rearing up on their hind legs, or leaping up to 2 metres in the air. Young caracals are born in litters of 2 to 4 in an old aardvark burrow, fox hole or hollow tree. Like any cat, the mother defends her young fiercely against intruders.
ORDER: Carnivora;
FAMILY: Felidae;
SPECIES: *Felis caracal.*

Cardinal

A finch-like songbird that is found naturally in temperate parts of the United States. It has been introduced to Bermuda and Hawaii. In Hawaii it breeds all year round and has become a pest because of the damage it does to fruit trees. Apart from a black bib the plumage is a mixture of scarlets, the female being slightly duller.
ORDER: Passeriformes;
FAMILY: Emberizidae;
SPECIES: *Pyrrhuloxia cardinalis.*

Cardinal fish

There are many different species of these small perch-like fishes that live mainly on coral reefs in tropical seas. Like many other fishes of this habitat, they have bright colours and patterns. Usually not more than 10 cm long, they appear to be the main food of many larger fishes of the reefs.
ORDER: Perciformes;
FAMILY: Apogonidae.

Caribou

The caribou belongs to the same species as REINDEER, but differs in several respects. Reindeer are domesticated or semi-domesticated in Greenland, Scandinavia and northern Russia, while caribou roam wild in North America and Siberia. Caribou have longer legs than reindeer. They stand 122 to 152 cm at the shoulder and can weigh 318 kg. The coat varies from near black to almost white, but most caribou are brownish or greyish, with light under-parts and rump. In winter, they become lighter and the hair lengthens. The ears and tail are short and the muzzle is furry.

These winter changes reduce the amount of heat lost from the body in cold weather. Caribou and reindeer are the only deer in which both sexes bear antlers.

At the beginning of this century, there were probably about 1,750,000 caribou in northern Canada. The population then declined through over-hunting, destruction of food by forest fires and high mortality in severe weather. In 1955, the population was 278,900, but numbers have been increasing recently because

Caribou crossing the tundra in Alaska. The annual migrations follow regular paths.

of an intensive programme of conservation.

Caribou live in small bands of 5 to 100, or in herds of up to 3000. In April and May, they migrate north to the open tundra, where they spend the summer. They winter in the woodlands at the southern end of their range. The annual migrations follow regular paths, which once made it easy for the American Indians to trap them. Caribou mate in late October to early November and the young are born in early June. Grizzly bears sometimes prey on young caribou, but wolves are their main enemy.

ORDER: Artiodactyla;
FAMILY: Cervidae;
SPECIES: *Rangifer tarandus*.

Carnivore

This name means flesh-eater and is applied to the cats and dogs and other members of the group of mammals called Carnivora. It is also used for meat-eaters in general.

These hunting flesh-eaters have evolved many different methods of catching their prey. Most cats stalk their prey slowly, and then pounce when they are near enough, using their large teeth to kill their victims. But CHEETAHS chase rapidly after their prey because they live on open plains and cannot stalk up on them unseen. WOLVES and hunting dogs also chase their prey, and often work together in packs. GOSHAWKS and PEREGRINES fly rapidly after smaller birds and snap them up in mid-air, while the DRAGONFLY does much the same to small insects. Good eyesight is obviously very important for these fast-moving predators.

A number of predatory animals actually shoot their prey. The SEA ANEMONES and their distant fresh-water relative HYDRA fire poison "harpoons" which paralyse small animals swimming nearby. The anemone's tentacles then draw the prey into its mouth. The ARCHERFISH, from South-East Asia, fires small water droplets at insects flying just above the surface, snapping them up when they fall into the water. Perhaps the most amazing of all is the spitting spider, which approaches its victim and then fires two sticky threads from its jaws. The

Lions hunt in groups, creeping silently through the long grass. It is usually the lionesses that do the actual killing.

victim is pinned down by these threads and rendered completely helpless.

Many creatures, including the praying MANTIS and the TRAPDOOR SPIDER, ambush their prey and some animals actually set traps. The most famous of these trappers are the SPIDERS, whose delicate silken webs form deadly traps for flies and other small insects. Some webs are sticky, but others work simply by entangling the unfortunate insect. The spider is always nearby to administer a paralysing bite and to wrap its victim in a silken shroud before sucking it dry. Some of the CADDIS larvae that live in fast-flowing water also spin silken snares. These are fairly simple nets suspended from water plants which trap debris and small animals.

Carp

The carp is the most widespread fish of the family to which it gives its name. Like its relative the GOLDFISH, the carp's original home was in the Far East, but it is now cultivated by man in many parts of the world. Carp live in the muddy bottoms of shallow waters where there are lots of water plants. They feed mainly on mud-dwelling animals. Sensory *barbels* under the mouth help in this hunting.

Carp have a reputation of long life, but this has often been greatly exaggerated. Perhaps a carp can live for as long as 50 years but 17 years is nearer the average life span. Similarly, their size is often exaggerated. Claims have been made for carp weighing 180 kg but the largest authentic weight of a European carp is about 27 kg for a fish over 1 metre in length.

ORDER: Cypriniformes;
FAMILY: Cyprinidae;
SPECIES: *Cyprinus carpio*.

The **carp** is a powerful fish that tests the angler's tackle to the full.

Cassowary

A large, timid bird of the rain forests of New Guinea and northern Australia. Cassowaries cannot fly, but they are well adapted to living in the dense undergrowth of the rain forests. The skin of their long neck and head is naked and brightly coloured, but the body is covered with coarse, bristle-like black feathers. On the head is a bony casque or helmet. The stiff plumage and bony helmet protect the cassowary as it runs through the undergrowth. Cassowaries are shy and secretive birds but, if cornered, they may leap and kick

out with their long, dagger-like claws. There are three species: the Australian cassowary, the one-wattled cassowary, and the Bennet's cassowary. The largest, the one-wattled cassowary, may be nearly 2 metres tall.
ORDER: Casuariiformes;
FAMILY: Casuariidae.

Cat

The domestic cat is a small member of the cat family, typically 76 cm long including a 23 cm tail, and weighing up to 9.5 kg. Unlike wild cats, domesticated cats usually hold their tails horizontally when walking. Their claws can be drawn in and these they keep in condition by scratching at trees, posts, furniture and carpets. They readily climb trees to escape dogs, to rob birds' nests, or to lie in the sun on branches. Long whiskers sprouting from the muzzle are probably used to feel the way in the dark. Coat colour varies, although tabby markings (greyish brown and black patterns, often striped) are dominant.

Cat hearing is acute. Cats can hear sounds above the range detected by the human ear: a cat beside a mousehole may hear rodent voices inaudible to us. Cats hunt silently, but in other situations produce a variety of sounds from the "meow" to the purr of pleasure. Male, or tom, cats seeking to impress a mate and deter rivals indulge in loud, insistent yowling.

There are more than 30 breeds of domestic cat, some long-haired like the Persian, but most short-haired like the Burmese. Several races of short-tailed cats exist, especially in South-East Asia, and there are also tailless cats, such as the Manx cat. Domestic breeds are

Left: The bony helmet and coloured wattles make the **cassowary** look like a creature from another planet.

probably a mixture of two wild species; the European wild cat and the African bush cat. The bush cat was tamed in ancient Egypt more than 3000 years ago.
ORDER: Carnivora;
FAMILY: Felidae;
SPECIES: *Felis catus*.

Catfish

The name of any of several hundred species of fishes, all of which have whisker-like *barbels* around the mouth. They fall into two groups: ARMOURED CATFISH, which are dealt with under that heading, and naked catfish, dealt with here.

Naked catfishes have an amazing variety of forms and habits. The European catfish, or wels, is a large, flattened fish with very long whiskers, which eats frogs and fishes. It can grow to a length of 2.7 metres or more. The banjo catfishes of South America have very flat bodies and long thin tails which give them their name. Another family of marine catfishes, Plotosidae, contains one of the most dangerous fishes of the coral reefs, with poisonous spines that can inflict fatal wounds. Equally to be feared are tiny catfishes of South American rivers which are parasites that enter body cavities and cause severe internal wounds.

Some small African catfishes are natural clowns, often swimming upside-down. In the mating season the males and females, in this position, repeatedly swim at one another and collide head-on.
ORDER: Siluriformes;

The wels is a **catfish** that can grow to a length of about 3 metres.

Two of the many kinds of **centipedes**. The longer species has from 77 to 83 pairs of legs; the other 15 pairs.

Cave fish

The name of 32 species of fishes that are largely unrelated to one another, but which all share features resulting from a life spent in darkness. All lack skin pigment so that they are pink in colour due to the blood showing through their skin. Most are quite blind, though in many cases the young fish start out with fully developed eyes which disappear as they mature.

Centipede

Any of about 3000 many-legged ARTHROPODS. Most centipedes have either 15 or 23 pairs of legs, one pair for each body segment, but one European centipede has up to 177 pairs. Centipedes vary in length from 2 cm to the 27 cm of a species which lives in the tropical rain forests of the Americas and has 23 pairs of legs. Because centipedes do not have a waterproof body covering, to prevent them drying out they have to live in damp surroundings. They are active predators, hunting insects, spiders, worms and other small animals. The front pair of legs act as poison claws and are used for paralysing and killing their prey. Many centipedes can run surprisingly quickly to capture their prey.

CLASS: Chilopoda.

Chaffinch

One of the commonest of all birds, the chaffinch is found throughout Europe, and large flocks migrate annually to North Africa and the Middle East. Like all FINCHES, chaffinches have stout bills for cracking seeds. They also eat insects, spiders and earthworms. Outside the breeding season, chaffinches form flocks several dozen strong which are often segregated into sex and can often be seen with other small species. They breed in woodlands. The females build a nest of grass, roots and moss.

ORDER: Passeriformes;
FAMILY: Fringillidae;
SPECIES: *Fringilla coelebs*.

Chalcid wasp

The chalcid wasps, of which there are thousands of species, are only distantly related to the true wasps and are mostly very small insects. Few are more than about 2.5 mm long, and the group actually contains the smallest of all insects – the fairy flies. These tiny creatures, some of them only 0.25 mm long, grow up inside the eggs of other insects. Most of the larger chalcids are also parasites of other insects. Eggs are often laid in the caterpillars and chrysalises of butterflies and moths, and large numbers of chalcid grubs grow up inside these hosts and kill them. Many chalcid wasps have beautiful metallic colours.

ORDER: Hymenoptera.

Chameleon

There are about 80 species of these slow moving lizards. Some are less than 5 cm long, while others grow to 60 cm. Most live in forests in Africa south of the Sahara Desert. The common chameleon ranges from the Middle East along the coast of North Africa to southern Spain.

Chameleons are probably the strangest of all lizards. Each has a high body, flattened from side to side. Jackson's chameleon has horns, and the flap-necked chameleon has a "helmet". Many species wrap their tails round a twig for extra grip. The toes of each foot are joined so as to produce feet like tongs, which give them a firm grip on the branches. The chameleons are slow-moving animals, rarely moving more than one leg at a time, and anchoring it firmly before moving the next. Their eyes move constantly in search of food or danger, each eye swivelling independently of the other. If a

A male **chaffinch** in flight shows clearly its characteristic double white wing bands.

chameleon sees an insect or some other prey within range, it shoots out a tongue longer than its own body length. The victim is trapped on the sticky tongue tip and whipped back to the mouth, the whole attack being over in a second.

Chameleons can change colour in response to changes in light, temperature or emotional state. Colour change may act as camouflage or as an indication of mood to other chameleons; for example, an angry chameleon turns black.

Some chameleons lay eggs, others bear live young. Within a day the young are catching prey.
ORDER: Squamata;
FAMILY: Chamaeleonidae.

Chamois

The chamois is a species of GOAT ANTELOPE. It stands about 80 cm at the shoulder and weighs up to 40 kg. Both sexes have horns, which can grow to 25 cm long. The coat is long, with a thick under-fur, tawny in summer and dark brown to black in winter. There is a dark line down the middle of the back. Most chamois live in alpine forests around the *tree-line*. Some reach the *snow-line* in summer, but they move down in winter. The chamois is found in southern Europe, Asia Minor and the Caucasus region. When alarmed, this agile animal can make tremendous leaps across ravines and up almost sheer rock faces. It is also noted for its excellent sight and hearing. Its enemies are wolves and lynxes. Foxes and eagles prey on the kids.
ORDER: Artiodactyla;
FAMILY: Bovidae;
SPECIES: *Rupicapra rupicapra*.

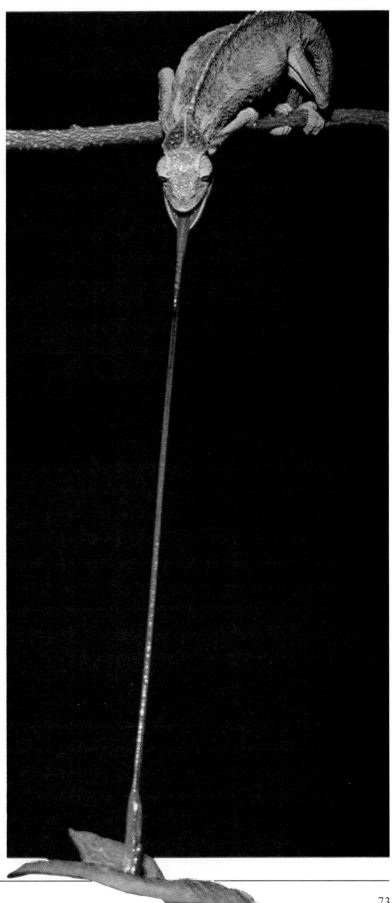

The **chameleon** is noted for three things: It can change colour to suit its surroundings or its mood; it can move its eyes independently of each other; and it has a tongue which shoots out at lightning speed to a length greater than that of the animal's body.

Char

Fish that are close relatives of SALMON and TROUT, which they greatly resemble. European char either spend their whole lives in lakes and streams, or else live mostly at sea, particularly in the Arctic Ocean. They return to inland waters only to breed.
ORDER: Salmoniformes;
FAMILY: Salmonidae.

Characin

A family of tropical freshwater fish well known to people who keep aquariums. Very familiar examples include the brilliant little TETRAS and the swordtail characin, another member of the same genus. Other well-known characins include the freshwater HATCHET FISHES and the dreaded PIRANHA of the rivers of Central and South America. Most characins live either in these rivers or in those of tropical Africa.

However, this huge family, which is often subdivided into as many as 30 sub-families, contains a host of other, less well-known fish. They range in size from just over 3 cm to 1.5 metres, and vary greatly in appearance. An out-standing feature of characins as a whole is the way in which they imitate fishes of other families. For example, one looks like a TROUT, another looks like a MULLET, a third resembles a HERRING, and so on. Most characins have the general appearance of MINNOWS and CARPS.

Examples of carnivores, omnivores and plant-eaters can be found among the characins. Spawning and egg-laying in general resemble those of many other freshwater fishes, although one member of the family, the spraying characin, has the curious habit of spraying its eggs on to land, where they develop with less risk of being eaten.
ORDER: Cypriniformes;
FAMILY: Characidae.

Cheetah

The cheetah is the fastest animal on land. Compared with the lion or leopard, the cheetah's legs are extremely long and the head is small. Head and body combined measure about 1.2 metres and the

The Congo tetra is one of the few **characins** from Africa.

tail is half as long again. It stands about 1 metre high and weighs over 45 kg. Closely spaced black spots cover most of the body, which is tawny or grey with white under-parts. Unlike other cats, the cheetah has blunt claws that can be only partly retracted. Cheetahs live in open countryside in Africa and south-western Asia. In India they are now thought to be extinct.

The cheetah's body gives a general impression of a lithe and speedy creature and it can certainly run very fast over short distances. Someone reportedly timed a cheetah running at 114 km/h over a distance of 640 metres. But many people accept a likelier top speed of about 97 km/h. Sprinting helps the cheetah catch its prey. Unlike other cats, who stalk their prey slowly or lie in wait and pounce, cheetahs walk towards their prey, and then speed up to a sprint. In this way they run down ANTELOPES, OSTRICHES and HARES. But if the chase proves long, the cheetah gives up, exhausted by its sudden and violent turn of speed.

Breeding is thought to take place at any time of the year, and litters contain 2 to 5 cubs. Studies in East Africa suggest that half of the young die in the first year of life.
ORDER: Carnivora;
FAMILY: Felidae;
SPECIES: *Acinonyx jubatus.*

Chicken

Although strictly defined as any young bird, this word is normally used for the domestic fowl – probably the commonest bird in the world. It was domesticated at least 4000 years ago and is thought to have been bred from the red jungle fowl of India and South-East Asia. It was first used for religious and sacrificial purposes, the eggs and flesh not being used until much later. There are now dozens of commerical breeds as well as ornamental ones bred for their attractive plumage. Like most game birds, the chicken is a vegetarian, eating mostly seeds, fruits, and leaves. It has a strong *gizzard* in which the seeds are ground up with the aid of small stones which the bird swallows. The bird also enjoys worms and insects. The wings are short and can sustain only short bursts of flight. Cock birds can be recognised by the larger wattles and combs on the head and also by the glossy greenish tail feathers.

ORDER: Galliformes;
FAMILY: Phasianidae.

Chimaera

A type of fish which in many ways comes between the bony fishes and the shark-like fishes. Like bony fishes, chimaeras have a gillcover protecting the gills. Details of their food canal and their upper jaw are also like those of bony fishes. But like sharks, chimaeras have a skeleton made of cartilage and not of bone. Their eggs are horny capsules like those of many sharks, and the male chimaera, like the male shark, has two claspers which he uses to impregnate the female during mating.

Chimaeras are strange-looking

A young **chimpanzee** with its parents.

fish – their name means "fabulous monster" – with a large head and eyes and a body tapering to an insignificant tail fin. The snout can be rounded, pointed, trunk-like or plough-like, depending on the species. The teeth may be large and rabbit-like, for cracking the shells of molluscs and crustaceans. Many chimaeras have a poisonous spine at the front of their DORSAL FIN. They can be large fishes, up to 1.5 metres long.

ORDER: Chimaeriformes.

Chimpanzee

The chimpanzee is one of the great apes. Because it is nearest in intelligence to man, it is one of the most studied and popular of animals. Chimpanzees are the best tool-makers apart from man – they can use sticks to extract honey, ants and termites from nests; and stones to crack nuts, or

A **chimpanzee** can communicate emotions by changing its expression. This one is showing great attention.

as missiles. They chew up leaves and make them into a sponge, which is then used to extract water from a hollow in a tree.

Chimpanzees live in tropical rain forests of Africa, ranging from the Niger basin to Angola. They are at home in trees and, at night, they sleep in nests made of branches and vines in the trees. They often search for food on the ground. They usually walk on all fours, although they sometimes run on three legs, leaving one free to hold food. They can walk upright, with their toes turned outward, standing 91 to 152 cm high. Their hair is long, coarse and black, except for a white patch near the rump. The face, ears, hands and feet are free of hair.

Chimpanzees live in groups of up to 40 but they often wander away from the troop on their own. Within a group, males are arranged in a social order, the inferior ones respecting the superior ones. The members of a group spend much time grooming themselves or others. Seven hours a day may be spent on feeding. Fruit, leaves and roots are the main foods, although it has been found that some chimpanzees like meat.

They have been seen catching young BUSHBUCKS, BUSHPIGS, COLOBUS MONKEYS and BABOONS.

The *gestation period* is about 230 days and the young depend entirely on their mothers for two years. Young chimpanzees are playful and friendly, but they may become ill-tempered in old age.
ORDER: Primates;
FAMILY: Pongidae;
SPECIES: *Pan troglodytes.*

Chinchilla

The chinchilla looks like a small rabbit with a squirrel's tail and is related to the VISCACHAS, AGOUTIS and GUINEA PIGS. Chinchillas once thrived all over the Andes mountains of South America. Valued for their soft fur, they were hunted so much that wild chinchillas are now found only in the high mountains of northern Chile. Chinchillas live in colonies in burrows among rocks. They come out at night and eat grasses and herbs.
ORDER: Rodentia;
FAMILY: Chinchillidae;
SPECIES: *Chinchilla laniger.*

In the year 1899, half a million **chinchilla** pelts were exported from Chile.

The western **chipmunk** above stores food in the autumn and sleeps much of the winter.

Chinese water deer

The Chinese water deer of China and Korea stands 44 to 55 cm at the shoulder and is about 90 cm long. It weighs up to 16 kg. This small animal is unique among deer as it can give birth to up to 7 fawns, although 4 or 5 is usual. The coat is a light yellowish-brown to pale reddish-brown in summer, turning dark brown in winter. There is little difference between the sexes. The males have no antlers, but their upper canine teeth are long and tusk-like. They are used in fights between males in the breeding season. This deer lives in swampy areas in its natural home, but it has become adapted to woodland life in other parts of the world where it has escaped from captivity.
ORDER: Artiodactyla;
FAMILY: Cervidae;
SPECIES: *Hydropotes inermis.*

Chipmunk

Chipmunks are common GROUND SQUIRRELS. There are about 20 kinds. The eastern chipmunk lives in the eastern United States and Canada. The slightly smaller western chipmunk is found throughout North America and northern Asia. The chipmunk's fur is reddish-brown with dark stripes on the back. The tail is not as bushy as that of tree squirrels.

Chipmunks live in burrow systems underground, usually in pasture land or open woodland. Their main foods are berries, fruits, nuts and seeds, but they also eat slugs, snails and small insects. Food not immediately needed is carried in cheek pouches and stored away for the winter.
ORDER: Rodentia;
FAMILY: Sciuridae.

Chiton

Chitons are a very old group of MOLLUSCS of which there are 700 species. They are flat and oval in shape, and cling to the undersides of seashore rocks. The chiton's shell is made up of eight plates, and the lower part of the body consists of a muscular foot, similar to that of a SNAIL. There are no eyes on the animal's head, but some species have eyes on the plates of the shell, sometimes as many as 11,500. Most chitons are small but one species that lives on the west coast of North America grows up to 33 cm long. Chitons feed on algae which they scrape off rocks.
CLASS: Amphineura;
ORDER: Chitonida.

The **chiton** is one of the most primitive of molluscs.

Chough

The name given to two species belonging to the CROW family, the common or Cornish chough and the alpine chough. Cornish and Alpine choughs are found all over Europe and southern Asia. Cornish choughs prefer sea cliffs, while the alpine chough lives inland and frequents mountain precipices. In the Himalayas they have been found breeding at 6500 metres. Choughs often behave as if they are enjoying themselves.

The **chough** has red legs and beak. Alpine choughs have a yellow beak.

weigh 2 kg. They live in rocky deserts of the south-western United States. Most lizards eat small animals, but wild chuckwallas eat the flowers of certain desert plants. If threatened by an enemy, a chuckwalla hides in the nearest rock crevice. It grips tightly with its toes and wedges itself firmly in by blowing up its body with air. In their hot desert homes, chuckwallas are active only from late March to early August, when food is abundant. They sleep for the rest of the year.
ORDER: Squamata;
FAMILY: Iguanidae;
SPECIES: *Sauromalus obesus*.

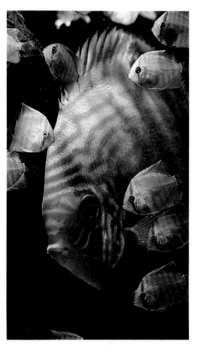

This **cichlid** is the Discus. Like all cichlids, it takes good care of its young.

They play elaborate games such as "follow the leader" and play in the air currents around cliff faces.
ORDER: Passeriformes;
FAMILY: Corvidae;
SPECIES: *Pyrrhocorax pyrrhocorax* (common); *Pyrrhocorax graculus* (alpine)

Chub

The chub is a freshwater fish of European rivers. It belongs to the CARP family. A fully grown chub is about 60 cm long, with a broad head and powerful jaws with which it catches smaller fish. Anglers often catch chub, but usually throw the fishes back in the river, because the flesh has an uninteresting taste and the texture of cotton wool.
ORDER: Cypriniformes;
FAMILY: Cyprinidae;
SPECIES: *Leuciscus cephalus*.

The **chub** is not a food fish.

Chuckwalla

The chuckwalla is a plump North American LIZARD. Some individuals grow to 46 cm long and

Below: **Cicadas** spend most of their time in trees, sucking sap from beneath the bark.

Cicada

The cicadas are fairly large sap-sucking BUGS that feed mainly in the trees. Their long beaks easily penetrate the bark of the smaller branches to reach the sap beneath. The insects are difficult to see when sitting on the bark, but the males give away their presence by their incredibly shrill calls. These are produced by a small membrane on each side of the body.

The membrane is vibrated very rapidly and it gives out a high-pitched, warbling whistle to attract the females. Eggs are laid in the soil, and the *nymphs* take sap from various roots. They have powerful front legs with which they dig their way through the soil. They remain under the ground for several years – 17 years for one American species – and come up only when it is time for the adult to break out of the nymphal skin. Most of the 1500 or so species are tropical.
ORDER: Hemiptera-Homoptera;
FAMILY: Cicadidae.

Cichlid

A family of fish containing 600 species, many of which are favourite fishes for tropical aquaria. Cichlids live in many rivers and lakes all over Africa and in Central and South America, southern India and Sri Lanka. The freshwater ANGELFISH and many other cichlids have deep, narrow bodies with colours which are always brilliant. These colours brighten even further in the male fish when he is attracting a female or frightening off a rival. Many cichlids have elaborate courting rituals, involving mouth-to-mouth tugging contests between male and female, and digging and cleaning activities that mime nest building.

After egg-laying and fertilization, both parent cichlids guard the nest. Later they may transport the eggs by mouth to nearby pits dug in the sand. Newly hatched cichlid *fry* are well looked after by their parents, who may take the fry into their mouths for protection.
ORDER: Perciformes;
FAMILY: Cichlidae.

Civet

Civets belong to the same family as the MONGOOSE and the GENET. They have a sharp muzzle and long body and tail. In habits and pattern of coat they resemble the small cats. The African civet lives in Africa south of the Sahara. The large Indian civet and the small Indian civet live in South and South-East Asia. Civets are forest-dwelling animals, eating insects, frogs, birds and fruit. They climb and swim well, and capture some of their food in water. Some have been seen catching crabs on the seashore. There are usually 2 to 3 young in a litter, born in a hole in the ground or in dense cover. Man's interest in civets has been mainly to collect the *musk* from glands near the reproductive organs. The concentrated substance smells offensive to the human nose but is pleasant when diluted. It is sometimes used in perfumes.
ORDER: Carnivora;
FAMILY: Viverridae.

Clam

Clam is a name given to many bivalve MOLLUSCS and it has different meanings in different parts of the world. In America it is applied to any edible *bivalves*, such as the soft clam, or the great clam. Elsewhere the term may apply only to freshwater MUSSELS. One species over which there is no dispute is the giant clam. These huge clams live in the shallow waters of the Indo-Pacific coral reefs, and can be more than 1.2 metres across and weigh up to 254 kg. The margins of the shell are corrugated in such a way that when the valves close they fit into each other. There have been many stories in the past of giant clams snapping shut on the leg of an unwary swimmer, trapping him until he drowns. In fact, this is most unlikely, as there are no such fatalities on record, and the clam probably closes its shell too slowly ever to trap anyone.
CLASS: Bivalvia.

Clawed frog

The clawed frog is a tongueless frog. Females are larger than the European common frog. Clawed frogs live in tropical and southern Africa, in swamps, streams and ponds. They seldom leave the water, where they are powerful swimmers. Their front legs are short and weak, and each ends in four straight fingers. Back legs are long and muscular, with large

The tridacna is a large **clam** of tropical reefs.

webs between the toes. Clawed frogs can change colour from mottled to black or pale buff to match their background. They seize their prey between their front feet and their mouths. At breeding time a female lays up to 2000 eggs.
ORDER: Salientia;
FAMILY: Pipidae;
SPECIES: *Xenopus laevis.*

The **click beetle** and its larva. The larva does damage to potatoes and cereal roots.

Click beetle

The click beetles are small, slender insects. They are able to right themselves when they fall on to their backs. They flick themselves into the air and turn over before they fall back to the ground. This action is accompanied by a loud click, from which they get their name. Some of the species have bright, metallic colours, but most are dull brown. Adult beetles chew pollen and lap nectar from flowers, but the *larvae*, known as wireworms, feed on plant roots and do much damage to crops.
ORDER: Coleoptera;
FAMILY: Elateridae.

Climbing perch

The climbing perch is a freshwater fish of South-East Asia. It is about 23 cm long and greyish-green in colour. This small fish is famous

The **clawed frog**, Xenopus, from South Africa. It can change its colour pattern to match its surroundings.

because it leaves its home pond when this is beginning to dry up, and travels overland for considerable distances to find another pond.

The fish "walks" overland with the aid of spines on its gill covers which dig into the soil, so giving it a purchase. It is also aided in walking by its *pectoral fins* and tail. In order to leave the water it has had to make a remarkable adaptation. A rosette-like development of the gills, richly supplied with blood vessels, acts like a lung, enabling the fish to breathe air directly and so to survive for long periods out of water.
ORDER: Perciformes;
FAMILY: Anabantidae;
SPECIES: *Anabas testudineus.*

Clothes moth

The name clothes moth is given to several species of small moths whose *larvae* feed on wool and other animal materials. They will feed on carpets and other furnishings, as well as on clothes, if undisturbed. They do not feed on vegetable or synthetic fibres. The adult moths are no more than 1 cm long and their wings are brown or silvery grey, with fringes around the edges. They are secretive insects, rarely flying and preferring to scuttle away into a crevice. The larva of the case-bearing clothes moth builds a tube of silk and fibre around itself and carries it about. The original home of the clothes moths must have been in birds' nests and similar places, where the grubs ate fur and feathers.
ORDER: Lepidoptera;
FAMILY: Tineidae.

The **clothes moth's** larva chews holes in anything woollen.

Coalfish

The coalfish is a marine food fish of European waters, a close relative of the COD. It grows up to a length of about a metre and has a silvery-dark body with three *dorsal fins* and two *anal fins*. The *pelvic fins* are just behind the gill covers. Like the cod, the coalfish has a short *barbel,* or feeler, on the lower lip.

The main spawning grounds of the coalfish are the Norwegian and British coasts, although the full range of the coalfish extends from the Arctic to the Mediterranean. Shoals of coalfish are inclined to feed on the *fry* of their larger relative the cod, but coalfish also take many other kinds of small fish and shellfish. The coalfish also has other names. In Europe it was

once known as the saithe. In America it is called the pollock or pollack.
ORDER: Gadiformes;
FAMILY: Gadidae;
SPECIES: *Gadus virens.*

Coati

The coatis are related to the RACCOON. They are up to 1.4 metres long, of which 0.75 metres is a striped tail which is generally

When frightened, the **cobra** rears up and spreads its hood.

A **coati** will poke his long nose into anything that promises food.

held vertically with the tip curled over. They have small ears and a flat forehead, which runs down to a long, mobile snout that extends beyond the jaw. The general colour is reddish-brown to black, with yellowish under-parts and black and grey face markings. The two main species are the ring-tailed coati which inhabits the northern parts of South America, and the brown coati, which lives in Central America and is occasionally seen in the southern United States.

Male coatis are solitary, but the females and young live in bands of up to 20. They travel through the forest foraging for fruit and small animals. Breeding takes place in the dry season, when each band is joined by a male. The young are born in a nest in a tree.
ORDER: Carnivora;
FAMILY: Procyonidae;
SPECIES: *Nasua nasua* (ring-tailed); *Nasua narica* (brown).

Cobra

Various species of true cobra live in Africa and Asia. They include the Indian cobra and the Egyptian cobra. Most cobras are medium-sized snakes, about 2 metres long. When frightened or excited they rear up, and movable ribs spread the skin behind the neck until it forms a flattish hood. Anyone who comes too near is likely to be bitten, and cobra venom is extremely poisonous. Victims suffer bleeding and swelling. But the venom's chief ingredients are nerve poisons that paralyse the nervous system. Victims of the Indian cobra may die of heart failure and breathing failure in only 15 minutes. Many experts believe the Indian cobra to be one of the most dangerous of all snakes. In India alone it kills about 10,000 people every year. Some cobras attack by spitting venom directly at the eyes of the victim. If their venom gets into the eyes it causes blindness for a time.

Cobras eat mainly rodents. Many accidents happen when the snakes enter homes in search of rats. Frogs, toads and birds are also eaten. Cobras climb trees to plunder nests. The Egyptian cobra will raid poultry runs. The Cape cobra often eats snakes, and the black-and-white cobra is said to hunt fish.

MONGOOSES and GENETS are among the cobras' enemies. But in a fight the cobra sometimes wins. Its inflated hood may help protect the neck from bites. Cobras also sham dead, going limp until danger passes.

ORDER: Squamata;
FAMILY: Elapidae.
SPECIES: *Naja naja* (India); *Naja haje (Egyptian)*.

Cockatoo

The cockatoos are a group of 16 species of the PARROT family. They include the cockatiels, gang-gangs and galahs. Cockatoos look like parrots, but have crests which they can raise at will. Most are white, sometimes with pink or yellow tinges and coloured crests, but some are black or grey.

A pink **cockatoo** from Australia displays its erect crest.

Cockatoos are found in the Australasian region, ranging from the Celebes in the west to the Solomon Islands in the east. They generally live in wooded country, though some extend to woodland borders and open scrub. Cockatoos are mainly vegetarian, eating seeds, fruits and nuts. Some are pests and raid cereal crops, trampling down the plants and taking the seeds. Others attack fruit trees. Cockatoos make good cage birds, being able to mimic human and other sounds.

ORDER: Psittaciformes;
FAMILY: Psittacidae.

Cockchafer

Also known as the may-bug, the cockchafer is a bulky brown beetle about 25 mm long. Its pointed hind end is black and sticks out beyond the *elytra*. It flies noisily in May and June and often crashes into lighted windows at night. The insect is a serious pest in both adult and larval stages. The adults strip the leaves from a wide variety of trees, while the fat white grubs live under the ground and do serious damage to the roots of cereal and other crops, as well as trees. The cockchafer is widely distributed in Europe and Asia, and several similar species live in other parts of the world.

ORDER: Coleoptera;
FAMILY: Scarabaeidae;
SPECIES: *Melolontha melolontha*.

Cockchafer and larva.

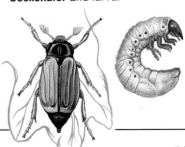

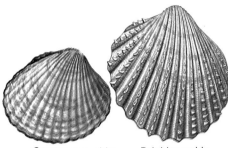

Common cockle   Prickly cockle

Cockle

Cockle is the name given to about 200 species of *bivalve* MOLLUSCS. They have unusually rounded, ribbed shells and are found from high-tide level down to 2400 metres deep in the sea. Most cockles live embedded in the sand or mud of the sea floor, with a pair of short tubes or *siphons* projecting above the surface. The cockle draws water in through one tube and ejects it through the other, filtering food and oxygen from it as it passes over the gills. The eyes are on tentacles on the siphons.
CLASS: Bivalvia;
ORDER: Heterodonta.

Cock-of-the-rock

The two species of cock-of-the-rock are ornate but uncommon South American birds belonging to the same family as the COTINGA. They are noted for their variety of crests and *wattles*. Cocks-of-the-rock live in the dense, damp forests around the Amazon basin. They are mainly fruit-eaters, but also take insects and snails. The males have elaborate displays.
ORDER: Passeriformes;
FAMILY: Cotingidae.

The collared dove has a black stripe edged with white on the back of its neck.

Cockroach

The cockroaches are flattened, greasy insects with long, spiky legs and very long *antennae*. Their bodies reach 8 cm or more in length, although most species are much smaller. Many can fly well, but others are wingless or have very short wings. When present, the front wings are rather leathery and they protect the more delicate hind wings. Cockroaches are scavenging insects and most of them live in the tropics. They come out at night to feed on dead animals and fallen fruit. A few of the 4000 or so species live wild in Europe, but the most familiar species are the "domestic" cockroaches – tropical species which have become established in heated buildings. The American cockroach is a typical example of this. Cockroaches lay their eggs in little "purses", which the females carry around with them for a time. The youngsters grow up without a pupal stage.
ORDER: Dictyoptera.

Cod

The cod is, in western countries, second only in importance to the HERRING as a food fish. The Atlantic cod is a large fish, up to two metres long and weighing as much as 96 kg, although the fish supplied to fish shops are much smaller. The cod has a plump, olive-green or brown body, patterned with spots, and a silvery belly. On its lower lip it has a prominent *barbel* or feeler. Most cod are trawled at depths of 20 to 200 metres, where they feed on smaller fishes and sometimes on SQUID. A female cod lays as many as six million eggs each year, but the vast majority get eaten by other fishes. Those tiny young, or fry, that do survive sometimes get protection by living between the stinging tentacles of JELLYFISHES.
ORDER: Gadiformes;
FAMILY: Gadidae;
SPECIES: *Gadus morhua*.

Coelacanth

The coelacanth is a living fossil, perhaps the most famous fish of this century. It belongs to a large order of fishes that were thought to have become extinct 70 million years ago, and is apparently its sole survivor. It is important to zoologists because the coelacanth and its extinct relatives belong to a larger group of fishes, the lobefins, from which the first land animals arose.

The first coelacanth to be identified was caught off the South African coast by a trawler in 1938. Unlike any coelacanth that had previously been caught, this one was seen by a zoologist, who recognized the large blue fish for what it was. Many more coelacanths have since been caught.

The living coelacanth is a large, deep-water fish with a heavy body weighing about 50 kg. Its body, about 1.5 metres long, is blue in colour and is covered with scales which, unusually for a bony fish, have many small tooth-like points. In some ways, these scales are more like those of non-bony fish such as sharks.
CLASS: Sareopterygii;
ORDER: Crossopterygii;
FAMILY: Latimeriidae;
SPECIES: *Latimeria chalumnae*.

Collared dove

A dove measuring 28 cm in length. It is distinguished by the narrow black collar around the back of the neck. Collared doves are birds of farmland and gardens, and can be seen in city centres. They feed mainly on seeds. Collared doves are found in Africa, Asia and Europe. Before 1930, they were confined to south-eastern Europe and then began a remarkable expansion to the north-west. They are now found throughout central Europe and extend to Britain, Ireland and Scandinavia, while some have bred in Iceland.
ORDER: Columbiformes;
FAMILY: Columbidae;
SPECIES: *Streptopelia decaocto*.

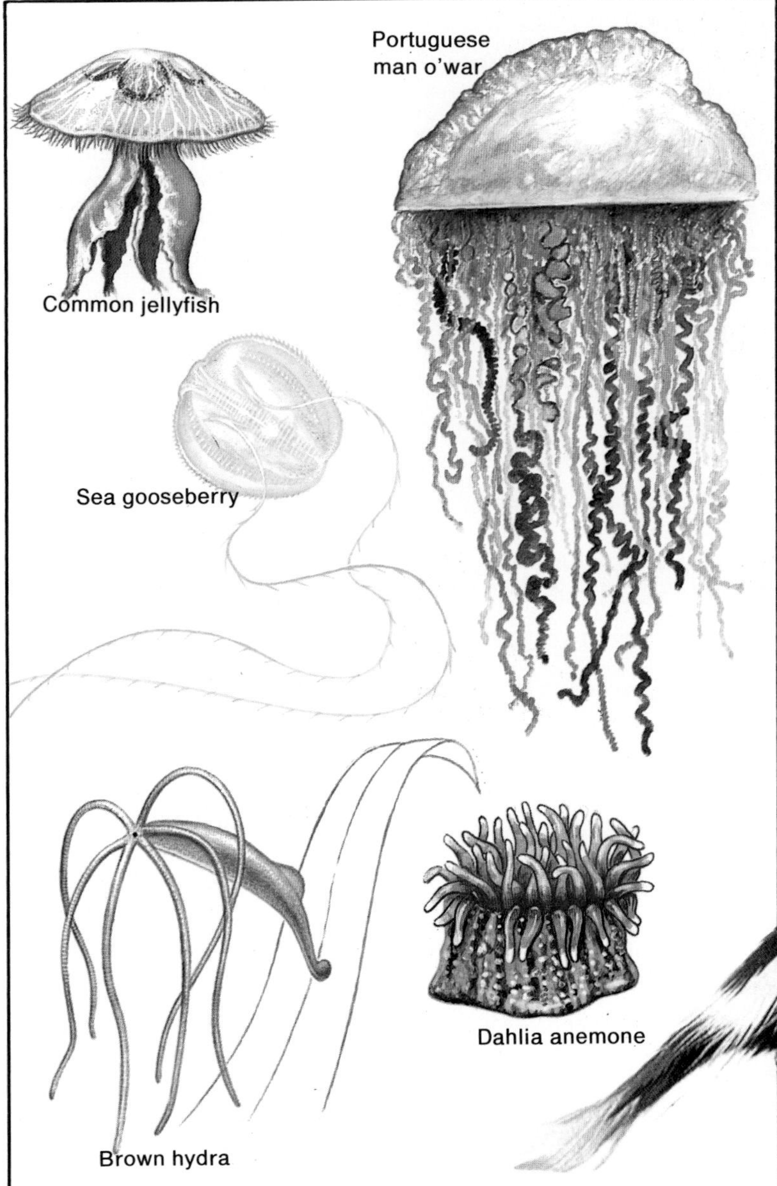

Portuguese
man o'war

Common jellyfish

Sea gooseberry

Brown hydra

Dahlia anemone

Coelenterates

This animal phylum contains more than 10,000 species of aquatic animals. They include CORALS, SEA ANEMONES, and JELLYFISHES, as well as the well-known HYDRA of ponds and streams. The soft body is little more than a bag whose walls consist of two layers of muscular cells separated by a layer of jelly. There is only one opening, which is surrounded by a number of arms or tentacles. These normally bear stinging cells with which the coelenterates catch their prey. There is no brain, but a network of nerves controls the actions of the tentacles and ensures that they push in the right direction. New individuals, known as *polyps*, grow from buds on the parent, but they do not always separate completely and they later produce buds themselves. A branching colonly thus builds up. The CORALS are the best known of these branching forms.

Colobus monkey

Colobus monkeys are shy animals, rarely coming out of the dense forest where they live. They range from Senegal to Ethiopia and southward to Angola, but despite this range, they are nowhere common. Of the three species, the black colobus is the best known. Although there are many variations in its coat it usually has short, black fur with long plumes of white on the tail and sides. There is also white on the chin, cheeks and forehead. The red colobus has a black body with chestnut-coloured head, arms and legs. The olive colobus is unusual in that the mother carries her newborn young in her mouth for the first few weeks of its life. This is probably because her hair is too short for it to grip. Colobus monkeys live in family groups.

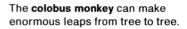

The **colobus monkey** can make enormous leaps from tree to tree.

They are mainly leaf-eaters. Their chief enemies are eagles and man.
ORDER: Primates;
FAMILY: Colobidae;
SPECIES: *Colobus polykomos* (black); *Colobus badius* (red); *Colobus verus* (olive).

Colorado beetle

The Colorado beetle is a serious pest of potatoes. It is one of a large

The **colorado beetle** is a dangerous pest. By chewing potato leaves it has been the cause of famine.

family of beetles known as LEAF BEETLES. Both the adult, easily recognized by its black and yellow stripes, and the bright pink grub feed avidly on the leaves and stems of the potato plant. Whole plants may be nibbled to the ground, so no tubers can develop. Adult beetles hibernate in the soil and emerge to lay eggs in spring. The beetle is a native of North America, but found its way to Europe in the 1920s.
ORDER: Coleoptera;
FAMILY: Chrysomelidae;
SPECIES: *Leptinotarsa decemlineata.*

Conch

A family of large sea snails, whose shells have been used as trumpets. The shells have a long and narrow opening and an outer lip which is generally expanded to form a broad plate. Conches range in size from 14 mm to 60 cm, the largest being the queen conch. They have two large eyes, carried on stalks on either side of a stout *proboscis.* Most conches live in warm, shallow tropical waters where they feed on seaweeds. At rest they tend to bury themselves in sand or gravel. Conches leap over the sea bed by means of their large foot, which has a sharp-edged *operculum,* on the hind end. The conch uses this operculum to push itself along and as a weapon.
CLASS: Gastropoda;
ORDER: Mesogastropoda;
FAMILY: Strombidae.

Condor

The condor is the world's largest flying bird, with a wingspan of 3 metres and weighing up to 11 kg. Of the two species, the Andean condor is still fairly common, but the Californian condor is almost extinct. Only about 40 birds survive. Hunters have found the large target of the condor irresistible and the condor's slow breeding rate handicaps its chances of survival. It lays one egg every other year.

Condors look like VULTURES, with the same naked heads and necks, and are mainly scavengers, feeding on carrion. But they are not related to the true vultures of the Old World. Condors are superb fliers, soaring to great heights on the thermal air currents over mountains. They have excellent eyesight and can spot a carcase at a great distance. If one condor suddenly drops towards the ground, other condors know it has found food and quickly fly to the feast. Apart from carrion, condors will also take live prey, such as lambs, young llamas and deer. Near coasts they will eat dead fish and seals, and also shellfish.
ORDER: Falconiformes;
FAMILY: Cathartidae;
SPECIES: *Vultur gryphus* (Andean); *Gymnogyps californianus* (Californian).

Cone shell

There are between 500 and 600 species of sea snails in the family Conidae, and they are known as cone shells from the shape of their shells. They range in size from very small up to about 23 cm long. They

The queen **conch** shell can be as much as 60 cm long. Conches have been used as trumpets from the earliest times. The Triton shell of Greek mythology was a conch.

The Andean **condor** is the world's largest flying bird. It can reach heights of over 4000 metres, gliding upwards on rising air currents.

live in the shallow tropical and sub-tropical waters of the Atlantic and Indian oceans, and around the East Indies. Cone shells are carnivorous, eating worms, molluscs or small fish. They have hollow teeth through which they inject poison into their victims. The sting of some of the large species can kill a man.
CLASS: Gastropoda;
ORDER: Neogastropoda;
FAMILY: Conidae.

Conger

The conger or conger EEL is a large marine eel which grows up to 3 metres long and weighs up to 45 kg. It has a light brown to dark brown scaleless body with large, keen eyes, strong jaws and sharp teeth, showing that it is a predator. One story says that a conger bit off the heel of a fisherman's seaboot!

Like the related freshwater EEL, the conger spawns only once, then dies. Also like its smaller relative, it begins life as a tiny, leaf-like fish which makes long migrations at sea, gradually changing in form to resemble the adult eel.
ORDER: Anguilliformes;
FAMILY: Congridae;
SPECIES: *Conger conger*.

Coot

The ten species of coots belong to the RAIL family and are closely related to the MOORHEN. They are found all over the world. Coots are dark-coloured water birds. Most species are distinguished by the white shield that lies above the bill. On each toe, coots have lobed flaps that open to act like paddles. These leave the toes free to move, so that coots are nimble on land, unlike birds with webbed feet. Coots are to be found on fairly large bodies of water, gathering in flocks outside the breeding season. They nest among tall water plants at the edges of lakes.
ORDER: Gruiformes;
FAMILY: Rallidae.

The **conger** can grow to a length of 3 metres.

Red-knobbed **coots** among water flowers at the margin of a lake in Kenya.

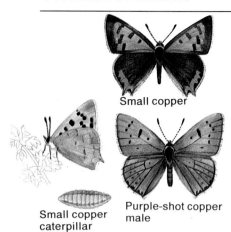

Small copper

Small copper
caterpillar

Purple-shot copper
male

Copper butterfly

The copper butterflies are quite small, fast-flying butterflies whose wings have the colour and lustre of polished copper on the upper surface. Many are marked with black spots and streaks, and several have a blue or purple sheen as well. They are related to the BLUE BUTTERFLIES and are widely distributed in the cooler parts of the northern hemisphere. There are many species, of which the small copper, also known as the American copper, is the most familiar. The butterflies frequent flowery places and often defend a particular clump of flowers against other butterflies by darting out at newcomers as they approach. The caterpillars of the coppers are somewhat slug-like in shape and almost all feed on docks and related plants.
ORDER: Lepidoptera;
FAMILY: Lycaenidae.

Coral

Corals belong to the class of sea creatures often called "flower-animals". They are similar to SEA ANEMONES except that they are surrounded and supported by a hard, chalky skeleton. True corals, often called stony corals, may be solitary or live in colonies. A solitary polyp lives in a chalk cup or on a mushroom-shaped chalky skeleton. The polyps of a colony-living coral unite in their thousands to form a sheet of tissue covering the chalky skeleton.

Although the skeleton is often white when dead, when the coral is alive and covered with a continuous layer of flesh it can be beautifully coloured and form a variety of shapes.

Most corals live in tropical seas. Only a few species thrive in temperate or polar regions. Reef-building corals form huge reefs along thousands of kilometres of tropical and sub-tropical shores, especially in the Indian Ocean. These corals grow only in very clear water and are absent from areas where large rivers flow into the sea. Corals feed by catching small swimming animals in their tentacles. Tiny single-celled plants live in the tissues of reef coral, and produce chemicals which help the polyps to make their lime skeletons. Corals reproduce in two ways; either sexually by producing eggs and sperm cells, or asexually by budding.

A living **coral** colony. The individual polyps that make it up are only 10 mm in diameter.

Soft corals are not true corals. They are usually tree-like, the centres of the stems and branches being strengthened by a chalky substance, coloured red or black. The polyps have eight tentacles, whereas those of true corals have six, or multiples of six.
CLASS: Anthozoa.

Coral snake

True coral snakes live in Asia and the Americas. They include two species found in North America: the common coral snake which lives in Mexico and the south-eastern United States, and the Arizona coral snake, which lives in Mexico and the south-western United States. The Arizona coral snake is shorter than the common coral snake, which measures about 1 metre when fully grown.

The jaws of coral snakes do not open wide, so they eat only slender prey such as lizards and other snakes. The common coral snake lays 3 to 14 soft, slim eggs in May

or June which take about 11 weeks to hatch. The. young measure about 18 cm long.

Coral snakes are slender, with a pattern of coloured rings running around the body and tail. In both North American species the rings occur in the same order: black, yellow or white, and red. These brightly coloured rings make coral snakes among the most gaudy of animals. They resemble the warning colours of creatures such as WASPS and FIRE SALAMANDERS. All these animals are poisonous. True coral snakes are close relatives of the COBRAS, and very poisonous, although they are not very aggressive.
ORDER: Squamata;
FAMILY: Elapidae;
SPECIES: *Micrurus fulvius* (common); *Micruroides euryxanthus* (Arizona).

Cormorant

There are 30 species of cormorants. They are found all over the world except for the central Pacific region. Their webbed feet, upright stance and long necks suggest that they lead an aquatic life. But they rarely fly far out to sea. Most are found along coasts or on inland waters.

The common cormorant is the

The **cormorant** is an expert fish-catcher. It can stay under water for more than a minute.

Continental form

Atlantic form

most widespread and largest of the species, being 100 cm long. It is also known as the great cormorant in North America, and the black cormorant in New Zealand. The plumage of the adult bird is generally glossy black with a white patch on the chin and cheeks. The green cormorant called the shag in Britain, has a glossy, bottle-green plumage. Cormorants are expert divers and swimmers, and feed mainly on fish. In north-eastern Asia, the Japanese cormorant is trained for fishing. A metal ring is placed around the bird's neck to prevent it from swallowing the catch.
ORDER: Pelecaniformes;
FAMILY: Phalacrocoracidae;
SPECIES: *Phalacrocorax carbo* (common).

The **corncrake** advertises its presence by the monotonous two-beat creaking call of the male, which is kept up for hours on end.

Corncrake

The corncrake breeds in the fields and grasslands of Europe and Asia, and migrates to southern Africa and Asia. It hides in the grass, feeding on insects and other small animals, and depends on its streaky, light-brown plumage for camouflage. The spread of agriculture originally helped the corncrake to expand, as it is a bird of grassland, but the introduction of mowing machines has harmed the birds.
ORDER: Gruiformes;
FAMILY: Rallidae;
SPECIES: *Crex crex*.

Cotinga

A group of birds found mainly in the dense forests of the Amazon basin. There are about 90 species and many of the males have ornate plumage as well as crests and *wattles*. The COCK-OF-THE-ROCK is the most ornate, together with the umbrella bird. Cotingas are best known for their constant calling – the BELLBIRDS are especially notable in this respect. Many cotingas are fruit-eaters, but some also eat insects. Males often have elaborate courtship displays.
ORDER: Passeriformes;
FAMILY: Cotingidae.

Cottontail

The cottontails are small RABBITS found throughout North and South America. The tail, brown above and white below, looks like a cotton ball and gives rise to the rabbit's name. The cottontail has shorter ears than the European rabbit, but its way of life is much the same.

There are about 13 species of cottontail, living in a range of habitats from woodland to desert. They feed on grass, and damage crops and young trees by nibbling and trampling them. The cottontail has many enemies, including foxes, skunks, owls, hawks and snakes. Its only defences are to crouch motionless or, if seen, to run for its life. Like all rabbits, cottontails breed almost continuously and can have as many as five litters a year. The young are born in a hollow in the ground rather than in a burrow, and are blind for about ten days.
ORDER: Lagomorpha;
FAMILY: Leporidae.

Courser

Coursers are long-legged, plover-like shore birds. There are nine species, the most familiar being the cream-coloured courser. It is a pale sandy colour, with creamy legs, distinctive black primary

Courtship and mating

After an animal has found enough food for its own survival, its next need is to find a mate which will ensure the survival of its species. For animals that roam together in

The magnificent male Prince Rudolph's **bird of paradise** woos the dull-coloured female by showing off its plumage and by strutting about.

herds, such as BISON, finding a possible mate is no problem. For species that lead solitary lives, finding another member of the same species may not be so easy.

Smell is one of the ways which help lone species to find a mate. Female moths, for example, release a faint perfume into the air, which will lure males from distances of over a kilometre. We cannot smell the scent, but to another moth it is so attractive and powerful that not even the smell of rotting eggs can mask it. In the same way, female fish release into the water a chemical substance that can be detected by males of their species.

GLOW-WORMS and FIREFLIES attract males by glowing brightly during the mating season. CRICKETS and GRASS-HOPPERS use sound to attract mates, but this time it is the male that attracts the female.

Once a mate has been found the ritual of courtship can begin. The courtship behaviour of many animals is remarkably similar to that of humans – males display their courage and handsome fea-

tures and even present the females with gifts. A male PENGUIN rolls a stone towards a female he is wooing. JACK-DAWS and other birds bring gifts of food or nesting material. A male HERON starts to build a nest before he woos the female of his choice. The BOWER BIRD goes a stage further and constructs an elaborate tentlike structure, which he decorates with berries, flowers and, if he can get them, bits of glass and jewellery!

The main aspect of bird courtship, however, is display. The male bird struts in front of his chosen partner. In most cases he is much more brightly coloured than the hen bird and he uses his colour to the full in his courtship. One of the most beautiful displays is that of the PEACOCK, which spreads out its elaborate feathers like a huge fan. With this display go various ritual dances, which differ from species to species. Many distinctive courtship songs also help to make the female more receptive to the male's advances. If the male and female birds are alike, like GREBES, both may dance.

Among mammals courtship tends to be less showy. Males are more likely to fight for the favours of the females or for the right to control a large harem. During the rutting season DEER make loud barking noises and two stags contest for superiority by a series of head-to-head charges, antlers clashing. These battles look and sound alarming, but fighting males rarely kill each other – the contest is over when the winner has chased off the loser. A fight to the death would not be in the interests of the species' survival.

wing feathers and a broad, black and white eye stripe. Other species, except for the Egyptian plover, are similar. The Egyptian plover, a courser despite its name, is a beautiful grey and white, with black and green markings. Coursers are good runners. They live in the Old World, from Africa to Australia.

ORDER: Charadriiformes;
FAMILY: Glareolidae.

Cowbird

Most species of cowbirds have the habit of laying their eggs in the nests of other birds. In this respect they are like CUCKOOS. Cowbirds are small birds with glossy, dark plumage. Most live in South America. The brown-headed cowbird is a North American species found right across the United States. Cowbirds eat seeds and insects and their name originates from their habit of following cattle and other large animals to feed on insects disturbed by the animal's hooves.

ORDER: Passeriformes;
FAMILY: Icteridae.

Cowrie

A group of sea snails with colourful, egg-shaped shells. The opening in the under-side of the cowrie shell is in the form of a narrow slit. The largest of the 150 species live in warm, tropical waters, but a few species are found around European shores. A live cowrie hides most of its shell by

Cowrie shells are popular with collectors. One species used to be used as money.

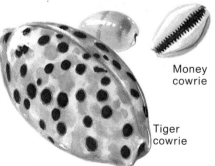

Money cowrie

Tiger cowrie

The **coyote** is found from Alaska to Central America.

folding part of the *mantle* (a soft layer of tissue on which the shell forms) over the top of the shell. Cowries crawl over the shallow sea bed, feeding on other sea creatures. The more colourful and shiny shells are popular with collectors. People in parts of Africa and southern Asia used to use shells of one species as money, while chiefs in Tonga and Fiji wore golden cowrie shells as badges of rank.

CLASS: Gastropoda;
ORDER: Mesogastropoda;
FAMILY: Cypraeidae.

Coyote

The coyote, also called a prairie wolf, is like a small version of the wolf. It measures about 1.2 metres from its nose to the tip of its tail and weighs 9 to 23 kg. The fur is tawny and the tail, which is bushy with a black tip, droops low behind the hind legs.

Originally, coyotes inhabited the plains of western North America. Today, they are even known to enter towns to scavenge among garbage. Despite persecution, they have extended their range and are now found all over North America, even as far north as Alaska.

Coyotes eat a wide range of food – small mammals, birds, fish, insects and sometimes vegetable matter. They pair for life. Mating occurs between January and March. The cubs (up to 19 in a litter) are born 63 days later and are reared for the first month in a den. This is usually an abandoned burrow, enlarged to form a long tunnel and a nesting chamber.

ORDER: Carnivora;
FAMILY: Canidae;
SPECIES: *Canis latrans*.

Coypu

The coypu is an aquatic RODENT found in South America. Although related to the PORCUPINE, the coypu looks more like a giant rat. It is over 1 metre long, has webbed hind feet and is an excellent swimmer. Its fur is known as nutria.

Coypus live solitary lives in rivers and swamps, feeding on reeds, water grasses and the roots of water plants. They also eat snails and mussels and will raid farm crops at night. In the 1930s coypus were brought to Europe and reared in captivity for their fur. Some animals escaped and there are now wild coypu colonies in many parts of Europe as well as in North America and the USSR. With no natural enemies to control their numbers, these immigrant coypu have become pests. In their native home, the animals are preyed upon by jaguars and caimans.

ORDER: Rodentia;
FAMILY: Capromyidae;
SPECIES: *Myocastor coypus*.

Coypus have become pests in some areas where they were reared for their fur.

Crab

Crab is the name given to about 4500 species of CRUSTACEANS. They range in size from the tiny pea crabs, which have shells only 6 mm across, to the giant spider crab of Japan which has a shell of 30 cm across and a claw span of up to 3.7 metres. Most species of crabs have hard shells. The hermit crab is an exception in that it does not have a shell covering the whole of its body, but makes its home in the shell of a sea snail or other MOLLUSC. The true crabs have five pairs of legs, though in some species not all the legs are visible. The front pair have well-developed pincers, which are used for picking up food, and many species use the back pair of legs as paddles for swimming. The tail is usually very small and folded forward under the rest of the body. On land, crabs walk with a side-long gait.

Most crabs live in the sea and those which live some distance

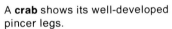

A **crab** shows its well-developed pincer legs.

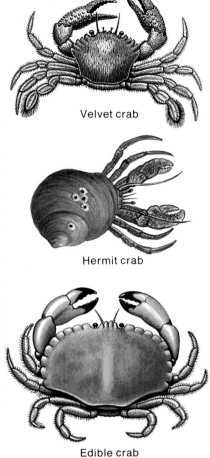

Velvet crab

Hermit crab

Edible crab

from it return to the water to breed. Some spend all their lives in fresh water; others, such as the Chinese mitten crab, spend most of their time in fresh water, but return to the sea to breed.

Crabs vary considerably in what they eat. Some are vegetarian, some are carnivores, while others eat anything and act as scavengers.

ORDER: Decapoda.

Crab spider

These spiders get their name because they resemble crabs in the shape of their legs and the way they scuttle sideways. Crab spiders eat a wide variety of animals. They do not make a web, but lie in wait for their prey among leaf litter or flowers which they often match perfectly. Indeed, the "white death" spider can change its colour from white to yellow and vice-versa to match different flowers. If it is moved from its white or yellow surroundings to a flower of a different hue it quickly looks for a flower of its own colour. The male of one species

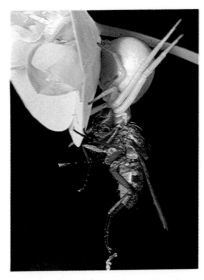

A **crab spider**, camouflaged against the flower in which it lies, has captured a fly.

binds the legs of the female to the ground with silk so that he does not get eaten by her after mating – a fate which often overtakes other male crab spiders.
ORDER: Araneae;
FAMILIES: Sparassidae, Thomisidae.

Crane

Cranes are long-necked and long-legged birds of marshlands and

One of the most handsome of **cranes**, the crowned crane of southern Africa.

swamps. The largest crane stands 150 cm high with a wingspan of 2.3 metres. Cranes live in North America and throughout most of Europe, Asia and Africa. They are mainly vegetarian, but may also eat frogs and other small animals.

Cranes are well-known for their spectacular dances, which are held throughout the year but are most often seen during the breeding season. The birds, in pairs or flocks, walk around each other with quick, stiff-legged steps and wings half spread, sometimes bowing and stretching. The tempo of the dance quickens and the birds leap 4.5 metres or more into the air and drift down in a slow-motion ballet. They also pick up sticks or leaves with their bills, throw them into the air and stab at them as they fall. Hunting and the drainage of marshes have caused the numbers of cranes to decline. The whooping crane of North America has declined to a single flock that has been down to 22 birds. A single disaster could wipe them out, particularly during migration, when the birds cannot be protected.
ORDER: Gruiformes;
FAMILY: Gruidae.

Crane-fly

The crane-flies are slim-bodied flies with long, slender legs, from

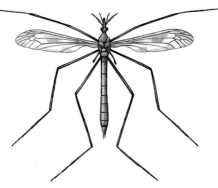

The female **crane-fly** one of the species known as daddy-long-legs.

which they get their popular name of daddy-long-legs. The legs break off very easily, but the insects are not inconvenienced as long as they keep three or four. The narrow wings span 5 cm or more in the larger species, and are often held well away from the body at rest. The *larvae* of many species live in mud and water, but some live in the soil and are troublesome pests because they damage plant roots. They are called leatherjackets. Adult crane-flies, which are most abundant in late summer, rarely feed.
ORDER: Diptera;
FAMILY: Tipulidae.

The **crayfish** usually hides by day under stones or in holes in the bank, and hunts by night.

Crayfish

Crayfish are freshwater CRUSTACEANS which look like small LOBSTERS. They are found in lakes and rivers of all the continents except Africa. Crayfish range in size from 2.5 cm to 40 cm.

The head and *thorax* of the crayfish are covered with a single shell. The crayfish has a pair of strong jaws and two pairs of smaller jaws, called maxillae. The thorax carries three pairs of appendages which are used to pass food to its jaws, a pair of stout pincers used to capture and hold the prey, and four pairs of legs used for walking. Other limbs called *swimmerets*, used for swimming, are on the abdomen. The crayfish can swim swiftly backwards to escape an enemy.

ORDER: Decapoda;

FAMILIES: Parastacidae, Astacidae, Austroastacidae.

Cricket

There are about 2500 species of cricket, most of which live in tropical regions. They are mainly nocturnal, but the European field cricket sings in the fields by day. The house cricket is found all over the world, but it is a native of the Middle East.

True crickets differ from BUSH-CRICKETS and GRASSHOPPERS in being flatter and broader across the back. Their jumping legs are also less obvious than in the other groups. The female has a long, needle-like *ovipositor*, with which she usually lays her eggs in the soil, and both sexes have two fairly long tails. Like the bush-crickets,

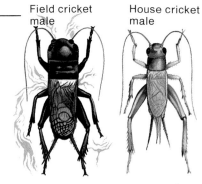

Field cricket male   House cricket male

Crickets can easily be distinguished from grasshoppers by their long thin antennae.

the males sing, by rubbing their wing bases together, and their calls are often very shrill. Crickets are OMNIVOROUS and most live on the ground. Some can fly, but many have no hind wings and some have no wings at all. Crickets grow up without a pupal stage.

The North American snowy tree cricket is commonly known as the "thermometer cricket". A listener can estimate the temperature in degrees fahrenheit by counting the number of chirps in 15 seconds and adding 40. In China, cricket fighting has been a popular sport for over a thousand years.

ORDER: Orthoptera;

FAMILY: Gryllidae.

Croaker

The name of perchlike fishes which are famous because they can make sounds, not only croaks but also drumming, purring, creaking and hissing noises. The 160 or so species of croaker, many of which live off the east coast of America, make their noises with their swim bladders, which they vibrate rather like a drumskin or a guitar string. Croakers may make their noises for the same reasons that birds sing, that is, to advertise their territory, attract a mate and warn off any rivals. They may even use their sounds like a submarine uses its echo-sounder, to discover the depth at which they are swimming.

ORDER: Perciformes;

FAMILY: Sciaenidae.

Crocodile

The crocodile family includes the largest of all living REPTILES. The biggest crocodile is the estuarine crocodile, which is said to reach 10

Two large **crocodiles** bask in the sun on a river bank. They are using the sun to regulate their body temperature.

metres in length. The smallest is the Congo dwarf crocodile, which is fully grown at about 1 metre.

Crocodiles are armoured, aquatic reptiles related to the ALLIGATOR to which they are similar. Crocodiles live in tropical parts of Africa, Asia, Australia and America. With their bulky bodies and short legs, adults are usually sluggish, although young crocodiles can gallop with the body high up off the ground. Unlike alligators, they are often found in brackish water and sometimes swim out to sea.

Although cold-blooded, crocodiles prevent their body temperature from varying too much by coming ashore at sunrise to bask and then cooling off in the water, as the sun becomes hotter. They float very low, with little more than eyes and nostrils showing.

An adult crocodile catches and eats fish and also traps larger mammals and birds. It captures its prey by lying in wait near game trails or water-holes, seizing an antelope or zebra in its jaws and dragging it under water or knocking it over with a blow from its head or tail. Drowning soon stills the victim's struggles. If its prey is large, the crocodile grips the body in its jaws and rolls over and over, tearing off large chunks of flesh.

The Nile crocodile breeds when 5 to 10 years old. Males fight for territories before mating. Each female lays up to 90 eggs in a specially dug pit. When, after four months, the eggs hatch, the mother takes the hatchlings in her mouth down to the water.
ORDER: Crocodilia;
FAMILY: Crocodylidae.

Crossbill

Crossbills belong to the FINCH family. They have characteristic bills in which the upper and lower parts cross each other. The common or red crossbill breeds all over the world. Crossbills breed only where there are coniferous trees, for they depend on pine, spruce and larch cones for food, feeding on the seeds which they gouge out with their bills. The female usually lays 4 eggs in an untidy, mossy nest. The chicks are born with ordinary bills: it is only after they leave the nest that the two halves cross over by growing crooked.
ORDER: Passeriformes;
FAMILY: Fringillidae;
SPECIES: *Loxia curvirostris.*

Crow

The family includes about 100 species. Hooded and carrion crows inhabit large areas of Europe and Asia, the common crow and fish crow live in North America, the collared crow in China and the pied crow in Africa. The carrion crow and hooded crow interbreed and are regarded as the same species by some. Carrion crows spend most of their time on the ground feeding or perched in trees. They are often confused with ROOKS but lack the grey skin at the base of the beak. They are black all over, though in strong sunlight the plumage is shot with purple and blue. Crows have a long, slow deliberate flight. Their food is very varied, including both plants and animals. The nest is usually in the stout fork of a tree. A female carrion crow lays 4 to 5 eggs at a time and incubates them.
ORDER: Passeriformes;
FAMILY: Corvidae.

Crowned eagle

This handsome bird of prey gets its name from the crest of black and white feathers on top of its head. It is the most powerful of the African eagles, although smaller than the MARTIAL EAGLE. Up to 76 cm long, the crowned eagle has the broad, rounded wings and long tail of the typical forest eagle. It is seldom seen, for it flies just above or within the forest canopy when hunting, and its nest is hidden in the tree-tops. Only the scattered bones of its prey beneath the nest site reveal the eagle's presence. Crowned eagles mostly prey on mammals, especially small antelopes and monkeys.
ORDER: Falconiformes;
FAMILY: Accipitridae;
SPECIES: *Stephanoaetus coronatus.*

The crossed bill of these birds is not always easy to see.

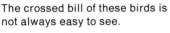

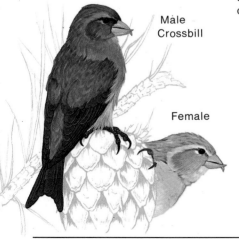

Male Crossbill

Female

Crows are among the cleverest of all birds. They may store food for the winter and open snails by dropping them on a stone.

Hooded crow

Carrion crow

Crustaceans

The Class Crustacea consists almost entirely of aquatic animals – SHRIMPS, CRABS, LOBSTERS, and a host of smaller, creatures, such as WATER FLEAS. Many are PLANKTON creatures, drifting in the surface waters of the oceans. The only really land animals in the class are the

Robber crabs are among the largest of crustaceans. They have lungs as well as gills and drown if kept under water.

WOODLICE, but even these cannot survive in really dry places. The crustaceans have many pairs of limbs, and in the most primitive kinds, such as FAIRY SHRIMPS, the limbs are all

alike. More advanced crustaceans have several types of limbs – some for walking, some for swimming, and some for catching food. The gills, which take oxygen from the water, are always modified limbs or outgrowths from the bases of the limbs. The *exoskeleton* is often very hard.

Cuckoo

The cuckoo family gets its name from the distinctive two-note call of the male common cuckoo. No other species in the family utters it. The common cuckoo ranges

Left: A common **cuckoo** just about to make its call. Only the male makes the "cuckoo" call; the female has a babbling sound. On the right are the two cuckoo forms.

across Europe, Asia and America, and all its members are birds that lay their eggs in the nests of other birds.

The common cuckoo has distinctive black and white barring on its under-side, which makes it resemble the SPARROWHAWK. This may help the cuckoo to frighten away birds from their nests when it wishes to lay its eggs. Other cuckoos are gaudy by comparison with the common cuckoo. Cuckoos mainly eat insects, worms, spiders and centipedes, and may help farmers by consuming pests.

Parasitic cuckoos lay their eggs in the nests of other birds. The foster parents instinctively feed the young cuckoo when it hatches, even though it pushes any other eggs and chicks out of the nest.
ORDER: Cuculiformes;
FAMILY: Cuculidae;
SPECIES: *Cuculus canorus* (common).

Curassow

Curassows are birds of the forests of Central and South America. There are 13 species, ranging in size from a pheasant to a small TURKEY, to which they are in fact related. Curassows are mostly black or brown in colour, and have crests and bony *casques* on their heads. Unlike other gamebirds, they nest in trees and not on the ground. They eat mainly fruit,

nuts, buds and leaves. Curassows would make good domestic birds, for their flesh is tasty. However, they lay few eggs and do not breed well in captivity.
ORDER: Galliformes;
FAMILY: Cracidae.

On the shore, **curlews** search with their long bills for small crabs, shrimps and fishes.

Curlew

Curlews are large wading birds which are distinguished by their 13 cm down-curved bill, and their two-syllable fluting call from which they get their name. The common curlew is found across Europe and Asia, usually on open plains, moors and marshes. Curlews feed on shellfish, snails, worms, insects, and fish, using their long bills to probe for them in the sand.
ORDER: Charadriiformes;
FAMILY: Scolopacidae;
SPECIES: *Numenius arquata* (common).

Cuscus

The cuscus is a noisy PHALANGER. Over 16 species live in the forests of Australia and Papua New Guinea. They are just over 1 metre long, including the curling *prehensile* tail, which is used when climbing. They are nocturnal animals which eat leaves, insects, eggs and small birds. When

alarmed they may snarl and bark with a guttural sound. They probably have no particular breeding season as most females carry one or more young at any time of the year. The cuscus can produce a repulsive odour that may be defensive.
ORDER: Marsupialia;
FAMILY: Phalangeridae.

Cuttlefish

The cuttlefish is a MOLLUSC related to the SQUID and the OCTOPUS. It has a shield-shaped body, inside which is a chalky plate containing gas-filled cells which make the animal buoyant. It has a small head bearing eight arms and two long tentacles which it can retract into pockets beside each of its large eyes. The smallest known cuttlefish is 4 cm long, the largest 1.5 metres. There are about 100 species.

The cuttlefish swims by waving fins on either side of its body, but when speed is required it can eject a stream of water from the funnel, producing a form of jet propulsion. It can also eject a blue-black "ink" which serves as a decoy when danger threatens. Cuttlefish are capable of changing their colour. A cuttlefish can change from grey to reddish-brown to a pale green as it passes over various patches of colour.
CLASS: Cephalopoda;
ORDER: Decapoda.

The **cuttlefish** catches its prey by shooting out its long tentacles at lightning speed.

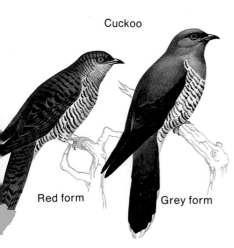

Cuckoo

Red form

Grey form

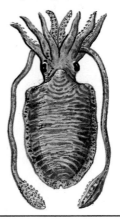

Cuttlebone

Dab

The dab is a flatfish, a relative of the PLAICE. Like other flatfishes of the sea, the dab lies on its side on the seabed, has a twisted mouth, and an eye that has migrated around the head so that both eyes lie on the same side. These peculiar developments happen as the dab grows up: its tiny young, or fry, have a more normal fish-like appearance.

The dab reaches a maximum length of about 40 cm. The upper surface of its body is brown, with red spots smaller than those of a plaice. The underside of the body is white.

ORDER: Pleuronectiformes;
FAMILY: Pleuronectidae;
SPECIES: *Limanda limanda*.

The **dab** is a common flatfish of sandy or shell grounds.

Damselfish

The damselfish, or demoiselle, is a brilliantly-coloured and patterned fish that lives on, or near, coral reefs. Damselfishes are aggressive fishes, usually not more than 15 cm long, but they attack and eat other small fishes.

The most famous damselfish is the clownfish, which shelters among the stinging tentacles of a giant sea anemone. The clownfish is not stung to death because a special slime on its scales stops the action of the deadly stinging cells. Other fishes, however, do get caught and killed by the sea anemone, and then the clownfish probably shares in the anemone's meal.

ORDER: Perciformes;
FAMILY: Pomacentridae.

Darwin's finches

A group of FINCHES which live only on the Galápagos Islands – except for one species which is also found on the Cocos Island. They are named after the naturalist Charles Darwin, who visited the islands during his famous voyage on HMS Beagle in 1835. Isolated on the islands for some time the finches have evolved into several distinct forms, so taking advantage of the different ways of life open to such birds on the islands. Darwin's observations on these birds were an important influence in helping him draw up his theory of evolution.

Damselfish are small, brightly-coloured and aggressive.

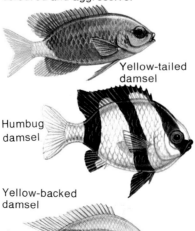

Yellow-tailed damsel

Humbug damsel

Yellow-backed damsel

These finches are presumed to have developed from ancestors on the South American mainland 960 km to the east. There are 14 species, each a drab greyish brown. There is little variation except in the bills. This is unusual as the mainland finches show different plumage rather than body form. The bills range from slender to stout, and are adapted for eating different kinds of food.

ORDER: Passeriformes;
FAMILY: Fringillidae.

Dasyure

Dasyures are known as the native cats of Australia, Tasmania and New Guinea. They are not in fact true cats but carnivorous MARSUPIALS, related to the marsupial mice. They have short legs and long, bushy tails, and their coats are marked with white spots. The head of some species is weasel-like with a pointed muzzle and long whiskers. Three of the five species of dasyure live mainly in trees, exceptions being the quoll and the western native cat. The tree-dwellers have roughened pads that give a good grip whilst climbing. Dasyures feed on birds, lizards, insects and young rabbits. They produce up to eight young, though some quoll females have been recorded as having as many as 24. Most of these must die as the mother is unable to feed them all.

ORDER: Marsupialia;
FAMILY: Dasyuridae.

Deathwatch beetle

The deathwatch beetle is about 6 mm long and a relative of the FURNITURE BEETLE. It is a serious

The **deathwatch beetle** can be a serious pest in the timbers of old houses, especially in oak.

pest in old buildings. Its grubs feed in old timbers and eventually destroy them. When the adult beetles are ready to emerge, they tap their heads against the wood, and the legend has it that the sound heralds a death in the house. The tapping noise is probably a signal which stirs all the new adults to emerge at about the same time. In the wild, the deathwatch beetle lives in old tree stumps.

ORDER: Coleoptera;
FAMILY: Anobiidae;
SPECIES: *Xestobium rufovillosum.*

Deer

LIKE ANTELOPES and cattle, deer are RUMINANTS (animals that chew the cud), but they are distinguished by their antlers, which are usually branched. Generally, only the male deer bear antlers, but both sexes of CARIBOU have them. Male deer, usually known as stags or bucks, are usually noticeably larger than the females, which are called hinds or does.

The antlers are shed each year, but buds soon appear on the skull and grow into tender stumps. These grow into new antlers within a few months. They are initially covered by "velvet", a layer of soft, hair-covered skin. When the antlers are fully grown, the skin peels away or is rubbed off by the deer. The tough antlers are then used to defend territory or, in the mating season, to fight to gain possession of females. Occasionally, the antlers of two warring deer become completely interlocked. The animals are unable to break away and finally die of

starvation. Each year's antlers are larger than those of the year before, until the animal is fully mature.

Deer are found throughout the Americas and Eurasia. Most deer are forest dwellers and grazers and browsers. They are graceful creatures, noted for their speed and their agility when jumping over obstacles. Deer vary in size from small species, such as the PUDU of South America, to the huge giant elk of Alaska.

Deer readily increase in num-

bers if they are not checked. Large, fast-increasing populations can cause great damage to tree plantations and to crops. The deer are then regarded as pests and herds are reduced in numbers by shooting. This not only safeguards plantations and farms, but also protects the deer's own habitat, which is also threatened when the population explodes.

ORDER: Artiodactyla;
FAMILY: Cervidae.

There are over 50 species of **deer**.

Spotted deer

Elk

The Development of Deer Antlers Each Year
The four stages cover the period from spring to autumn

1 2 3 4

Devil fish

The popular name for large, flattened fishes related to RAYS, SHARKS and SKATES, which flap through the waters of tropical seas like giant bats. The manta ray looks most like a fish of the devil, being 9 metres or more across and weighing upwards of 2 tonnes when fully grown. Lesser devil rays are down to about 1 metre in width.

Devil fish get their name not only from their wing-like fins but also from horn-like projections in front of their eyes. Despite these sinister features, however, they are harmless creatures which feed on the smallest of sea food. Indeed, their devilish horns are employed to scoop up this food from the floating plankton, as the fish flaps gracefully along.

ORDER: Rajiformes;
FAMILY: Mobulidae.

Diamond-backed terrapin

The diamond-backed terrapin gets its name from the bold, angular sculpturing on the plates of its shell. Up to 20 cm long and weighing about 1 kg it is found in most coastal regions of North America. It lives in estuaries and salt marshes and, like most other terrapins, it feeds mainly on other small animals. Crabs, worms, and winkles form a large part of its diet, while the terrapin itself is regarded as a delicacy in many areas. Large numbers of animals are reared commercially to meet the demand for terrapin flesh. A female may lay five clutches of eggs each year, with as many as 20 eggs in a clutch.

ORDER: Chelonia;
FAMILY: Emydidae.
SPECIES: *Malaclemys terrapin.*

Dik-dik

The six species of this small ANTELOPE live in dry scrub in many parts of Africa. They are named after the call of the female when alarmed, which sounds like "zik-zik" or "dik-dik". Hunters dislike them because they alert other animals to the hunters' presence. If they are flushed from the scrub into the open, dik-diks race away with erratic leaps, rather like hares, on zigzag courses. They are up to 70 cm long, standing 30 to 40 cm at the shoulder, and they have incredibly thin legs. The females are larger than the males. The coat is grey to reddish-brown and the tail is a mere stump. Only the males have horns.

ORDER: Artiodactyla;
FAMILY: Bovidae.

Dingo

The dingo is the wild dog of Australia. It stands about 50 cm high at the shoulder. Its colouring varies from light red to brown and some individuals are brown with black streaks.

The dingo is unusual in that it is one of the few *placental* mammals found in Australia.

In the wild, dingos hunt in small groups and catch animals, such as kangaroos, wallabies and, unfortunately, sheep and cattle. Consequently, they are relentlessly hunted by man. However, they are extremely cautious and despite the fact that thousands have been killed, they are still common.

ORDER: Carnivora;
FAMILY: Canidae;
SPECIES: *Canis dingo.*

Dipper

The four species of dipper are unusual perching birds because they are water birds. They live by clear, fast-flowing streams, flitting about the rocks, and walking and flying in and out of the water. They even appear to walk along the bottom of the stream, in search of insect larvae, crustaceans, worms and molluscs, which form their main diet. Dippers have a thick layer of down and large *preen glands* to supply the oil needed to keep the plumage waterproof. They nest in banks or stone walls overlooking water.

ORDER: Passeriformes;
FAMILY: Cinclidae.

The **dik-dik** is a small African antelope, little more than 30 cm tall.

Dingos, the wild dogs of Australia.

Diver

Divers, or loons, are water birds. They have streamlined bodies, with short tails and strong, sharp bills. Like other good swimmers, they have powerful legs which are set well back, and large webbed feet. They can swim long distances underwater and dive to great depths, but they are clumsy on land and only come ashore to breed. There are four species, which live in the northerly parts of the hemisphere, partly on inland waters and partly on coastal waters. The great northern diver has a black and white, spotted body and collar. The white-billed diver, the largest species, has a whitish-yellow bill. The black-throated diver has black and white barrings on its back, and the red-throated diver has a dove-grey head and neck.

ORDER: Gaviiformes;
FAMILY: Gaviidae.

Dog

The dog was probably the first animal to be domesticated. As long as 10,000 years ago there appear to have been at least two domestic breeds. However, the origins of the domestic dog are uncertain. Theories range from the belief that the wolf is the

Winter

Great northern diver summer

Winter Summer
Red-throated diver

In winter, all **divers** become grey-brown above and white below.

Summer

Winter
Black-throated diver

ancestor, to the idea of a long extinct North American or even Asian ancestor.

Whatever the case, there are now over 100 breeds of domestic dog. The smallest is the chihuahua, which is only 18 cm high and may weigh 0.8 kg, a breed developed from the Mexican hairless dog. The largest are the St Bernard, which grows up to 70 cm high and weighs 90 kg, and the mastiff, which is slightly taller, but lighter.

ORDER: Carnivora;
FAMILY: Canidae;
SPECIES: *Canis familiaris.*

Dogfish

The name given to several species of small SHARKS common in coastal waters. They include what are perhaps the best-known of all sharks, because for many years

The **lesser spotted dogfish** is about a metre long. It lives in sandy or gravel bottoms in shallow water.

biology students have studied and dissected the bodies of these fishes as a necessary part of their courses. These laboratory dog-fishes include the lesser spotted dogfish and the spiny dogfish. Larger dogfishes include the nursehound or greater spotted dogfish, and the alligator dogfish which has the habit of eating spiny dogfishes.

Dogfish are the enemy of fishermen, partly because they are so common and so take the bait offered to more valuable fish, and partly because their too-plentiful bodies clog and foul nets.

ORDER: Lamniformes;
FAMILIES: Scyliorhinidae (cat-sharks); Squalidae (spiny dog-fishes).

Dolphin

Dolphins are small members of the WHALE family, found in seas all over the world, both in deep water and near to coasts. People have long admired the dolphin's grace and playfulness in the water – a school of dolphins will follow a ship for days. Recent studies have revealed that the dolphin is among the most intelligent of all animals,

A **dipper** at rest on a rock by a fast-running river. The bird gets its name from the way in which it bobs up and down as it perches.

Dormouse

This **dolphin** in a Florida aquarium appears to enjoy doing tricks.

Above right: Common **dormice** at their summer nest in a bramble bush.

with a communications system which some scientists believe is a form of language.

There are several species of dolphin and they can be distinguished from the PORPOISES, to which they are related, by their beaked snouts. Like all whales, dolphins give birth to live, fully-developed young. They are born tail first and are supported by their mothers (and sometimes by other "midwife" dolphins) until they are able to swim to the surface and take their first breath of air. During these first moments, the "midwives" stay close to guard the young from sharks. The young remain dependent on their mothers for up to six months after birth.

Dolphins live together in schools. There is no single leader of the school, although members observe an order of rank. If a member is injured, other dolphins will assist it, swimming alongside and supporting it. They can stay submerged for up to 15 minutes. Their sense of hearing is acute and is probably the chief sense used when hunting food, which consists mainly of fish with some shrimps and cuttlefish.

The best known dolphin is the bottlenose, which is found along the Atlantic coasts of North America and also in European waters. Up to four metres long, the lively bottlenose dolphin has become a star performer in oceanaria and zoos.
ORDER: Cetacea;
FAMILY: Delphinidae.

Donkey

The donkey is a domesticated ASS. It was derived from the African wild ass, but it has undergone various changes in appearance and temperament during its history. By the 1700s, the donkey had become an important beast of burden in most parts of the world. It was also used for riding and for pulling many kinds of equipment. It remains important today in developing countries. Donkey breeds vary from nearly white to almost black. Many have lived more than 20 years although some are claimed to have lived for 50 years or more.
ORDER: Perissodactyla;
FAMILY: Equidae;
SPECIES: *Equus asinus.*

Dormouse

The name dormouse means "sleeping mouse" and there are

species of dormice in many parts of the world. The edible dormouse is the largest and most squirrel-like, with a bushy tail. The Romans fattened this species in special jars and thought it a great delicacy.

Dormice are night creatures, spending the day asleep in nests in trees or in the ground. During HIBERNATION, the dormouse rolls itself up in a ball and becomes rigid. Its temperature drops and its heartbeat almost stops. It remains in this state until spring when, much thinner, it emerges to feed hungrily on nuts, seeds, young shoots and bark. Hibernation is a dangerous time; perhaps four out of every five dormice fall prey to predators while in their winter sleep.

ORDER: Rodentia;
FAMILY: Gliridae.

Dotterel

The dotterel is a small wading bird belonging to the PLOVER family. But it is rarely found near the shore and is a bird of cold, desolate places, notably in Scandinavia and parts of Siberia. It also occurs in North America, in mountainous parts of Europe and, recently in the polders (reclaimed areas) of the Netherlands. The plumage is grey-brown, with white cheeks and throat and a white eye-stripe. The breast is chestnut below and grey-brown above, the colours being separated by a white stripe. The belly is black. However, in winter the bird is mostly brown.

ORDER: Charadriiformes;
FAMILY: Charadriidae;
SPECIES: *Eudromias morinellus*.

The **dotterel's** plumage is paler in winter.

Winter

Summer

Douroucouli

The douroucouli, also called the night monkey, is the only noc-turnal monkey. Its loud and resonant call echoes around the forests at night. It lives in the dense rain forests of Central and South America from Nicaragua in the north, to north-eastern Argentina in the south. Douroucoulis are omnivorous, eating fruit, insects, small birds and small mammals. They have large eyes set in a flat face which have earned them their third name of owl monkey. The head and body measure only 24 to 37 cm, with a tail of equal length and the fur is short, soft and woolly. They are silvery or dark

The **douroucouli's** large eyes tell us that it is a creature of the night.

grey above, with grey or brown under-parts.

ORDER: Primates;
FAMILY: Cebidae;
SPECIES: *Aotus trivirgatus*.

Dove

Dove is a name given to several members of the pigeon family. There is no real difference between a pigeon and a dove. The smaller members with more pointed tails are often called doves, and the larger birds with more rounded tails are usually called pigeons, but the names have no special signifi-cance. For example, the ROCK DOVE and feral pigeon are the same species and can interbreed.

ORDER: Columbiformes;
FAMILY: Columbidae.

Dragonfly

The dragonflies are fairly large insects with slender bodies and gauzy, transparent wings. Many of the larger species make rustling noises as they fly, but they are quite harmless. They feed on small flies and other insects, which they usually catch in mid-air with their spiky legs. Their large compound eyes, some with as many as 30,000 tiny lenses, enable them to detect their prey most efficiently. There are two main groups – damselflies and the true dragonflies. The damselflies are delicate creatures with bodies generally about the size of a matchstick. Their flimsy wings are all the same size, and the insects fly weakly. The males often have bright blue or metallic green colours, but most of the females are less bright. The true dragon-flies are larger and much faster insects, with hind wings somewhat broader than the front ones. Their bodies are usually beautifully coloured and often metallic.

Eggs are laid in water, with the female often submerging com-pletely for this task. The *nymphs* spend a year or more in the water, catching other small creatures. When fully grown, they climb up the reeds and split their skins to allow the adults to emerge. There are more than 5000 species, most of them living in tropical regions. ORDER: Odonata.

Drongo

There are 20 species of drongo. These birds are usually black with a green, blue or purplish gloss on some parts, but two species are

A blue **dragonfly** rests on the stem of a rush at the edge of its native stream.

pale grey. Their eyes are usually red and there are bristles around the nostrils. They often have ornate tails, forked, curled or with long, trailing flags. From 18 to 38 cm long, they perch on bran-ches waiting for insects to catch on the wing. Inhabiting the tropical parts of Africa and Asia, they usually live in dense forests or shrubberies, and are difficult to study. Drongos lay from 2 to 5 eggs in a frail nest high in a tree. ORDER: Passeriformes; FAMILY: Dicruridae.

Duck

Ducks are water birds related to the SWANS and geese. They have short legs, webbed feet and large flattened beaks with comb-like edges. The females generally have a dull plumage, but the males are often brightly coloured.

Ducks have thick plumage. Next to the skin is a dense layer of downy feathers, which keeps out the cold. Outside this is a layer of oily, waterproof feathers, which prevents the bird from becoming waterlogged. Most ducks live on fresh water, but some, such as EIDERS and scoters, are true seabirds. Ducks use their webbed feet as paddles, folding them on the forward stroke. They nest on the ground or in burrows and the young can run and swim soon after hatching.

There are two main types of duck. Divers, of which there are many, include the POCHARDS, EIDERS and scoters. The deepest diver is the long-tailed duck which dives to about 55 metres to find molluscs on the sea bed. The second type are the surface feeders, which eat small animals and weed. They include the mandarin, (one of the wood ducks), the PINTAIL, and the northern green-winged TEAL. Some ducks feed on land. For example, the wigeon crops grass leaves. Generally, surface feeders can get into the air quickly, but divers have to taxi along the water in order to get airborne.

Ducks are found in all the northern regions of the world and a few are found south of the Equator. The most northerly ducks are the eiders of the Arctic. Species common to Europe and North America include TEAL, MERGANSERS, scoters, the PINTAIL, the MALLARD, (from which most domestic ducks are descended), the gadwell, and the shoveler. A few species are exlusively European and Asian, such as the SHELDUCKS, and some are exlusively North American, such as the surf scoter and the ruddy duck. Many northern ducks migrate southwards in winter.

South American ducks include the TORRENT DUCK, the STEAMER DUCKS and the muscovy duck. The comb duck is found in South America and in Africa, where the southern POCHARD is also found. ORDER: Anseriformes; FAMILY: Anatidae.

Female / Male

Female / Male / Shoveler

Below: The gorgeously-coloured **mandarin duck** was once given as a wedding present in China.

Female / Male / Gadwall

Female / Male / Goldeneye

The **gadwall** is a dabbling duck that prefers inland waters. The **tufted duck** is a diver, often seen on lakes and ponds, also at the seashore in winter. The **goldeneye** is also a diver. The male raises its bill in a courting display.

Male / Female

Tufted duck

Duiker

These small ANTELOPES have been so named after the Afrikaans word "duiker" meaning "diver", because they dive for cover at the slightest alarm. They have short legs, pointed hooves and arched backs. The common or grey duiker is the only species that lives in open grassland. It stands about 60 cm at the shoulder. The dozen species of forest duiker belong to the genus *Cephalophus*. Some reach 90 cm at the shoulder, but most are less than half this height. Their coat varies from buff to black, or yellowish red in the grey duiker. The banded duiker, or zebra antelope, which is the one species currently threatened by extinction, has black stripes across its back. Both sexes usually have short, pointed horns, although female grey duikers often only have stunted horns or none at all. These shy animals are swift runners. They are generally solitary or go in pairs.

ORDER: Artiodactyla;
FAMILY: Bovidae;
SPECIES: *Silvicapra grimmia* (common).

Dung beetle

Dung beetles are mostly heavily-built, black, and often rather rounded beetles that feed on and breed in mammal dung. There are many hundreds of species. Some species merely eat the dung where they find it, others bury it before eating it or laying eggs on it. The digging is done with their broad and powerful front legs, and burial is often effected simply by digging a shaft under the dung and pulling some of it down into the soil. The beetles are all strong fliers and their large antennae ensure that they find fresh supplies of dung without trouble. Surrounded by food, the grubs do not have to move much and they all have soft, podgy bodies. (See also SCARAB BEETLE).

ORDER: Coleoptera;

E

Bonelli's eagle

Light form

Short-toed eagle

Booted eagle

Dark form

Dark form

Light form

Eagle

Eagles are birds of prey belonging to the same family as HAWKS, HARRIERS and VULTURES. A large, powerful bird with a hooked beak, strong curved talons, and keen eyesight, the eagle has been a symbol of power and courage since ancient times. Eagles are found world-wide, in both northern mountainous regions and equatorial forests. The GOLDEN EAGLE is a typical species, having the feathered legs found in many eagles. The sea eagles, of which the BALD EAGLE is one, have naked lower legs. Among the most splendid birds of prey are the HARPY EAGLE and the MARTIAL EAGLE.

ORDER: Falconiformes;
FAMILY: Accipitridae.

Earthworm

Earthworms live in warm, moist soil, and are continually churning up the ground as they swallow the soil and excrete it as worm casts. They digest decaying plant matter in the soil. The number of worms in the ground varies from 32,000 to 17 million per hectare according to the kind of soil.

Earthworms range in size from 1 mm to 3.4 metres long, and there are several hundred species. The longest is the Gippsland worm of Australia. Like many other worms, earthworms have long, slender bodies marked off into segments. Each segment has just a few short bristles which help it to move through the soil. The animal cannot move on a sheet of glass

because there is nothing for the bristles to push against.
PHYLUM: Annelida;
CLASS: Oligochaeta.

A male common **earwig**. The male sometimes has larger pincers.

Earwig

Earwigs form a complete insect order on their own. There are about 1200 species throughout the world, and except for variations in size they are much the same in shape and habits. Earwigs are small insects with a formidable-looking pair of pincers at the hind end. The insects can use these pincers to grip with some strength, but they are not such fearsome weapons as they appear. Earwigs spend the day hidden away in crevices, and hunt for food at night. They eat a great variety of plant and animal matter. Many earwigs are completely wingless, but some can fly on their delicate hind wings. The front wings, when present, are small, and the hind wings are elaborately folded beneath them.

Their popular name reflects the belief that earwigs like to enter people's ears. They have been known to do so, but only because they like hiding in cracks and folds.
ORDER: Dermaptera.

Eel

The name of 16 species of fish with snakelike bodies, small fins and a slimy skin. This article deals only with freshwater eels: the larger MORAY EELS and CONGER being covered under those headings. Freshwater eels are common

An **earthworm** starts to burrow into the soil.

inhabitants of rivers and lakes of Europe and eastern North America. They are popular sport for fishermen, who hunt them at night when the eels are most active. These fishes are mostly less than 1 metre in length, although females may reach 1.5 metres.

Freshwater eels are famous for their migrations. Despite their name, they spend much of their lives at sea. As adults, the eels leave their native fresh waters on a long journey to an area of the South Atlantic, near the Sargasso Sea, where they spawn. At the start of their migration they may travel overland for considerable distances, to reach a river which connects with the sea. The parent eels never return from spawning, dying in the far-off Atlantic. Their tiny young, transparent leaf-like creatures called leptocephali, make the return migration over a period of one to three years, changing on the way into more recognizably eel-like juveniles called elvers. These elvers find their way back up their home rivers to begin their adult life.
ORDER: Anguilliformes;
FAMILY: Anguillidae.

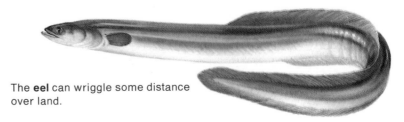

The **eel** can wriggle some distance over land.

Eelworm

Eelworms are a group of ROUND-WORMS which live in the soil and are parasitic on plants. They are tiny, thread-like creatures, some being too small to see with the naked eye. Many of them browse on the roots of plants doing little damage, but others carry viruses which cause serious diseases. Some, such as the potato root eelworm, bore their way into roots and cause severe damage to crops.
PHYLUM: Nematoda.

Egg-eating snake

The common African egg-eating snake is one of six species which feed almost entirely on eggs, and are specially adapted for this purpose. It is usually about 70 cm long, varying in colour between slate-grey and olive-brown, with large, square patches on its back that sometimes form a zig-zag pattern.

The snake finds an egg by smell and tests it with its tongue to see if it is addled. If the egg is satisfactory, the snake coils up around it

The picture shows the enormous distension of the **egg-eating snake's** jaws.

and begins to swallow it. This may take up to 15 minutes for a large egg: the eggs are frequently larger than the snake's head. Inside, a series of sharp projections from the snake's backbone jut into the throat. The snake rocks his head back and forth so that these "teeth" saw through the shell. Having swallowed the contents of the egg, he then spits the crushed shell out as a neat pellet.
ORDER: Squamata;
FAMILY: Colubridae.

Egret

Egrets belong to the HERON family and, like herons, they frequent pools, streams and marshes. In summer the male egrets develop long, lacy plumes, which they display during courtship. These were once much sought after for the millinery trade, and in the east the plumes were prized as ornaments in ceremonial dress. This demand resulted in the near extinction of these lovely birds. Fortunately, egrets are now protected by law.

Most egrets are white. They feed in shallow waters with the exception of the cattle egret of Africa and Asia which feeds on insects, often following other animals that

A snowy-white **common egret** in the Florida Everglades. The heron-like features are clearly seen.

stir up insects from the grass. The common egret, or great white heron, ranges from the central United States to Argentina and across Europe, Asia and Africa to Australia. The little egret occurs from central Europe to South Africa, and in Australia.
ORDER: Ciconiiformes;
FAMILY: Ardeidae.

Eider

Eiders are diving DUCKS that feed in shallow water on shellfish, barnacles, cuttlefish and starfish. They are found around the Arctic coasts of Canada and Siberia, moving farther south in winter. The king eider breeds in the Arctic. The common eider breeds as far south as Nova Scotia, northern Britain and Holland. In the breeding season a male eider is white, with a black crest on the head, and black under-parts and tail. The female incubates her eggs

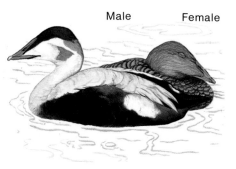

Male   Female

Eider ducks are seldom found inland. They breed at the seashore.

in a nest on the ground lined with down feathers. Eiders are noted for this wonderfully soft down which is widely used in making warm bed coverings. In some places, such as Scandinavia and Iceland, there are special farms where these duck are encouraged to breed. The down is then removed from the nests with no harm done to either parents or eggs.

ORDER: Anseriformes;
FAMILY: Anatidae;
SPECIES: *Somateria spectabilis* (king eider); *Somateria mollissima* (common).

Eland

Eland are the largest ANTELOPES. There are two species; the common eland, which lives in central and southern Africa: and the Derby eland, which is mostly restricted to central Africa and is in danger of extinction. The common eland has a greyish-fawn body. The Derby eland is a rich fawn colour, but its neck is black, with a white band at the base. Eland stand 152 to 183 cm at the shoulder and measure up to 4 metres from nose to tail. Both sexes have spiral horns that can be 120 cm long, and there is a well developed dewlap below the throat.

These heavy, ox-like beasts live in herds of between 17 and 100. When threatened, the bulls utter deep warning barks. When all the herd has been alerted, it takes flight with the bulls at the rear. Eland can reach speeds of 64 km/h

over short distances. They live mainly in savanna lands, but are also found in forests or on desert fringes.

ORDER: Artiodactyla;
FAMILY: Bovidae;
SPECIES: *Taurotragus oryx* (common); *Taurotragus derbianus* (Derby).

Electric catfish

The electric catfish lives in many rivers and lakes of tropical Africa. It is a typical catfish in that it has long *barbels* or feelers around its mouth, used for the detection of worms and other food animals living in the mud. It is plump-bodied, as opposed to being flat like many other catfishes, but its most remarkable difference from other catfish is its electric organ. This is formed from a layer of muscle that lies just under the skin that covers the trunk and part of the tail.

The electric organ is divided into a series of living electric batteries, negative at the forward end and positive at the rear end. Altogether, these batteries can deliver 350 volts, more than enough to stun any smaller creature. It seems to use its electric organ both for the purpose of catching prey and also to deter enemies. The electric catfish was well-known to ancient Egyptians, who fished it – with caution – and ate its flesh.

ORDER: Siluriformes;
FAMILY: Malapteruridae;
SPECIES: *Malapterurus electricus*.

Electric eel

This electric fish is eel-like in shape but is not related to the eel. It belongs to a family of South American freshwater fish that also includes KNIFE-FISHES. It is a large fish up to 1.8 metres long and thick-bodied, with a long, conspicuous *anal fin* running from the throat to the tail. Its eyes are very small and the surface of its mouth contains patches of blood vessels which absorb oxygen when the

fish takes a gulp of air at the surface. Both these features are adaptations for life in muddy waters, and so too, is the fish's large electric organ. This extends under the skin from immediately behind the head right to the end of the tail. It is the most powerful of electric fish batteries, delivering 550 volts that can stun a horse. The electric poles of this battery are positive in front and negative to the rear – the opposite arrangement to the ELECTRIC CATFISH. The electric eel uses its battery continuously when swimming, to generate electric pulses like beams, to find its way about its murky habitat.

ORDER: Cypriniformes;
FAMILY: Gymnotidae;
SPECIES: *Electrophorus electricus*.

Electric ray

More than 30 species of flatfish related to SHARKS are called electric rays. Most, if not all, skates and rays have electric organs in the tail, but in the electric rays there are two large electric organs under the skin on each side of the head. These fishes, which are often known as torpedoes, live in tropical and temperate seas and include fishes as small as 43 cm and as large as 1.5 metres which may weigh up to 90 kg.

Electric rays use their batteries to capture their prey. Although the batteries operate at an average of only about 60 volts (much less than the ELECTRIC EEL voltage), by wrapping its pectoral fins around the prey the ray gives out enough electricity to stun the fish.

ORDER: Rajiformes;
FAMILY: Torpedinidae.

Elephant

Elephants are the largest living land animals. There are now only two surviving species: the African and the Indian. Formerly there were many species, including the extinct mammoths and mastodons. The African elephant is the larger of the two. A bull (male)

may stand up to 3.5 metres high and weigh as much as 6 tonnes. The African elephant can be distinguished from the Indian by its large ears, which reach below the mouth, its sloping forehead and hollow back, and its trunk, which has two "lips" at the end. The Indian elephant, in comparison, has a domed forehead, a high-domed back, and a single lip on its trunk. It also has much smaller ears.

Elephants are massively built. Their heavy bodies are supported by thick pillar-like legs and broad feet. The remarkable trunk is in

The **African elephant** is the larger of the two species.

fact a long, flexible snout with nostrils at the tip. The elephant uses its trunk for carrying food and water to its mouth, for spraying water over itself, for smelling, and for lifting and investigating objects. The tusks on either side of the upper jaw are extra-long *incisor* teeth.

The **Indian elephant** is widely used for logging operations.

The African elephant lives south of the Sahara, in bush, forest or even semi-desert country. The Indian elephant lives in South-East Asia as well as India, and prefers thick forests. Both species are herd animals. Each herd is normally led by an old cow. The adult bulls live alone, joining the herd during the breeding season. A female gives birth to a single calf after a gestation period which on average lasts 22 months. At birth, the young elephant is about a metre tall and weighs some 90 kg.

Elephants can sleep either standing up or lying down, sometimes using a pillow of vegetation as a head rest. Their diet includes grass, leaves, fruit and young tree branches. The broad *molar* teeth are used to grind the food. As each tooth is worn down, another moves along the jaw to replace it, rather like a conveyor belt. In old age – elephants live to around 70 years – the supply of new teeth is exhausted and the elephant then faces death from starvation.

In the wild, elephants have no natural enemies, although very young elephants may fall prey to lions and tigers. But their majestic size and the valuable ivory of their tusks has made them a target for hunters and poachers, and the numbers of elephants in the wild is now much reduced. Herds survive only in game parks, but their natural instinct to migrate in search of fresh food poses problems. Elephants are intelligent and respond well to training. Indian elephants are used to haul logs in lumber forest and are often seen marching in processions, colourfully decorated. But the African elephant has only rarely been domesticated.

ORDER: Proboscidea;
FAMILY: Elephantidae;
SPECIES: *Loxodonta africana* (African); *Elephas indicus* (Indian).

Elephant seal

These are the largest of the SEALS. They may be 7 metres long, and the bulls weigh up to 3630 kg. Ungainly to look at, the bull elephant seal has a large drooping nose, which gets even bigger during the

The roaring head of an **elephant seal** bull.

breeding season. Rival bulls fight fiercely for ownership of territories on the breeding beaches, each striving to gather a harem of females.

There are two species, both very alike in size and appearance. The northern elephant seal lives on islands off the coast of California and Mexico. The southern elephant seal is found in the southern Atlantic and Antarctica, and is the more numerous of the two. Elephant seals eat fish and squid. Sealers almost wiped them out in the 19th century but these seals are now protected by international law.

ORDER: Pinnipedia;
FAMILY: Phocidae;
SPECIES: *Mirounga leonina* (southern); *Mirounga angustirostris* (northern).

Emperor moth

The emperor moth is a handsome,

day-flying insect related to some of the silk moths. It is found in most parts of Europe and northern Asia. The male, about 63 mm across the wings, is richly patterned with brown, orange, and purple, while the female, a good deal larger, is greyish purple. Each wing bears a large eye-spot resembling the eye of a much larger animal. This is a form of bluff or deception and it undoubtedly deters some birds from attacking the insect. Freshly emerged females emit a strong scent which the males pick up with their large, feathery antennae. Using this scent trail, the males can find their way to the females from well over a kilometre away. The caterpillars are green and black and feed on a wide variety of shrubs including heather, bramble, and blackthorn.

ORDER: Lepidoptera;
FAMILY: Saturniidae;
SPECIES: *Saturnia pavonia*.

Emu

The emu is a tall flightless bird of Australia. It grows to a height of almost 2 metres and is only rivalled in size by the ostrich. Emus are found in deserts, plains and forests in most parts of Australia. Outside the breeding season, they live in nomadic flocks. They raid crops and waterholes, and farmers consider them a pest. There were once several other species of emu, but they have all been wiped out by man. The male emu builds the nest, incubates the eggs and raises the young.

ORDER: Casuariiformes;
FAMILY: Dromaiidae;
SPECIES: *Dromaius novaehollandiae*.

The male **emperor moth** is much brighter than the female, seen here. The caterpillar can be 70 mm long.

F

Fairy shrimp

The fairy shrimp is widespread in western Europe and North America. Fairy shrimps are transparent and almost completely colourless except for a pair of black eyes set on movable stalks. They appear, often in large numbers, in temporary pools of water which are most common in dry grasslands and semi-desert regions. Even if these pools dry up suddenly, the fairy shrimps survive because they lay eggs which can resist being dried out. Some of the eggs hatch at once when wetted, the rest after varying periods of time. The animals grow up very quickly.

Fairy shrimps feed on single-celled plants and other small particles of matter. They swim about on their backs, beating their 11 pairs of legs a little out of step. This not only propels them along, but helps to waft food particles towards them to be trapped by a sticky substance near the mouth. The legs also serve as gills, extracting oxygen from the water as it flows over them.

ORDER: Anostraca;
FAMILY: Chirocephalidae;
SPECIES: *Chirocephalus diaphanus*.

Falcons

Falcons and HAWKS are both day-flying birds of prey. Falcons are usually the faster fliers, with long, pointed wings, whereas hawks' wings are shorter and broader. Long admired for their speed, grace and hunting prowess, fal-

The **hobby** usually takes over the nest of another bird in which to lay its two or three eggs.

cons are used in the ancient sport of falconry. Among falconers, the PEREGRINE is the most favoured bird. In this, as in all true falcons, the female is the larger and most aggressive. Other members of the falcon family include the GYRFALCON, HOBBY and KESTREL. The little falconets of the Tropics are hardly bigger than sparrows.

ORDER: Falconiformes;
FAMILY: Falconidae.

Fallow deer

European fallow deer live in open woodlands and are often kept in parks or on country estates. A second species is native to Iran and Iraq, but it is close to extinction.

The European fallow deer, which has also been introduced into the United States and other countries, has a coat which is

Fallow deer bucks are elegant animals, but they can be dangerously aggressive.

reddish-yellow to greyish-brown. In summer the back and sides are dappled with white spots, but in winter the deer becomes darker and loses its spots. Some animals remain dark brown. The rump is white, with a black margin, and the upper side of the tail is black. When alarmed, the deer raises its tail and the white hairs of the rump are erected. The rump is thus made very conspicuous and serves as a danger signal to other deer. The buck stands up to 90 cm at the shoulder, but the doe is smaller.

The males' antlers resemble the palm of a hand, drawn out into finger-like points. Grass is their main food. They mate in September, when their antlers are fully grown, and fawns are born in late May or early June.

ORDER: Artiodactyla;
FAMILY: Cervidae;
SPECIES: *Dama dama* (European).

False scorpion

False scorpions are tiny ARACH-NIDS, rarely more than 8 mm long. They bear some resemblance to true scorpions, but lack the tail which has the poisonous sting in it.

The best-known is the book scorpion, sometimes found in old books. There are about 1000 species, mainly living in vegetable litter. Many false scorpions build igloo-like shelters with silk and debris. The silk comes from glands in the body and emerges through pors on the mouthparts. The animals feed on various other small creatures, which they catch with their large pink pincers. The latter sometimes possess poison glands. They are also used to cling to larger animals so that the false scorpions are carried from place to place.

ORDER: Pseudoscorpiones.

Fanworm

Fanworms belong to two related families of marine BRISTLEWORMS. They live in tubes attached to the sea bed. These tubes may be composed of sand grains glued together, or of limestone secreted by the animal. The fanworms build them up as they grow, and if they are removed from their tubes they cannot normally build new ones. They filter their food from the surrounding water with a fan, or crown, of stiff, feathery filaments or tentacles. The crown also acts as a gill to take in oxygen. However, many species also breathe by driving water through tubes.
PHYLUM: Annelida;
CLASS: Polychaeta.

Like miniature ostrich plumes, the feathery tentacles of the **fanworm** wave in the sea. This fanworm has built itself a protective tube from small stones.

Feathers

Birds are the only animals to have feathers. Although they look so different from the scales of reptiles, the birds' ancestors, feathers are made of the same substance, keratin. Keratin is also the material of hair. Feathers grow unevenly on a bird's body. Some parts are well covered, others very lightly protected.

There are several types of feathers. Flight feathers, those on the wing, are called primary feathers when attached to the "hand" part, and secondary feathers when on the bird's "forearm". Contour feathers cover the body. Other kinds include the fine, downy feathers of the breast.

The number of feathers on a bird varies with its size, ranging from 1300 up to 12,000 or more. Birds change their feathers by moulting every year.

Fennec

The fennec is the smallest of the FOXES and the one with the longest ears. Its head and body measure up to 40 cm and its ears are 15 cm long. It lives in the desert regions of North Africa, Arabia and the Sinai peninsula, and its large ears are an adaptation to life in such arid surroundings. They act as radiators with large surface areas over which excess heat can be lost quickly. Its thick, silky coat (pale fawn or white, with white under-parts) insulates it against the heat – as do the thick clothes of desert Bedouins.

The fennec drinks when water is available, but it can survive for long periods without water. It avoids the worst of the desert heat by spending the day in its deep, long burrow, coming out at night to feed on insects, spiders, scorpions, lizards, snakes and rodents. Its hearing is extremely acute.

ORDER: Carnivora;
FAMILY: Canidae;
SPECIES: *Fennecus zerda*.

The **fennec** is a small desert fox with extra large ears.

Fer de lance

The deadly fer de lance gets its name from its lance-shaped head and body. This PIT VIPER lives on hot coasts from Mexico to Argentina and also in some West Indian islands, including Martinique. The fer de lance, which is usually 122 to 152 cm long, is brown or grey and patterned with dark, diamond-shaped blotches. Fer de lances eat small animals, such as opossums, frogs, rodents, snakes and lizards. They sometimes bite humans – agricultural workers clearing away undergrowth or working in plantations – and invade poor dwellings and outhouses in search of rodents. The young are born alive in litters of 60 to 80 and are dangerous from birth.

ORDER: Squamata;
FAMILY: Crotalidae;
SPECIES: *Bothrops atrox*.

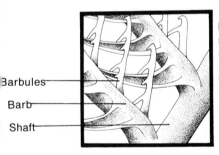

Feathers consist of a hollow central shaft or quill, with numerous barbs on either side. Barbules – tiny hooks – link the barbs. The inset on the left shows the construction of a contour feather. The diagram below shows the wing feathers of a bird.

Barbules
Barb
Shaft

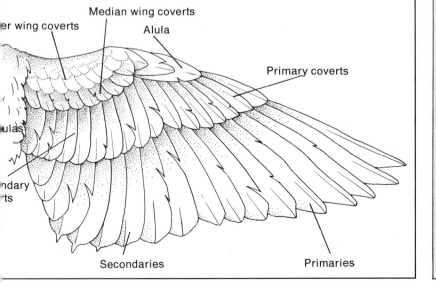

Median wing coverts
er wing coverts
Alula
Primary coverts
ulas
ndary
ts
Secondaries
Primaries

Feet

The feet of animals vary greatly, depending largely on how much they climb, walk or run. Bears and monkeys stand on the whole foot, from the toes to the heel. Members of the dog and cat families stand and run only on their toes. The foot is greatly elongated, so that the heel appears to come a long way up the leg. All these animals have five toes. But in the last adaptation, the number of toes decreases. The *ungulates*, such as antelopes, pigs, horses and cows, stand right on the tips of their toes, and often do not have all five. For example, the rhinoceros has three toes, the camel two and the horse only one. The nail on the horse's single toe has become greatly enlarged to form a hoof. The cloven hoof of pigs and cattle is really two separate toes. The ungulates include all the mammals with horns. They are all plant-eaters.

Fiddler crab

Fiddler crabs are small, brightly coloured crabs whose males have one claw very much larger than the other. The crabs live in burrows on tropical beaches and in mangrove swamps. Most of them are about 2 cm across, or less. The large claw is too big to be used for feeding, and the male crab uses it for signalling. The male waves his claw every few seconds to warn other crabs off his territory. At courtship times he waves it to attract females, often with a beckoning movment, or to fight rival males. The claw can also be used to make a sound similar to the song of a cricket.
CLASS: Crustacea;
ORDER: Decapoda.

Fighting fish

The fighting fish is also called the Siamese fighting fish after its homeland. This brilliantly decorative little fish owes much of its pugnacity and also its gorgeous appearance to the fish breeders of Thailand. The wild fish is yellowish-brown with indistinct dark stripes along its flanks, and

These Siamese **fighting fish** are about 60 mm long.

Male

Female

The firefly looks ordinary by day, but sparkles at night.

although pugnacious, the males rarely fight for any length of time. By contrast, the domestic breeds of fighting fish will battle to the death, which is the inevitable result if the fishes are badly matched in size. The extra-long, flowing fins of the bred fish also result in injury because they prevent the fish turning quickly enough to escape its rival's jaws.

Besides their pugnacity, fighting fish have other items of interesting behaviour. While courting, the male builds a floating raft of air bubbles coated with mucus. After fertilizing the female's eggs, he catches these in his mouth and transfers them to the underside of the raft, which he then guards until the eggs have hatched.
ORDER: Perciformes;
FAMILY: Anabantidae;
SPECIES: *Betta splendens.*

Finch

A small, usually colourful seed-eating bird. The typical finch has a stout, but pointed and sharp-edged, bill for cracking seeds. Many birds have evolved bills of this type, and not all of them are finches of the family Fringillidae, even though finch may be part of their common name. Most finches are sociable birds found in flocks outside the breeding season. They live in trees and shrubs, coming down frequently to the ground to feed. Finches are found throughout the world. Many species take part in long migrations, nesting in the warmer northern summers and wintering in the Tropics. Others travel much shorter distances, their movements determined more by availability of food than an inbuilt urge to travel. Yet others move from higher to lower altitudes in winter. Female finches are mainly responsible for building the nest, incubating the eggs and caring for the young. The majority of species build simple, cup-shaped nests and the eggs are usually pale-coloured, from white to a pale blue.
ORDER: Passeriformes;
FAMILY: Fringillidae.

Firefly

The fireflies, like the GLOW-WORMS, are small beetles. Both sexes give out light, usually from the hind end, and they may light up while flying or while sitting on vegetation. The lights are usually flashed for short periods only, and each species has a distinct on/off rhythm. Males and females can thus recognize and reply to members of their own species. In some parts of the world, fireflies gather in the trees in their thousands and flash in unison night after night. Most species live in tropical regions, but several occur in Europe. In North America, they are often called "lightning bugs". The grubs of most species eat snails, but the adults eat little.
ORDER: Coleoptera;
FAMILIES: Lampyridae and Elateridae.

Fish Eagle

The fish eagle is found all over Africa south of the Sahara. About the size of a herring gull, it lives along rivers, lakes and seashores. The eagle usually feeds on fish, which it catches in its talons as it flies slowly over the surface of the

The **fish eagle** has been described as the most handsome of the African eagles.

water. A handsome, black and white bird, the fish eagle has a characteristic yelping cry. Usually seen in pairs, fish eagles spend much of their time perched in trees on the lookout for prey.
ORDER: Falconiformes;
FAMILY: Accipitridae;
SPECIES: *Haliaeetus vocifer*.

Flamingo

The beautiful flamingos are un-usual birds. Their necks and legs are proportionately longer than in any other bird. They feed in a peculiar manner, with their heads upside down in foul, alkaline or salty water. To extract the tiny plants and animals from it, the water is filtered through comb-like bristles in the bill. The food is swallowed after the water has been expelled.

The bird's plumage is tinged with pink, except for the black flight feathers. There are four species. The greater flamingo is found in the Americas, from the Bahamas to the tip of South

Statuesque greater **flamingos** in the weedy shallows of a lake. They stand about 120 cm tall.

America, and from southern Europe to South Africa and across to India. The lesser flamingo lives in East Africa and India. The other two species, the rare James' flamingo, and the more common Andean flamingo, live in the high Andes mountains in Argentina, Bolivia and Chile.
ORDER: Ciconiiformes;
FAMILY: Phoenicopteridae.

Flatworm

This name most commonly applies to the turbellarians, although the FLUKES and TAPEWORMS, are also referred to as flatworms. Turbellarians are free-living animals, found mostly in fresh or salt water. Mostly under a centimetre long and only a millimetre or so wide, their dark bodies glide smoothly along like small pieces of ribbon. They have a primitive brain, but appear to be able to learn. In laboratory experiments scientist have "trained" turbellarians to turn right or left to find water.

Many worms reproduce by splitting in half, each half growing the missing part. Even a very small piece can grow into a complete animal. Experiments suggest that when cut in half, a worm can pass on its memory to the two new worms formed. Turbellarians, also called planarians, are carnivores, eating a variety of small animals.
PHYLUM: Platyhelminthes;
CLASS: Turbellaria.

Flea

The fleas are wingless, blood-sucking insects that live as para-

The human **flea** is a blood-sucker only in the adult stage.

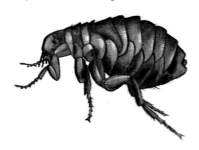

sites on birds and mammals. The largest is about 8 mm long, although most are less than half this size. They are generally brownish and flattened from side to side for easy movement through fur and feathers. The back legs are long, enabling the insects to jump very powerfully. Each kind of flea has its own host species. Although fleas will often bite various kinds of animals, they cannot breed without the proper host. This is because the flea *larvae* live in the host's nest or home and require just the right conditions. The larvae are maggot-like and feed on debris in the nest, including pellets of undigested blood passed out by the adult fleas. The larvae pupate in the nest, and the new adults emerge when they are disturbed. This usually happens when an animal is in the nest, and so the new fleas get a host right away. There are about 1800 species.
ORDER: Siphonaptera.

The **flounder** is equally at home in saltwater or freshwater.

Flounder

The common flounder is a marine flatfish closely related to the PLAICE and DAB, which may weigh up to 2.5 kg. Like those fishes, both eyes of the adult fish are on the same side of its flattened body, and its mouth is twisted sideways. These are both adaptations for a life spent largely lying on the seabed, although the flounder is equally at home in freshwater. Also like its cousin flatfishes, the flounder can change its colour-pattern to camouflage itself against the sandy or pebbly sea bottom.
ORDER: Pleuronectiformes;
FAMILY: Pleuronectidae;
SPECIES: *Platichthys flesus*.

Fluke

Flukes are parasitic flatworms, many of which have extremely complex life cycles which may involve several hosts. Of the thousands of species, many attack sheep and cattle, causing great loss to farmers, and at least 36 are known to infect man, sometimes with fatal results. The varieties of fluke which infect man include lung flukes, intestinal flukes, blood flukes and liver flukes. A mature liver fluke lays about 20,000 eggs a day inside its host. The eggs are excreted by the host and under suitable conditions hatch into *larvae*. These must then seek a new host, which must be one of a number of species of water snail. Having changed form within the snail, the larvae leave and attach themselves to vegetation, where they undergo a final change into cysts. No further developments occur unless the cysts are eaten by a suitable host. Then the cycle begins again. Other flukes have a simpler life cycle which they complete in or on a single host.
PHYLUM: Platyhelminthes;
CLASS: Trematoda.

Fly

The true flies are a very large group of insects which includes BLOW-FLIES, CRANE-FLIES, HOVER-FLIES, MOSQUITOS, and many others. Most of the 90,000 or so known species have wings but, unlike most other insects, they have only one pair. The hind wings have been converted into little pin-like balances which act like gyroscopes in flight, and help to keep the insects stable. The balancers are concealed under flaps of skin

Robber-flies catch other insects, such as this fruit fly.

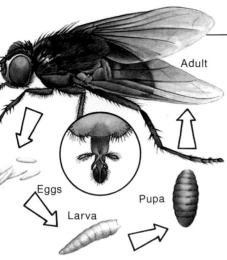

Adult

Eggs

Larva

Pupa

Flies lay their eggs in decaying matter. The life cycle can be complete in a week. The fly has a sponge-like mouth (circled) with which it mops up liquid food.

in most of the stouter species, but are clearly visible in crane-flies and their relatives. The *antennae* of most flies are short and bristle-like, but craneflies and other slender-bodied flies have longer, thread-like antennae.

The flies are all liquid feeders, although the materials they feed on vary enormously, from dung and other decaying materials to blood and nectar. The mouthparts are also extremely varied. Blow-flies and HOUSE-FLIES have mop-like mouthparts which soak up surface liquids. The insects deal with solid materials, like sugar, by pouring digestive juices over them and then mopping up the resulting liquids. Blood-feeders possess piercing mouthparts enclosing a narrow tube through which blood can be sucked, but the actual structure of these piercing organs varies a great deal.

Larval flies are also extremely variable in form and habit, although they are always legless. Many live in decaying matter and take in semi-liquid food, and several parasitic forms live inside other animals and plants. Crane-fly grubs (leatherjackets) chew plant roots, while many hover-fly grubs eat aphids. A good many fly larvae live in water. All pass through a pupal stage before becoming adult flies.
ORDER: Diptera.

Flycatchers' plumage (right) varies with sex and time of year.

Flycatcher

The name given to two different families of insect-eating birds, most of which catch insects on the wing. The New World, or tyrant flycatchers, belong to the Tyran-nidae family. Members of the second family, sometimes called Old World flycatchers, are found throughout Europe, Africa and Asia. The most beautiful are the paradise flycatchers found in Africa, Asia and Australia. Males and females are always differently coloured. The upper half of the bill in Old World flycatchers has a fringe of bristles which helps the bird catch insects on the wing. The young generally have spots, like the THRUSHES to which they are related. Many species live in woodlands and they nest in trees and crevices in rocks.
ORDER: Passiformes;
FAMILY: Muscicapidae, Tyranni-dae.

Flying fish

Several kinds of fish are called flying fish because of their ability to fly or glide above the surface of the water. The marine flying fishes fall into two groups. One group, referred to simply as flying fish, have streamlined, herring-like bodies. The other group, known as the flying gurnards, have a large head and tapering body similar to that of other GURNARDS, to which, however, they are not related.

Herring-like flying fish range in length from 25 to 46 cm. They are either two-winged or four-winged. A single flight above the water can cover 150 metres, at a speed of 55 km/h. However, since the flying fish does not flap its fins, this flight is really a glide.
ORDER: Atheriniformes;
FAMILY: Exocoetidae (flying fishes);
ORDER: Dactylopteriformes;
FAMILY: Dactylopteridae (flying gurnards).

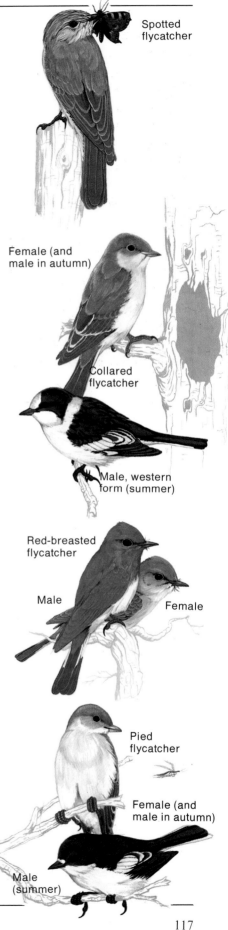

Spotted flycatcher

Female (and male in autumn)

Collared flycatcher

Male, western form (summer)

Red-breasted flycatcher

Male

Female

Pied flycatcher

Female (and male in autumn)

Male (summer)

The Seychelles **fruit bat** or flying fox can be a menace to fruit farmers.

Flying fox

About 60 of the largest species of fruit bats are called flying foxes. Flying foxes are found in southern Asia, nothern Australia, Madagascar and a few South Pacific Islands. The largest has a body length of 41 cm. It is covered with reddish brown fur, and has black wings that span 1.8 metres. Unlike most bats, flying foxes depend mainly on sight and scent to locate their food. After a day spent sleeping while hanging upside down by their feet, the flying foxes leave their roosts in the treetops and fly in masses to seek the banana, pawpaw, guava and other fruits that are their diet.

ORDER: Chiroptera;
FAMILY: Pteropidae.

Flying lemur

Among the mammals, only the bat can truly fly. But the flying lemur, which is not related to the LEMURS, despite its name, is the best equipped mammal for gliding. It can glide because it has a skin which extends down the side of the chin and continues in a broad web down both sides of the body, taking in the forearm with all the fingers the hind legs and toes, and going up to the tip of the tail. When disturbed, the animal launches itself into a flying leap, gliding anything up to 140 metres. Over that distance, it loses less than 12 metres in height. It is a tree-dweller and rarely comes to ground.

Flying lemurs have no close relatives, but their anatomy suggests links with both bats and insectivores. This cat-sized animal is 46 cm long, with a tail of nearly 30 cm. It has a sharp muzzle and large eyes. It feeds on leaves, flowers and buds. There are two species, one of which occurs only in the Phillippines. The other is found in South-East Asia.

ORDER: Dermoptera;
FAMILY: Cynocephalidae.

Flying squirrel

The flying squirrel is capable of controlled gliding flight. There are 37 species, most of which are asiatic, but the one about which most is known is the North American flying squirrel. When flying, the squirrel spreads its legs, extending the web of skin which acts as a parachute, and uses its tail for balance. It can bank and turn, land on all fours and can even turn round in mid air.

Flying squirrels rest by day and come out at night to feed on nuts, fruit, seeds, insects and birds' eggs. As the days shorten towards autumn, the northern flying squirrels hoard food, and in cold weather they become inactive although they do not really hibernate.

ORDER: Rodentia;
FAMILY: Sciuridae.

Fossa

Madagascar's largest CARNIVORE, the fossa is a cat-like creature in the same family as the CIVETS and may be descended from an ancestor of both civets and cats. Like cats, fossas can retract their sharp claws. Head and body measure up to 90 cm, and the narrow tail is as long again. Their soft, short fur is normally reddish-brown. They are usually solitary forest dwellers, but roam in small bands during the breeding season. At this time they are very aggressive, liable to set upon any animal that disturbs them. At night, fossas hunt LEMURS, which they chase through the trees. They also take domestic ducks and chickens, so they are unpopular with local farmers. But very little is known about these animals, despite the fact that they are not uncommon.

ORDER: Carnivora;
FAMILY: Viverridae;
SPECIES: *Cryptoprocta ferox.*

Francolin

Francolins are among the largest birds of the PHEASANT family, reaching a length of 45 cm. A few male francolins are brightly coloured, but most males and all females have dull plumage. There are 36 species living in Asia and five in Africa. Francolins are found in wooded or brush country, and are very shy and secretive. They rely on their plumage to camouflage them in the long grass or undergrowth, and rarely fly. They nest on the ground and scratch for food like domestic chickens, pecking up the small animals and plants that are uncovered.

ORDER: Galliformes;
FAMILY: Phasianidae.

Frigatebird

Frigatebirds are superb fliers and are recognizable in flight by their long, narrow wings and deeply forked tails. They use their hooked bills to attack and rob other sea birds of their fish. They are also known as man-o'-war birds. Piracy is a source of food only during the breeding season. For most of the year, frigatebirds catch their own food. They never stray far from land and they prey on newly hatched turtles on tropical beaches. Frigatebirds have weak legs and leap from trees or rocks to become airborne. The plumage is mainly black. Male frigatebirds have red throat pouches which they inflate when courting. The five species all live in the warmer parts of the world.

ORDER: Pelecaniformes;
FAMILY: Fregatidae.

Frilled lizard

The frilled lizard lives mainly in dry sandy parts of northern Australia. It grows to about a metre long. Its strangest feature is a large frill around the throat, which is made of skin supported by rods of cartilage. Normally the frill lies folded over the shoulders, but in moments of excitement muscles pulling on the rods can raise the frill to 20 cm or more across. If danger threatens, the lizard runs away on its hind legs, fore legs held close against its body, but if it is cornered it

Male

Male

Silver-washed fritillary

Female

Caterpillar

Dark green fritillary

Male

High brown fritillary

Marbled fritillary

Niobe fritillary

There are several hundred species of **fritillary butterfly**. The upper wings are generally orange-brown with black markings.

A **frilled lizard** putting on its threatening display.

spreads its frill, opens its mouth wide and hisses and steps towards its enemy. Even hunting dogs used to attacking larger lizards are scared by this display.

ORDER: Squamata;
FAMILY: Agamidae;
SPECIES: *Chlamydosaurus kingii*.

Fritillary butterfly

The fritillaries are a large group of butterflies in which the upper surface of the wings is generally a bright orange-brown chequered with black markings. The undersides are beautifully patterned, often bearing silvery spots or stripes. There are several hundred species of widely differing sizes. They are found mainly in the temperate and cool regions of the

northern hemisphere, where they live in woodlands and open country, including high mountain tops and the Arctic tundra. Most are strong-flying insects. In the colder areas, the butterflies tend to be somewhat darker, a feature which helps them to absorb warmth from the sun more easily. The Arctic fritillary has been found within 9° of the North Pole. Fritillary caterpillars tend to be rather spiky, brownish creatures and they feed on a wide variety of low-growing plants. The caterpillars normally hibernate when very small and complete their growth in the spring. The *pupae* always hang upside down from a small silken pad attached to the food plant or some other suitable support.

ORDER: Lepidoptera;
FAMILY: Nymphalidae.

Frog

The common frog occurs nearly everywhere in Europe and temperate Asia, although its numbers have been greatly reduced in recent years through the filling in of ponds and other breeding sites. It has a maximum length of about 10 cm and its colour ranges from dirty green or yellow to deep brown or even red. The darker markings vary, but there are always a number of bars on the hind legs. There is also a dark streak running back from the snout on each side and widening out to enclose the ear-drum.

Outside the breeding season, the common frog is a solitary creature, living in marshes and damp woodlands and also many damp grasslands. In some places it is called the grass frog. It is quite common around the *snow line* on many mountains. As the temperature falls in the autumn, the frogs go into HIBERNATION, usually burying themselves in the soft mud of marshes and ditches or in the mud at the bottom of ponds. They wake early in spring and make their way to the breeding ponds, preferring shallow water with a slight flow. The males arrive first and begin their chorus of rasping croaks. When present in large numbers they sound like motor cycles roaring by in the distance. They can even croak under the water. Their vocal sacs are internal, and a croaking frog merely seems to puff out its throat. Females are attracted by the noise, and when they arrive at the ponds they are grabbed by the males.

The eggs are laid in large masses and the tadpoles grow up in typical AMPHIBIAN fashion. Each egg is surrounded by protective jelly which swells up as soon as it makes contact with the water. The egg produces a fish-like youngster called a tadpole, which breathes by means of feathery gills behind the head. After a few days the mouth opens and the tadpole begins to feed. The external gills are soon replaced by internal ones. The

Above: A **gliding** (or flying) **frog** from Costa Rica has feet like parachutes.

Below: A solitary common or grass **frog** resting on a damp waterside rock.

tadpole continues to live in the water while its limbs develop. Just before the animal is ready to leave the water, the gills are replaced by lungs and the tail is absorbed. The miniature but fully-formed froglet becomes sexually mature at three years. *Metamorphosis* may be complete in ten weeks, but it takes longer in cool regions. In the coldest areas, the tadpoles may hibernate and complete their growth the following year.

ORDER: Salientia;
FAMILY: Ranidae;
SPECIES: *Rana temporaria* (common).

Fruit Bat

There are 160 species of fruit bats. They live only in the Old World and are confined almost entirely to the Tropics. However, not all eat fruit. Fruit bats either have no tail or only a stump, so they have no tail membrane, or only a small one. The folds of skin on the faces of insect-eaters, which aid echo location, are absent in fruit bats. Some use a less developed system of echo location, listening to clicks instead of high-pitched squeaks. But most fruit bats use mainly sight and smell to find their food. As well as eating fruit, most fruit bats also drink nectar, and feed on blossoms.

ORDER: Chiroptera;
FAMILY: Pteropidae.

Fruit-fly

The fruit-flies are small insects with a passion for ripe fruit and fermenting materials. Vast clouds of these insects can often be seen where jams or wines are being made. Their bodies are usually brown or yellow, and their eyes are normally red. The larvae develop in rotting fruit. There are several hundred species, of which the best known is *Drosophila melanogaster*. This species is widely used in studying genetics.

ORDER: Diptera;
FAMILY: Drosophilidae.

A spectacled **fruit bat** enjoying a meal of figs in Australia.

Fulmar

The fulmar is an ocean bird the size of a large gull. The name fulmar possibly comes from two old Norse words meaning "foul smell". The birds are so-called because of their musky odour and their habit of spitting an evil-smelling oil at intruders. This habit is shared by many other members of the petrel family. The fulmar has a short, stocky body, 50 cm long, with long, narrow wings. In the North Atlantic, the fulmar is silvery grey above and whitish below. In the Arctic Ocean and North Pacific, many fulmars are sooty brown, with light undersides. In flight, fulmars resemble small ALBATROSSES as they glide along with only occasional wingbeats. They feed on the surface, sometimes upending themselves like ducks.

ORDER: Procellariiformes;
FAMILY: Procellariidae;
SPECIES: *Fulmarus glacialis*.

Furniture beetle

The furniture beetle, or woodworm, is a notorious pest of furniture and other household timber. It is a reddish-brown insect, about 4 mm long, and the female lays her eggs in minute cracks in timber. The grubs then tunnel through the wood for two or more years before pupating there. The new adults emerge through the familiar little holes which they cut with their jaws. Out of doors, the beetles breed in tree stumps and even in dead twigs, and the adults commonly visit flowers to sip nectar.

ORDER: Coleoptera;
FAMILY: Anobiidae;
SPECIES: *Anobium punctatum*.

Fur seal

Fur seals are closely related to SEA LIONS and, like them, they have small external ears. They are also called eared seals. Like sea lions, they turn their hind flippers forwards when moving overland, thus raising their bodies and giving them greater agility on dry ground than the true seals. In the water their powerful front flippers are used like oars and the hind flippers act as a rudder. They have dense fur, for which in the past they were slaughtered in their thousands.

One species lives in the northern hemisphere, and six species in the southern. They eat mostly fish, sometimes diving to great depths to find food. The southern fur seals also feed on krill. Fur seals congregate on beaches to breed, each bull fighting for possession of a harem of females. After being on the edge of extinction, due to hunting by sealers, the fur seals have now regained something like their former numbers.

ORDER: Pinnipedia;
FAMILY: Otariidae.

Fulmars often follow ships, but may come ashore and occupy buildings.

G

Gallinule

Gallinules, together with COOTS, are members of the RAIL family. There are two genera, which live in most temperate and tropical parts of Europe, Asia and Africa, and America. They are closely related to the MOORHEN, which is in fact called the common gallinule in North America. Like the moorhen and coots, gallinules have shields above their bills. They live secretively among dense water plants surrounding lakes, pools, streams and marshes. Their long toes enable them to walk about on lilies and other surface vegetation.
ORDER: Gruiformes;
FAMILY: Rallidae.

Gall Wasp

Gall wasps are small, ant-like insects, with or without wings and usually black or brown in colour. They are only distantly related to the true WASPS. The insects themselves are rarely seen, but their effects are often obvious, for they cause the formation of the abnormal plant growths known as *galls*. Most of the species affect oak trees. The wasp lays eggs in the tissues of the plant and the grubs start to feed there. Their

This **gall wasp** develops inside oak apples on oak twigs.

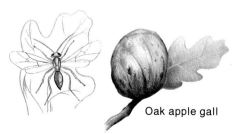

Oak apple gall

A pair of **gannets** greet one another. The gannet is a spectacular diver.

presence triggers off unusually rapid growth in the surrounding tissues, which swell up round the grubs to form the galls. There may be one or more grubs in each gall, according to the species. Many of the oak-inhabiting species have complex life histories. The disc-like spangle galls that grow on the undersides of oak leaves in late summer contain grubs that mature early in spring, after the leaves have fallen. The gall wasps that emerge can all lay eggs without mating, and they lay the eggs in the oak buds. The new grubs start to

feed as the buds open, and they cause the formation of currant galls on the young leaves and catkins. These galls produce male and female wasps. After mating, the females lay their eggs in the leaves to produce another generation of spangle galls.

Other familiar galls induced by gall wasps include oak apples and marble galls on oaks, and the bedeguar gall, or robin's pincushion, on roses.
ORDER: Hymenoptera;
FAMILY: Cynipidae.

Gannet

Gannets are large seabirds which only come ashore during the breeding season. They live in temperate regions and are closely related to the tropical BOOBIES. The common gannet is 90 cm long, with a wingspan of 168 cm. The body is white with dark wing-tips, but immature birds are brown. Like all gannets, they have straight, sharp bills and webbed feet. Gannets are strong fliers and can cover great distances. During feeding, they make spectacular dives from heights of 30 metres, plunging underwater to emerge a few moments later with their prey. They eat fish and squid. The birds make nests of seaweed and live in colonies, usually on small off-shore islands or rocks.

The common gannet, breeds on both sides of the North Atlantic Ocean. The Cape gannet breeds off South Africa. The Australian or Pacific gannet breeds in the Bass Strait between the Australian mainland and Tasmania, and in the North Island of New Zealand.
ORDER: Pelecaniformes;
FAMILY: Sulidae.

Gar

Gars should not be confused with garfishes (also called NEEDLE-FISHES), which are much smaller and marine. There is only one family with seven species of gar remaining in this primitive order, which flourished in the Age of the Reptiles 65–225 million years ago. They have long, thin, pike-like bodies with an armoured covering of diamond-shaped scales. These are joined to each other (interlinking rather than overlapping) and coated with a hard shiny layer. The jaws are elongated like a bill, bearing long sharp teeth. These features have earned one species the name alligator gar, also known as the "shark" of freshwater in Mexico because it tears up fishing nets and preys on other fish.

The gar is a solitary fish, preferring quiet shallow waters. Like the PIKE, it lies in wait for passing prey then darts out to grab its victim. Even quite large fish are not safe

The **chinkara** is a small gazelle from the Indian subcontinent.

from this predator, because its mouth floor is flexible and the jaw arches to make room for its dinner!
ORDER: Semionotiformes;
FAMILY: Lepisoosteidae.

Garter Snake

Garter snakes are commonly found in Canada and the United States, and they include the common garter snake and the ribbon snake. Their range extends farther north than any other American reptile. Garter snakes are non-poisonous, slim, up to 1 metre long, and marked with yellow, red or orange stripes running down the body. Young snakes feed on worms and older ones also eat toads, salamanders and frogs. Unlike many other snakes, the garter snake does not lay eggs but bears its young live. The young are born in summer in litters of about 50 to 60, and many live for 12 years. There is, however, a very heavy death-rate

during the first few months, due mainly to predators and death from starvation.
ORDER: Squamata;
FAMILY: Colubridae.

Gaur

The gaur lives in mountain forests in South-East Asia, from India to Vietnam. It is the largest species of wild cattle, the males averaging nearly one tonne in weight, and usually standing 168 to 183 cm at the shoulder. Females are rather smaller. These black animals have whitish legs below the knees. The horns curve over the head in a semi-circle. The domestic gaur, called the gayal or mithan, is sometimes said to be a separate species, formed by the crossing of wild gaur and common cattle.
ORDER: Artiodactyla;
FAMILY: Bovidae;
SPECIES: *Bos gaurus*.

Gazelle

Gazelles are slender, graceful ANTELOPES. There are 10 species of

The **genet** is about 50 cm long, with a tail of the same length.

true gazelle, but several other similar antelopes, belonging to different genera, are also called gazelles. The true gazelles are found in Asia and in northern and eastern Africa. The males have sweeping, lyre-shaped horns while the females have short spikes or no horns at all. The smallest species, the Dorcas gazelle, ranges from Algeria to Egypt and Sudan. It stands only 53 cm at the shoulder. Two well-known East African species are the Grant's gazelle and the Thomson's gazelle. Enormous herds of these animals once roamed the savanna, but they have been much reduced by hunting and by the invasion of their territory by farmers.

All gazelles are fawn-coloured, with a white rump and belly and black and white face markings. There is often a dark band along the flanks. Most species live in fairly dry country and they dislike areas with many bushes. Gazelles eat grass, but they also browse on bushes and fleshy plants in dry country. They can go without drinking for long periods. Various kinds of social behaviour occur. Thomson's gazelle bucks will establish territories which they defend against other males. When a herd of does passes through the territory, the buck will mate with several of them. In the dry season, the bucks return to the main herd, migrating to better pastures.

When endangered by lions, cheetahs, leopards and hyenas in Africa, or by wolves and tigers in

Asia, the long-legged gazelles do not use their natural speed to escape. Instead they dart about, or run for about 200 metres and then stop, in order to turn around and look back at their enemy.
ORDER: Artiodactyla;
FAMILY: Bovidae.

Gecko

Geckos form a large family of LIZARDS best known for their nocturnal way of life and the ease with which some species run up walls. Geckos are the only lizards that utter special calls. The largest is the tokay gecko which lives in South-East Asia and catches mice as well as insect food. It measures up to 36 cm. The smallest species is about one-tenth that length. Geckos live in all warm countries. Most live in trees, some among rocks, and others in the desert.

Tree geckos can often be found in buildings. They hide in crevices by day, and at night they feed on insects attracted to the artificial lights. The underside of a gecko's toes have countless tiny hooks that catch in the slightest roughness, even in a sheet of glass. This is why geckos are such expert climbers. Night-active geckos have vertical-slit pupils like cats. The few that run about by day have eyes with rounded pupils.

Some geckos bear live young, but most lay two eggs with a tough white shell. These are hidden under bark or stones and take months to hatch.
ORDER: Squamata;
FAMILY: Gekkonidae.

Genet

These slender-bodied, long-tailed mammals look like a cross between a domestic tabby cat and

a MONGOOSE. There are six species of genet, all of which live in Africa. The feline genet has the widest distribution. It lives in most of Africa outside the Sahara, and in Arabia, Spain, and southern France. The blotched genet is the most common in much of Africa.

Genets are typical CARNIVORES, with small but needle-sharp *canine teeth*. They hunt small rodents, birds and insects – particularly night-flying moths and beetles. Sure-footed climbers, feline genets stalk and pounce on prey as cats do. They are most at home in trees and bushes.
ORDER: Carnivora;
FAMILY: Viverridae.

Geometer moth

The geometers are mostly rather small moths with slender bodies, although there are some exceptions to this rule. The PEPPERED MOTH, for example, is quite stout, while the swallowtailed moth spans 63 mm or more across the wings. The moths normally rest with their wings spread out flat on each side of the body, although a few species hold their wings vertically above them in the manner of butterflies. The females of some species are wingless. The name geometer literally means "ground measurer" and refers to the behaviour of the caterpillar, which has only two pairs of stumpy legs at the hind end. The creature's normal method of progression is to extend the body and take a grip with the front legs, and then to bring the hind legs up close to the front, arching the body upwards in the process. This

A **gecko's** foot. It uses the hooked ridges to cling to smooth surfaces.

action is repeated again and again, giving the impression that the caterpillar is measuring the ground. In North America the caterpillars are known as inch-worms. They are also known as loopers. All are slender and many bear striking resemblances to twigs. There are several thousand species in this family and many of them are serious pests of fruit trees and other crops.

ORDER: Lepidoptera;
FAMILY: Geometridae.

Common emerald

Yellow shell

Garden carpet

Lime-speck pug

Magpie moth

Two young **gerbils** peer short-sightedly at the camera.

Gerbil

Gerbils are mouse-like creatures with long hind legs and a long tail. They often move in great bounds like tiny kangaroos, and one species, the Indian gerbil, can make leaps of up to 5 metres.

Left: Some **geometer moths**. Below: The caterpillar of the **magpie moth** in its typical looping attitude.

Gerbils are also called sand rats as they live in the desert or semi-desert parts of Africa and Asia. Most species spend the heat of the day in underground burrows, only coming out at night, although there are some gerbils which are active during the day. They eat leaves, seeds, flowers and roots and store food in their burrows for use during the dry season. They can live for many days without drinking. A few gerbils are carnivorous, eating locusts or birds' eggs. The habits of gerbils in the wild are not well known, but many are now kept in laboratories as experimental animals and they are also popular as pets.

ORDER: Rodentia;
FAMILY: Cricetidae.

Gerenuk

The gerenuk is also called Waller's gazelle and the giraffe-necked gazelle, because of its long neck. It stands up to 107 cm at the shoulder. The head, and body measure 137 cm in length and the

tail is 23 cm long. The coat is fox-red on the back, lighter on the flanks and white below. This shy animal lives singly, in pairs, or in herds of 3 to 10 in the drier parts of Ethiopia, Somalia and northern Kenya. It browses on foliage, particularly acacia, and often stands on its hind legs to eat leaves which are otherwise beyond its reach. The gerenuk can go for long periods without water. Little is known of its breeding habits.
ORDER: Artiodactyla;
FAMILY: Bovidae;
SPECIES: *Lithocranius walleri.*

Gharial

The rivers Indus, Ganges and Brahmaputra are the homes of this long, slim-snouted croco-dilian. A gharial can grow to 6 metres long. Its eyes are high on its head and its nostrils lie at the tip of its snout. Because its snout is thin, a gharial is able to turn its head quickly in the water. In this way it can seize fish with a sideways snap of its jaws, which are armed with sharp teeth. In the breeding season each female lays about 40 eggs in the sand on the river bank. The hatchlings are about 36 cm long.

Unlike more aggressive croco-diles, gharials offer little danger to people, and are considered sacred by the Hindus. Even so, they have now become very scarce; no more than a few hundred are believed to survive.
ORDER: Crocodilia;
FAMILY: Gavialidae;
SPECIES: *Gavialis gangeticus.*

Giant tortoise

Giant tortoises reach lengths of about 1.5 metres and weights of over 250 kg. They are found on the Galapagos Islands in the Pacific Ocean and on the Aldabra Islands in the Indian Ocean. It is thought that the ancestors of these TOR-TOISES arrived on the islands by floating across from the mainland on tree trunks or other driftwood. With little competition on the

The **gibbon** is the acrobat of the tropical rain forests. It swings through the trees with great ease.

islands, the tortoises were able to grow to their unusually large size. Giant tortoises are vegetarians and some of the Galapagos animals have long necks which allow them to reach the branches of shrubs. Both the Aldabra tortoises and the Galapagos species are long-lived, reaching ages well in excess of 100 years.
ORDER: Chelonia;
FAMILY: Testudinidae.

Gibbon

Gibbons, the smallest of the APES, have long arms, which may be one and a half times as long as the legs. They travel through the trees by swinging by their arms, often making leaps of 9 metres or more between the branches. They are the only apes to walk upright habitually, most reaching a height of about 90 cm, though the tallest, the siamang, stands up to 120 cm high.

There are six species of gibbon. The siamang lives on the Malay

peninsula and in Sumatra, and the dwarf siamang lives on small islands west of Sumatra. Both species are completely black. The concolor gibbon occurs in Laos, Vietnam and Hainan. The hoo-lock gibbon is found in Burma. The black-capped gibbon occurs in Thailand. The male of the last three species are black, and the females are fawn. The sixth species, the Lar gibbon, is found in Thailand, the Malay peninsula, Sumatra, Java and Borneo. Gibbons live in small groups, often consisting of a pair, which mate for life, and up to four offspring. The group occupies a small territory and the animals hoot and call noisily each morning to let other groups know they are there. The gibbons' main food is fruit. They breed all the year round and the gestation period is seven months. They live about 25 years.
ORDER: Primates;
FAMILY: Hylobatidae.

Gila monster

The Gila monster is one of only two poisonous lizards in the world. Its name is pronounced "heela" and comes from the Gila basin in Arizona where the lizard is plentiful. The Gila monster lives in deserts of the south-western

Right: The **giraffe's** long neck enables it to browse the tops of trees.

The **gila monster** is a poisonous lizard of the south-western United States.

United States and nearby parts of Mexico. The animal measures nearly 60 cm and has a stout body, large blunt head, thick tail, and short legs. It is mainly black with pink and yellow patches.

Gila monsters spend much of their time in burrows in the sand. They come out in the rainy season, mainly at night. Because they move slowly they cannot catch fast moving prey and instead feed on eggs, and baby birds and rodents. When food gets scarce their body fat yields the nourishment they need; one survived a three-year drought without a meal. Gila monsters probably use their poisonous bite mainly for defence.

ORDER: Squamata;
FAMILY: Helodermatidae;
SPECIES: *Heloderma suspectum.*

Giraffe

The giraffe is the world's tallest animal. An old bull may measure 5.5 metres to the top of its head, although females are smaller. Giraffes live in the savanna of Africa south of the Sahara, but populations have been greatly reduced and the animal was once much more widespread. The long neck allows the animals to browse on high foliage and to watch out for enemies. The main source of food is the acacia, but giraffes also eat other plants gathering in the leaves with a tongue up to 45 cm long. They can go for long periods without drinking. When they come to water, they move their front legs wide apart in an ungainly manner in order to bring their heads down to the water. When resting, they crouch with their legs folded under their bodies, often laying their heads along their back while they sleep. But adult giraffes do not sleep much and some zoologists say that they do not sleep at all.

The giraffe has large eyes and a head which tapers to mobile, hairy lips. On the head, there are two to five bony knobs, covered with

skin. The shoulders are high and the back slopes down to the long, tufted tail. The coat is boldly marked with irregular chestnut, dark brown or liver-coloured blotches against a pale buff background.

Giraffes live mainly in herds, moving around slowly, unless alarmed. Males often live in groups in forested areas, while old males may live on their own. The females and the young live apart in more open country. Males visit them mainly for mating, which seems to take place all the year round. The gestation period is 420 to 468 days and only one calf is born at a time. The calf, when born, is 1.8 metres high and weighs about 50 kg.

Giraffes have few enemies. Lions may take a calf and several lions may bring down an adult, but most predators fear the giraffe's powerful long legs and heavy hoofs, which can severely damage any attacker.
ORDER: Artiodactyla;
FAMILY: Giraffidae;
SPECIES: *Giraffa camelopardalis.*

Glass snake

Although these reptiles look more like snakes they are, in fact, legless LIZARDS. They include the European glass snake and the Eastern glass lizard of North America. The European species is bronze, yellow, and brown and measures up to 1 metre or more. It occurs in south-eastern Europe and south-western Asia. Glass snakes are supposedly so brittle that they break into pieces if struck. In fact, they merely shed their long tails, which fracture into several parts. They mainly eat insects but also take other lizards and even mice. Glass snakes are said to live up to 60 years.
ORDER: Squamata;
FAMILY: Anguidae.

Glow-worm

The European glow-worm is actually a beetle, belonging to the same family as the FIREFLIES. The

A female **glow-worm**, glowing to attract a mate. She can switch off her light at will.

female is wingless and looks rather like a brown WOODLOUSE. She sits in grassy places on summer nights and gives out a bright greenish light from her hind end. The male can fly, and when he sees the female's light from the air he drops down to mate. The male is about 13 mm long – slightly shorter than the female – and brown in colour. Glow-worm *larvae* look rather like the females, but they lack *antennae*. They feed on snails. Adult glow-worms do not feed. Several species live in other parts of the world. In North America, the term glow-worm refers to any of various luminous insect larvae.
ORDER: Coleoptera;
FAMILY: Lampyridae;
SPECIES: *Lampyris noctiluca.*

Gnu

There are two species of gnu, or wildebeest, as they are also known: the white-tailed gnu or black wildebeest and the brindled gnu or blue wildebeest. The white-tailed gnu is extinct in the wild, but is preserved on private land in South

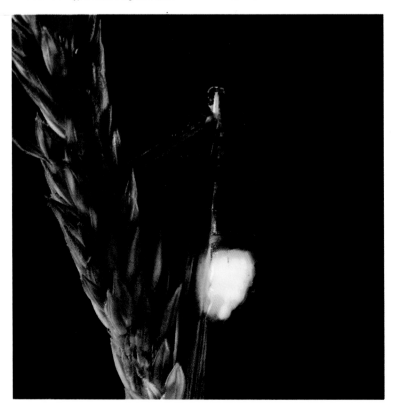

Africa. It is a blackish animal with forward-curving horns, while the grey, brindled gnu has horns that curve sideways and a horse-like black tail.

Gnu are cow-like antelopes which stand 120 cm at the shoulder. They have short, thick necks and large heads, a throat fringe and a mane. Males weigh up to 200 kg and females up to 160 kg. The brindled gnu is still fairly common on the savannas of southern Africa. It mates in April and May and calves are born in January and February. They live for about 20 years. Their chief predator is the lion.

ORDER: Artiodactyla;

FAMILY: Bovidae;

SPECIES: *Connochaetes gnou* (white-tailed); *Connochaetes taurinus* (brindled).

Goat

There are several species of goat, including the IBEX and MARKHOR. The wild goat, from which came the domesticated goat, ranges from southern Europe through south-western Asia to Pakistan. It

A rock **goby** lurks in a tidal pool.

usually lives in herds of 5 to 20 individuals in rugged or mountainous country, each herd being led by an old female. Agile and sure-footed, these goats are excellent climbers and frequently climb trees. They have been known to jump onto the backs of donkeys to reach otherwise inaccessible boughs.

A group of **gnu** drink from a pool in the African veld.

The head and body of the wild goat measures about 137 cm. The animal stands 90 cm at the shoulder and weighs up to 120 kg. The males are larger than the females. The horns of the males are sweeping, scimitar-shaped and up to 130 cm long. The horns of females are shorter and more slender. The coat is typically reddish-brown in summer and greyish-brown in winter, with black markings on the body and limbs.

ORDER: Artiodactyla;

FAMILY: Bovidae.

SPECIES: *Capra hircus*.

Goat moth

The goat moth is a large moth found in most parts of Europe and western Asia apart from the far north. Its wings, which span up to 90 mm, are mottled greyish brown, and the insect is hard to see when resting on tree trunks. It gets its name from the goat-like smell of its fleshy, pink caterpillar, which spends three or four years tunnelling in a tree trunk – often a willow. It may pupate in the trunk, or chew its way out of the timber and pupate among the moss and debris at the base of the trunk.

ORDER: Lepidoptera;

FAMILY: Cossidae;

SPECIES: *Cossus cossus*.

Goby

A family of small fish living in seas and estuaries in many parts of the world. Gobies reach a maximum length of about 60 cm, but most gobies are less than 8 cm long and the smallest, the Luzon goby, is a tiny fish that grows to only 1.3 cm and so holds the record for the smallest backboned animal.

Gobies are usually colourful little fish. Their eyes are placed close together at the top of the head and their *pelvic fins* are jointed to form a sucker, which they use for holding on inside rock crevices. Some gobies share their crevices with other animals, the relationship being useful to both animals. For example, a pair of gobies may share a burrow with SHRIMPS. The shrimps dig and maintain the burrow and the gobies mount guard at the entrance. Whenever danger threatens, the gobies retreat into the burrow, so warning the shrimps.
ORDER: Perciformes;
FAMILY: Gobiidae.

Godwit

Godwits are wading birds with long legs and bills, which enable them to wade in shallow water and probe the water or mud for food. They are related to the SNIPE and SANDPIPERS. Godwits live in most parts of the world. They mainly

The **godwit** is becoming rarer in many parts as its breeding haunts have been cultivated.

nest inland on marshes or moors, digging worms and insects from the soil. During the winter, they seek shellfish and worms in the sand or mud of the marshes or seashore.
ORDER: Charadriiformes;
FAMILY: Scolopacidae.

Goldcrests are active little insect-eaters.

Goldcrest

The smallest European bird, the goldcrest breeds from the British Isles to Japan, though its distribution through this range is very patchy. Usually it inhabits dense forests. The goldcrest is a dull green bird with whitish underparts but its crown bears a bright golden-yellow patch bordered with black. Goldcrests are insect-eaters, picking their food from leaves and bark in much the same way as TITS. In winter they also eat buds and small seeds. Their nest is made of moss, with a little grass,

bound together with spiders' webs and lined with feathers. They lay from 7 to 10 eggs which are incubated by the females.

The firecrest is similar to the goldcrest but has black stripes on its head and a more orange-coloured patch on its head.
ORDER: Passeriformes;
FAMILY: Regulidae;
SPECIES: *Regulus regulus.*

Golden eagle

The magnificent golden eagle has long been thought of as a royal bird. In the Middle Ages, only kings could hawk with a golden eagle, and it has remained perhaps the most admired of all birds of prey. Its range extends right across the northern hemisphere.

The golden eagle is up to 90 cm long, the female being larger than the male. The plumage is dark brown. In flight it spreads its broad wings with the main primary feathers separated and curving upwards, as does the smaller BUZZARD. The eagle lives in open mountainous country, hunting over a wide territorial range. It preys mainly on rabbits, hares and other mammals, together with birds, snakes and occasionally carrion. Eagles pair for life, and a pair will often hunt together, co-operating to attack prey. The nest, either on a rock ledge or in a tree, is used from year to year and is known as an eyrie. The golden eagle normally lays two eggs, the helpless chicks being fed by the parents until they leave the nest at the age of about 10 weeks. Contrary to legend, there are few recorded cases of golden eagles attacking people.
ORDER: Falconiformes;
FAMILY: Accipitridae;
SPECIES: *Aquila chrysaetos.*

Goldfinch

The goldfinch gets its name from a yellow line across each wing that is only clearly visible when the bird is in flight. Another distinctive

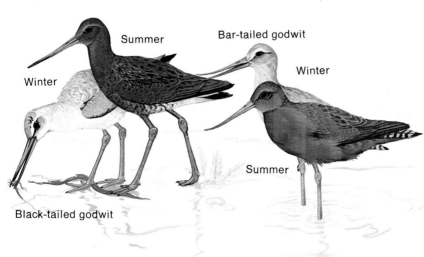

Summer

Bar-tailed godwit

Winter

Winter

Summer

Black-tailed godwit

feature is the head which is boldly marked with red, black and white. The beak is typical of seed-eating birds, being short and cone-shaped. Except in the breeding season, goldfinches move about in flocks. They chatter continuously and cling to seed heads when feeding. They build their nests in the branches of trees or hedges. The nest is made of interwoven roots, moss and lichens and lined with thistledown and wool. Goldfinches usually lay 5 to 6 eggs.
ORDER: Passeriformes;
FAMILY: Fringillidae;
SPECIES: *Carduelis carduelis*.

The proud head of a **golden eagle**.

Goldfinches can be identified by the red patches on their faces.

Goldfish

This most widely-domesticated of all fishes is really a CARP from China. The wild form of this species is green or brown in colour but occasionally red-gold individuals are found and it is from these that the ancient Chinese bred the first domestic goldfish, including many fancy breeds. These include veil-tail, telescope, calico, tumbler, lionhead, pompom and fantail, to name only a few. Some fancy breeds are freaks or monstrosities which in the wild would quickly die off in competition with more ordinary goldfish. This is shown by cases where domestic goldfish have escaped into rivers and lakes. After a few generations they have changed into fishes more closely resembling the wild goldfish.

On the other hand, because pet goldfish have no natural enemies except, perhaps, for a visiting heron, they tend to live much longer than wild goldfish, sometimes reaching an age of 25 years.
ORDER: Cypriniformes;
FAMILY: Cyprinidae;
SPECIES: *Carassius auratus*.

Goose

Geese are water birds related to the DUCKS and SWANS. They have webbed feet and oily feathers, but their necks are longer than those of ducks and shorter than those of swans. Many species migrate south in winter, usually flying in V-formation and making easily recognizable honking and gabbling noises as they fly. Usually, the sexes are alike.

The best known species are the CANADA GOOSE, the BARNACLE GOOSE, the greylag goose and the pink-footed goose. The HAWAIIAN GOOSE is a species famous for the fact that it has recently been saved from extinction.

The greylag goose is one of five grey geese, the others being the bean goose, the white-fronted goose, the lesser white-fronted goose and the pink-footed goose. The greylag breeds in Iceland,

A red lionhead veil-tail **goldfish**.

Scotland and northern Europe and is believed to pair for life. It is the ancestor of the domestic goose, which is well-known for its "watch dog" abilities – flocks of geese set up a loud cackling when they sense an intruder. The pink-footed goose and bean goose, which some ornithologists believe to be different races of the same species, breed in the tundra.

Grey geese are generally found on inland waters, whereas black geese, such as the Brent goose are usually found near the sea. The Brent goose also breeds in the tundra.
ORDER: Anseriformes;
FAMILY: Anatidae.

Gorilla

The gorilla is the largest of the APES. Males are sometimes over 1.8 metres tall and weigh between 180 and 200 kg. These powerful animals have broad chests, muscular necks and broad, strong hands and feet. But they are not the savage beasts of popular imagination. They are peaceful, gentle animals, which never attack unless provoked, and are at least as intelligent as CHIMPANZEES.

Gorillas live in troops, comprising one or more adult males with several females and their young. Each troop is led by an old male. The animals normally walk on all fours, with the knuckles on the ground, and adults seldom climb trees. Territories often overlap,

Right: A **greylag goose**. Greylags are ancestors of the farmyard goose. Below: **Brent geese** can be identified by the black head and neck, with a small white mark.

A powerful old male **gorilla** eating a melon. Gorillas are vegetarians.

but when troops meet, no aggression is shown. Gorillas in lowland forests eat fruit and leaves, often raiding banana plantations, whereas those living in mountains eat bark, stems and roots. They get nearly all their water from their food. The *gestation period* is about 255 days and the animals may live up to 37 years. Leopards may take young gorillas but they have no other enemies except man.

There are three races. The grey-black to brown-black western gorillas live in the lowland rain forests from sea-level to about 1800 metres in Cameroon, Equatorial Guinea, Gabon, Congo, the extreme south-west of the Central African Republic and the extreme south-west of Nigeria. The jet black eastern lowland race occupies a similar habitat in eastern Zaire, ascending to about 2400 metres in the highlands bordering the East African Rift Valley. The black mountain gorilla occurs in the Virungu Volcanoes and Mount Kahuzi in eastern Zaire and parts of Rwanda and Uganda between 2700 and 3600 metres above sea-level.

ORDER: Primates;
FAMILY: Pongidae;
SPECIES: *Gorilla gorilla*.

Goshawk

The goshawk is a large bird of prey found throughout the northern hemisphere. It looks like a SPARROWHAWK, but is much larger, with a body length of about 60 cm. Goshawks live in woodlands and forests. They are superb fliers, flitting among the trees and pouncing suddenly on prey.

Gamekeepers dislike and hunt down goshawks, because they kill pheasants and other gamebirds. But they prey on a variety of birds and animals, including squirrels, pigeons, and even foxes. Goshawks often concentrate on one form of prey, if it is plentiful. One Danish pair was seen to eat only gulls, while a another pair ignored the gulls and hunted crows. Related to the northern goshawks are the African black goshawk and the crested goshawk of South-East Asia.

ORDER: Falconiformes;
FAMILY: Accipitridae;
SPECIES: *Accipiter gentilis*.

Grasshopper

The grasshoppers are familiar insects in grassy places all over the world, although they are most common in the warmer regions. They can be distinguished from the related CRICKETS and BUSH CRICKETS by their short *antennae*. Most are quite sturdily built, and their tough wings, when present, are wrapped around the top and sides of the body at rest. Some fly quite strongly although rarely far. Many species, especially in upland areas, have greatly reduced wings or none at all. They all have long hind legs which enable them to jump. Most species are brown or

The **goshawk** is similar to the sparrowhawk, but larger in size.

A nymph of the Egyptian **grasshopper**. The adults are brown.

green and match their surroundings well, although some have brightly coloured hind wings.

Grasshoppers are best known for the males' chirpy calls, which fill the air on sunny days in summer. The sounds are produced by rubbing the hind legs against the wings, and each species has its own call, designed to attract females. Eggs are laid in the ground after mating, and the young grasshoppers grow up through a series of *nymphal* stages without a *chrysalis*. They all feed on grass and other low-growing plants. There are about 9000 species, including the LOCUSTS.
ORDER: Orthoptera;
FAMILY: Acrididae.

Grass snake

The harmless grass snake is found all over Europe except Ireland, the Isle of Man and the far north. It also ranges east to Central Asia. Grass snakes are usually 1 metre long. The longest known individual measured almost 2 metres. They are usually grey or olive brown with black and yellow

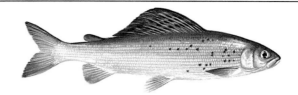

patches on the back of the neck. The yellowish patches generally form a distinct collar just behind the head. Grass snakes swim well and hunt mainly in and near ponds, eating frogs, newts and fish. If threatened, a grass snake hisses and strikes with its mouth shut. If that fails to scare an enemy it produces a foul smell. Finally it will sham dead.
ORDER: Squamata;
FAMILY: Colubridae;
SPECIES: *Natrix natrix.*

Grayling

An elegant fish of the SALMON family, the grayling lives in the swift-flowing streams of Europe and Scandinavia. Up to 2.3 kg in weight, it is a fast-swimmer which gives good sport to the angler.

A **grass snake** feigns death. This is one of the snake's main lines of defence.

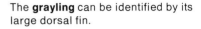

The **grayling** can be identified by its large dorsal fin.

Shaped like a salmon, the grayling's body has an overall, greenish-gold sheen but its large, sail-like *dorsal fin* is purplish in colour and dark, zig-zag lines run the length of its body. The grayling is a delicate fish which is easily damaged by handling and is also sensitive to pollutants in water, so that in many parts of Europe it has become rare.
ORDER: Salmoniformes;
FAMILY: Salmonidae;
SPECIES: *Thymallus thymallus.*

Great white shark

Also called maneater shark, the great white is a fearsome-looking CARNIVORE of the sea, up to 13 metres long and with a frightful array of saw-edged teeth which may be 7.5 cm long. Its body has the streamlined shape associated with killer sharks, but with a tail fin that is more symmetrical than in most sharks. Its colour is bluish grey or slate grey above, shading to white below. The great white shark lives mainly in warmer seas but is by no means unknown in temperate waters. It lives in the open, coming inshore only when the shallow seas are near deep water. Its attacks on man have occurred during these visits to shallower waters.

The great white shark is the largest member of the family of mackerel sharks, which has a bad reputation for causing injury and death. However, the great white is, probably, one of the least dangerous to man of this family, the mako and PORBEAGLE sharks having a much worse record of attacks.
ORDER: Lamniformes;
FAMILY: Isuridae;
SPECIES: *Carcharodon carcharis.*

A **great-crested grebe** on its grassy nest.

Greenfinch

A species of FINCH that ranges across Europe and Asia. The greenfinch is only tinged with green. The bright yellow edges to each wing are more prominent. Except during the breeding season, they move about in flocks, though they tend to nest in groups and among bushes and hedges. They have voracious appetites and around harvest time can consume large amounts of grain. The nest is typical of finches and females lay between 4 and 6 eggs. Like most small songbirds, many of the young are killed by predators.
ORDER: Passeriformes;
FAMILY: Fringillidae;
SPECIES: *Chloris chloris.*

Green turtle

The green turtle is a large marine turtle, about 1 metre long and weighing up to 180 kg. The adult

The **green turtle** is becoming scarcer because its meat and eggs are sought after as human food.

Grebe

Grebes are elegant water birds. They look like DIVERS but are smaller and have lobed toes. In the spring and summer, most species can be distinguished by their colourful nuptial plumes. They live on lakes and reservoirs and, rarely, on slow-moving rivers. Some stay in one place, but others, such as the great crested grebe, migrate to the coast in winter. Generally, however, grebes do not fly much. They have to run across the water to take off. They are famed for their courtship dances.

Of the 18 species, the 48 cm long great crested grebe is the largest. It is found in most of Europe and many parts of Africa, Asia and Australasia. The upper parts are light brown and the under-parts are white. The black ear tufts and, in the breeding season, the chestnut and black frills on the side of the head are very distinctive. The Slavonian grebe has dark upper-parts. It lives in the Arctic region. The little grebe, or dabchick, is the smallest species. It is found in much of Europe, Asia and Africa. Ten other species are confined to the Americas. For example, the flightless giant pied-billed grebe is confined to Lake Atitlan, in Guatemala. The best known species in America is the pied-billed grebe.
ORDER: Podicipediformes;
FAMILY: Podicipedidae.

shell is dark brown or olive, but the animal gets its name from the greenish colour of its fat. Green turtles live in tropical and sub-tropical seas, keeping mainly to shallow, coastal waters where they feed on seaweeds. The breeding beaches, on to which the females struggle to lay their eggs, are often far from the main feeding grounds and the turtles sometimes swim 2000 km to reach them. The young turtles are carnivorous during their first year of life, while they gradually make their way to the adult feeding grounds. Green turtles have become scarce in most regions because both adults and eggs are sought after as human food.

ORDER: Chelonia;
FAMILY: Chelonidae;
SPECIES: *Chelonia mydas.*

Grey fox

The grey fox, or tree fox, is a skilled tree-climber. This short-legged fox is found in southern Canada, the United States, Central America and northern South America. Its head and body measure up to 70 cm and it weighs up to 7 kg.

Other foxes climb trees, but the grey fox is unusual in that it grips the trunk with its fore feet and pushes upwards with its hind feet – like a cat. On the ground it is not a fast runner. The grey fox hunts mice, squirrels, small birds and insects. It also eats eggs and is particularly fond of fruit.

ORDER: Carnivora;
FAMILY: Canidae;
SPECIES: *Urocyon cinereoargenteus.*

Gribble

Gribbles are small wood-boring CRUSTACEANS, closely related to WOODLICE. The 21 species live in coastal waters; 14 of them attack timber, the rest burrow into the large seaweeds known as oar-weeds. Gribbles attack woodwork in pairs, the female doing most of

the work. They feed mainly on fungi growing in the wood. A fully-grown gribble is 3 mm long, and there may be as many as 20 to 25 in each cubic centimetre of infested wood.

ORDER: Isopoda;
FAMILY: Limnoridae.

Ground squirrel

There are numerous species of ground squirrel, most of which live in North America, although some live in Africa and Europe. Some members of the group are known as MARMOTS, CHIPMUNKS, susliks, and gophers (see POCKET GOPHER). Two of the most interesting are the antelope ground squirrel, which can stand exceptionally high temperatures, and the Barrow ground squirrel of Alaska, which HIBERNATES for nine months of the year.

Ground squirrels can measure between 18 and 74 cm long, although as much as half this length may be tail. Most are yellowish-grey in colour. Their ears are small, their legs short and their feet large by comparison with tree

Ground squirrels have much less bushy tails than tree squirrels.

squirrels such as the grey and the red.

Some ground squirrels live in colonies, others are solitary. They dig burrows or make their home under logs, under rocks or in other sheltered places. In northern regions, ground sqirrels hibernate during the winter. They eat plant food (nuts, seeds, roots), insects, birds, eggs and also carrion.

ORDER: Rodentia;
FAMILY: Sciuridae.

Ground beetle

The ground beetles are sturdily built and generally long-legged beetles which, as their name suggests, spend most of their time on the ground, although some tropical species live in the trees. Many lack hind wings and are unable to fly. There are more than 20,000 species, most of them black, but often with metallic sheens. Their eyes are generally large, and their jaws are quite prominent. Most are nocturnal. They run well, and capture other small animals. The elongated *larvae* are also carnivorous.

ORDER: Coleoptera;
FAMILY: Carabidae.

Grouper

A family of mainly marine fish, containing 400 species. These fishes live mostly in warmer waters and range enormously in size, the smallest being little more than 2.5 cm long when fully grown. The largest are heavy-bodied fishes up to 4 metres in length and half a tonne in weight. The largest and best known groupers have a rather sinister reputation for stalking skin-divers, a habit which can be unnerving because the grouper's enormous gape reveals many strong, needle-sharp, backward-pointing teeth.

This wide-ranging family has many strange members. The soapfishes are so-called because when alarmed they exude a slime, which they beat into a foam with thrashing movements of their bodies. Other members of the family are *hermaphrodites*, having both male and female sex organs. Yet other members are quick-change artistes among fishes; they are able to change their colour-patterns rapidly. The Nassau grouper, for example, has no fewer than eight colour schemes, or phases.

ORDER: Perciformes;
FAMILY: Serranidae.

Far right: A hen **blue grouse** poses on a branch in a willow thicket in British Columbia. The cock will be a richer, blue colour. Right: **Black grouse**. Below: **Red grouse**.

Grouse

The 18 species of grouse make up a family of gamebirds. They range from the size of a domestic hen to the size of a turkey, and live mainly in the northern parts of the Northern Hemisphere. In all grouse, the male is larger than the female. Their legs and feet are completely or partially feathered to protect them from the cold. Grouse are mainly ground-living birds and mainly vegetarian, but they also eat insects.

The red grouse lives among heather on the uplands of Britain and Ireland. It is a sub-species of the willow grouse which ranges across northern Europe and Asia and northern Canada. The red grouse retains its red-brown plumage throughout the year, camouflaging itself among the heather. The willow grouse is faced with winter snows, living farther north, and becomes white in winter to match the change in its surroundings. The ruffed grouse is a common North American species, ranging from Alaska south to Georgia. The male performs his mating dance on a log, beating his wings to give a drumming sound which attracts the female. The black grouse lives in Europe and Asia on the fringes of moors. Unlike the red or the ruffed grouse, it is polygamous, having a special courting ground at which the male displays a white fan of plumage to the assembled females. Grouse are sought by hunters outside the breeding season, but are protected while raising their young.

ORDER: Galliformes;
FAMILY: Tetraonidae.

Grunion

The grunion is a MULLET-like fish that spawns at night. It is famous for its spectacular spawning display. For example, on the beaches of California, countless thousands of these fishes can be seen at high tide after a full or new moon, riding in on the surf. The female grunions, each accompanied by one or more males wrapped around her to fertilize the eggs as they are laid, leaps out on to the sand and lays her eggs. The grunions then heave themselves back into the sea but their eggs remain high and dry buried in the sand until the next high tide, about a fortnight later. Within three

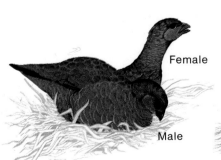

Female

Male

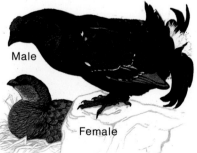

Male

Female

minutes of being wet by the tide, the eggs hatch into grunion *fry*, which are then swept into the sea to start their active lives.
ORDER: Atheriniformes;
FAMILY: Atherinidae;
SPECIES: *Leuresthes tenuis*.

Gudgeon

A small member of the CARP family, the gudgeon is very closely related to, but smaller than, the BARBEL. It lives in slow waters of European rivers, often in large shoals which keep near the bottom. Like its larger relative, the gudgeon has a *barbel* or feeler at each corner of its mouth which it uses to detect prey in the muddy sediments. It is coloured blackish or greenish on the back and has a silvery underside with dark spots. Like the barbel, it is tasty when cooked.
ORDER: Cypriniformes;
FAMILY: Cyprinidae;
SPECIES: *Gobio gobio*.

The **gudgeon** is a round-bodied fish with a large head.

Guenon

There are between 10 and 20 species of these medium-sized or small monkeys. They occur in a wide variety of colours. They have skilled, grasping hands and feet, short faces and brightly-coloured fur. For example, the green or VERVET MONKEY is greenish, with a black face, white throat and white whiskers. It ranges throughout most of Africa south of the Sahara in open grassland. The blue monkey is blue-grey, with black arms and legs and bushy cheek whiskers. It lives in forests in eastern and central Africa. The red-tailed monkey of East Africa is olive green, with a red tail and a white nose.
ORDER: Primates;
FAMILY: Cercopithecidae.

Guillemot

Guillemots are auks, and, like diving petrels and PENGUINS, spend all their time at sea except when breeding. On land they stand with an upright stance, similar to penguins, but in water they are more duck-like. Guillemots are birds of the northern seas. They suffer greatly from oil pollution, because they tend to dive when they come into contact with it. In this way, they become even more coated with oil. The common guillemot is 40 cm long. The upper-parts are black or dark brown. The under-parts are white and there is a white stripe on the wings. The neck and throat turn white in winter. In North America, guillemots are usually called common murres.
ORDER: Charadriiformes;
FAMILY: Alcidae.

A colony of **guillemots** on a rocky islet off north-east England. Lower down are kittiwakes.

Summer

Winter

Left: The **guillemot** breeds in large colonies on coastal cliffs and on offshore islands.

Below: The vulturine **guinea fowl** is the largest species of these African birds.

Guinea fowl

Guinea fowl live wild in Africa, and there are seven species. They are related to pheasants and chickens but, unlike these birds, both sexes are alike. Guinea fowl have also been domesticated, but have never been kept with such success as chickens. Some species of guinea fowl live in open country in flocks of as many as 200. During the day the birds wander in search of food, but return to regular roosts at night. Other species inhabit thick forest or woods and thickets. The birds disperse to nest, laying up to 20 eggs on the ground.

ORDER: Galliformes;
FAMILY: Numididae.

Guinea pig

The domestic guinea pig has been selectively bred from the wild guinea pigs, or cavies, of South America. There are several varieties, the most common being: the short-haired, which is most like the wild type; the wirey-haired Abyssinian, which has a coat arranged in rosettes; and the Peruvian, with its long, soft fur. Guinea pigs are not, in fact, pigs as the name suggests, but RODENTS. They are kept as domestic pets throughout the world, and are also widely used as laboratory animals.

ORDER: Rodentia;
FAMILY: Caviidae;
SPECIES: *Cavia porcellus* (domestic).

Gull

Gulls are white or greyish sea-birds, although a few have dark upper-parts. Some, such as the BLACK-HEADED GULL, are distinguished by the fact that the head plumage changes colour in the breeding season. Gulls have hooked bills, sometimes with red patches on the under-side. The wings are long and pointed and the tails are usually squarish. The legs are strong and the feet are webbed. These medium- and large-sized birds range in length from 30 to 75 cm.

Left: A handsome **herring gull**.

Below: A flying **gurnard** spreads its winglike pectoral fins as it rests on the seabed. The flying gurnard is not related to the true gurnard.

No two male **guppies** are ever exactly alike.

Nearly all gulls live in coastal regions. Only the KITTIWAKE lives far out to sea. Most gulls nest in colonies, which may consist of thousands of pairs, on cliffs and islands. But some breed inland, and others move inland for the winter. They are noisy birds and have elaborate courtship displays.

This **gyrfalcon** has a particularly white plumage. Gyrfalcons are the largest type of falcon.

There are more than 40 species of gull. One of the most common is the HERRING GULL.
ORDER: Charadriiformes;
FAMILY: Laridae.

Guppy

A popular aquarium fish, the guppy is a native of the Caribbean islands and northern South America. It is a hardy little fish. It matures rapidly, breeds prolifically, and can stand a wide range of temperatures and water that is polluted with organic matter. Because of its hardiness and lack of discrimination as to food, the guppy is frequently used for experiments on breeding and physiology and has also been used to control malaria by consuming the aquatic larvae of malaria mosquitos. The male guppy is a colourful little fish, hence its alternative name, rainbow fish, and is rarely more than 2.5 cm long. His bright colours are an advertisement of his virility, because he is almost incessantly sexually active. He fertilizes the large, less brightly coloured female guppy internally, using a special tube. Young guppies hatch inside their mother and when they are born, many are likely to be eaten by her.
ORDER: Atheriniformes;
FAMILY: Poeciliidae;
SPECIES: *Poecilia reticulatus.*

Gurnard

A family of marine fishes, with box-like heads on which the eyes are set high up. They have wing-like *pectoral fins*. Two or three bony rays in these fins have become separated into long finger-like projections on which the gurnard walks on the seabed. These rays also possess taste buds which help the fishes to detect small prey. Some deeper water species, called armoured sea-robins, have bodies covered with bony plates from which project a forest of spines.

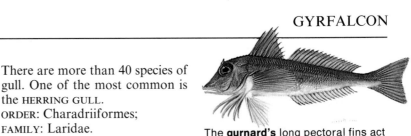

The **gurnard's** long pectoral fins act as feelers.

Gurnards live in tropical and temperate seas and may be up to 60 cm long. They are caught for food, and some are renowned for the grunting noises they make when removed from the water.
ORDER: Scorpaeniformes;
FAMILY: Triglidae.

Gymnure

Gymnures look like large SHREWS. They are related to the HEDGEHOG, and are sometimes called hairy hedgehogs. The moon rat is the largest species. It is 25 to 45 cm long from nose to rump and its scaly tail adds another 20 cm. Its outer fur is harsh and rough with a dense, shorter under-fur. All gymnures live in South-East Asia, in forests near streams or swamps, and swim readily. They feed on insects and earthworms. The moon rat eats fish and frogs as well.
ORDER: Insectivora;
FAMILY: Erinaceidae.

Gyrfalcon

The handsome gyrfalcon is the largest and the most northerly of the FALCONS, being found only in northern Europe, Scandinavia, Siberia and northern Canada. In colour, it ranges from grey brown to almost white. The gyrfalcon is said by falconers to have greater stamina than the PEREGRINE, and will pursue its quarry to the ground. It hunts ptarmigan, lemmings, rabbits and sea birds, and normally nests on rock ledges. Unlike the peregrine, the gyrfalcon does not migrate but keeps to its harsh haunts even in the winter.
ORDER: Falconiformes;
FAMILY: Falconidae;
SPECIES: *Falco rusticolus.*

H

Haddock

The haddock is a close relative of the COD and an important food fish. It is most easily distinguished from the cod by a dark, oblong patch on its flank, just behind the gills. Otherwise, the haddock is very cod-like, with three triangular *dorsal* and two *anal* fins, and a greyish-brown colour above, shading to white on the belly. However, the haddock is a smaller fish than the cod, reaching 120 cm in length and 16 kg in weight. It lives in the Arctic ocean and on both sides of the North Atlantic. Haddock feed on a variety of small *invertebrates* as well as small fish and squid. At times they gorge themselves on HERRING eggs. Young haddock swim in the mid-depths until they are about 5 cm long, after which they become bottom-feeders.

ORDER: Gadiformes;
FAMILY: Gadidae;
SPECIES: *Melanogrammus aeglefinus*.

Hairstreak butterfly

The hairstreak butterflies belong to the same family as the BLUES and COPPERS. They are all relatively small butterflies which get their name from the fine streaks on the undersides of the wings. There are generally one or more tails on the hind wing, usually hair-like but sometimes very long and ribbon-like in tropical species. Several of these tropical hairstreaks have "false heads" at the hind end like some of the blue butterflies. The upper surfaces of the wings are mainly brown in temperate species, although there may be orange patches or purple sheens. Tropical species are often much more colourful. The undersides are generally brown or grey, with a certain amount of orange and blue decoration, but the green hairstreak has a leaf-green underside. Most hairstreaks are woodland butterflies. Their *larvae* are rather slug-like in shape.

ORDER: Lepidoptera;
FAMILY: Lycaenidae.

Hagfish

The hagfish is a strange eel-shaped sea animal. Like the LAMPREY, it is a direct descendant of the first backboned animals. It lacks any trace of jaws. Unlike the lamprey, however, its body is not armoured with bone but is scaleless and very slimy.

Hagfishes, like sea lampreys (to which they are not closely related) are parasites of other fishes. The hagfish's way of life is generally regarded as horrifying, because it feeds by burrowing into the bodies of other fishes. However, these fishes are usually dying or already dead by the time the hagfish can attack them. A hagfish finds its prey by smell, with the aid of a single nostril. Its eyesight is bad, although a third eye on the top of its head is thought to detect light and dark. Around its mouth are six *barbels* or tentacles which also aid in food detection. Its anatomy is extraordinary in several ways. For example, its gut is a simple tube, lacking a stomach; its skeleton has no bone, being formed entirely of *cartilage*, and it possesses both male and female sex organs.

ORDER: Cyclostomata;
FAMILY: Myxinidae.

Hake

The hake is a deep-water fish closely related to the COD. The common hake lives in the north Atlantic and the Mediterranean; the silver hake lives off the Atlantic coast of North America; and other

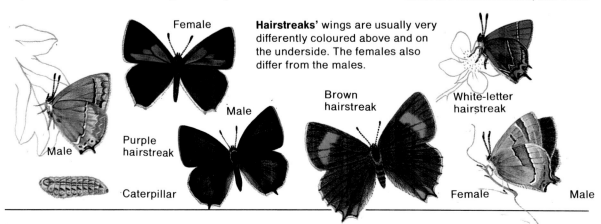

Female

Hairstreaks' wings are usually very differently coloured above and on the underside. The females also differ from the males.

Male

Brown hairstreak

White-letter hairstreak

Male

Purple hairstreak

Caterpillar

Female

Male

species of hake live off the Pacific coast of America and in South African waters.

Hake are fierce hunters, catching other fish in the middle deeps and devouring them with their sharp-toothed jaws. During winter and spring most hake live at depths of 150–600 metres but from April to August they move into shallower waters to spawn. Hake can be regarded as their own worst enemies because they frequently catch and eat their own young. Males of the common hake grow to about 30 cm long but the females may reach a length of 76 cm. Hake is a valued and tasty food fish.

ORDER: Gadiformes;
FAMILY: Merlucciidae.

Halibut

The halibut is a bottom-living flatfish. There are two species, one living in the North Atlantic, the other is a native of the North Pacific. Both can be very large fishes, occasionally reaching 4 metres long and weighing as much as 320 kg. Halibut are intermediate in shape between ordinary round-bodied fishes and the more extreme type of flatfish, such as the PLAICE, SOLE and DAB. Although flattened, the halibut is plumper than these fishes. Like the flatfishes, both of the halibut's eyes lie on the same side of its head. But its jaws have remained normal in shape and have not become twisted to one side. Like other flatfishes, halibut are able to change the colour of their upper surface – normally dark – to match their background.

ORDER: Pleuronectiformes;
FAMILY: Pleuronectidae;
SPECIES: *Hippoglossus hippoglossus* (North Atlantic); *Hippoglossus stenolepsis* (North Pacific).

Hammerhead shark

Five species of hammerhead SHARK live in warm oceans. They have extraordinary heads which

are drawn out sideways into the shape of a hammerhead. In every other respect, they are like ordinary sharks. The largest hammerhead sharks are 6 metres or more in length and weigh as much as a tonne. On the whole, hammerhead sharks have rather a bad reputation for aggression towards man, although authentic reports of their attacks are few.

The very unusual shape of the head of these sharks has still not been fully explained. Large hammerheads feed mostly on other fish, which demands accurate hunting. Perhaps, because the nostrils are so widely separated, the hammerheads are better able to pinpoint their prey, rather in the way that binocular vision aids in the judging of distances.

ORDER: Lamniformes;
FAMILY: Sphyrnidae.

Hamster

The Hamsters are a short-tailed *rodents* similar to VOLES and GERBILS. There are 14 kinds, of which the best known is the golden hamster, which has reddish-brown fur and is an easily-kept children's pet. Golden hamsters are all descended from a single family caught near Aleppo, Syria, in 1930. They are less robust than the common or black-bellied hamster of Europe. Various other species of hamster are found in Europe and Asia.

The **common hamster** digs extensive burrow systems with many chambers.

Hamsters mostly come out at night. They eat cereal, fruits, roots, leaves and occasionally insects, stuffing food into pouches in their cheeks and carrying it off to storage chambers in their underground burrows. They live alone, except during the breeding season.

ORDER: Rodentia;
FAMILY: Cricetidae.

Hare

Although similar in appearance, a hare can be distinguished from a rabbit by three chief points: it is bigger; has longer ears; and much longer hind legs. In winter the coat of the mountain or blue hare may turn white, as does the fur of the North American snowshoe rabbit.

Unlike rabbits, hares live solitary lives. They never burrow, but spend the day lying in hollows in the grass. These are known as forms, for they retain the shape of the animal. When pursued by an enemy, a hare is capable of great speed, but relies on twisting and leaping to evade capture.

In spring, male hares indulge in wild pre-mating antics. They buck, bound, kick and stand on their hind legs to box with one one another. Deaths sometimes occur during these displays. Young hares are called leverets. Unlike rabbits, they are born with their eyes open and can use their legs

Brown hare

Summer coat

Winter coat

Mountain hare

The **mountain hare** is more heavily built than the **brown hare**, with shorter ears and longer legs.

Above: The largest of all eagles, the **harpy eagle**, lives in dense forests in South America.

almost from birth. Each soon makes its own form and is visited by the doe to be suckled.
ORDER: Lagomorpha;
FAMILY: Leporidae.

Harpy eagle

The harpy eagle is the largest of the eagles. It is a forest-dweller. It has short, broad wings and a long tail and flies about the tree tops, hunting monkeys. It also descends to the forest floor to catch small animals. Like the CROWNED EAGLE, the harpy bears a crest of long plumes on its head. Its plumage is black, with white underparts and it has immensely strong talons. There are two species, the South American and the New Guinea harpy eagle. The female, which is one third as large again as the male, weighs 7 to 8 kg. Although not particularly rare, the harpy is seldom seen and little is known about its habits, since it rarely

emerges from the dense foliage of the treetops. However, it is known that this impressive eagle can fly at up to 80 km/h while hunting prey through the forest.
ORDER: Falconiformes;
FAMILY: Accipitridae;
SPECIES: *Harpia harpyja* (South American); *Harpyopsis novaeguineae* (New Guinean).

Harrier

Harriers are HAWKS which live in open country. They fly low over the ground, then drop down for the kill. They have rather owl-like heads, long wings and long legs and are found throughout the world, except in polar regions. Species seen in Europe include the hen harrier, the marsh harrier and Montagu's harrier. Harriers have been hated by farmers over the centuries for taking poultry and gamebirds. They congregate in flocks, and sometimes nest in colonies of 15 to 20 pairs.
ORDER: Falconiformes;
FAMILY: Accipitridae.

Below: The **hen harriers** and **Montagu's harriers** have very similar flight and nesting habits. They both hunt while flying low over moors, fields and marshes.

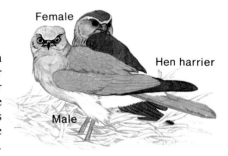

Female

Hen harrier

Male

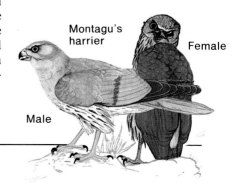

Montagu's harrier

Female

Male

Hartebeest

The hartebeest is a large, ungainly looking ANTELOPE with a long, narrow face. It stands 120 to 170 cm at the shoulder but the back slopes steeply down to the hind quarters. There are three species, all of which are abundant. The common hartebeest ranges across Central Africa from Guinea to Ethiopia. Lichtenstein's hartebeeste ranges from Tanzania to Mozambique. The Cape or red hartebeest is now extinct in South Africa but it is found in Angola, Botswana and Namibia. Hartebeests were once spread throughout Africa. All three species have brown coats, but there are varying amounts of black on the limbs. They live in herds of up to 15 in well-established territories, defended by the single male. They mate in mid-April to mid-May and the young are born eight months later. The chief enemy is the lion.
ORDER: Artiodactyla;
FAMILY: Bovidae.

Harvestman

Although often called harvest spiders, the harvestmen are not closely related to true spiders. Their body lacks the distinct "waist" seen in the spiders and carries just two eyes mounted on a "turret" on the back. Harvestmen are unable to spin silk and, although they have strong jaws, they have no poison fangs. They are scavenging creatures, feeding on a variety of living and dead insects, fruit, and decaying matter in general. Some species live in leaf litter and have quite short legs, but the best known are the long legged species that amble over low-growing vegetation at harvest time, hence their common name. The second pair of legs are very long and are used to feel and smell, just like insect's antennae. The animals often lose legs, and can survive with just three or four as long as they have at least one of the second pair. There are about 3000 species. In the United States harvestmen are known as daddy-long-legs, a name more commonly applied in Europe to the crane-fly.
CLASS: Arachnida;
ORDER: Opiliones.

Harvest mouse

The tiny harvest mouse is only about 13 cm long, nearly half of which is tail. It is one of the smallest mammals. Found from Europe to eastern Asia, it lives in ditches, pastures and fields, and spends much of its time climbing nimbly on the stalks of cereals or other plants. The harvest mouse

The **harvest mouse** is so small, it does not even bend the cereal stalks.

uses its long tail as an extra limb. It can hang from its hind feet and tail, leaving its front paws free for feeding.

Female harvest mice make a round nest of woven grass for their young. Modern harvesting methods, which use machinery, are thought to have caused a drop in the numbers of these inoffensive creatures.

ORDER: Rodentia;
FAMILY: Muridae;
SPECIES: *Micromys minutus.*

Hatchet fish

Freshwater hatchet fish and marine hatchet fish are quite different, but share the same name because of their similar shapes. Both have compressed, flat bodies with deep chests.

Marine hatchet fish are small, silvery and extremely thin. They live deep off the Atlantic, Indian and Pacific oceans. Numerous light cells, or photophores, on the lower body make these fish glow in the murky waters. Their eyes are telescopic and point upwards, to detect food in the faint light from above.

Freshwater hatchet fish are the only true flying fish. Their deep chests contain strong muscles which power the pectoral fins. These are expanded like wings, and flap rapidly with a buzzing sound as the fish makes a short dash across the water surface. It can take off and "fly" several metres through the air – a habit evolved for catching insects and used in courtship. Freshwater hatchet fish live in the tropics of South America and Panama, and are commonly kept in aquaria.

ORDER: Salmoniformes (marine); Cypriniformes (freshwater);
FAMILY: Sternoptychidae (marine); Gasteropelecidae (freshwater).

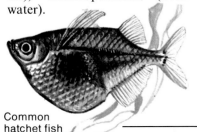

Common hatchet fish

Hawaiian goose

The Hawaiian goose, or ne-ne is a close relative of the CANADA GOOSE and may be descended from the Canada geese that settled in Hawaii thousands of years ago. It is a medium-sized bird and its plumage is grey brown with whitish barring. It feeds on leaves, stems and flowerbuds and will strip seeds from grasses. Hawiian geese feed together in flocks until the breeding season, when the males become bad-tempered and each pair defends its own territory. Unlike most birds, they breed when the days are shortest, from November to January.

The population of Hawaiian geese was once about 25,000, but by 1950 there were only 17 left in the wild. Three were taken to the Wildfowl Trust at Slimbridge, England, where they bred. In 1962, 30 were released in Haleakala crater on Maui Island and there is now an established wild population again.

ORDER: Anseriformes;
FAMILY: Anatidae;
SPECIES: *Branta sandvicensis.*

Hawfinch

The common grosbeak or hawfinch is one of the larger FINCHES and characterized by its large bill. It ranges across Europe from the British Isles to Japan. In spring and summer the male is more brightly coloured, but in winter both sexes look alike. They nest high up in trees and bushes, especially evergreens, and the nest is made of twigs and roots lined with finer roots, hair or fibre. Hawfinches use their stout beaks to crack open hard seeds. They can even crack open cherry pips and olive stones, which most people

Left: Freshwater hatchet fish live near the surface and can fly short distances, using fins like wings. The **common hatchet fish** is popular in aquaria.

Right: The **hawfinch's** large beak is a powerful nut-cracker.

would find difficult to break with a hammer.

ORDER: Passeriformes;
FAMILY: Fringillidae;
SPECIES: *Coccothraustes coccothraustes.*

Hawk

Popular names for birds of prey often confuse hawks with FALCONS. The European KESTREL, for example, is a falcon, but the American kestrel is popularly known as the sparrowhawk. The European SPARROWHAWK is a typical hawk, with broader wings and tail than a falcon. Most hawks hunt by pouncing on their prey, often flying in a series of short dashes followed by a long glide. Their prey includes small birds and mammals.

ORDER: Falconiformes;
FAMILY: Accipitridae.

Hawkmoth

Hawkmoths are fast-flying insects with stout bodies and rather narrow wings. The wings may be quite long, however, and several species exceed 15 cm in wingspan. One of the best known species is the death's head hawkmoth, which has a skull-like pattern on its *thorax* and which can squeak when handled. Many species feed by hovering in front of flowers and sucking up the nectar with their long tongues, but some other species have no tongue and do not feed as adults. Most are nocturnal,

Hawfinch

although the bee hawkmoths, which have transparent wings, fly by day. Most of the 900 species are found in tropical regions all over the world. Hawkmoth caterpillars usually have a horn on the hind end. They frequently rest with the front part of the body reared up, resembling the Egyptian sphinx in profile.

ORDER: Lepidoptera;
FAMILY: Sphingidae.

Hedgehog

The common or European hedgehog is one of 15 species found in the Old World. All species are alike in habits, and their appearance differs in small details only.

Almost all adult **hawkmoths** feed on nectar, probing the flowers with a long tubular tongue.

The common hedgehog is about 25 cm long, and weighs up to 1.2 kg. The animal has small eyes, short ears and legs, a short tail and a long snout. The hedgehog's back and top of its head are covered with sharply-pointed spines, and each spine stands nearly at right-angles to the skin. The rest of its body is clothed with coarse hair. All four feet have five toes and five pads on the sole.

Hedgehogs sometimes eat plants, but the main part of their diet consists of snails, slugs, insects and worms. Occasionally they eat lizards, mice, frogs and snakes, and have also been seen to eat bird's eggs. The hedgehog searches for its food at night, generally close to a supply of leaf litter where it can sleep through the day. Its sight is poor but smell and hearing are acute.

When alarmed, the hedgehog curls into a ball so its enemy can find no way past the prickly spines. It can swim and climb well, but usually stays on the ground. In winter, some hedgehogs hibernate completely, while others hibernate only intermittently.

ORDER: Insectivora;
FAMILY: Erinaceidae;
SPECIES: *Erinaceus europaeus* (European).

Herbivore

Those animals which feed only on plants are known as herbivores. They range from zooplankton – minute creatures that swim in the sea – to the huge ELEPHANT.

Herbivores are peaceful creatures. In most places vegetation is so abundant and varied that there is little competition between the species. Several different kinds of herbivores may graze together because they eat different kinds of plants. And, in some cases, different species may even feed on the same plant because their eating habits are different. GIRAFFES, GERENUKS and GAZELLES, for instance, all feed at different levels and may peacefully share a meal from one acacia tree. The giraffe's height allows it to feed from the topmost branches of the tree, while, beneath it, the little gazelle browses on the lower branches. In between them, the gerenuk stands on its hind legs to reach the middle branches.

A great many insects also feed only on vegetable matter. Harvester ants, for example, gather the seeds of grasses, remove the kernels and store them in their nests to provide a food stock for future needs.

BEES are among the insects that work hardest to gather their food. Bees fly from flower to flower, gathering nectar and pollen. By transfering the pollen from one flower to another they help to fertilize the plants. A bee will fly a considerable distance in order to find its food.

Zebras, antelopes and giraffes are all peaceful plant-eaters.

Hermit crab

Hermit crabs have rear parts that are not protected by the shell. For shelter, a hermit crab backs into the disused shell of a sea snail. Some crabs use a shell of a dead snail, others kill and eat the snail to get both a meal and a home. The front end of the body is hard, and the crab uses its right claw as a stopper to close the entrance to the shell when it is in residence. The crab moves around dragging the shell with it. If it outgrows its home it looks for a larger shell and moves in. Hermit crabs feed on small animals and plants.
ORDER: Decapoda;
FAMILIES: Paguridae, Coenobitidae.

Only the armoured part of the **hermit crab** projects from the shell.

Heron

Herons are wading birds, belonging to the same family as BITTERNS, EGRETS and NIGHT HERONS. Their main food is fish, but they also eat water voles, frogs and many other animals. Their flight is low and graceful, with the head drawn back and the legs trailing behind. Herons spend much time on the ground, roosting with one leg raised, or waiting for prey on a bank or in shallow water. They nest in colonies. The most common European heron is the grey heron, which is also found in parts of Asia and Africa. It has a long neck and long legs, and is closely related to the great blue heron of North America. The little green heron of North America and the squacco heron have shorter necks and legs.
ORDER: Ciconiiformes;
FAMILY: Ardeidae.

Herring

The most important of all food fishes, the Atlantic herring is a torpedo-shaped fish about 30 cm long, which spends much of its life swimming near the surface, feeding on floating plankton. Vast shoals of herring occur in the

The **grey heron** stands motionless in or near water, then suddenly darts its head down after its prey.

fishing grounds of the Atlantic, the total yearly catch from these and adjacent grounds being no fewer than 3000 million herrings. Various races of the Atlantic herring, distinguished by the different numbers of bones in their backbone, are named after the particular areas of the Atlantic in which they occur. Examples are the Icelandic race, the Norwegian race, the Channel race and the Baltic race. The Pacific herring is a closely related species. It is another important food fish which inhabits northern parts of the Pacific and the adjacent Arctic oceans. In human history, the abundance of herring has often strongly influenced the development of nations, such as Holland, Norway and Japan.
ORDER: Clupeiformes;
FAMILY: Clupeidae;
SPECIES: *Clupea harengus* (Atlantic); *Clupea pallasi* (Pacific).

Herring gull

The herring gull is one of the most successful of birds. Originally a fish-eater, it has become a scavenger and a predator. Flocks of these large, noisy gulls are a common sight around many European shores, and the species also breeds in North America. The herring gull is white, with a yellow bill and black wingtips. It sometimes interbreeds with the lesser black-backed gull, which is usually considered to be a separate species.

Herring gulls will eat practically anything. They are common around refuse tips, and are frequently seen inland, far from the sea. They plunder the nests of other birds for eggs and chicks, and will also attack sick or injured seabirds and small mammals. Shellfish, such as MUSSELS, are carried aloft and dropped so the shell is broken. At sea, herring gulls dive to feed on shoals of fish swimming close to the surface.
ORDER: Charadriiformes;
FAMILY: Laridae;
SPECIES: *Larus argentatus.*

Hibernation

As winter approaches and the weather turns cold, BATS and HEDGEHOGS, together with DORMICE and a few other rodents, disappear from the countryside. They go into a very deep sleep called hibernation. Stimulated by the shortening days of autumn, they take on extra food and then hide themselves away. Their body temperature drops drastically until it is only just above that of the surroundings, and their heart and breathing rates slow almost to a stop. Very little energy is used up in this condition and the animals can sleep for several months. The warm sunshine wakes them up again in the spring. Hibernation is essential for the bats' survival, because there are no insects for them to eat in the winter. It is less easy to see what value it has for hedgehogs and rodents, because related animals survive the winter quite happily without a long sleep. Although some birds hide away and become drowsy during the winter, none is known to go into true hibernation. Birds have solved the food problem in cold climates by migrating. Most cold-blooded animals pass the winter in a state of suspended animation, but this is less complex than the hibernation of the warm-blooded mammals. Cold-blooded animals depend on the Sun's warmth to keep their bodies at working temperature and, as the weather turns colder, they become completely dormant, but not usually until they have fed themselves up and found a snug corner in which to hide away.

Hippopotamus

The hippopotamus rivals the RHINOCEROS as the second largest living land animal. Nearly 430 cm long and standing up to 150 cm at the shoulder, it weighs about 4 tonnes. It once lived throughout Africa, but it is now extinct north of Khartoum, in the Sudan, and south of the Zambezi River, except in protected areas. The smaller pygmy hippopotamus is a separate species and is only about 150 cm long. It lives singly or in pairs in Liberia, Sierra Leone and southern Nigeria.

The word "hippopotamus" means "river horse" and the animal spends most of the day lazing in rivers or lakes, or basking on sandbars. At night, it comes on land to feed, mainly on grass. When frightened, it can run with surprising speed on its short thick legs. The hippopotamus can stay under water for as long as five minutes. Its eyes are raised on the top of its large flattish head. It has small ears and its slit-like nostrils are high up on the muzzle. The animal can thus bask below the surface of the water with its nostrils just breaking through into the air. The barrel-shaped body is hairless, except for some bristles on the muzzle, in the ears, and at the tip of the short tail. The enormous mouth contains large *canine* tusks which may be over 1.5 metres long.

The hippopotamus lives in groups of between 20 and 100. The female selects her mate. After mating, the baby is born about eight months later. During the mating season the males are aggressive. Fights are vigorous and large gashes are inflicted with the tusk.

ORDER: Artiodactyla;
FAMILY: Hippopotamidae;
SPECIES: *Hippopotamus amphibius.*

The **hippopotamus** is about the size of the white rhino. These animals are exceeded in size among land animals only by the elephants.

Hoatzin

The hoatzin is a bird of the forests of northern South America. It is about the size of a ROOK and lives along river valleys, where it can find the two particular plants on which it mainly feeds. Hoatzins cannot fly well but may use their wings to clamber about in trees and find food.

Young hoatzins are born with claws on the front edges of their wings. These claws help the young bird to clamber through the trees when it leaves the nest. The nest is built out over the river, and the young will dive into the river if it cannot escape danger by leaving the nest. It climbs back to its nest when danger is past.

The claws on the young hoatzin's wings are very like those of Archaeopteryx, the first known bird, which probably lived the same kind of life as the hoatzin.
ORDER: Galliformes;
FAMILY: Opisthocomidae;
SPECIES: *Opisthocomus hoatzin.*

Honey badger

The honey badger resembles other badgers in size and build but lacks the striped head. The under-parts and sides of the body are dark brown or black while the top of its head, neck and back are usually white or greyish. Honey badgers are ferocious, aggressive animals and can produce an evil-smelling fluid from their tail glands. They are not often seen as they tend to be nocturnal prowlers. During the day they lie in holes or burrows or under rocks. Also known as ratels, they are found in Africa and Asia, but are beoming increasingly rare.

Honey badgers eat almost any kind of food including fruits and insects, as well as a variety of larger animals. They use their powerful jaws to crack open the shells of TURTLES and TORTOISES and there is one story of a honey badger tackling and eventually overpowering a PYTHON over 3 metres long.

Honey badgers like honey, and they have developed an associa-tion with a bird called a HONEY-GUIDE. This bird uses a special call to lead the badger to a bees' nest. The badger breaks the nest open and proceeds to feed on the honey and grubs within, whilst the honeyguide eats the wax comb.

ORDER: Carnivora;
FAMILY: Mustelidae;
SPECIES: *Mellivora capensis.*

Honey bee

The honey bee is a native of tropical Asia, but it has been semi-domesticated for centuries and has been taken to most parts of the world to provide honey. Many different strains, or races, have been bred, but the insects still behave in exactly the same way as their ancestors. Unlike bumble bee colonies, the honey bee colony goes on year after year.

Most honey bees live in hives provided by bee-keepers, although there are plenty of "wild" bees which have escaped and estab-lished nests in hollow trees. Each colony is ruled by a queen, who exerts her influence by spreading chemical signals through the hive. As long as she is there and in good health, everything runs smoothly. She is quite helpless, though, and cannot even collect food for her-self: she is always surrounded by attentive workers. The workers are sterile females, and there may be 60,000 in the colony in mid-summer. They build the wax combs of the nest, collect the nectar and pollen from the flowers, and feed the young.

The workers have evolved some wonderful ways of telling each other where to find rich sources of food. They "dance" on the combs when they return to the hive, and the speed and direction of the dances tells the other bees how far to go and in which direction. Much of the pollen and nectar brought back is given to "house-maid" bees, who pass it to the grubs in the cells. The rest of the nectar is converted to honey and stored in the cells. Excess pollen is also stored.

If conditions in the hive get too crowded, the queen leaves with a swarm of workers to start a new nest. The remaining workers then rear a new queen by giving one of the young grubs extra-rich food. This enables the grub to develop into a fully fertile bee instead of a sterile worker. The young queen flies out to mate with a number of male bees, or drones, of which there are always a few hundred in a hive in summer. Then she returns to devote the rest of her life to laying eggs. New queens are also reared when the old ones begin to fail.

When autumn comes and food becomes scarce, the bees cluster in

An alert pair of **honey badgers**. This African animal has a reputation for ferocity.

Honey bees build thousands of wax cells. They store honey and pollen in some, and rear the young in others.

Above: A **honey eater** sips nectar from a flower. Left: a **honey bee** drops in for a meal.

the centre of the hive and stay there for the winter, feeding on the pollen and nectar that they stored up during the previous summer.
ORDER: Hymenoptera;
FAMILY: Apidae;
SPECIES: *Apis mellifera.*

Honeyeater

A diverse group of birds that eat mainly nectar and fruit, honey-eaters are very varied in form and habits. The o-o-aa of Hawaii searches for insects in tree trunks, propping itself on its stiff tail like a WOODPECKER. The leatherheads resemble JACKDAWS but several have horny growths on their bills and vulture-like bald heads. The spinebills have long, curved bills and hover near flowers like hummingbirds. Others resemble TITS, FLYCATCHERS or WARBLERS. Half of the species live in Australia, the remainder are found in New Zealand and the islands of the south-western Pacific, though some have reached Hawaii and one species lives on the Bonin Islands off Japan.
ORDER: Passeriformes.

Honeyguide

The 12 species of honeyguide live in Africa and southern Asia. They are small birds of forest and brush country, mostly dull in colour. Some honeyguides are fond of bee *larvae* and bees' wax, but cannot break open bees' nests unaided. The birds therefore attract the attention of HONEY BADGERS, man and other animals to the nests by excited chatterings. They then wait for the nests to be opened and feed on the wax and larvae.
ORDER: Piciformes;
FAMILY: Indicatoridae.

Hoopoe

The hoopoe is found in Africa, Asia and Europe, preferring warm dry climates with open woodland. It likes to perch on a branch and then fly down to the ground to feed on insects, grubs, spiders and worms. Hoopoes are 30 cm long and pinkish-brown in colour with conspicuous black and white bars on the lower back and wings. When excited, they raise a crest of chestnut, black-tipped feathers. To frighten away birds of prey, hoopoes spread their wings to display the bold black and white

stripes, and point their long, curved bill into the air.
ORDER: Coraciiformes;
FAMILY: Upupidae;
SPECIES: *Upupa epops.*

Hornbill

Hornbills live in tropical forests, from Africa south of the Sahara across tropical Asia to the Philippine and Solomon Islands. Their huge and often bizarre bills which may be surmounted by a large bony *casque*, give these birds their name. Hornbills eat mainly fruit, and berries which they gather by hopping about the larger branches of trees. In this respect, they are remarkably similar to the unrelated TOUCANS of the Americas. Hornbills also attack snakes. Sometimes several birds band together to kill one large snake. They rain blows on their prey with their large, sharp-edged bills while shielding themselves with their wings. Hornbills vary in length from 40 to over 120 cm.

Many hornbills have unusual ways of nesting. They use holes in trees, like many other birds, but to prevent any animals from raiding the nest-hole, the female seals

The **hoopoe** is named after its call.

Crest up

Hoopoe

Crest down

herself in with the eggs by building a wall of mud or dung across the entrance to the hole. A small slit is left, through which the male feeds the female. While imprisoned, the female moults. She may stay in the nest-hole until the young can fly.

ORDER: Coraciiformes;
FAMILY: Bucerotidae.

Horned toad

Despite ther toad-like faces and squat bodies, horned toads are LIZARDS. The Texas horned toad and more than a dozen other species live in the desert lands of North America. They drink dew and hunt insects, particularly ants. The head and neck are protected by several backward-projecting spines and smaller spines cover the back. The toad's dull colours help camouflage it in the sand. If threatened or alarmed, a horned toad may squirt blood from its eyes. It is thought that the blood irritates the eyes of the enemy.

ORDER: Squamata;
FAMILY: Iguanidae.

Hornet

The name "hornet" refers to any one of several large social wasps. The European hornet is easily identified by its large size and distinct coloration, which is brown and yellow instead of the black and yellow of most species. The common white-faced hornet of the United States has a black body with white markings and a white face. Like other social wasps, hornets build their nests with paper made from chewed wood. The nests are usually sited under eaves or in hollow trees. The habits and life cycle of these insects are like those of other wasps. (See WASP).

ORDER: Hymenoptera;
FAMILY: Vespidae.

Horse

Wild horses belong to the same family as ASSES and ZEBRAS. They were widespread in Europe and Asia in prehistoric times, but their numbers were reduced through hunting and domestication. Only two remnants of wild horses persisted: the tarpan, which survived in the Ukraine until 1851 and Przewalski's horse of Central Asia. The domesticated horse was probably derived from one of these. The tarpan was a small, shy, swift-running animal, with a long, mouse-coloured coat. Przewalski's horse was discovered by the Russian explorer Nicolai Przewalski in 1881. It nearly became extinct, but the surviving stock is now protected. This stocky horse stands 135 cm at the shoulder. It is sandy-orange brown, with an erect black mane, no forelock and a black tail.

In many areas, domesticated horses have escaped and reverted to the wild. These are called feral horses. They include the half-wild mustangs of the United States and the brumbies of Australia. Wild horses live in herds on steppes or grassy plains. A herd consists of mares, foals, and colts led by a stallion. As male colts reach maturity, the stallion drives them to the outside of the herd. Stallions use the hooves of the forefeet in fights, rearing up on their hind legs to do so. They also bite. Foals are born 11 months after mating and horses commonly live to 20 years or more, the record being 62.

ORDER: Perissodactyla;
FAMILY: Equidae.
GENUS: Equus.

Horsefly

The horseflies are rather stout insects whose females feed on blood – especially that of horses, deer, and other large mammals, including man. They pierce their victims with very sharp, blade-like mouth-parts, but the males lack this equipment and they feed on nectar. Horseflies are sometimes known as stouts, and the largest approach 5 cm in length. Their large eyes often display wonderful metallic colours in life, but the rest of the body is generally rather sombre. The *larvae* live in water or damp soil, feeding on other small animals and on decaying matter. There are about 2000 species.

ORDER: Diptera;
FAMILY: Tabanidae.

Horseshoe bat

About 50 species of horseshoe bats inhabit temperate and tropical areas of the Old World. The bats derive their name from the shape of their nose leaves. The nose leaf is the skin that covers the upper lip and surrounds the nostrils. In the horseshoe bat, the lower part of the nose leaf is shaped like a horseshoe. The nose leaves play a major role in the production of sounds for echo-location in all

The **hornet** is a large wasp that nests in hollow trees.

Only the female **horsefly** feeds on blood.

The **lesser horseshoe bat** is only about 63 mm long.

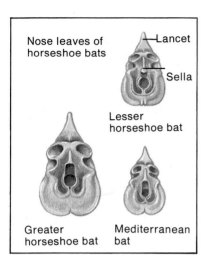

Nose leaves of horseshoe bats

Lancet

Sella

Lesser horseshoe bat

Greater horseshoe bat

Mediterranean bat

The **housefly** mops up all kinds of liquid food.

BATS, and the horseshoe bats are particularly efficient because the horseshoe can be moved round to beam the sounds. These bats depend on echo-location when seeking the insects that form the principal part of their diet.
ORDER: Chiroptera;
FAMILY: Rhinolophidae.

Housefly

The housefly is one of the world's most widely distributed insects, being found almost everywhere that man lives. Its *larvae* – little white carrot-shaped creatures – feed on domestic refuse and dung. When fully grown, they seek slightly drier places and then pupate in little brown barrel-shaped cases. In warm places, the adult flies emerge only a week after the eggs are laid, but the life cycle may take two months in cooler climates. The adult fly has a grey-ish *thorax* and a yellowish abdomen. It is very common in houses, especially in late summer, but also lives happily out of doors, around rubbish tips and manure heaps. It does not bite, but it is a dangerous insect because it feeds indiscriminately and often carries germs from dung to our food.
ORDER: Diptera;
FAMILY: Muscidae;
SPECIES: *Musca domestica.*

House mouse

The house mouse, the most familiar of all rodents, is now found wherever man lives. Once a resident of woods and fields, this adaptable animal has taken to life alongside humans, and has travelled as a stowaway wherever man has settled.

House mice mainly eat seed and grain, but will feed on a wide variety of other foods. Some even live permanently inside meat cold stores, nesting in the carcases and surviving by virtue of extra thick coats. House mice can climb well, can squeeze through tiny holes as they are only 9 to 13 cm long, and give birth to up to five litters in a year. This helps to explain their spread to all parts of the world.

House mice have many enemies among the birds and beasts of prey, such as HAWKS, OWLS, WEASELS, FOXES and CATS. They cannot see very well, but have keen senses of smell and hearing.

Though pests in the house, these small animals are of great importance in scientific research. The *albino* strains in particular are used in laboratory work.
ORDER: Rodentia;
FAMILY: Muridae;
SPECIES: *Mus musculus.*

Hoverfly

The hoverflies are a large family of true flies, named for their marvellous ability to hover in mid-air. There are thousands of species, some fat and some incredibly thin, but all can be recognized by looking at the wings. The veins turn sharply near the edge and form a "false margin" a little way in from the true edge. The head is relatively large and nearly all eyes, and the body generally has little hair. Many species are brightly coloured and many of them mimic bees and wasps. The flies feed mainly on nectar, although some can actually crush pollen in their mouths.

Hoverfly *larvae* are extremely varied. Many are pale and slug-like and feed on APHIDS, others feed on decaying matter in soil or water, and a few live inside plants.

This **hoverfly** is a superb wasp mimic.

The **greater horsehoe bat** has quite a slow flight, rather like that of a butterfly.

Some are scavengers in the nests of BEES and WASPS. One of the most interesting larvae is that of the drone-fly. It lives in ditches and muddy pools and has a telescopic breathing tube with which it obtains oxygen from the air. It is called a rat-tailed maggot.
ORDER: Diptera;
FAMILY: Syrphidae.

Howler monkey

Howler monkeys, the largest of the South American MONKEYS, are so named because of their loud calls. They live in groups of 2 to 30. They usually howl at dawn, and when they wish to warn others off their territory. The colour of the fur is usually black, brown or red, but it differs between the five species. The hands and feet are large but, like other South American monkeys, the thumbs cannot be opposed to the fingers. Hence, these monkeys pick up objects with the second and third fingers. Both sexes are nearly 120 cm long, including the tail. The mantled howler lives in Central America and north-western South America. The other species are the red howler, the brown howler, the red-handed howler and the black howler.
ORDER: Primates;
FAMILY: Cebidae.

Hummingbird

The 300 species of hummingbirds live in the New World forests. The largest hummingbird is only 22 cm long while the smallest, the bee hummingbird, is little more than 5 cm long. It is the world's smallest bird.

Hummingbirds are most common in the forests of South America, but they range from southern Alaska to Tierra del Fuego. Some undertake long migratory flights, for which they prepare by storing body fat to fuel the journey. The ruby-throated hummingbird migrates between North and South

A **hummingbird** hovers before a hibiscus flower to suck nectar through its long, tubular tongue.

America, crossing the gulf of Mexico on each trip.

Hummingbirds have brilliant, often iridescent, plumage which has led to their being given names like "ruby" and "topaz". They are called hummingbirds because the wings beat so fast that they produce a low humming sound. Small species have wingbeats of 50 to 80 per second, and in courtship displays even higher rates have been recorded. The fast wingbeats enable hummingbirds to dart to and fro through the air, and they reach speeds of about 110 km/h in straight flight. Flying with such rapid wingbeats consumes a large amount of energy. Hummingbirds obtain this energy by taking nectar from flowers and eating soft-bodied insects and spiders. The bird uses its long tubular tongue to probe flowers for insects and nectar while hovering in mid-air.
ORDER: Apodiformes;
FAMILY: Trochilidae.

Humpback whale

One of the whalebone, or baleen WHALES, the humpback grows to around 15 metres in length. It is found in all oceans and is remarkable for its extremely long flippers, which can be up to a third of its body length.

Humpbacks migrate every summer to polar seas to feed on KRILL, returning to tropical waters in winter to breed. When in warmer waters, humpbacks feed very little, building up sufficient blubber reserves in summer to last the rest of the year. When they migrate, they usually keep close to the coasts, which makes them an easy prey for whalers.

ORDER: Cetacea;
FAMILY: Balaenopteridae;
SPECIES: *Megaptera novaeangliae.*

Hydra

Hydra are small, fresh water animals related to JELLYFISHES and SEA ANEMONES. They have thin cylindrical bodies 6 to 13 mm long, and several tentacles – usually five or six, but sometimes as many as 12 – surrounding the mouth. At the other end of the body is a sticky disc with which the hydra anchors itself to solid surfaces.

Hydras capture their prey with their tentacles. The tentacles have stinging cells which are fired out like miniature harpoons. Hydras eat insect larvae, water fleas, worms, tadpoles and newly-hatched fishes. They reproduce in two ways. The most common way is by budding. A bud or bulge grows on the side of the hydra's body, and eventually breaks off and begins a new existence as a separate animal. Alternatively, at certain times of the year, particularly autumn and winter, hydras reproduce sexually, from female cells and male sperm cells which join together to produce new animals.

PHYLUM: Coelenterata;
CLASS: Hydrozoa.

Hyena

Hyenas are dog-like animals found in Africa and Asia. Although they are carrion-eaters, their reputation for cowardice is unfounded. They frequently hunt quite formidable prey, such as ZEBRA and WILDEBEEST. They hunt at

The **spotted hyena** is a powerful and aggressive animal. Hyenas hunt at night in packs of up to 20.

night in packs of up to 20 individuals, chasing their prey at speeds of up to 60 km/h. They have strong shoulders which are higher than their hindquarters, powerful jaws and strong teeth that can crush large bones.

There are three species, of which the largest and most aggressive is the spotted or laughing hyena. It can be up to 1.5 metres long and weigh as much as 82 kg. Its coat is grey to tawny or yellowish-buff, with numerous brown spots. The spotted hyena is found in Africa south of the Sahara desert. It lives in clans of up to 100. By day it rests in lairs – either caves or burrows – or simply hidden among rocks and dense vegetation.

The brown hyena of southern Africa is slightly smaller with a dark brown coat and distinct stripes on the legs. It lives near the shore, feeding on anything from dead crabs to the carcasses of stranded whales.

The smallest and rarest species is the striped hyena which is yellowish-brown with dark stripes. There is a long, shaggy mane along its back. It is found in North Africa, Arabia, the Middle East and India.

ORDER: Carnivora;
FAMILY: Hyaenidae.

Hyrax

The hyrax is a zoological puzzle. A small rabbit-sized animal, it has a skeleton similar to that of a RHINOCEROS and its nearest relative seems to be the ELEPHANT!

There are 12 species of hyrax divided into two groups: the rock hyraxes; and the tree hyraxes. They live in colonies in Africa and the Middle East. Both kinds have rubbery pads on their feet, which help them to climb over rocks and up trees. They eat leaves and grasses, but their teeth are unlike those of the RODENTS, which hyraxes resemble in appearance. The hyrax's brain is also unlike a rodent's and its stomach is nearer that of a horse. This curious mixture of rodent and hoofed animal may in fact be the nearest living relation to the long-extinct common ancestor of HORSES, TAPIRS, RHINOCEROSES, HIPPOPOTAMUSES and ELEPHANTS. To complete the confusion, the name hyrax is Greek for "shrew".

ORDER: Hyracoidea;
FAMILY: Procaviidae.

I

Ibex

Seven species of wild GOAT are called ibex. They all live high in the mountains but are a varied group. Most are larger and more thickset than the true wild goat or bezoar and their horns are broad and rounded in front with prominent ridges, especially among the males. The European ibexes are the Spanish ibex and the Alpine ibex. The walia is found in northeast Africa and the Nubian ibex occurs in Egypt, Arabia and eastern Mediterranean countries. Two species in the Caucasus region of the USSR are called tur, and the Siberian ibex is found in parts of central Asia.
ORDER: Artiodactyla;
FAMILY: Bovidae.

Ibis

Ibises are wading birds related to SPOONBILLS but with long, downward-curving bills. They have long spindly legs and long necks. Ibises inhabit marshes and mudflats, feeding on small aquatic animals. They usually nest in colonies in reeds or trees. Most ibises have magnificent plumage. There are about 25 species. The smallest, the glossy ibis, is about the size of a CURLEW. Its dark plumage shines with iridescent greens and purples. It occurs in southern Europe, Asia, Australia, Africa and around the Caribbean Sea. The sacred ibis lives in Africa south of the Sahara and Arabia. The scarlet ibis lives in tropical America, while the white ibis, also known as the

The **ibex** is one of the most nimble of mountain animals.

white curlew, ranges from the southern United States to northern South America.
ORDER: Ciconiiformes;
FAMILY: Threskiornithidae.

Ice fish

These pale fishes inhabit freezing-cold seas from the Antarctic to Patagonia. There are about 18 species, the largest being about 30 cm long and 2 kg in weight.

Ice fishes are pale because their blood lacks the red pigment haemoglobin, used in other animals to carry sufficient oxygen to meet the body's metabolic needs. Since ice fishes live in near-freezing water, they are sluggish – low temperatures slow down *metabolism*, so less oxygen is required. The amount absorbed into the blood plasma is sufficient for their needs.

Ice fishes having gaping, beaked mouths and goggling eyes. They feed on other fishes and shrimp-like KRILL, plentiful in Antarctic waters.
ORDER: Perciformes;
FAMILY: Chaenichthyidae.

Ichneumon

The ichneumons, or ichneumon flies, are parasitic insects belonging to the same large group as the

Left: A **scarlet ibis** of tropical America. Above: An **ichneumon** that develops in moth caterpillars.

BEES and ANTS. There are many thousands of species, nearly all of which grow up as parasites of BUTTERFLY and MOTH caterpillars. Adult ichneumons are generally fully winged, slender-bodied insects, and the female has a more or less prominent *ovipositor*. When searching for a caterpillar, she taps her long antennae on the vegetation to pick up the scent, and when she finds a suitable victim she injects one or more eggs into it with her ovipositor. The eggs hatch, and the ichneumon *grubs* begin to eat the host tissues. They

The green **iguana** is dewlapped and elegantly crested.

avoid vital parts, however, until they are nearly full grown. They then finish off the host and pupate either inside or outside its shrivelled skin. The host may have pupated itself by then, but it will never become an adult insect. The little yellow *cocoons* so common around shrivelled cabbage white caterpillars belong to a small ichneumon. The most spectacular ichneumon is *Rhyssa persuasoria*, with a 25 mm body and an ovipositor even longer. Although no thicker than a human hair, the ovipositor can be driven deep into a pine trunk to lay an egg with unerring accuracy on the grub of a horntail tunnelling in the wood.
ORDER: Hymenoptera;
FAMILIES: Ichneumonidae and Braconidae.

Iguana

The iguana family is one of the largest groups of LIZARDS, and includes such creatures as the BASILISK and HORNED TOAD, as well

as those lizards commonly known as "iguanas". Nearly all the 700 or so species live in the Americas.

The green iguana can grow about 1.8 metres long, but much of it is tail. Green iguanas have a crest and a large skin flap beneath the throat. Their pale green colour conceals them among the leafy branches where they live. These agile climbers eat shoots, fruits, flowers and leaves. They are at home among the tropical forests of Central and northern South America. Their worst enemies are birds of prey, cats, dogs and humans who kill them for their flesh.

Most iguanas live on the ground. Among these are the land iguanas of the Galapagos Islands. Males hold territories which they defend against other males. The Galapagos Islands are also home to the marine iguana. These big black or black and reddish creatures are the only lizards that swim beneath the sea to browse on underwater seaweed. The lizards crawl ashore to bask before the cold water chills them.

ORDER: Squamata;
FAMILY: Iguanidae.

Impala

One of the most graceful ANTE-LOPES, the impala is found in many parts of eastern and southern Africa. Impala like being near water and they avoid open country, preferring scrub and thornbush country. They mate at the start of the dry season and the single lamb is born after 180 to 210 days, early in the wet season when there is plenty of food. Impala live in herds except during the mating season, when the males establish territories, through which groups of ewes pass for mating.

The main predator is probably the leopard. When in danger, impala display an unusual alarm reaction; the whole group begins to leap into the air in all directions. This display may be intended to confuse the predator, which is trying to single out its victim. Impala are about 70 to 100 cm at the shoulder and weigh 60 to 70 kg. They are chestnut brown, with lighter brown on the flanks and a white belly. The male has lyre-shaped, ribbed horns which make one spiral turn. The female is hornless.

ORDER: Artiodactyla;
FAMILY: Bovidae;
SPECIES: *Aepyceros melampus*.

A handsome **impala** buck displays his lyre-shaped ribbed horns.

Indian buffalo

The Indian or water buffalo of Asia is an important domestic animal, noted for its docility. In this, it is most unlike its aggressive wild relatives. It stands 150 to 180 cm at the shoulder and weighs $\frac{1}{2}$ to 1 tonne. Wild buffaloes are black, but domesticated animals may be grey, black, pink or white. The horns are semicircular, spreading out sideways and backwards. There are populations of wild Indian buffalo in Sri Lanka, Nepal, North-eastern India and parts of South-East Asia. Wild Indian buffalo live in small herds, usually in swampy areas or near rivers.

ORDER: Artiodactyla;
FAMILY: Bovidae;
SPECIES: *Bubalus bubalis*.

The **Indian buffalo** is a useful domestic animal.

Insects

Of all forms of life, the most varied are the insects. More than 900,000 different species are known, and more are being classified each year. The number of individual insects is almost beyond calculation.

An adult insect has six legs, and a body in three sections covered with a hard casing known as an exoskeleton. Most insects have wings. Their eyes are made up of up to 30,000 tiny lenses, each lens contributing a tiny part of the whole view to the insect's brain. Insects have senses of smell and taste, and many kinds can hear, too. They breathe through fine tubes which branch throughout the body.

Some stick insects have bodies more than 30 cm in length, and some moths have wingspans of 25 cm, but their bodies are never very large.

The fist-sized Goliath beetle is the bulkiest insect, and probably as large as any insect could be.

Insects are grouped into 29 orders, each containing many families, genera and species.

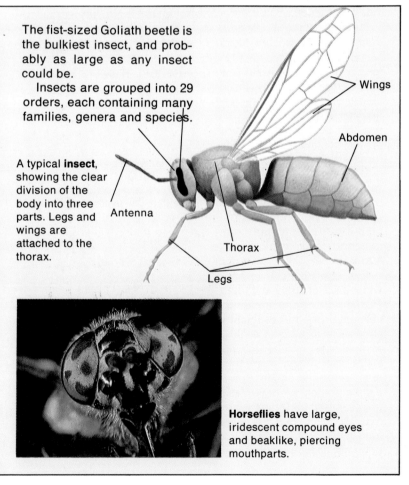

A typical **insect**, showing the clear division of the body into three parts. Legs and wings are attached to the thorax.

Wings

Abdomen

Antenna

Thorax

Legs

Horseflies have large, iridescent compound eyes and beaklike, piercing mouthparts.

Instinct and Learning

Every member of the animal kingdom is programmed rather like a computer. There are a great many actions that each performs automatically, with no experience and no lessons. We call this programming instinct. A good example of instinct is the first journey taken by a baby kangaroo after it is born. Kangaroos, like other marsupials, are born only partly developed. The tiny creature, only a little larger than a haricot bean, crawls through its mother's fur until it reaches the pouch on her abdomen. There it attaches itself to a mammary gland which supplies it with milk. Nothing can teach the baby what to do. Only two senses have developed, those of smell and touch.

Throughout the life of every animal, instinct will tell it to do certain things automatically — to run or growl if it sees an enemy, for example. In most invertebrate animals, such as insects and crustaceans, the brain is very simple. Almost all the actions of these creatures are instinctive. In vertebrate animals, such as fish, reptiles and mammals, the brain development is much greater. These creatures, particularly mammals, supplement their instinct with learning.

It is often difficult to know when instinct stops and learning begins. For example, the chick of a ground-nesting bird, such as a SNIPE or a GROUSE, instinctively crouches low and stays still when something flies overhead, even if it is only a falling leaf. But as it grows older the chick learns that the outline of a leaf or any long-necked bird is safe and does not crouch when it sees them. It crouches only when it sees a less familiar outline, such as the short neck and broad wing of a bird of prey. Instinct is still working but it is blended with knowledge acquired through experience.

Sometimes instinct triumphs over learning. Some infant monkeys separated from their mothers were given two "substitute mothers" — one a dummy consisting of a plain wire frame, the other consisting of a wire frame covered with soft cloth. Even when the wire "mother" was provided with a bottle from which the babies could suck milk, they invariably preferred the cloth "mother", which felt more like a real animal. The babies would also desert a heated pad which provided warmth and comfort in order to hug the cloth "mother".

The marvellous and apparently highly organized lives of such insects as BEES, WASPS, ANTS and TERMITES are controlled almost completely by instinct. The built-in "programme" leads each HONEYBEE in the hive to do a specific task or switch to another when required. For example, if an ants' nest is damaged the insects will at once try to repair it. This may be the result of learning or it may be yet another instinct that only comes into play when the nest is threatened.

Most bird behaviour is instinctive. Without ever having built a nest before, the SWALLOW piles pellets of mud on a ledge to form a hollow cup and the STORK makes a large, untidy nest on top of some tall object, such as a chimney stack. Birds migrate entirely by instinct. But learning also plays a large part in their lives. Though the first flight of a young bird is very wobbly, its flying improves with practice. Young birds also soon learn where the best food is and where danger lurks.

Learing plays a much larger part in the lives of mammals, particularly carnivores that have to learn to hunt. The most intelligent animals are APES, ELEPHANTS and DOLPHINS. One CHIMPANZEE under test even learned the value of money. It could obtain tokens from one vending machine by pulling the lever, and raisins from a second machine by inserting tokens. When the machines were set to work at different times, the chimpanzee learned to stockpile tokens ready for the raisin machine. And elephants hauling logs in the teak forests of Burma are always learning new ways to do their work. They have even been known to plug the bells they wear with mud and raid a nearby banana plantation unheard!

A **potter wasp** makes a clay cell, fills it with food, lays her eggs in it, then flies away. Later, a female offspring will instinctively do the same thing.

J

Jacana

The jacana is a wading bird related to the AVOCET, CURLEW and SNIPE but looks more like a long-legged COOT. Jacanas are often found in ponds, lakes and slow-moving rivers where they can run over soft water plants because their long toes spread their weight like snow-shoes. Also known as lily-trotters and lotus birds, the jacana often appears to be running over clear water when in fact its weight is being supported by just two or three stems. It feeds on water plants and small animals. There are seven species, living in the Americas, Africa south of the Sahara, Asia from India to the Malay peninsula, and eastern Australia.

ORDER: Charadriiformes;
FAMILY: Jacanidae.

A **jacana** steps out with a flourish of its immensely long toes.

The **jackal** is smaller and more lightly built than the wolf.

Jackal

Jackals are close relatives of the DOG and WOLF. They are found in wooded and savanna country in Asia and Africa though they often venture into inhabited areas to scavenge and feed on refuse. Jackals are hunters as well as carrion-eaters and scavengers. They prey mainly on GAZELLES. They are usually seen in pairs, but often hunt in packs of 5 to 20.

There are three species, all about the same size, with a body length of 64 cm and standing about 40 cm at the shoulder. The golden or Indian jackal, found in North Africa, Asia and south-eastern Europe, is a dirty yellow colour. The black-backed jackal, found in eastern and southern Africa, is greyish black on the back and light underneath, and has a black-tipped tail. The side-striped jackal, found in parts of central and southern Africa, has a pair of light and dark stripes on each side of the body and a white-tipped tail.

ORDER: Carnivora;
FAMILY: Canidae.

Jackdaw

The jackdaw is a member of the CROW family. It is renowned for its talkative nature and habit of stealing bright objects. It is 30 cm long and has black plumage shot with blue on the back and head and with a grey nape and pale blue eyes. Its short, but strong bill is black and so are the legs and toes. The jackdaw ranges through Europe except for the extreme north, across into North Africa, and into much of western and central Asia. Jackdaws live in flocks. Their natural home was probably cliffs and craggy hills, but they have readily adapted to

The **jackdaw** is usually seen in flocks, walking jerkily or playing acrobatically.

buildings, especially around farms. They feed on insects, particularly grubs, small vertebrates and seeds. The nest is a small platform of sticks with a lining of wool, fur, hair, grass and paper in any kind of hole in a tree, building or even a rabbit burrow.
ORDER: Passeriformes;
FAMILY: Corvidae;
SPECIES: *Corvus monedula*.

Jack rabbit

The jack rabbits are actually HARES, not rabbits. They live in the western United States and, like all hares, live above ground rather than in burrows. They can run at up to 72 km/h in a series of bounds, and the long ears help to detect enemies. Jack rabbits are found on dry plains and seldom drink, getting all the moisture they need from the plants they eat.
ORDER: Lagomorpha;
FAMILY: Leporidae.

Above: The long-eared **jack rabbit** of the western United States is always alert to danger.

Below: **Jaguars** are more heavily built than leopards and their coats have larger spots.

Jaguar

The jaguar resembles a heavily-built LEOPARD. It is the largest of the American cats. Head and body are up to 1.8 metres long and the tail is about 1 metre. It may weigh up to 136 kg. The mainly yellowish coat is patterned with black spots. Like those of a leopard, these spots are grouped in rosettes, but unlike the leopard's, the rosettes have a central spot. Black and *albino* jaguars also occur. Jaguars range from the southern United States to Patagonia.

The main home of jaguars is dense tropical forest, especially near water: jaguars are extremely strong swimmers. They climb well, often hunting their prey along branches. Among trees, their spotted coats provide extremely effective camouflage. Little is known about their habits, but it seems likely that they hunt in territories, each defending its own against other jaguars. These big cats take a wide variety of food. Their main prey is CAPYBARAS and PECCARIES, but they will tackle beasts as big as domestic cows, and will fight, kill and devour ALLIGATORS. They also catch fish: lying in wait on a low branch or river bank, and using a front paw to flip the fish from the water.

Jaguars breed at any time of year. A female produces 2 to 4 cubs every other year but little is known of their care. They have few natural enemies but sometimes PECCARY herds are said to corner and kill them. Jaguars are hunted where they prey on domestic animals and are also shot for their beautiful skins.

ORDER: Carnivora;
FAMILY: Felidae;
SPECIES: *Panthera onca.*

Jaguarundi

The jaguarundi or otter-cat, looks more like a weasel than a cat. It has a weasel-shaped head, short ears, a long neck and body, short legs and a long tail. The coat colour may be red or grey. Jaguar-

The colourful but elusive **jay** is best known for its harsh, scraping call.

undis live in warm forests and grasslands from the southern United States south to northern Argentina. They kill rodents and ground birds but instead of stalking and pouncing on their prey, as do most cats, they chase it. Jaguarundis readily take to water and often climb trees in search of fruit.

ORDER: Carnivora;
FAMILY: Felidae;
SPECIES: *Felis yagouaroundi.*

Jay

Jays are colourful members of the CROW family. There are over 40 species of jay, 32 of which are American. The most widely ranging is the common jay of Europe and Asia. It is 34 cm long and has a reddish-brown plumage, darker on the wings and back than on the breast. It has a white head streaked with black and the feathers are raised in a crest when excited. There is a conspicuous black moustache from the corner of the bill, but the most noticeable feature is the patch of bright blue feathers barred with black on each wing.

Jays are shy birds. The common jay lives in woods but comes out into the open at night to feed. It has a harsh cry and its flight is heavy and laboured. The diet is varied, and includes seeds, fruit and small invertebrates. Jays also eat the eggs and nestlings of small song-birds.

ORDER: Passeriformes;
FAMILY: Corvidae.

Jellyfish

Jellyfish are free-swimming members of the COELENTERATES. The typical jellyfish is shaped like an umbrella and may have four or eight tentacles around the margin. Some jellyfish have a great many

Above: A **jellyfish** trails its long, stinging tentacles.
Above right: A common jellyfish, seen from below.

tentacles forming a ring. Underneath the umbrella-part of the jellyfish is a short tube containing the mouth. The body of a jellyfish is nearly 99 per cent water. Yet despite this, jellyfish can be venomous for they have a great many stinging cells. A few species produce enough poison to kill a man. Most of them feed on small planktonic animals, but some of the larger species trap fish.

Jellyfish lay eggs, which soon develop into small *larvae*, and these in turn become *polyps* which are like very small sea anemones. The polyps in time produce jellyfish by budding. Jellyfish vary in diameter from 1 to 1800 mm.
PHYLUM: Coelenterata;
CLASS: Scyphozoa.

Jerboa

Known as the desert rat, the little jerboa looks more like a miniature kangaroo. It has hindlegs four times as long as its forelegs, and a tail longer than its body. When chased, it escapes in a series of hops, covering up to 3 metres in each bound.

Several species of jerboa live in North Africa and Asia. They survive the heat by living in burrows, coming out at night to feed on desert plants. They dig very rapidly, but normally escape by leaping rather than by burrowing. Jerboas need little water; they have survived in captivity for three years on a diet of dry seeds.
ORDER: Rodentia;
FAMILY: Dipodidae.

John dory

The John dory is a fish of the Mediterranean and eastern Atlantic Ocean. From the side, its body appears roundish but from the front the John dory looks very narrow bodied. Its fins are high and spiny and there is a round black spot on each flank. A legend says that the marks are where the thumb and finger of St. Peter pressed when he took a coin from the fish's mouth. When it is stalking its prey, which it has to do because its heavily-plated body prevents it giving chase, excitement causes its many-coloured body to blush and fade alternately.

It feeds mainly on small fishes such as young herrings, pilchards, and sand eels.
ORDER: Zeiformes;
FAMILY: Zeidae;
SPECIES: *Zeus faber.*

Jungle fowl

There are four species of jungle fowl. They belong to the PHEASANT family. The best known is the red jungle fowl of the warm regions of Asia. The male has magnificent red plumage with an iridescent sheen, and a bright red comb on the head. The female is duller. The domestic chicken is descended from the red jungle fowl, and the original plumage can still be seen in some chickens. The other three jungle fowl are the grey jungle fowl of India; the green jungle fowl of Java; and the Ceylon jungle fowl of Sri Lanka. All jungle fowls live in forests and are extremely wary. They scratch for food on the forest floor, just as domestic chickens do, and eat virtually anything they find. Breeding takes place during most of the year, but more often in the rainy season.
ORDER: Galliformes;
FAMILY: Phasianidae.

K

Kangaroo

Among the 55 species of kangaroo, the most readily recognized are the great grey and the red kangaroos. These Australian animals are the world's largest living MARSUPIALS.

The great grey or forester kangaroo lives mainly in open forest lands of Australia, where it browses on the vegetation. It stands up to 1.8 metres high and weighs about 90 kg. The thick muscular tail may be over 1.2 metres long. The coat is mainly grey in colour, paling to a whitish shade on the legs, the under-parts and under the tail.

The red kangaroo is found over most of Australia. It is similar to the great grey in build and size, but the male has a reddish coat. The female is generally a smoky blue colour. Red kangaroos graze in herds of about a dozen on the open plains.

The smaller rock kangaroo or wallaroo, sometimes called a euro, lives among rocks mainly in a few coastal areas. Its hind legs are more stockily built than those of the red or great grey kangaroo.

Kangaroos feed mostly at night. They move on all four feet when proceeding slowly, but bound on their powerful hind legs only, using the tail for balance. They can attain speeds of up to 48 km/h for short distances.

Baby kangaroos are called joeys. As a rule there is only one young in a litter. The joey is born at a very early stage of development when it is little more than 2.5 cm long. But it can find its way to its mother's pouch where food and warmth are available. The joey remains in the pouch for about six months. Even after leaving the pouch, the joey will return to suckle.

ORDER: Marsupialia;
FAMILY: Macropodidae;
SPECIES: *Macropus giganteus* (great grey); *Macropus rufus* (red).

The baby **kangaroo** remains in the pouch for about six months.

Kangaroo rat

Like JERBOAS, the kangaroo rats are well adapted to desert life.

They live in the dry regions of North America west of the Missouri river. There are 24 species, the largest being about 20 cm long.

All kangaroo rats have extra-long hind legs and long tails. Their only protection against their many enemies, such as foxes, owls and snakes, lies in their keen hearing and their leaping power. Kangaroo rats are active only in the cool of the night. They eat a variety of plants and collect food stores for use in times of shortage, carrying food in cheek pouches and burying it in pits, sealed with pressed down soil. The animals do not need to drink and get all the water they need form their food.
ORDER: Rodentia;
FAMILY: Heteromyidae.

Kestrel

The kestrel is a small FALCON found on all continents except Antarctica. The common kestrel often lives in towns, as well as in open woodlands. It can be seen hovering on gently fanning wings while searching the ground below for prey. Like most kestrels, it feeds on mice, voles, small birds and insects. The American kestrel, also known as the sparrowhawk, looks much like the common kestrel. The rarest of all falcons is the Mauritius kestrel.
ORDER: Falconiformes;
FAMILY: Falconidae;
SPECIES: *Falco tinnunculus* (common); *Falco sparverius* (American).

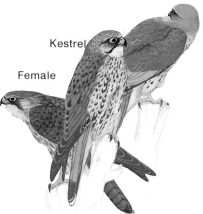

Lesser kestrel

Kestrel

Female

The **kestrel** is usually seen hovering close to the ground. The male **lesser kestrel** has unspotted wing feathers.

In captivity, **killer whales** are often playful and intelligent.

Killer whale

The killer whale or grampus is related to the DOLPHIN. But, unlike the dolphin, it has a reputation for ferocity and is one of the most feared hunters of the seas. Killer whales are boldly marked in black and white, with a large *dorsal fin* not unlike that of a shark. The males average 9 metres in length, the females being only half as long.

Killers hunt in packs. Included in their diet are whales, dolphins, seals, penguins, fish and squid. Killer whales have been seen to tip up ice floes to dislodge sheltering penguins, and the sight of a killer seems to terrify the victim so that it makes little effort to escape. Yet, in captivity, killer whales have proved intelligent and playful.
ORDER: Cetacea;
FAMILY: Delphinidae;
SPECIES: *Orcinus orca*.

King crab

The king or horseshoe crab is not a true crab but is related to the ARACHNIDS such as spiders. It has a horseshoe-shaped body, up to 60 cm long, covered with a tough

Above: The **kingfisher** captures its prey with a single, swooping dive.
Left: **King crabs** are not crabs at all, but are related to the spiders.

leathery *carapace*, a long tail spike and four pairs of jointed legs, three with pincers. The animal uses its spike as a lever to plough through sand or mud, or to right itself when it has turned over onto its back. It feeds mainly on molluscs and worms along ocean shores. There are four species: one in Nova Scotia, two in southeast Asia, and another in the Gulf of Bengal, Malaysia and along the Phillipine coast.
ORDER: Xiphosura;
FAMILY: Limulidae.

Kingfisher

Kingfishers are a large family of water and woodland birds. They are stocky birds, with long bills, short tails and often brilliant plumage. There are over 80 species, living mainly in the Tropics. The common kingfisher of Europe, North Africa and Asia is one of the most beautiful European birds. This sparrow-sized bird with its iridescent blue plumage is often found near rivers and streams. The only North American species, the belted kingfisher is a bigger bird. It is blue-grey above and white below and has a bushy crest. The largest member of the family is the Australian KOOKABURRA. Kingfishers nest in holes in banks or in hollow trees. The 6 to 8 white eggs are laid on the floor of the burrow.

ORDER: Coraciiformes;
FAMILY: Alcedinidae;
SPECIES: *Alcedo atthis* (common).

King snake

King snakes are harmless North American snakes that eat other snakes, even the venomous RATTLESNAKES. King snakes are immune to snake venom. But lizards, frogs and rodents form their usual prey. They attack by biting, coiling around the victim's body, and suffocating it. The common king snake grows to a length of almost 2 metres. The related milk snakes are sometimes called king snakes.

ORDER: Squamata;
FAMILY: Colubridae;
SPECIES: *Lampropeltis getulus.*

Kinkajou

The kinkajou is a relative of the PANDA and is found in Central and northern South America. It feeds at night, and spends the day resting on a branch or a hollow in a tree trunk. Although it is a *carnivore*, its diet is mostly fruit. Its soft, woolly fur is gold to brown in colour with lighter parts underneath. The kinkajou can be kept as a pet and is often called a honey-bear, for it is especially fond of honey.

The kinkajou is well-adapted to life in the trees. It has a long, supple body and its forelegs are shorter than its hind legs. The strong tail is adapted for grasping branches and can be used as a fifth limb. The young, which are born blind in litters of one or two, can hang by their tails by the time they are seven weeks old.

ORDER: Carnivora;
FAMILY: Procyonidae;
SPECIES: *Potos flavus.*

Kissing gourami

A South-East Asian river fish which has become popular in domestic aquaria. It is called the kissing gourami from its habit of pressing its thick lips against those of a member of the other sex of the same species. Quite possibly, this means the same thing as it does with human beings! These fishes are greenish or pinkish-white in colour and although small in aquaria, they can grow up to a

The gaily coloured Californian mountain **king snake** is harmless to man but attacks other snakes.

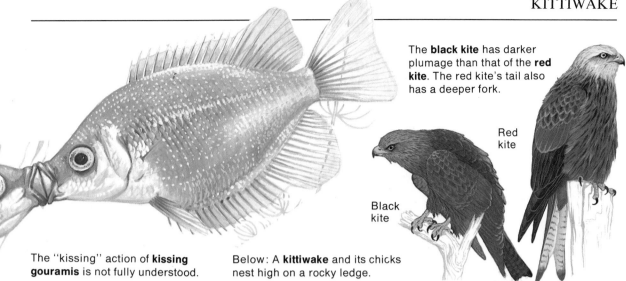

The **black kite** has darker plumage than that of the **red kite**. The red kite's tail also has a deeper fork.

Red kite

Black kite

The "kissing" action of **kissing gouramis** is not fully understood.

Below: A **kittiwake** and its chicks nest high on a rocky ledge.

length of 30 cm or more in the wild. Gouramis are among the labyrinth fishes, so called because they have a special organ in the gills which allows them to breathe air at the surface as well as under water.

ORDER: Perciformes;
FAMILY: Anabantidae;
SPECIES: *Helostoma temmincki*.

Kite

The kite is a bird of prey and a master of soaring flight. It has long, pointed wings and a forked tail. There are two species of true kite: the black kite and the red kite. Both are found throughout Europe and Asia, living in wooded river valleys or on the edge of forests. They hunt live prey and are great scavengers, feeding on any kind of dead animal food. They were once a common sight in many European cities. Similar birds include the Brahminy kite, which is the sacred kite of India, and the white-tailed kite of Africa.

ORDER: Falconiformes;
FAMILY: Accipitridae;
SPECIES: *Milvus migrans* (black); *Milvus milvus* (red).

Kittiwake

Unlike other GULLS, the kittiwake spends most of its time on open water, far from the shore. It nests in large colonies on cliff ledges and is rarely seen inland. The kittiwake

is a small bird, about 40 cm long. It is white with grey wings and back. It has a yellow bill and black legs. The bird feeds on a variety of marine animals such as crustaceans, squids and small fishes. It will sometimes follow fishing boats to feed on scraps.

Kittiwakes live in the North Atlantic Ocean and have been found within 200 km of the North Pole.

ORDER: Charadriiformes;
FAMILY: Laridae;
SPECIES: *Rissa tridactyla*.

Kiwi

The three species of kiwi are found only in New Zealand. They are flightless birds each about the size of a domestic fowl. They have a rounded body, no tail, stout but short legs with three toes on each foot, and a long slender bill with slit-like nostrils at its tip. The wings are only 5 cm long, and are hidden among the hair-like body feathers.

Kiwis live in pine forests. They spend the day hiding away in burrows or among tree roots, and come out at night to seek food. They move quietly, probably feeling their way with the bristles around the bill. Kiwis sniff out their food, which consists of earthworms, insects when the ground is moist, and fruits and leaves when it is dry.

Kiwis nest in hollow logs, among the roots of large trees, or in burrows in soft banks. The male incubates the eggs for as long as 80 days.

ORDER: Apterygiformes;
FAMILY: Apterygidae.

Koala

Looking much like a small bear, 60 to 90 cm long and weighing up to 15 kg, the koala lives mostly in trees. It is an expert climber and can scale smooth tree trunks with ease and speed. Koalas are reluctant to descend to the ground, but occasionally do so to lick earth,

The strange **kiwi** is a flightless bird the size of a chicken.

Right: A **koala** clings to its favourite eucalyptus tree.

possibly as an aid to digestion.

The koala has thick, ash-grey fur, tinged with brown on the upper parts and yellowish-white on the hindquarters. The animal's under-parts are whitish. One of the five toes on each of the front feet is opposed to the others, and the first toes of the hind feet are opposed. This allows the koala to grip branches more firmly than it could if it had a more bear-like paw.

Koalas feed at night. They climb up to the top branches of eucalyptus trees to eat the tender shoots. Most koalas eat only the shoots of 12 species of this tree, although koalas of certain regions of Australia restrict their diet to even fewer of these species. Like other MARSUPIALS, koala young are minute at birth and remain in their mother's pouch for at least six months.

ORDER: Marsupialia;
FAMILY: Phalangeridae;
SPECIES: *Phascolarctos cinereus.*

Kob

Kob are close relatives of the WATERBUCK and LECHWE. There are two species: the true kob, which ranges from Guinea to Uganda; and the puku, which is found in Zambia and part of Malawi. The true kob stands 90 cm at the shoulder and weighs 90 kg. The coat varies from orange or red to blackish, with white round the eyes and at the bases of the ears. The puku is smaller with similar coat coloration which differs only in detail.

ORDER: Artiodactyla;
FAMILY: Bovidae;
SPECIES: *Kobus kob* (true kob); *Kobus vardoni* (puku).

Komodo dragon

The Komodo dragon is the largest living LIZARD. It is a member of the MONITOR family. Males grow up to 3 metres long and weigh up to 136 kg. The dragons inhabit a few

The **kookaburra** is clearly a member of the kingfisher family.

small Indonesian islands: Komodo, Rintja, Flores and Padar. A Komodo dragon has a stout, powerful body and its toes end in long claws. It sleeps in holes among rocks at night and hunts for food such as deer, pigs and monkeys during the day. It also feeds on carrion which is found by smell. The larger lizards drive smaller individuals away from food by lashing at them with their powerful tails. Females lay their eggs in August, and these take until the following April to hatch.

ORDER: Squamata;
FAMILY: Varanidae;
SPECIES: *Varanus komodoensis.*

The **komodo** dragon grows to a length of over three metres.

Kookaburra

The two species of kookaburras belong to the KINGFISHER family. They are found in Australia but do not live near water. Their original habitat is open forests, particularly favouring gum trees, but kookaburras are now found in parks and gardens in Australia. The two species are the kookaburra, which is also known as the laughing jackass because of its chuckling cry, and the blue-winged kookaburra. Kookaburras eat anything animal, including large insects, crabs, fish, reptiles and birds. They are well-known as snake-killers.

ORDER: Coraciiformes;
FAMILY: Alcedinidae;
SPECIES: *Dacelo gigas; Dacelo leachi* (blue-winged).

Kudu

There are two species of kudu: the greater kudu and lesser kudu, antelopes with spiral horns. The greater kudu lives in remote, dry, hilly areas from lake Chad, through East Africa, to South Africa. The lesser kudu lives in scrub and desert bush in Ethiopia, Kenya and Somalia.

Kudu live in small groups, which may be all males, or all females with their calves. Some larger groups are mixed, with roughly two females for every male. Mating takes place all the year round and the young are born about seven months after mating. The chief enemies of kudu are leopards, lions and wild dogs. The greater kudu stands 127 cm or more at the shoulder. It has a thick mane extending to the back and a throat fringe. Its coat is reddish-fawn or blue-grey in old males. There are between 4 and 10 white stripes on the flanks. The lesser kudu is smaller. It has a yellow-grey coat and a scanty mane.

ORDER: Artiodactyla;
FAMILY: Bovidae;
SPECIES: *Tragelaphus strepsiceros* (greater); *Tragelaphus imberbis* (lesser).

L

Lacewing

The lacewings, or lacewing flies, are slender and often very beautiful insects with four delicate, gauzy wings. Most of the insects have a rather feeble flight. Best known are the green lacewings, with wingspans of about 25 mm, but there are many smaller brown species and a number of larger ones as well. Green lacewings are abundant in shrubs and hedgerows in summer, feeding voraciously on APHIDS. The females lay their eggs at the ends of hair-like stalks, which they produce from quick-setting gum. The *larvae* are flat, bristly creatures with large, curved jaws. The jaws are hollow and they are used to suck the juices from aphids. Many green lacewing larvae then fix the empty aphid skins onto the spines on their backs, making themselves look like piles of rubbish. Fully grown larvae pupate in silken cocoons. The adults are generally active by night, and often come into houses. ORDER: Neuroptera.

Ladybird

Ladybirds are predatory BEETLES with oval bodies in most species. The *elytra* are generally bodly marked with red and black or yellow and black patterns, to warn of their unpleasant taste. When handled, they give out a very pungent fluid. APHIDS and SCALE INSECTS are the main prey of both adult and larval ladybirds. The *larvae* are generally steely blue in colour, and they have an enormous appetite for aphids. One larva will eat several hundred aphids during its three-week-development. The ladybird *pupa* looks

Ladybird larva

Wings closed

Left: The **green lacewing** is one of several similar species. The adults and the larvae eat aphids.

Below: Like other kinds of **ladybird**, the 7-spot has a warning coloration that tells birds to keep off. The 7-spot larva (left) is steely blue with a few yellow spots.

rather like a shrivelled larva, attached to a leaf with a few strands of silk. Adults often hibernate in dense masses in roof spaces and other undisturbed places, and the same sites are often used year after year, although the individual ladybirds are different. There are hundreds of species.

ORDER: Coleoptera;
FAMILY: Coccinellidae.

Lammergeier

The lammergeier is a large VULTURE which lives in the high mountains of the Old World. It has a wing-span of nearly 3 metres and is a magnificent flier, gliding high over the peaks or close to the ground with equal ease. Tufts of

The **lammergeier** is a large, handsome vulture.

feathers either side of the bill give the bird its other name of bearded vulture.

Like all vultures, the lammergeier eats carrion. Despite its size, it is cowardly and will not approach a carcase until other vultures have eaten their fill. Lammergeiers are fond of bone marrow, and will drop bones onto rocks to split them. The nest is a mass of sticks lined with wool and other material. One or two eggs are laid, and the chicks are covered with white down. The lammergeier has been seen at great heights in the Himalayas, where it is quite common.

ORDER: Falconiformes;
FAMILY: Accipitridae;
SPECIES: *Gypaetus barbatus*.

Lamprey

Like the HAGFISH, the lamprey is an eel-shaped, jawless fish. Both are survivors of the earliest vertebrates. Its skeleton is made entirely of cartilage. It is easily distinguished from an eel by the seven circular gill openings behind each eye. The slimy body has no scales or paired fins. The only fins are the dorsal ones on the rear half of the body and a small one around the tail. There are about 30 species of lamprey, ranging up to about a metre in length. Most of them live in the sea when they are adult, but they all swim up the rivers to breed. In the sea the lampreys attack other fishes, clinging on with their sucker-like mouths and drinking the blood after rasping away the flesh with their horny teeth. In aquaria, lampreys may remain attached to the same prey for several days. They also eat carrion. Their well-developed eyes suggest that they hunt by sight and not by scent like the hagfishes.

Female lampreys lay eggs which give rise to slender *larvae* called ammocoetes. These live on the river bed for up to eight years, feeding by filtering small creatures from the mud and water. The larvae eventually change into

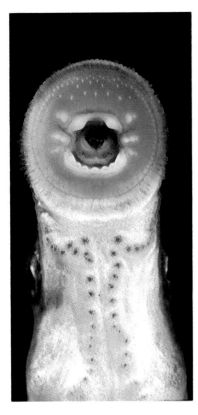

The **lamprey** has teeth on the surface of its mouth and on the tongue.

adults and swim down to the sea. Some species, known as brook lampreys, stay in the rivers all their lives, but the adults do not feed.
ORDER: Cyclostomata;
FAMILY: Petromyzontidae.

Lampshell

Lampshells are a group of about 260 small sea animals which look rather like *bivalve* MOLLUSCS. A typical lampshell is about 5 cm long, and has two unequal valves or shells, one forming the top of the animal, the other the bottom. The shell is usually a dull grey or yellow, but it may be red or orange. A short fleshy stalk projects from the rear of the shell, and most species use this stalk to anchor themselves to a solid surface such as rock. The lampshell has a complex feeding organ inside its shell. This consists of coiled arms covered with cilia – small beating hairs. These draw in a current of water, from which is filtered small food particles. Lampshells are found mostly in warm seas. The animals first appeared 600 million years ago, and fossils of 30,000 species have been found.
PHYLUM: Brachiopoda.

Lancelet

The lancelet is a small, fish-shaped sea animal. It is considered a link between the vertebrates and the invertebrates. Instead of a backbone it has stiff horny rod called a *notochord*. It has numerous gill slits, and also has many well-developed muscles all along the body. The animal lives in coastal waters, normally half-buried and straining food from the water with its gill slits. It is not difficult to imagine lancelet-like animals developing fins and backbones and evolving into the first fishes.
PHYLUM: Chordata;
FAMILY: Branchiostomidae.

Langur

Langurs are MONKEYS found in India and South-East Asia. One species, the golden snub-nosed monkey, lives in China. Langurs have crests of hair on the head and contrasting patches of naked skin. Most of them are slender with long fingers and toes and a long tail. Most langurs spend their lives in trees, the only exception being the Hanuman langur of India and Sri Lanka which spends more than half of the day on the ground. Langurs are leaf-eating monkeys.
ORDER: Primates;
FAMILY: Colobidae.

Lantern fish

More than 250 species of deep-sea fish are called lantern fish. They are so called because their small bodies bear one or more rows of light organs on each side. These look like brightly glowing yellow or green buttons. Each species has a particular pattern of light organs, which are used mainly as recognition signals between members of the same species. This idea is supported by the fact that lantern fish have large, keen eyes. Although they are deep-sea fishes, lantern fish rise to the surface frequently in search of PLANKTON food. At night this creates vivid displays of flashing, coloured lights.
ORDER: Salmoniformes;
FAMILY: Myctophidae.

Lapwing

The lapwing is the most familiar wading bird in many parts of Europe. It is distinguished by its long crest and black-and-white plumage. The black plumage has a green sheen, which accounts for its alternative name – green plover. It is also known as the peewit, after its call. Lapwings are found in Europe and Asia, extending from the British Isles to Manchuria. They live on open ground and perform spectacular flying displays, often plummeting to earth in a dizzy spin. Outside the breeding season, they gather in vast flocks that may number thousands of birds.
ORDER: Charadriiformes;
FAMILY: Charadriidae;
SPECIES: *Vanellus vanellus*.

The **lapwing** is also called the peewit after its loud call. It is found in fields and marshes and on moors; also at the coast in winter.

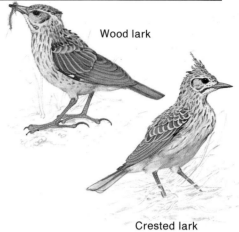

Wood lark

Crested lark

Above: The **woodlark** has a black and white mark at the front of the wing. The **crested lark** has a pronounced crest.

Left: A **skylark** feeds its young at the nest. The youngsters gape as soon as they see the parent with food.

Lark

There are 78 species of larks. They are found throughout the world, except in parts of South America and Antarctica. Most species are native to Africa; the New World has only one, and Australia two species. Small to medium-sized perching birds, larks have long pointed wings. They are birds of open areas, frequenting grassland, beaches and desert areas. They have a very musical song, often singing in flight – that of the SKYLARK being particularly well-known as the bird soars upwards. Most larks forage on the ground for insects and their *larvae*, small CRUSTACEANS, and plant food such as berries. Larks nest on the ground, making a scraped hollow near a grass tuft and lining it with grass and hair.
ORDER: Passeriformes;
FAMILY: Alaudidae.

Leaf beetle

The leaf beetles are a very large group of BEETLES whose *elytra* are generally smooth and shiny and often brightly coloured. Many have beautiful metallic sheens. With a few exceptions, both adult and *larva* feed on leaves. Several species, including the notorious COLORADO BEETLE, cause severe damage to crops. The flea beetles, named for their extraordinary jumping abilities, are very small leaf beetles which attack the seedlings of turnips and cabbages. The tortoise beetles appear to live under a shell, for the edges of the *thorax* and the elytra are drawn out well beyond the margins of the body. At rest, the "shell" is pulled right down to protect the beetle. Some tortoise beetles are brightly coloured, while others are green and blend in perfectly with the leaves. The bloody-nosed beetle is one of the largest and most fasci-

Leafcutter bees look something like small honey bees. The female cuts neat semicircular pieces from leaves.

nating of the 30,000 or so leaf beetle species. When disturbed, it often exudes red blood from its mouth, and the sudden appearance of the red colour alarms the would-be attacker.
ORDER: Coleoptera;
FAMILY: Chrysomelidae.

Leafcutter bee

Neat holes cut in the leaves of roses and other plants are usually the first signs that leafcutter bees are about. This bee, which is a solitary species, cuts pieces from the edges of leaves with its jaws, and uses the pieces to furnish its nest. The nests are generally situated in dead wood, and each consists of a narrow tunnel. The female bee carries the leaf segments one by one, neatly rolled under her body, and she fits them together in the nest tunnel to make a row of short, sausage-shaped cells. Each cell is provisioned with enough honey and pollen to support one bee grub. An egg is then laid in each one, and the nest tunnel is sealed up.
ORDER: Hymenoptera;
FAMILY: Apidae.

The nymph of a **leaf insect** blends perfectly with a leaf.

Leaf insect

Closely related to the STICK INSECTS, the leaf insects display some of the most amazing examples of camouflage found in the animal kingdom. Their bodies are green and almost as thin as the leaves on which they sit. Their wing veins are almost indentical to the veins of the leaves. Their short legs bear flanges which look like torn leaves and so conceal the outlines of the legs very effectively. The insects even sway gently as they sit on the foliage, thus copying the effect of the wind on the leaves. There are several species, all living in tropical Asia. They feed on the leaves of various trees and shrubs.

ORDER: Phasmida;
FAMILY: Phylliidae.

Leathery turtle

The largest turtle in the world, the leathery turtle differs from other marine turtles in that its upper shell consists of hundreds of bony plates embedded in a thick, leathery skin. Other marine turtles are covered in hard plates. Seven ridges run down the back, and five along the lower shell. Leathery turtles grow to 2.7 metres long and weigh up to 820 kg. Long, broad fore-flippers propel the turtles through the sea.

Stomach contents show that these REPTILES eat JELLYFISH and other slow-moving soft-bodied sea creatures. Females lay their eggs at night on warm, sandy shores. Each digs a pit with her hind flippers. She lays 60 to 100 white eggs the size of billiard balls. Then she fills the nest with sand. The eggs hatch in seven weeks, and the young race to the sea.

ORDER: Chelonia;
FAMILY: Dermochelidae;
SPECIES: *Dermochelys coriacea.*

Leech

Leeches are related to the EARTH-WORM. They all have 33 segments, and suckers at each end which are used as anchors during locomotion. The posterior sucker is usually much larger. Some have toothed jaws. Most small leeches live in ponds and streams and are predatory, feeding on other small *invertebrates* such as worms, insect larvae and snails. They may suck out body fluids or eat their victims whole. Others live on land in damp environments and are parasitic, sucking the blood from larger animals.

Best known is the medicinal leech, once used by doctors for "blood-letting". They attach themselves to the host's skin and inject saliva which contains an anaesthetic and an anticoagulant called hirudin, which prevents the host's blood from clotting. They gorge themselves, injesting many times their body weight in blood and storing it in special pouches. A fully grown medicinal leech can survive up to a year on one meal.

PHYLUM: Annelida;
CLASS: Hirudinea.

The **horse leech** is 30 cm long when extended, but can contract to an oval blob. It has nothing to do with horses.

Lemming

Lemmings are rodents found in the Northern hemisphere. Of the 14 species, the best known is the Norwegian lemming, whose mass migrations often end in death by the thousand.

The lemming is a plump little animal, 10 to 15 cm long, including its short tail. It has a thick grey or brown coat. Some species have a dark stripe running along the back. The lemming lives in the mountains, tunnelling under the winter snow to make snug burrows. It feeds on lichens, mosses and grasses. Winter is the safest time in a lemming's life, when predators such as HAWKS and OWLS cannot find it under the snow. STOATS and WEASELS can still find the lemmings, but these predators are less common in winter.

Every few years the lemming population builds up to abnormal levels. This usually happens after mild winters (during which lemmings continue to breed) followed by early springs and an abundance of food. As their numbers increase, the lemmings become agitated and begin marching in hordes. They will cross glaciers and lakes, and when they reach the coast, they swim out to sea. Although good swimmers, with waterproof fur, large numbers of lemmings inevitably drown when this happens. The ones to benefit from this behaviour are those that stayed behind, but then their numbers begin to build up again. There may be a population crash without emigration when numbers reach a certain level. It seems that during these population explosions, the lemmings become agitated and their body balance is upset, causing exhaustion and finally death. Afterwards the survivors settle down once more.

ORDER: Rodentia;
FAMILY: Cricetidae.

Norway
lemming

Wood
lemming

The **Norway lemming** has long
yellow-brown fur, with a bold
pattern of black streaks. The **wood
lemming** looks like a short-tailed
vole.

Lemur

Lemurs are a group of small
animals related to, but more
primitive than, MONKEYS. Lemurs
have bushy tails and large eyes.
They are confined to Madagascar,
living mostly in the forests but also
in dry scrubland. The word lemur
means "ghost" and some lemurs
have weird-sounding calls. They
eat fruit, insects and sometimes
small birds and reptiles. Apart
from humans, eagles are their
main enemy.

With the exception of the
specialized AYE-AYE, INDRI and
SIFAKA, scientists divide the lemurs
into three groups. The first group
contains the mouse and dwarf
lemurs, which are rarely more than
30 cm long, with bushy tails and
short, pointed faces. The coats
range from red to grey, with white
or yellow under-parts.

The second group contains
lemurs between 51 and 102 cm
long. They, too, have bushy tails.
The ring-tailed lemur is grey, with
a black and white, ringed tail. The
ruffed lemur is the largest lemur. It
is PANDA-like, black and white,
sometimes with some red.

The third group contains only
one lemur, the sportive or weasel
lemur, which is about the size of
the largest dwarf lemur. It has long
hind legs and is entirely vegetarian.

ORDER: Primates;
FAMILY: Lemuridae.

A pair of **ring-tailed lemurs** at ease
in their native Madagascan forest.
Some lemurs have weird, ghostly
cries.

Leopard

The leopard is a big cat of southern Asia and much of Africa. Males are up to 2.5 metres long, including the tail, and weigh about the same as an average man. Females are smaller. The colour and length of the fur vary with the locality and the climate. The background colour is usually a tawny yellow with whitish under-parts. The body is covered with small black spots, many arranged in rosettes. Some of these cats are black all over and are called black panthers.

Leopards live wherever there is plentiful cover: in forest, bush, scrub or on rocky hillsides. They are mainly solitary except during the breeding season. In areas where they are hunted they are nocturnal. Elsewhere they are active in early morning and from late afternoon into the night. They rest in thick undergrowth. A leopard will eat almost anything that moves, from DUNG BEETLES to ANTELOPES larger than itself. Generally it preys on the small and medium sized antelopes. Some leopards are partial to DOGS as food. When hunting for prey, a leopard may simply lie in ambush, camouflaged by the play of light and shade on its coat. It then leaps

Shaded from the noonday heat, a **leopard** rests in an African tree.

on passing prey, seizing it by the throat or sinking its teeth into its skull. Individuals sometimes develop a taste for just one kind of prey. This may explain the occasional man-killers and cattle raiders.

Leopards are very powerful for their size, and can carry a large kill up into a tree, where it is safe from theft by LIONS and HYENAS.

Breeding probably occurs at any time of the year. A female bears between one and six cubs, although three is the usual number. The cubs stay with the parents until nearly adult.

Hunters have killed countless leopards as farm pests or for their skins. At one time 50,000 were poached annually in East Africa alone.
ORDER: Carnivora;
FAMILY: Felidae;
SPECIES: *Panthera pardus.*

Leopard seal

The leopard seal is a true seal living on the outer fringes of the Antarctic pack ice. Up to 3.5 m long, it gets its name for its spotted grey coat. Unlike other seals, the female is always larger than the male. It is normally a solitary creature and, despite many statements to the contrary, it is inoffensive unless provoked. Its main foods are fish and SQUID,

which are easily caught and held by the large, cheek teeth. PENGUINS are regularly caught in some areas, the seal lying in wait near a rookery for a bird to dive into the water. The leopard's seal's mouth is so large that the smaller penguins can be swallowed whole. Leopard seal pups are born on the pack ice during the Antarctic summer, between November and January.
ORDER: Pinnipedia;
FAMILY: Phocidae;
SPECIES: *Hydrurga leptonyx.*

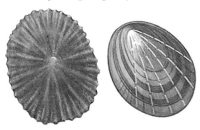

Common limpet   Blue-rayed limpet

The **blue-rayed limpet** is smaller than the **common limpet**.

Limpet

Limpets are a group of sea snails which have tent-shaped shells and cling tightly to rocks and other surfaces. Once atached, they are extremely difficult to dislodge. Under its ribbed, conical shell, which may reach 8 cm in length, the common limpet has a grey-green oval foot with a large flat adhesive surface. At the front is the head with its big, ear-like tentacles, each with an eye near its base. The limpet moves around underwater, and also when the tide is out at night, to feed, scraping algae from the rocks. But it returns to the same spot afterwards. It avoids drying up by holding a little water in its gills when the tide is out.
ORDER: Archaeogastropoda;
FAMILY: Patellidae;
SPECIES: *Patella vulgata* (common).

Ling

The common ling is one of several species of sea fish called ling. These

fishes are relatives of the COD, growing up to two metres in length but with narrow, rather EEL-shaped bodies. A closely related freshwater fish is the eel-pout or burbot. Ling are fond of pressing themselves into crevices, and for this reason they are often found in, or near, submerged wrecks. Ling feed on smaller fishes, and are themselves a valuable source of food for human beings.

ORDER: Gadiformes;
FAMILY: Gadidae;
SPECIES: *Molva molva* (common).

Linnet

An attractive-looking FINCH when in summer plumage, the linnet is an inhabitant of Europe, North-

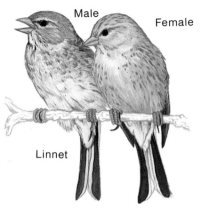

The male **linnet** has a reddish forehead and breast. The bird nests in low bushes and hedges, usually in open country.

Lionesses take their ease in a typical catlike way. In the evening, however, they may be very active at the kill.

West Africa, South-West Asia and parts of Central Asia. It is found wherever cover is provided by bushes, trees, hedges and brambles. The linnet is noted for its song, which is mainly learned, not inborn. They eat mainly seeds, especially flax seeds, and some insects and spiders. Linnets tend to nest in groups, their nests sited not far above ground. They lay 4 to 6 eggs at a time and there may be several broods a year.

ORDER: Passeriformes;
FAMILY: Fringillidae;
SPECIES: *Carduelis cannabina*.

Lion

This tawny-coated big cat is better known than its more solitary and

secretive relatives, the LEOPARD, JAGUAR and TIGER. Male lions are up to 2.7 metres long, including the tail, stand 1 metre high at the shoulder and weigh up to 250 kg. They have black or tawny manes covering the head, neck and shoulders. Lionesses are smaller and have no mane.

Lions were once common from southern Europe to northern and central India, and over the whole of Africa. The last lion died in Europe between AD 80 and 100 and in Asia they survive only in India's Gir Forest. They have been wiped out in northern Africa, and in southern Africa, outside the Kruger Park.

Lions live in open country where there is scrub, spreading trees or reed-beds. Their tawny coats camouflage them well among the tall tropical grasses of savanna lands. They live in groups called prides of up to 20 individuals, but occasionally as many as 40. Each pride contains one or more mature lions and a number of lionesses with their cubs. Members of a pride cooperate in hunting, to stalk or ambush prey. A lion is capable of speeds of up to 60 km/h, but only in short bursts.

In a hunting group, the lionesses most often kill the prey. The male lions eat first, the lionesses next and the cubs last. ANTELOPE and ZEBRA form the bulk of a lion's kill but almost any animal is taken, from cane rat to ELEPHANT. When age or injury prevents a lion catching large, agile prey it may turn to PORCUPINES or smaller rodents,

or to sheep and goats for its food. Occasionally they have been known to take to man-eating, attacking especially women and children.

Lions reach their prime at five years. A male will fight rival males and mate with several females. Pregnancy lasts 105 to 112 days. A lioness usually has 2 to 5 cubs, which are born blind. They are weaned at three months and start hunting for themselves at a year old. Meanwhile, because they feed last at kills, many cubs die from lack of food. This serves as a natural check on numbers. Apart from humans, lions have no natural enemies.

ORDER: Carnivora;
FAMILY: Felidae;
SPECIES: *Panthera leo*.

Little auk

The little auk is the smallest of the Atlantic auks and, perhaps, the most abundant of all the birds in the North Atlantic. It is only 20 cm long, and looks very different from other auks. It has a short, almost FINCH-like bill. Its plumage is black, with white under-parts and white patches on the wings and eyes. In winter, the upper part of the breast, throat and sides of the head become white.

Little auks breed in colonies on cliffs around the Arctic ocean. They range as far south as the shores of the British Isles and New England. Occasionally they may fly as far as the Mediterranean. The great auk, a flightless bird the size of a goose, was hunted to extinction in 1844.

ORDER: Charadriiformes;
FAMILY: Alcidae;
SPECIES: *Plautus alle*.

Lizard

Lizards are reptiles related to the SNAKES. Unlike snakes, lizards have an outer ear opening, and moveable eyelids. They cannot "unhinge" their jaws like snakes to swallow prey much wider than their heads. The 18 lizard families include about 3000 species – more than any other kind of reptile.

Lizards are mostly rather small, very active reptiles. The ocellated lizard is the largest of those illustrated, being 25 cm long, with a 50 cm tail.

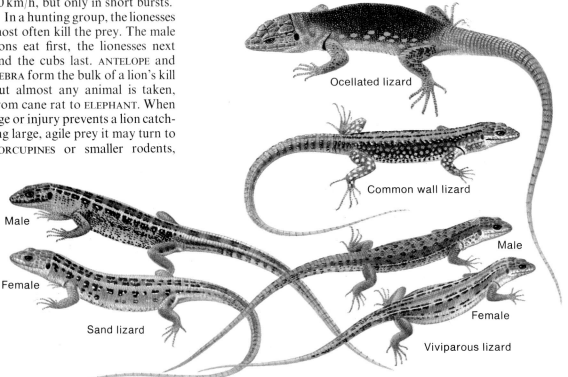

Ocellated lizard

Common wall lizard

Male

Female

Sand lizard

Male

Female

Viviparous lizard

The **little auk** nests in the arctic and spends the winter in northern seas.

At least one species ranges north inside the Arctic Circle. But most lizards live in warmer regions of the world and control their body heat by basking, then burrowing or lying in the shade. Some use special tricks like flattening the body to warm up quickly or standing on alternate feet to stop their toes burning on hot desert sand.

Usually, lizards have four well-developed limbs. But some have limbs modified especially to help them run, climb, or burrow. The FRILLED LIZARD sprints on its long hind legs. The GECKO family have toes that help them run up walls. The GLASS LIZARD group have smooth, limbless bodies that help them burrow.

Lizards generally eat live insects, spiders and other small creatures, although members of the MONITOR LIZARD family hunt larger prey and the IGUANA lizards include one *herbivore* that eats fruit, and one that feeds on seaweed. Lizards have many enemies and rely mainly on speed, camouflage, or hiding to protect themselves.

Most lizards lay eggs, but some bear fully-formed young. In a few kinds, mothers nourish unborn young by means of a *placenta*.
ORDER: Squamata.

Llama

The llama is a domesticated member of the CAMEL family. It is used as a beast of burden in Peru and other parts of South America. It is

Left: The **llama** is the most useful of the domesticated, camel-like animals of South America.

Below: Aquaria **loach** come in many colours and sizes. They all have pronounced barbels, seen head-on in the photograph.

well adapted to working at high altitudes and is sure-footed on steep mountain trails. It can be stubborn, however, when it is tired or when it considers a load to be too heavy. The llama weighs up to 136 kg and stands 120 to 150 cm at the shoulder. The llama is also kept for its meat, wool and hide. Its dense, coarse coat is white, brown or black in colour.
ORDER: Artiodactyla;
FAMILY: Camelidae;
SPECIES: *Lama peruana*.

Loach

The loach is a freshwater fish, living in the rivers and lakes of Europe, North Africa and South-East Asia. They are bottom-living fish with several pairs of *barbels* or feelers around the mouth that they use for detecting small prey. The smaller species are popular in aquaria, which they keep tidy by their "vacuum-cleaning" activities. Some species have adapted their intestine to absorb oxygen from the air.
ORDER: Cypriniformes;
FAMILY: Cobitidae.

Lobster

Lobsters are among the largest CRUSTACEANS. They live mainly

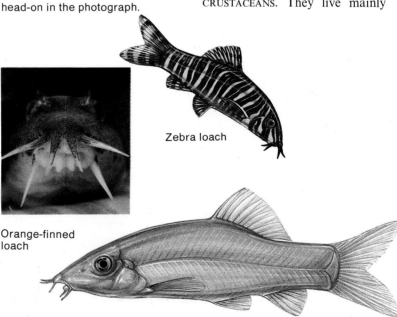

Zebra loach

Orange-finned loach

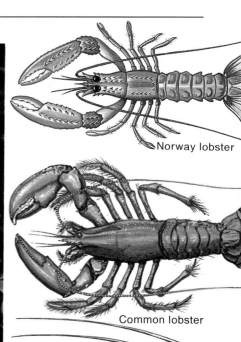

Norway lobster

Common lobster

Spiny lobster

around rocky shores and move over the sea-bed on four pairs of walking legs. They are often propelled forward by the beating of *swimmerets* under their abdomens. They have a pair of large pincers which reach out in front and are used for capturing prey such as CRABS, small fish, soft MOLLUSCS and even other lobsters. Lobsters have many enemies and often escape by shedding a limb

Above: A common **lobster** in its true colours.
Above right: The **Norway lobster** is only 10 to 40 cm long. It is marketed as scampi or Dublin Bay prawns. The spiny lobster is also called crawfish.

Below: A migratory **locust** perches on a leaf.

that is being held. They can also dart backwards to escape a predator. Lobsters grow by moulting the hard outer skeleton every so often. They replace "lost" limbs at the same time. They have dark green or dark blue shells which turn red when cooked.

The common lobster of Europe is found along the European coast from Norway to the Mediterranean. The closely related American lobster ranges from Labrador to South Carolina. It is similar to the European lobster but larger. Other kinds of lobster include the Norway lobster, or "Dublin prawn" which is flesh-coloured and the source of scampi, and the SPINY LOBSTER, CRAWFISH, or langouste.
ORDER: Decapoda.

Locust

Locusts are just large GRASS-HOPPERS, but they differ from or-

dinary grasshoppers in their tendency to form dense swarms and to migrate. They have huge appetites, and do immense damage to many kinds of crops. There are several species in the warmer parts of the world. The migratory locust ranges from southern Europe to Japan and Australia, although major plagues seem to build up only in West Africa. The most destructive species is the desert locust which inhabits dry areas from West Africa to India.

Locusts do not always live in great swarms. For much of the time, they lead solitary lives like other grasshoppers, but from time to time they congregate in particularly favourable areas – perhaps attracted by a good food supply. Once they become crowded, their behaviour changes and they bunch together in dense swarms.

Eggs are laid, and the resulting *nymphs*, called hoppers, band together in their thousands and march across the land, eating almost every plant on the way. They turn into adults, and these still bunch together in huge swarms. This phase, where individuals differ slightly in shape and colour from the solitary locusts, may last for several generations. During this time the insects cover vast areas. Swarms of more than 100 million locusts may build up, blackening the sky as they fly. Eventually the swarms decline and the locusts return to the solitary phase, in which insects do little damage.

ORDER: Orthoptera;
FAMILY: Acrididae;
SPECIES: *Locusta migratoria* (migratory); *Schistocerca gregaria* (desert).

Loggerhead

A marine turtle, the loggerhead lives in warm seas around the world. It swims farther into cool waters than other turtles and is the only turtle to breed on mainland coasts of the United States. Individuals wander far up river. Loggerheads grow to about 1 metre and weigh up to 130 kg. The loggerhead is olive or reddish-brown above and yellowish below. The arrangement of the shell plates and this REPTILES's large head distinguish it from the GREEN TURTLE. Loggerheads are extremely aggressive and eat fish, jellyfish, seaweed and other foods. They lay their eggs on beaches guarded by rocks and reefs.

ORDER: Chelonia;
FAMILY: Chelonidae;
SPECIES: *Caretta caretta*.

Longevity

All animals and plants, whether they live in the wild or in zoos, eventually grow old and die. No matter how well cared for, their bodies will age and deteriorate. Some animals have only a short life-span. MAYFLIES may live only a day or two as adults. Others, such as WHALES and ELEPHANTS, may live to be as old as humans. But no matter what age they live to be, they all go through the process of aging. A mayfly can be said to be old on the morning of the second day after it emerges form its nymphal stage; an elephant at 60. Both animals, although they live to very different ages, are going through a similar process. The difference lies only in the speed of the process. It is known that DOGS age six to seven years for every year a man does.

The length of life among animals is closely related to their size and the speed of their growth. Large MAMMALS live longer than small ones. Animals which mature slowly have longer life-spans than animals which mature rapidly.

Human beings outlive all other mammals, with proven records of 110 years and more. The oldest aquatic mammal on record was a KILLER WHALE which lived over 90 years, while the longest living land mammal, besides humans, was an Asiatic elephant which died at 69 years of age. On average, however, the longest-living *vertebrates*

The adult **mayfly** only lives for a few hours and never feeds.

are the TORTOISES. The oldest on record was a Mediterranean spur-thighed tortoise which died in a British zoo at the age of 116.

The average life-span of BIRDS is longer than that of mammals of the same size. The oldest age reported for any bird is 68 years for a female European EAGLE OWL. The oldest fish known is a STURGEON caught in Ontario, Canada, believed to be 150 years old. The oldest recorded age of an insect is of a wood-boring BEETLE known to have lived to 37 years of age. Some queen TERMITES are also believed to live as long as 50 years.

The life-spans of animals are shorter in the wild than they are in captivity. This is because an animal has to face harsher conditions in its natural environment. Mice live only a few months in the wild, even when they are not hunted. In the laboratory, the same strain of mice may live two to three years.

Above and right: Two **long-horned beetles** show something of the variety nature demonstrates in these insects. There are over 20,000 different kinds.

Long-horned beetle

Very long *antennae*, often much longer than the body, are responsible for the name of this group of BEETLES. Many of the insects are large, and many are brightly coloured. Their *grubs* develop in living or dead wood, and often cause damage to structural timbers. They can take many years to mature, for wood is not a very nutritious food. The adults eat pollen and nectar and the occasional small insect.
ORDER: Coleoptera;
FAMILY: Cerambycidae.

Lorikeet

Lorikeets are colourful little PARROTS distributed over the Malay Archipelago, Polynesia and Australia. There are 31 species, ranging in size from 15 to 40 cm. They are all mainly green, with patches of other colours – red, blue, yellow, purple, brown or black – on the head, neck and breast. Lorikeets feed on buds, fruit and flowers, which they crush to obtain nectar. They move about in flocks, following the seasonal blossoming of eucalyptus and other flowering trees. Flocks of lorikeets may descend on orchards and rob the fruit crop.
ORDER: Psittaciformes;
FAMILY: Psittacidae.

Above: The slender **loris** has huge, close-set eyes, adapted for its nocturnal life-style.
Left: The rainbow **lorikeet** of Australia.

Loris

Lorises are LEMUR-like mammals of the forests of southern Asia. They are closely related to the African ANGWANTIBO and POTTO. They have broad, grasping hands and feet and they climb with a very slow hand-over-hand movement. Lorises are nocturnal and have big eyes to help them see in the dark. They feed mainly on fruit and insects. They are solitary animals and sleep rolled up in a ball. Like lemurs, they have a claw on the second toe and comb-like front teeth. Both are used in grooming.

There are three species. The slender loris is found in southern India and Sri Lanka. It is 25 to 40 cm long and is grey-brown with black eye-rings. The slow loris is much plumper, with shorter, stouter limbs. It ranges from India through South-East Asia. Its colour is a greyish brown. The lesser slow loris has less woolly hair and is only 20 to 25 cm long. It is found only in Vietnam.
ORDER: Primates;
FAMILY: Lorisidae.

Lory

Lories are small parrots closely related to LORIKEETS. There are 25 species that live on the islands of the East Indies, notably New Guinea; and on islands in the south-western Pacific. Lories are somewhat bigger than lorikeets but have shorter tails. They are predominantly red in colour, with patches of yellow and green. Lories are very like lorikeets in their habits. They are also popular as cage birds, both for their bright colours as well as their "talking" ability.

ORDER: Psittaciformes;
FAMILY: Psittacidae.

Louse

Lice are small parasitic insects that live on the bodies of birds and mammals. There are two distinct groups – biting lice and sucking lice. All have very flat, leathery and wingless bodies. Strong claws help them to cling to the host's fur or feathers and, unlike FLEAS, there is no *metamorphosis* – lice spend all their life on the host. Their eggs are usually glued to the fur or feathers. Most of the 3000 or so species of biting lice attack birds and feed by scraping skin and chewing feathers. Their heads are usually as broad as their bodies. Sucking lice have very narrow heads. They live only on mammals, including people, and they suck blood.

ORDER: Mallophaga (biting lice) and Anoplura (sucking lice).

Lice cluster on a pigeon's feather. These lice have often evolved with the birds they parasitize, so that dissimilar birds can sometimes be shown to be related because their lice are similar.

Lovebird

Lovebirds are small PARAKEETS found in Africa. The six species are all about 10 cm long, and pairs of lovebirds spend much of their time huddling together bill-to-bill. This trait gives them their name; indeed, lovebirds do mate for life, unlike most birds. Lovebirds look like very small parrots and are generally green in colour. They are popular cage birds, because of their bright colours as well as their "loving" habits. They eat a variety of food, including seeds, fruit, nectar and insects. Flocks of lovebirds may damage crops.

ORDER: Psittaciformes;
FAMILY: Psittacidae.

Lugworm

Lugworms are BRISTLEWORMS which live in sand on the seabed.

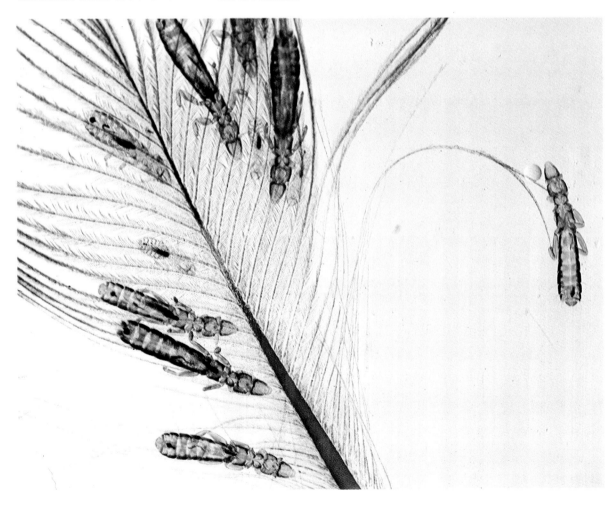

Lugworms are up to 30 cm long. They live in U-shaped burrows in the sand, where they stay swallowing sand from time to time. Small particles of dead animal and plant matter are digested, and the sand is passed through the lugworm, producing cylindrical casts which can be seen on beaches at low tide.
PHYLUM: Annelida;
CLASS: Polychaeta.

An attractive pair of red-headed **lovebirds**. The hen bird is on the right.

In an aquarium, a **lugworm** buries itself in sand. Its reddish, feathery gills are still just visible.

Lumpsucker

A fish of the North Atlantic, the lumpsucker gets its name from the sucker on the underside of its body. It is also called the henfish because of the devotion with which the male fish guards the eggs. The male is a dark-coloured fish, smaller than the bright-green female which may be up to 30 cm long. Both are stocky fishes who spend most of their time fixed to rocks or weeds by their powerful sucker. The female lays up to 136,000 eggs on the shore between low tide and high tide, so that the eggs are uncovered by water for part of the time. The male sits close by and whenever the eggs are covered with water he fans them with his fins to make sure they are all properly aerated, until they hatch.
ORDER: Scorpaeniformes;
FAMILY: Cyclopteridae.

Lungfish

A fish with a very long history, going back 350 million years. Today only six species remain; their only living relative – not a very close one – is the COELACANTH. As their name implies, as well as gills, lungfish have lungs with which they breathe air at the surface, although the various species do this to a varying extent. Also, all lung fishes use their gills to a greater or lesser extent for breathing under water. Most primitive of the lungfishes is the Australian lungfish. This large river fish may be 2 metres long and weigh 45 kg. It has large scales and flipper-like fins. It has a single lung and does not need to use this for breathing air when the water contains enough dissolved oxygen. The African and South American lungfishes are more slender, eellike fish with narrow fins. They have paired lungs and need to gulp air at the surface – if they are held under water they will drown. When the water in their shallow streams and pools dries up, these lungfishes burrow into the mud and remain there until the rains come, breathing air through pores in the dried mud. This summer rest is called AESTIVATION.

CLASS: Sarcopterygii;
ORDER: Dipnoi;
FAMILIES: Ceratodontidae (Australian lungfish); Lepidosirenidae (South American and African lungfishes).

Lynx

Lynxes are bobtailed members of the cat family, which include the CARACAL and BOBCAT. The European lynx which lives in northern Europe and Asia, can exceed 1.2 metres in length, including its short tail and weigh up to 18 kg. It has a short body, tufted ears, cheek ruffs, strong limbs and broad feet. The fur is sandy-grey or rusty red with white underparts, and black spots in summer. The Canadian lynx of northern North America is larger with longer hair and often lacks spots. The Spanish lynx of southern Europe is smaller and more heavily spotted.

Lynxes live in forests, especially of pine. They hunt by night using their keen sight and smell. Tireless walkers, they follow scent trails for hours and can climb and lie in

ambush for prey on branches. Lynxes hunt hares, rabbits, birds and even small deer. They also catch fish. A litter of 2 to 5 young is born in the spring. The kittens stay with their mother for 9 months.

ORDER: Carnivora;
FAMILY: Felidae;
SPECIES: *Lynx lynx* (European).

Lyrebird

The name given to two species of perching birds, native to Australia. Lyrebirds were discovered by explorers in New South Wales in 1798, and then called mountain

The **lynx** has tufted ears and a ruff round the face.

pheasants. The male superb lyrebird has a remarkable tail some 60 cm long. While displaying, the tail of the male is unfolded and raised like a canopy over its back, assuming the lyre shape which gives the bird its name. Albert's lyrebird is small and its tail less well-developed. Lyrebirds are also accomplished singers and can mimic other birds.

ORDER: Passeriformes;
FAMILY: Menuridae.

M

Macaque

Macaques are Old World monkeys, most of which live in southern Asia. They live in large social groups made up of both sexes and all ages. Macaques are difficult to define. Some species have long tails, some have short tails and some have no visible tails. Most are brown, but some are black. They have pink or red skin on the

face and rump. They are larger and longer-faced than GUENONS, but smaller and shorter-faced than BABOONS.

The two best known species are the BARBARY APE and the RHESUS MONKEY. Other species include the large Assamese macaque, the crab-eating monkey of South-East Asia, the bearded Tibetan macaque, and the sad-looking, pink-faced Japanese macaque.

ORDER: Primates;
FAMILY: Cercopithecidae.

Macaw

Parrots of the tropical forests of Central and South America, that extend from Mexico to Paraguay. There are 18 species in all. The biggest is the scarlet macaw or red and blue macaw which is 90 cm long. It is mainly scarlet except for

A family group
of **long-tailed
macaques**. The various
species of macaques
are the most numerous
of the Old World
monkeys.

Right: A blue and
yellow **macaw**, one of
South America's largest
parrots.

yellow and blue wing feathers, and blue lower back feathers and outer tail feathers. Other macaws, well known as cage birds, include the yellow and blue macaw, which is a rich blue on the head and back and golden yellow underneath, and the all-cobalt hyacinthine macaw.

Macaws move about the forest in screeching flocks, except when breeding. Most feed on fruits, seeds and Brazil nuts which they crack with their strong beaks. Their bright colours and social habits made them an easy prey for hunters, and several species have died out in the West Indies.
ORDER: Psittaciformes;
FAMILY: Psittacidae.

Mackerel

The common European mackerel is a streamlined food fish belonging to the same family as the TUNA and the BONITO. Several other species of mackerel are also important food fishes in various parts of the world. In their Atlantic home waters, common mackerel travel in big shoals to their spawning grounds, but then break into smaller groups for the rest of the time. They are caught in large numbers in nets or on long lines, or by spinning. In the water, and when first caught, a mackerel looks very handsome. Its ripple-patterned body shines blue-green above and silvery below – but its colours soon fade with death. Mackerel feed on small animals of the floating PLANKTON, except in winter months when they descend to the sea bottom to feed on SHRIMPS and other small crustaceans.
ORDER: Perciformes;
FAMILY: Scombridae;
SPECIES: *Scomber scombrus* (common).

The first dorsal of the **mackerel** has 11 to 13 slender spines.

The **magpie** may steal bright objects and store them in its nest.

Magpie

Magpies are members of the CROW family. Like their close relatives the JAYS, and unlike other crows, they are brightly-coloured birds. They have long tails which account for over half the total length of the birds. Magpies are found throughout the world. The common magpie is as familiar in Europe as it is in Alaska and Siberia. But it also lives in northern Africa, southern China and the western United States. In North America it is known as the black-billed magpie, to distinguish it from the similar yellow-billed

Most domestic ducks, though different in colour, are descended from wild **mallards**.

magpie of California. Magpies will eat almost anything from insects, slugs and earthworms to young rabbits, rats and mice. They are notorious egg-stealers, and also eat plant food. The nest is an elaborate structure made of sticks, cemented with mud and lined with fine roots, dry grass or hair. Usually 5 to 6 eggs are laid. In spring magpies are sometimes seen in excited groups of 20 or so.
ORDER: Passeriformes;
FAMILY: Corvidae;
SPECIES: *Pica pica* (common); *Pica nuttalli* (yellow-billed).

Mallard

The mallard is the most wide-spread of all the DUCKS. It breeds in most of Europe, Asia and North America. Throughout their range, the mallards move south in autumn to southern Asia, North Africa and, in America, to Florida and Mexico.

Mallard are often found on dry land, but are attracted to any water, from woodland ponds to large lakes. They are shy birds that feed mainly on leaves, seeds, fruits and tiny water animals. They either dabble in the mud or up-end in deeper water to feed from the mud at the bottom.

The male is brightly coloured from September to June, the most striking feature being the dark, glossy, green head and neck. Mating is preceded by a courtship ritual and the eggs are incubated in a down-filled nest either on the ground or in a tree.

ORDER: Anseriformes;
FAMILY: Anatidae;
SPECIES: *Anas platyrhynchos.*

Mallee fowl

The mallee fowl belongs to a family of turkey-like birds known as the megapodes, a name simply meaning "big feet". The megapodes, range from islands in the Indian Ocean to Polynesia and Australia, the mallee fowl itself being found in the dry scrub of Australia.

The **green mamba** is less venomous than the black species. It is a tree-living snake.

The megapodes are renowned for the way they hatch their eggs without using their own body heat. Some lay their eggs in ground heated by volcanic steam, while others lay their eggs in cracks in sun-heated rocks.

A pair of mallee fowl dig a deep pit in the sand and fill it with vegetable litter. When the rains come, the dead plants get wet and start to rot, giving off heat. The birds lay their eggs in the litter and tend them to make sure they do not get too hot to too cool. When the young hatch, they scramble to the surface unaided and can immediately seek food.

ORDER: Galliformes;
FAMILY: Megapodidae;
SPECIES: *Leipoa ocellata.*

Mamba

The mambas of Africa include one of the most venomous of all snakes, the black mamba. This is the largest of the mamba group, sometimes measuring up to 4.3 metres. It is also the fastest snake on earth, with an accurately recorded speed of 11 km/h. Speeds of 24 km/h may be possible in short bursts. A black mamba lives in dry, open bush country hunting birds, rodents and rock hyraxes. If scared, it speeds homeward to a hole in the ground, attacking any living creature in its path. Green mambas are shorter, less aggressive snakes, with weaker venom. Unlike black mambas, green mambas live in trees, seeking lizards, birds, bird's eggs and small mammals. All mambas lay eggs. Newly hatched black mambas measure 38 to 60 cm, and within a year, they may be 2 metres or more.

ORDER: Squamata;
FAMILY: Elapidae;
SPECIES: *Dendroaspis polylepsis* (black).

Mammals

Mammals belong to the animal Class Mammalia, and their most important characteristic is the feeding of the young with milk from the mother's body. They are all warm-blooded and, with the exception of a few WHALES, they all have a certain amount of hair or fur. Most live on the land, but the BATS have taken to the air and several orders contain aquatic species. The whales and SEA COWS are entirely confined to the water. The most primitive mammals are the echidnas and the duck-billed PLATYPUS, and, unlike all other mammals, they lay eggs.

The marsupial order contains pouched mammals such as the KANGAROOS, WOMBATS, and KOALAS. Their babies are born at a very early stage and then kept for some time in a pouch on the mother's body.

The other 17 orders of mammals are known as placentals. Their babies remain in the mother's body for a longer period and are nourished through a special organ called the *placenta*. Food from the mother's blood passes into the baby's blood stream where the two sets of blood vessels come together in the placenta. There are about 4000 species of placental mammals, of which almost half are rodents (rats, mice, squirrels etc.) The bats account for about a quarter of the placental species, and other major orders include the Carnivora (the cats and dogs and other flesh-eaters), the Primates (monkeys, apes, and man), and hoofed mammals.

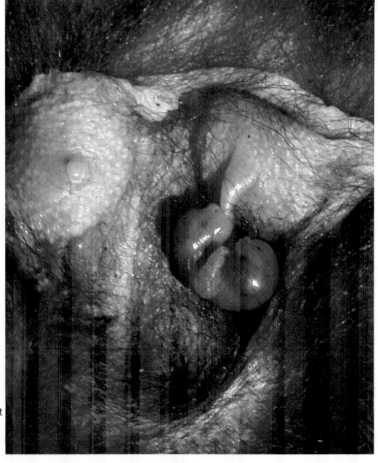

Top: The **orang utan** is one of 4000 kinds of warm-blooded animals that suckle their young.
Right: The pouch of an **opossum**, opened to show the newborn baby.

Mandrill

The mandrill is a forest-living BABOON, found in Cameroon, Equatorial Guinea, Gabon and Zaire. It grows up to 84 cm long. The male has a striking appearance. His coat is generally dark brown, with white cheek whiskers, an orange-yellow beard and a dark crest on the head. The nose is bright red and the ridges of the muzzle are bright blue. There is also a blue patch on the rump. The female, in comparison, is quite drab. The drill is related to the mandrill, but is slightly smaller and less colourful. It has a black face, surrounded by a white ruff, and is found in Cameroon, Gabon and south-eastern Nigeria Mandrills and drills live in small family groups, spending most of the time on the forest floor.

ORDER: Primates;
FAMILY: Cercopithecidae;
SPECIES: *Papio sphinx* (mandrill); *Papio leucophaeus* (drill).

Maned wolf

The maned wolf is a South American FOX and one of the largest members of the dog family. It has long, slim legs, and stands 76 cm at the shoulder. Its body length, including the head, is 127 cm, and it weighs 23 kg. Its coat is reddish-brown and it has a mane of long hair on the back of its neck, and shoulders. The mane rises when the animal is excited.

The maned wolf has no natural enemies, but is hunted by humans in Brazil and Argentina, where it lives in small areas of forest interspersed with open country. It is a solitary nocturnal animal that preys on small rodents, birds, reptiles and insects. It also eats fruit, sugar cane and other plant food.

ORDER: Carnivora;
FAMILY: Canidae;
SPECIES: *Chrysocyon brachyurus.*

A leaflike **mantis** makes short work of a moth it has seized with its long, hooked forelegs.

Mannikin

Mannikins are small seed-eating birds, measuring up to 110 mm long. There are several species, the largest of which is the Java sparrow. Two common species, popular as cage birds, are the spice finch and the Bengalese finch. The latter has been produced by breeding, and is unknown in the wild. Mannikins are found mainly in the tropics of Asia, ranging from India to New Guinea. Some are found in northern Australia and Africa. They frequent open country, especially near water.

ORDER: Passeriformes;
FAMILY: Estrildidae.

Mantis

The mantises, better known as praying mantises, are predatory insects related to the COCKROACHES. They feed on a wide variety of other insects, especially grasshoppers, flies, moths and butterflies. Prey is caught mainly by ambushing. The mantis sits still, usually well camouflaged by the surrounding vegetation, and waits for the victim to appear. The large eyes pick up the slightest movement, and the mantis swivels its head to face the prey. The spiky front legs are held up in front of the head at this stage – hence the name praying mantis – but when

the prey comes within range the legs shoot out at high speed and the victim is seized and held. The legs are drawn in just as quickly and the strong jaws get to work to chew up the food. A very hungry mantis will stalk prey instead of waiting for it to arrive.

The females are larger than the males, and often start to eat them before mating is complete. Mantises themselves have enemies among the birds, but they often defend themselves by making a hissing noise. They do this by raising the wings and rubbing the abdomen against them. Mantises seldom use their wings to fly far.

There are about 1800 species, most of which live in tropical regions, but several occur in Europe and North America. The European mantis lives in the Mediterranean region and has been introduced into eastern North America. The Chinese mantis a native of eastern Asia, has also been introduced to North America. It is the largest mantis in that continent.

ORDER: Dictyoptera.

Mantis fly

Mantis flies look and behave like praying MANTISES, but have more delicate wings. They are actually close relatives of the LACEWING and are not true flies. The resemblance to a mantis is a good example of how nature causes two creatures to come to look alike because they have similar habits. Young mantis flies grow up inside the egg *cocoon* of WOLF SPIDERS. Most mantis flies live in the Tropics, but a few species occur in southern Europe and the Americas.

ORDER: Neuroptera;
FAMILY: Mantispidae.

Marabou

The marabou is a most unattractive STORK, with a pink, almost bald, head and neck, a long, thick bill, and an ugly fleshy pouch hanging from its throat. The lack of feathers is probably an adap-

The nearly naked head of the **marabou** is an advantage when the bird is feeding on carrion.

tation for eating dead flesh, for feathers would become matted with bood while feeding on a large carcass. The marabou lives in eastern Africa, where it feeds, as VULTURES do, on the carcasses of big game. But marabou also flock around slaughter-houses and rubbish dumps in human settlements. On lake shores they clear up fish offal left by fishermen. Marabou are 120 cm tall and the wingspan is more than 2.4 metres. The back, wings and tail are dark grey and the under parts are white. The legs are mainly grey. Closely related birds are the adjutant STORK and the lesser adjutant of India and Borneo.

ORDER: Ciconiiformes;
FAMILY: Ciconiidae;
SPECIES: *Leptoptilus crumeniferus*.

Markhor

The markhor is a magnificent wild GOAT. The male stands 90 cm at the shoulder and his spiral horns measure between 76 to 165 cm. Females are smaller and have far shorter horns. The coat is light

The **markhor** is a wild goat with magnificent twisted horns.

foxy to sandy in summer and grey in winter. Both sexes have beards which reach lengths of 20 cm. The markhor lives in small herds in the mountains of Afghanistan, Pakistan, Kashmir, and Turkmenia in the USSR.
ORDER: Artiodactyla;
FAMILY: Bovidae;
SPECIES: *Capra falconeri*.

Marlin

Probably the fastest of all swimmers, marlins are powerful, streamlined fishes. They have a long, slender beak rather like that of a swordfish. The *dorsal fin*, however, is lower and longer than the swordfish's. The largest of the various species of marlin can reach a length of 4 metres and a weight of more than 680 kg. Even the smaller white marlin grow as long as 3 metres. Swimming at speeds of up to 80 km/h or more, they pursue shoals of smaller fish for days on end, catching up and striking with their beaks, and then feeding at leisure on the dead prey. They are sometimes the prey of large SHARKS – but few sharks swim fast enough to catch them.
ORDER: Perciformes;
FAMILY: Istiophoridae.

Marmoset

The marmosets of South America are the smallest of all the MONKEYS. These lively animals live in family groups in the upper parts of trees, feeding on insects, fruit and leaves. Most marmosets are about 20 cm long, with a 30 cm long tail. But the brown pygmy marmoset is less than 15 cm long and is the world's smallest monkey. It occurs in the upper Amazon region. The common marmoset lives in the coastal region of Brazil. It has silky fur, marbled with black and grey. The head is black, with long, white tufts of hair around the ears. Three or four other species are also found in the Brazilian coastal

Young prairie **marmots** at the entrance to their burrow. The members of a family show great affection for each other.

region. Marmosets are regarded as primitive because they have claws instead of nails on their toes and fingers (except the big toe). Hence they are put, together with TAMARINS, in a separate family from the other South American monkeys.
ORDER: Primates;
FAMILY: Callithricidae;
SPECIES: *Callithrix jacchus* (common).

Marmot

These burrowing rodents occur in Europe, Asia and America. Among the best known species are the alpine marmot and the bobak (both European) and the prairie marmot or prairie dog of North America.

The alpine marmot grows up to

60 cm long, and lives on mountain pastures. The bobak prefers the steppes or grasslands. Marmots are stout, short-legged animals with coarse brownish fur. The hoary marmot is silvery grey. All marmots are vegetarian but unlike most other ground squirrels, they have no cheek pouches for carrying food. They make nests in burrows, sleeping in nests of dry grass.

The marmot's main enemies are foxes and eagles. Living in colonies gives some protection to the marmots, who appear to post sentinels to keep watch while the rest feed. At the first sign of danger, the sentinels' shrill whistles send the marmots scurrying for the safety of their burrows. In practice, it is individuals feeding on the edge of the colony who first spot danger and whistle, so alerting the others. But whether planned or not, the marmot's "early warning system" works very well.

ORDER: Rodentia;
FAMILY: Sciuridae;
SPECIES: *Marmota marmota* (alpine); *Marmota bobak* (bobak).

Marsupial frog

The females of these South American tree frogs carry their spawn in a pouch on their back. When a female lays eggs, she raises her back so the eggs roll into the pouch. Then the mouth of the pouch closes, and the eggs inside hatch into tadpoles that are released in water, or stay in the pouch until they are froglets.

ORDER: Salientia;
FAMILY: Hylidae.

Marsupial mole

Most marsupial moles grow to a length of only 9 cm, but a few reach 18 cm. They range from the deserts of south-central to northwestern Australia. The marsupial mole is much like the true mole, except that the female has a pouch for her young. The mole tunnels about 8 cm below the surface, using cloven scoops formed by enlarged curved claws on the third and fourth toes of its forefeet.

ORDER: Marsupialia;
FAMILY: Notoryctidae;
SPECIES: *Notoryctes typhlops.*

Marsupial mouse

Several kinds of marsupial mice live in the scrub and desert of Australia. True mice – which marsupial mice closely resemble – have a pair of *incisors* in each jaw, but marsupial mice have eight in the upper and six in the lower jaw. They are flesh or insect-eaters and belong to the same family as the other marsupial carnivores, such as the TASMANIAN DEVIL and the thylacine. Marsupial mice have pouches for their young, but in some species the pouch is no more than a fold of skin round the teats.

ORDER: Marsupialia;
FAMILY: Dasyuridae.

Marten

Martens belong to the same family as BADGERS and WEASELS. About 10 species are found in Europe, Asia and North America, ranging from 40 to 100 cm in body length. They are excellent climbers, ascending and descending trees headfirst. They leap from branch to branch using their tails as para-

Marsupial

A marsupial is an animal with a pouch in which the mother can carry her young. Marsupials were common in many parts of the world about 100 million years ago, when dinosaurs were stll roaming the Earth. But they died out everywhere except Australia, New Guinea and South America. In these places, more advanced animals did not develop to compete with the marsupials. Eventually, South America joined up with North America and one group of the South American marsupials moved north. These are the OPOSSUMS.

Ordinary mammals produce fully developed young,

One of the smaller marsupials, a **bandicoot** forages for food on a forest floor in Australia.

even though they are small and helpless. But marsupial babies are much smaller and only partly formed. When they are born they have just enough strength to make the difficult journey across their mother's abdomen and into her pouch. There they stay, sucking milk from teats, until they are big enough to venture into the outside world.

There are about 250 species of marsupials. Many are the equivalents of ordinary mammals in other parts of the world. For example, there are marsupials similar to DOGS, CATS, MICE, RATS, MOLES, BADGERS and SQUIRRELS – but they have all evolved quite independently.

chutes. They are solitary, nocturnal animals.

The pine marten and the beech marten are European species. They hunt squirrels and other rodents, rabbits and birds, and will also eat insects and fruit. The American marten has a similar diet. The fisher is so called because it is said to catch fish. But it probably eats only spent salmon, and fish stolen from traps and

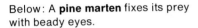

Below: A **pine marten** fixes its prey with beady eyes.

Beech marten

Cretan form

The **beech marten** is similar to the pine marten but with a pure white throat patch. In Crete the throat patch is much reduced.

The **pine marten** has a conspicuous yellowish throat patch.

nets. It also catches BEAVERS, American martens and PORCU-PINES

Martens mate in July or August, but the young are not born until April, due to a delay in the gestation process. The young (usually 3 or 4, but sometimes as many as 7) are reared in a grass nest among the rocks, in a hollow tree, or in a crow's or squirrel's nest.
ORDER: Carnivora;
FAMILY: Mustelidae.

Martial eagle

The largest African eagle is the martial eagle. It is found south of the Sahara, usually in grassland or semi-desert. Like the CROWNED EAGLE, it has a crest of feathers on its head. It has large wings, spanning almost 3 metres, and its plumage is dark grey above with white, speckled under-parts. Martial eagles prey on small mammals and birds, swooping down on their victims from a great height.

Unfairly persecuted by farmers, these rather shy eagles do less damage to domestic animals than was formerly thought.
ORDER: Falconiformes;
FAMILY: Accipitridae;
SPECIES: *Polemaetus bellicosus*.

Martin

The name given to a number of birds in the SWALLOW family. The house martin breeds in Europe, most of Asia as far east as Japan, and in North Africa. Its tail is less forked than a swallow's, the upper-parts are blue-black, the under-parts are white, and it has a white rump which easily distinguishes it from a swallow. The sand martin, which is smaller and more slender than the house martin, ranges around the world. It is found in most of America north of Mexico, and in most of Europe and Asia. It is also found from Egypt to Ethiopia.
ORDER: Passeriformes;
FAMILY: Hirundinidae;
SPECIES: *Delichon urbica* (house); *Riparia riparia* (sand).

The **house martin** builds a mud nest with a tiny entrance hole. The **sand martin** nests in holes dug in banks of rivers, and also in cliffs.

House martin

Sand martin

Mayfly

Mayflies are slender insects with large flimsy wings, and two or three long tail filaments. Adult insects never feed, and often live for only a few hours – but the *nymphs* live in water for one or more years. The nymphs eat a variety of plant and animal materials, and all have three tails. They breathe with the aid of feathery gills on the sides of the body.

A cluster of **mayflies** on a branch.

When fully grown, the nymphs come to the surface. The winged insects rapidly break out of their skins and fly away.

Mayflies are unique among insects because they undergo one further moult after getting their wings. The final moult may occur within minutes of leaving the water, transforming a rather dull, hairy insect into a shiny one. The mayflies may swarm over the water prior to mating, but are generally weak fliers. There are over 1000 known species, but only those in Europe and North America have been studied. Many more species must still exist, undescribed.
ORDER: Ephemeroptera.

Menhaden

A close relative of the HERRING, the menhaden is also an important food fish. It lives in enormous shoals off the eastern coast of the USA. About 40 cm long, it has a deeper body and a larger head than a herring, and its body is covered with scales of a bluish-silvery colour.

Large catches of menhaden are made from boats using purse seine nets. They are used for fish meal, as fertilizers, and for their oil. But menhaden are food fishes not only for people but also for many other fishes, including TUNA and BLUE-FISH. Schools of bluefish often cause tremendous carnage in shoals, killing tens of thousands of menhaden and driving thousands more on to the shore.
ORDER: Clupeiformes;
FAMILY: Clupeidae;
SPECIES: *Brevoortia tyrannus*.

Merganser

Mergansers are often called saw-bills because of their long, pointed bills set with backward-pointing "teeth". There are several species of the bird, all of which migrate south in winter. The red-breasted merganser breeds in the northern parts of Europe, Asia and America. The male has a chestnut breast, bottle green head with a stiff double crest sticking out backwards, and a red bill. The common merganser, or goosander, which lives farther south, does not have the chestnut breast. Mergansers eat fish and other freshwater animals. Mating occurs with the female underwater, pushed there by the weight of the male on top and is preceded by a spectacular courtship, involving much racing to and fro. Red-breasted mergansers nest on the ground; goose-anders nest in trees.
ORDER: Anseriformes;
FAMILY: Anatidae;
SPECIES: *Mergus serrator* (red-breasted); *Mergus merganser* (common).

A male **red-breasted merganser** performing its courtship dispay. The colours of the female are quite different (below).

Female

Male

Merlin

The merlin is also known as the pigeon hawk. It is a small FALCON, slightly larger than a THRUSH, and breeds in both the Old and New Worlds. It prefers open country, such as moorland, and preys on

The **merlin** catches its prey with swift pounces.

small birds, reptiles and insects. When hunting, the merlin does not dive down like other falcons but chases its prey in rapid dashes, pouncing on it in the air or on the ground. Merlins are unusual for birds of prey in that they sometimes store food beneath clumps of heather. They nest among low ground vegetation, or in abandoned crows' or ravens' nests and defend their territories aggressively. Ground nests are seldom more than a shallow scrape, lined with a little vegetation.
ORDER: Falconiformes;
FAMILY: Falconidae;
SPECIES: *Falco columbarius*.

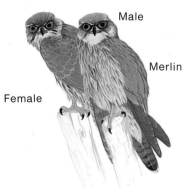

Male

Merlin

Female

The male **midwife toad** carries a string of eggs wrapped round its hind legs.

Midwife toad

The midwife toad is so named because of its strange breeding habits. By manipulating the female's body, the male persuades her to lay her eggs. Then he wraps the string of 20 to 100 yellowish eggs around his hind legs, and walks off. For the next three weeks he carries the eggs, resting in a burrow by day and feeding by night. On dry nights he moistens the eggs in water. When they are ready to hatch he enters the water and the tadpoles swim free. Midwife toads are greyish or light brown and are only 4 to 6 cm long. They live in western Europe.
ORDER: Salientia;
FAMILY: Discoglossidae;
SPECIES: *Alytes obstetricans*.

Migration

Of all the journeys undertaken by animals, the best known are the annual migrations of birds. A great many birds rear their young in the temperate lands of the north, where insects and other food are plentiful during the summer. When the food grows scarce and the weather is cold, they migrate south to warmer places where food is available.

Birds find their way over enormous distances with astonishing accuracy. A swallow, for example, can fly from France to South Africa, and return not only to the same country but to the very place it built its nest the year before.

It seems that birds navigate in much the same way as sailors once did, using the Sun, Moon and stars to guide them. To navigate in this way a sailor needs to plot the position of the Sun or other heavenly body and to have an accurate clock so that he can tell in which direction the Sun should be in relation to himself. It took men thousands of years to make instruments that do this. But birds apparently have such devices built in.

Birds, and many other animals, do have some form of internal chronometer by which they can tell the time of day. We do not yet know what it is or how it works. But we do know that in a bird's eye, attached to the retina, is a tiny projection rather like a sextant, helping the bird to calculate the Sun's positon.

Birds, however, fly at night and in cloudy weather when there is no Sun to help them. Experiments with birds in a planetarium show that they use star patterns to guide them when the stars are visible. When there is no visible aid they seem to use the Earth's magnetic field as their guide. Tests with birds in metal chambers shielding them from the Earth's magnetism have proved that a bird's brain also has a built-in compass.

Birds also use ordinary vision for finding their way over short distances, just as the pilot of a light aircraft uses landmarks to find his way back to an airfield.

In some ways even more amazing, because of their size, are the journeys made by insects. Monarch butterflies spend the summer in Canada and the northern United States. In autumn they fly south to winter in the southern states and Mexico. Other butterflies and moths make similar journeys every year, some of them across the sea.

Comparatively few mammals migrate, though many of them lead nomadic lives, wandering in search of food. The CARIBOU of North America wander northward to breed in the tundra, the region of winter ice and summer vegetation that borders the Arctic Ocean. At the end of the brief northern summer they return to the wooded regions further south. Similar migration patterns have been noted for the reindeer of northern Europe and Asia.

Migration is common among fish and other animals that make the sea their home. The European EEL, for example, breeds in the Sargasso Sea, in the western Atlantic Ocean. The eel *larvae*, barely 8 cm long, swim to the shores of Europe and North America. During the journey they change into elvers – young eels. The elvers swim up rivers and spend several years in fresh water. When they are about 10 or 12 years old they return to the Sargasso Sea, where they spawn and die.

SALMON spawn in fresh water and then die. The young salmon, at the age of about a year, swim down river and out to sea where they travel thousands of miles feeding and growing. They then return to the rivers where they were born.

WHALES make regular migrations across the oceans in search of food. PLANKTON, the main food of most whales, abounds in polar seas in summer, and the whales go there to feed. In winter, whales are found in warmer waters. SEALS, SEA-LIONS and WALRUSES migrate every year to their breeding grounds, returning always to the same deserted stretch of shore. They spend several weeks on shore or near it, while the young are born. Then they put to sea again.

In early autumn, birds get ready for their long migration flight. Because the journey is so dangerous, they frequently band together and travel in large flocks.

Millipede

Like CENTIPEDES, millipedes are many-legged animals. Although their popular name means "thousand legged", no millipede has that many. The most that have been counted is 750. Millipedes vary in size from 2 to 280 mm, but the longest millipedes do not have the most legs. The smallest millipedes are soft-bodied, while some of the largest are heavily armoured. Their bodies are generally more rounded than those of the centipedes.

There are about 6500 species, mostly living in moist soil, leaf-mould or crevices. They are active at night, feeding on vegetable matter, in contrast to centipedes which are *carnivores*. For example, the spotted snake millipede chews potatoes. Millipedes are comparatively slow-moving, and when walking, each leg is a little out of step with the one in front, so that waves appear to sweep back along each side of the body. Two pairs of legs are attached to each body segment, except for the first four. Many species are protected by poisonous glands in the skin.
CLASS: Diplopoda.

Mink

There are two species of mink: the European mink and the American mink. They belong to the WEASEL family and are very similar in appearance. Males are 43 to 66 cm from the snout to the tip of the bushy tail. Females are about half the size of the males. The fur is light to dark brown with a white patch on the chin. Mink live in dens among rocks, in trees or in the burrows of other animals. They are nocturnal and hunt both on land and in water. On land they catch small mammals and birds; in water they feed on CRAYFISH, FROGS, and fish such as TROUT.

Mink are valuable fur bearers and have been bred commercially since 1866. A number of colour varieties, from white to almost

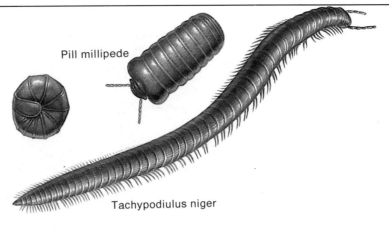

Pill millipede

Tachypodiulus niger

black, have been bred on farms. The European mink is becoming rare in places, and the American mink has been introduced into European farms. Unfortunately, a number of mink have escaped. Wild populations are now a nuisance as they prey on local wildlife and on poultry.
ORDER: Carnivora;
FAMILY: Mustelidae;
SPECIES: *Mustela lutreola* (European); *Mustela vison* (American).

Minnow

Many small, freshwater fishes of temperate and tropical waters are called minnows. Not all these fishes are closely related, although many belong to the CARP family. The common European minnow is one of the most widely-known freshwater fishes in Europe, and its range extends as far as Lake Baikal in Siberia. Its streamlined body is not more than about 10 cm long, and is pale in colour, with

The **minnow** is commonly found in stony bottomed streams, and is popular prey for larger fish.

European mink

reddish-tinged fins. Most minnows live in the deeper parts of clear brooks and streams. Where there is a sandy or gravelly bottom. They are numerous, easily caught, and easy to keep in aquariums, so they are often used as laboratory animals.
ORDER: Cypriniformes;
FAMILY: Cyprinidae;
SPECIES: *Phoxinus phoxinus* (common European).

Mite

Mites are relatives of the SPIDERS, with rounded bodies, usually about 0.5 mm long. There are many thousands of species and they live in all sorts of odd places, including the nostrils of seals the hearing organs of moths and decaying cheese.

The red spider mite is a garden pest that weaves sheet webs on plants. The mites live in large numbers within the webs and suck the plants' juices. The *larvae* of the harvest mite wait in low-growing vegetation and cling on to any warm-blooded animals which pass by. They pierce the skin of their host and suck out fluids, causing severe irritation.
ORDER: Acari.

Above: An unfortunate butterfly is being parasitized by **red mites**.

Mitten crab

The mitten crabs are fresh water animals 6 to 9 cm long, brownish-green above and yellow underneath. The popular name comes from the ruffle of silky brown "hairs" on each pincer, which is more obvious in the male crab. The crabs live in the streams of China, Japan and Korea. About 80 years ago the Chinese mitten crab was accidentally introduced into European rivers. Like most crabs, mitten crabs are scavengers, and they also eat water snails, small crustaceans and insect larvae. They burrow into river banks, often causing serious damage.
ORDER: Decapoda;
GENUS: *Eriocheir*.

Mockingbird

Mockingbirds are members of the same family as catbirds. They are 25 to 30 cm long, and have more slender bodies than the THRUSHES which they resemble. Their tails are longer too, and their bills thinner. The mockingbird's ability to mimic other birds has made them extremely popular in the United States, and they are the state bird of five states. Mockingbirds are found in North, Central and South America and the West Indies. The Galapagos mockingbird has evolved separately, just as DARWIN'S FINCHES have. Mockingbirds eat fruit and insects.
ORDER: Passeriformes;
FAMILY: Mimidae.

Below: A galapagos **mockingbird**.

Mole

The mole family includes about 20 species.

The European mole ranges across Europe and much of Asia. It is one of the busiest of mammals. It is a voracious eater and is constantly hunting for earthworms, its favourite food. The mole is well adapted to life underground. Its cylindrical body, about 13 cm long, is carried on short legs. Its forefeet are extremely broad, and function ideally as diggers of the tunnels in which the mole spends most of its life. The mole's skin has more organs for detecting touch than any other mammal.

The star-nosed mole of North America has the most unusual organ of touch. The tip of its muzzle is surrounded by a fleshy fringe of feelers, forming a star. The animal has a much longer tail than its European relative. It is an expert swimmer and often finds its food in the water. It also eats earthworms.

ORDER: Insectivora;
FAMILY: Talpidae;
SPECIES: *Talpa europaea* (European); *Condylura cristata* (star-nosed).

Mole rat

Because its way of life is so like that of the MOLE, the mole rat has evolved a similar appearance. It is a burrowing rodent, with short,

The **mole** spends most of its time digging underground. Occasionally, as here, it pops to the surface.

thick fur, small ears and short, powerful legs. The eyes have virtually disappeared and the mole rat's most distinctive features are its large front teeth, which it uses for digging.

There are several kinds of mole rat, most of which are found in Africa. Others live in the Middle East, southern Russia, and South-East Asia, where they are called bamboo rats. Typical, is the Palestine mole rat, which is up to 30 cm long. The mole rat digs food chambers in which it stores roots, bulbs and the other underground parts of plants on which it feeds. It usually remains below ground, but occasionally visits the surface after dark.

ORDER: Rodentia;
FAMILIES: Spalacidae; Rhizomyidae; Bathyergidae.

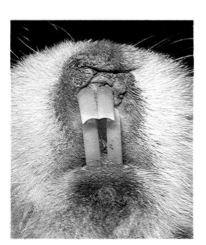

Left: The head of an African **mole rat**, showing the long gnawing teeth.

Greater mole rat

Molluscs

Second largest of the animal phyla, with about 120,000 species, this group contains the SLUGS and SNAILS, the BIVALVES, and the SQUIDS and OCTOPUSES, as well as the CHITONS and several other minor sections. The bodies of these animals are soft and unsegmented, but many are protected by shells.

The slugs and snails belong to the Class Gastropoda – a name which means "belly-footed", because the animals appear to glide along on their bellies. In fact, the muscular part on which they glide is called the foot. As well as slugs and snails, the class contains POND SNAILS, SEA SLUGS, and numerous sea snails, such as WHELKS, winkles, and TOPSHELLS. Many of the more advanced land-living species are *hermaphrodite*. Many aquatic species, in common with many bivalves, pass through *larval* stages.

Bivalves, whose shells consist of two parts hinged together, include COCKLES, MUSSELS, SCALLOPS, OYSTERS, and RAZOR SHELLS. They all live in water, fresh or salt, and they all feed by sucking in water and filtering out food particles.

Squids and octopuses, together with CUTTLEFISHES and the NAUTILUS, make up the Class Cephalopoda. They are all marine, predatory molluscs with very highly developed brains and sense organs. The pearly nautilus has a coiled shell similar to those of the extinct ammonites but other cephalopods have no real shells, although there may be a horny or chalky plate under the skin for support. The head is surrounded by eight or ten arms which bear suckers and which are used to capture fish and other prey.

Above: The **squid** is a mollusc wth highly developed brain and sense organs.

Below: Inside and outside a **bivalve mollusc**. Siphons draw in water and drive out waste. This bivalve moves on a foot poked out between both valves.

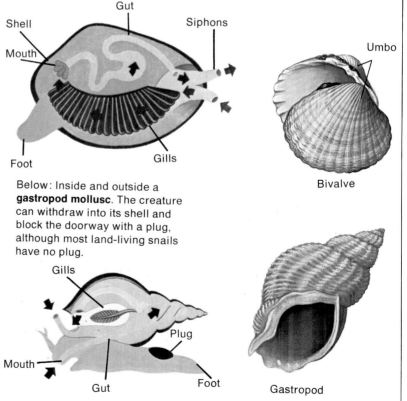

Below: Inside and outside a **gastropod mollusc**. The creature can withdraw into its shell and block the doorway with a plug, although most land-living snails have no plug.

Bivalve

Gastropod

Moloch

Australian desert and semi-desert regions are the home of this strange, prickly LIZARD, sometimes called the thorny devil. Its total length is 15 cm and it is covered in thorn-like spikes. A moloch feeds mainly on ANTS, flicking them up one at a time with its tongue as they pass. One lizard may eat up to 5000 ants at a sitting. Before laying eggs, a female moloch spends 2 to 3 days digging a nest hole in soft sandy soil. The completed tunnel may be as much as 60 cm long.
ORDER: Squamata;
FAMILY: Agamidae;
SPECIES: *Moloch horridus.*

Monarch butterfly

Also known as the milkweed, the monarch is one of the world's most widely distributed butterflies. It occurs throughout the Americas and has spread through the Pacific islands to Australasia and South-East Asia. Its bold orange and black pattern, which it shares with several other species, is a good example of warning coloration, for the insect is poisonous to birds and other insect-eating animals.

In autumn, butterflies from Canada and the northern United States gather together and fly down to California and Mexico, where they spend the winter in a state of semi-hibernation, clustering on trees in huge numbers. The reverse journey takes place in spring. Monarch caterpillars feed on various plants in the milkweed family.
ORDER: Lepidoptera;
FAMILY: Danaidae;
SPECIES: *Danaus plexippus.*

Mongoose

Mongooses are slim, low-slung animals related to CIVETS. They have a sharp muzzle, bushy tail and small ears almost hidden in their long, coarse, speckled hair.

Above: a **monarch butterfly** clings to its empty pupa case soon after emerging.

Left: The **mongoose** is well known for its ability to kill snakes by agility and speed of attack.

Mongooses live in southern and South-East Asia, Africa and Madagascar. There are 48 species (the SURICATE is a rather specialized kind). Among the largest is the crab-eating mongoose of South-East Asia. At 1.2 metres long it is nearly three times longer than the smallest species, the dwarf mongoose of Africa south of the Sahara. The best known is the Egyptian mongoose, which is 1 metre long. This species occurs in much of Africa and part of south-western Europe.

Mongooses are alert, active animals, but love to lie and bask. Most of them live on the ground, but a few species are known to climb trees. The water mongoose is aquatic. Most mongooses hunt by day, their favourite foods being eggs and snakes. Some crack eggs by throwing them against a stone. They also have a special method of killing snakes: as the snake rears to strike, the mongoose darts in at lightning speed to attack the head. It can kill a cobra far longer than itself. If bitten, the mongoose may survive, for snake venom has only a mild effect upon it. Besides snakes, mongooses eat small animals of many kinds. Females give birth to 2 to 4 in a litter, at almost any time of the year.
ORDER: Carnivora;
FAMILY: Viverridae.

Monitor lizard

This family includes the largest lizards alive. After the KOMODO DRAGON the next largest is the water monitor, up to 2.7 metres long. Monitors are a slim stream-lined shape and, like snakes, they have long, forked tongues. If cornered they hiss and lash with their whip-like tails, bite, and slash with their claws. Monitors eat a wide variety of animals, as well as carrion, and all of them enjoy eating eggs. The Nile monitor swims well, while some other species are expert tree climbers. Monitors occur in most warm Asian and African regions. They are among the earliest group of lizards to appear, and date back about 130 million years.
ORDER: Squamata;
FAMILY: Varanidae.

Monkeys

Monkeys are animals of the highest order of mammals, the Primates. This order also includes the apes and Man. Monkeys are characterized by usually living in trees, by being covered with hair, and by having nails, not claws, on each of their five fingers and toes. They live in the warm climates of Central and South America, Africa, Asia and the East Indies.

Monkeys can be divided into two main groups: the Old World species of Africa and Asia, and the New World species of the Western hemisphere. The monkeys of Central and South America are distinguished from the Old World monkeys by having nostrils which tend to be wider apart, and by their long prehensile (gripping) tails. Most of the New World monkeys are not so intelligent as the Old World monkeys, and they are much less lively in their behaviour. Some of the Old World monkeys have cheek pouches for storing food and have hardened areas on the buttocks which are at times very brightly coloured. They all have 32 teeth.

Monkeys are not found in Europe, apart from the BARBARY APE of Gibraltar.

One **monkey** grooms another. Many apes and monkeys groom each other to remove parasites and dirt, taking turns at grooming or being groomed. Being groomed is a pleasant feeling and so helps to keep harmony among the members of monkey or ape groups.

A **moorhen** on its nest among the reeds.

Monkfish

Flat-bodied and clumsy-looking, the monkfish looks unlike most people's idea of a SHARK. It is, however, a true shark but one that lives mostly on the sea bottom, using its crushing teeth to feed on shellfish, flatfish and worms. There are eleven species, the largest of which reaches a length of 2.5 metres and a weight of 72 kg. Monkfishes are widespread in tropical and temperate seas.

Monkfish is sometimes also called angelfish, after the wing-like appearance of its *pectoral fins*. This name, however, is confusing when used in this way, and is best left applied to certain freshwater bony fishes.

ORDER: Lamniformes;
FAMILY: Squatinidae.

Moorhen

The moorhen is a water bird belonging to the RAIL family. In America, it is known as the common gallinule. It lives in swamps, lakes and rivers throughout the world, except for Australia and New Zealand. The moorhen is 28 cm long. It has black plumage, but can be distinguished from the COOT by the red shield above the bill and by the white line running along each side. Moorhens are common on park lakes. They nest in bushes or vegetation beside water, but sometimes build floating nests attached to water plants.

ORDER: Gruiformes;
FAMILY: Rallidae;
SPECIES: *Gallinula chloropus*.

Moose

The moose is the largest living DEER. It stands 2.4 metres at the shoulder, but the back slopes

This bull **moose's** antlers are still covered with velvet.

sharply down to the lower rump. The male's antlers have a span of up to 2 metres. In summer, the coat is greyish or reddish-brown to black above, and lighter beneath and on the legs. In winter, the coat is greyer. The moose lives in well-watered, wooded areas of Alaska and Canada and in the Rocky Mountains of the north-western United States. In Europe, where it is called the elk, it is found in Norway and Sweden. It spreads eastwards through the USSR to Mongolia and northern China.

Moose tend to be solitary. But, in winter, several may combine to form a "yard". This is an area of trampled snow in a sheltered spot where there are plenty of bushes for feeding. Bark and small branches are their main food at this time of the year. When the food is used up, they move to another yard. In summer, moose often wade into lakes and rivers to feed on water plants. This gives them some relief from mosquitos and other flies. The males, known as bulls, shed their antlers in December. New antlers sprout in April or May and are fully grown in August. The breeding season is September to October. This season is marked by fights between the bulls, but the fights normally do little damage. Calves are born 240 to 270 days after mating. Moose sometimes live for 20 years. Their main enemies are BEARS and WOLVES and, to a lesser extent, PUMAS, COYOTES and WOLVERINES, which prey on the young.

ORDER: Artiodactyla;
FAMILY: Cervidae;
SPECIES: *Alces alces*.

Moray eel

There are 120 species of moray eel, all of which inhabit tropical and subtropical seas, especially around CORAL reefs. They have elongated, bodies ranging in length from 15 cm to 3 metres or more. Moray eels have a bad reputation for attacking divers but this is most

This **moray eel** is accompanied by a tiny blue cleaner fish.

probably unearned. Morays have large mouths full of sharp teeth, with which they bolt their prey whole, but generally they will attack man only when in a tight corner. Then, they can inflict severe injury. However, morays may become rather more vicious during the breeding season, which may explain why members of the Kon-Tiki expedition were attacked by them in the lagoon of a coral island.

Many morays are brilliantly coloured and patterned, an adaptation for life on brightly-coloured coral reefs. The zebra moray, for example, is brightly ringed in ochre and white stripes. Morays like to lurk in crevices and holes in the reef, emerging to grab a passing CRUSTACEAN, MOLLUSC or fish. They need a continuous flow of water through their mouths to breathe, and often seem to be panting because they swim open-mouthed.

ORDER: Anguilliformes;
FAMILY: Muraenidae.

Morpho butterfly

Morphos are among the world's largest and most brilliant butterflies. There are less than 50 species, all living in the forests of tropical America. The largest species has a 23 cm wing-span. The males of most species have iridescent blue wings, which appear to change colour as the angle of the light changes. These wings are in great demand for the jewellery trade. The females are beautifully coloured, but much less showy.

ORDER: Lepidoptera;
FAMILY: Morphidae.

The wings of this South American **morpho butterfly** are iridescent blue and gold on the upper side.

Mosquito

Mosquitos are slender FLIES, rarely more than about 1 cm long, whose wing veins are clothed with tiny scales. The females are blood-suckers, and need a meal of blood before laying their eggs. They suck the blood through a needle-like beak, which they plunge into birds and mammals, including humans. At the same time, they pump in a substance to prevent the blood from clotting right away, and this is responsible for the irritation produced by many mosquito bites. Far more serious, however, are the various diseases transmitted by the insects, including malaria and yellow fever.

Male mosquitos have no sharp beak, and they feed on nectar. They have fluffy *antennae*, with which they detect the high-pitched whine of the females. Eggs are laid on the water surface, either singly or in raft-like masses. The *larvae* feed on minute organisms in water. The comma-shaped *pupae* can swim but they do not feed. They spend most of the time hanging from the water surface. The adult mosquitos can fly as soon as they break out of the pupal' skins. There are about 2500 species.
ORDER: Diptera;
FAMILY: Culicidae.

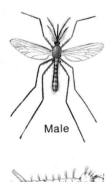

Male

Larva

The male **mosquito** has feathery antennae. Only the female sucks blood. There are many species.

Motmot

Eight species of birds make up the Motmot family. They live in the forests of Central and South America, ranging from Mexico to Argentina. They are about 36 cm long, with a long tail, and are brownish-green with patches of blue and brown on the head and breast. Motmots feed mainly on flying insects, which they are able to catch in flight; they also eat snails, lizards and fruit. They are related to the KINGFISHERS, and like kingfishers, they often take their prey to a perch and pound it before swallowing. Motmots nest in burrows that they dig in banks.
ORDER: Coraciiformes;
FAMILY: Momotidae.

Mouflon

The only European wild sheep is the mouflon. It is found truly wild only on the Mediterranean islands of Corsica and Sardinia, but it has been introduced into many other parts of Europe. Standing 70 cm at the shoulder, it is reddish-brown with a whitish saddle and black marks on the limbs. The male's horns form a close spiral and the tips may curve slightly inwards. Some females have short horns but normally they have none. Breeding begins in autumn and lambs are normally born in April. Apart from the breeding season, the rams live in separate flocks from the ewes and the young.
ORDER: Artiodactyla;
FAMILY: Bovidae;
SPECIES: *Ovis musimon*.

Mouse

The name is applied to a number of small RODENTS, but most often to the common HOUSE MOUSE. Other examples are the HARVEST MOUSE, POCKET MOUSE and SPINY MOUSE. The MARSUPIAL MOUSE is so named for its mouse-like appearance, but it is not related to true mice.

Mice are found in most parts of

Male

Female

Below: The **house mouse** can be a serious pest.

The **wood mouse** is a rodent food-hoarder. It has rather kangaroo-like hopping legs.

the world, and are often pests, since many of them live close to man; eating his foodstuffs, gnawing his materials, and carrying diseases. Mice will eat almost anything, although plant food is the most usual. They breed prolifically, and their ability to produce large litters of young several times a year explains why mice remain so numerous, in spite of a wide variety of predators. Mice are a vital link in the natural food chain, and, as laboratory animals, they are of considerable value to scientific research.

ORDER: Rodentia.

Mousebird

Also known as colies, mousebirds inhabit the forests of Africa south of the Sahara. There are six species, all about 30 cm long and grey or brown in colour. They have long thin tails and prominent crests. One toe on each foot can face either backwards or forwards, giving mousebirds an agility which

allows them to feed in any position, even upside-down. Mousebirds get their name from their habit of scurrying through the foliage like mice. Outside the breeding season, they travel in flocks, eating buds, leaves, berries and fruit as well as insects.
ORDER: Coliiformes;
FAMILY: Coliidae.

Mouth-breeding frog

This midget frog is only 2.5 cm long, yet it is perhaps the most remarkable of all the AMPHIBIANS. In the breeding season each female lays 20 to 30 eggs. Males guard groups of eggs for 10 to 20 days. When the eggs are about to hatch, each male picks some up with his tongue and they slide down into his vocal sacs. Nourished by egg yolk enclosed in their intestines, the tadpoles turn into froglets inside the male. Then they hop from his mouth. Mouth-breeding frogs live in the cool, moist beech forests of southern South America. They are greenish-brown in colour, with darker stripes and patches.
ORDER: Salientia;
FAMILY: Rhinodermatidae;
SPECIES: *Rhinoderma darwinii.*

Mudpuppy

The mudpuppy is a large SALA-MANDER, living in the ponds and rivers of North America. Individuals are usually 30 cm long, with four weak legs which are used only for crawling, and are held by the sides for swimming. Mudpuppies never become fully adult, and their three pairs of gills are kept throughout life. They take 5 to 7 years to become sexually mature, and may live for 20 years. They eat small water creatures such as worms, fish and frogs' eggs.
ORDER: Caudata;
FAMILY: Proteidae;
SPECIES: *Necturus maculosus.*

Mudskipper

Mudskippers are fishes which remain on the exposed mud at low tide, instead of staying in the water. They move quickly over the mud on their large *pectoral fins*, keeping watch for predators with eyes which are set on the top of the head and can swivel in any direction. Many species of mudskipper live in mangrove swamps and muddy estuaries from West Africa to South-East Asia. Most are 13 to 30 cm long, with mottled bluish or brownish bodies.

Mudskippers can breathe air through membranes lining the back of the throat, and their enlarged gill chambers hold a good supply of water. This dual system allows them to remain out of water for long periods. From time to time they return to pools to renew their gill water supply, and to keep their skin and eyes moist. On the mud, they feed on tiny plants which they skim from the surface water layer, or insects, crabs and worms which have fallen into the mud. In the water they swim as other fishes do, but unlike other fishes they generally keep their head above water.
ORDER: Perciformes;
FAMILY: Gobiidae.

The **mudskipper** is a successful "fish out of water".

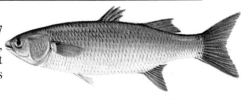

The thick-lipped **grey mullet** above feeds on rich organic mud. The **red mullet** below is smaller and a bottom-living fish.

Mule deer

The mule deer of western North America stands nearly 120 cm at the shoulder and weighs up to 130 kg. The does are about one-third smaller than the bucks. The coat is tawny or yellowish-brown in summer. In winter, it is longer and greyer. The rump is white, with a contrasting, black-tipped tail. The antlers divide into two almost equal branches. They are shed in January to March and grown in April or May. In the wild, mule deer live about 10 years. During the 20th century, populations of mule deer have increased because their enemies, such as COYOTES, PUMAS, and WOLVES, have been killed. Today, the population of mule deer is controlled by hunting.
ORDER: Artiodactyla;
FAMILY: Cervidae;
SPECIES: *Odocoileus hemionus.*

Mullet

The name belongs to two groups of fish, the grey mullets and the red mullets, which are not closely related to one another. Grey mullets, a group of 100 species, are streamlined fishes of temperate and tropical in-shore waters, up to about 90 cm in length and weighing up to 6 kg. They feed on vegetable and animal matter in mud and sand, picking this up with their mouths and sieving out the edible matter with their gills. They also feed on

the surface, especially where there is rotting seaweed or rubbish.

The red mullet is a marine fish mainly living in tropical and subtropical waters. It can easily be distinguished from grey mullets by its smaller size, its reddish colour, perhaps streaked with yellow, and by the two *barbels* or feelers on the lower jaw. The red mullet feeds mostly on small shellfish and worms from the sea-bed, using its barbels like fingers to search the sand for food.

ORDER: Perciformes;
FAMILY: Mugilidae (grey mullets), Mullidae (red mullets).

Muntjac

Muntjac are small, solitary, shy DEER. They are often called barking deer, because they bark a warning when predators are near. There are five species: the Indian muntjac, the Pleihari muntjac of Borneo, the Chinese muntjac, Fea's muntjac of Burma and the hairy-fronted muntjac of the Ningpo district of China. Muntjacs stand 40 to 64 cm at the shoulder, but the rump is somewhat higher. The males have long, tusk-like upper *canine teeth*, and small antlers. The Chinese muntjac is quite common in England, having escaped from various parks and zoos.

ORDER: Artiodactyla;
FAMILY: Cervidae.

The male **muntjac** has simple antlers pointing backwards. Females carry tufts of hair in place of antlers.

Musk-deer

Musk-deer, the most primitive members of the DEER group, are in a family of their own. There are three species: the brownish Siberian Musk-deer, which is the largest, the light grey mountain musk-deer of the Himalayas, and the dark grey dwarf musk-deer, which lives on the slopes below the mountain musk-deer. They all feed on grasses, lichens, and young conifer shoots in the forests. Musk-deer have no antlers. Both sexes have a gland under the tail which gives off a substance with a goaty smell. Adult males secrete a jelly-like musk (a strong smelling substance) from a pouch on their

Musk-oxen form a tight circle when an enemy attacks. The young stay in the middle for protection.

abdomen. It is used to make perfumes. Both sexes have long upper *canine teeth* which are pulled upright when the animal opens its mouth. They use these sabre-like teeth to defend their territories. The Siberian musk-deer stands up to 56 cm at the shoulder. Dwarf musk-deer are 40 to 46 cm high.

ORDER: Artiodactyla;
FAMILY: Moschidae.

Musk-ox

The musk-ox is found in the Arctic tundra of Canada and Greenland.

It is usually seen in herds of between 20 and 30 but, sometimes, up to 100. During blizzards, the animals huddle together with their backs to the wind, sheltering their calves in the centre of the herd. Mating occurs in August and the single calf is born in the following April or May. When wolves threaten, the bulls move to the outside of the herd, facing the wolves and completely surrounding the young musk-oxen. If the wolves attack, they may be trampled or gored to death by the bulls. This method of defence proved to be useless against armed men and by 1917 the musk-ox was so rare that the Canadian government ordered its protection. Since then, it has been slowly gaining in numbers.

Although the musk-oxen resembles CATTLE, it is probably more closely related to SHEEP and GOATS. The bulls emit a strong odour from musk glands on the face which can be smelt 90 metres away. The bulls stand 150 cm at the shoulder and weighs up to 320 kg. The cow is nearly as big. Sideways-curving horns are joined in the centre of the head. The shaggy mantle of long hairs, which almost reach the ground in winter, is dark brown. A thick, woolly undercoat enables the animal to withstand the cold and damp. The musk-ox remains on the tundra throughout the year, grazing on lichens and mosses that they dig from beneath the snow.

ORDER: Artiodactyla;
FAMILY: Bovidae;
SPECIES: *Ovibos moschatus*.

Muskrat

The muskrat is a large VOLE up to 60 cm long, including the tail. Both it and its cousin, the Newfoundland muskrat are native to North America, but have been introduced to several parts of Europe.

The muskrat has two scent glands at the base of its tail: hence its name. It has adapted to living in the water. Its scaly tail, flattened

Common **mussels** (left) are attached to rocks by tough threads. The **painter's mussel** above shows the frilly edges of the siphons.

from side to side, acts as a rudder when it is swimming and the hind feet are partly webbed. The fur colour is silvery brown to black. The short undercoat is sold commercially under the name musquash.

Muskrats nest either in bulky nests of plants on open swampland, or in tunnels dug into river banks above the high water mark. They eat the roots and leaves of water plants, but will also catch CRAYFISH, MUSSELS and the occasional fish. When diving, a muskrat can stay submerged for up to 12 minutes.

ORDER: Rodentia;
FAMILY: Cricetidae;
SPECIES: *Ondatra obscura*; *Ondatra zibethica* (Newfoundland).

Mussel

The name mussel is given to various species of *bivalve* MOLLUSCS. All feed by filtering small particles from the water.

The best known is the common or edible mussel. It is found on the

Muskrats are nocturnal animals that live near water and swim well.

temperate and sub-tropical coasts of the northern hemisphere. Most common mussels are 1 to 10 cm long. Usually brown-blue-black in colour, the two halves or *valves* which make up the shell are hinged with elastic ligament, allowing them to open and close. The animal has a long, brownish "foot" which produces tough threads. These form a byssus, or beard, to anchor the mussel.

Freshwater mussels live partly buried in mud. They use their foot for burrowing and a *siphon* for drawing in water.

CLASS: Bivalva;
ORDERS: Anisomyaria; Schizodonta.

Mynah

Mynahs are birds belonging to the STARLING family. The best-known is the hill mynah, which lives in the tropical forests of southern Asia. It is from 30 to 38 cm long, and has glossy black plumage with yellow head wattles. This mynah is renowned for its ability to "talk", so it is a popular cage bird. In the wild, mynahs travel through the forest in noisy flocks, feeding on fruits. Other varieties, more colourful than the hill mynah, extend into the Pacific islands.

ORDER: Passeriformes;
FAMILY: Sturnidae;
SPECIES: *Gracula religiosa* (hill mynah).

N

Narwhal

The narwhal is related to the BELUGA or white whale. It lives in Arctic waters, growing to about 5 metres in length and is a fast swimmer and deep diver. Known as the "unicorn" of the whale family, its peculiar feature is the single twisted horn on its forehead, which can be 2.7 metres long. This horn is, in fact, an outsize tooth and is usually found only on the males. There is no satisfactory explanation of how the narwhal uses its horn, for the animal feeds mainly on CUTTLE-FISH, which it seizes in its mouth. The horn is much prized by Eskimos for its ivory.

ORDER: Cetacea;
FAMILY: Monodontidae;
SPECIES: *Monodon monoceros.*

Natterjack

A yellow line down the head and back helps to identify the natterjack toad. This European AMPHI-BIAN has short legs and runs rather than hops after its prey, which includes insects and spiders. They burrow in sand, often in dunes on the coast, and, when alarmed, exude a white liquid which smells like boiling rubber.

ORDER: Salientia;
FAMILY: Bufonidae;
SPECIES: *Bufo calamita.*

The **natterjack** usually has a clear yellow strip on its back.

The beautiful **pearly nautilus** swims in tropical waters. It is related to the octopuses, squids and cuttlefishes.

Nautilus

The nautilus differs from other living *cephalopods* because it has an external shell. In this respect it resembles the extinct ammonites more closely than the OCTOPUSES and SQUIDS. The shell, never more than about 30 cm across, is ivory coloured with a zebra-like pattern of reddish stripes. Inside, it is lined with mother-of-pearl and divided into about 30 chambers. The animal itself lives in the outermost chamber and the other chambers contain gas to give buoyancy. The nautilus swims freely in the water, driving itself along by jet propulsion and trailing its numerous tentacles behind it. The tentacles have no suckers, but they are strongly ridged and can grip the fishes and other animals on which the nautilus feeds. There are six species, all living in the south-west Pacific.

CLASS: Cephalopoda;
ORDER: Tetrabranchia.

Needlefish

Needlefishes, or garfishes are slim, fast-swimming fishes with long, beak-like mouths. They are closely related to the FLYING FISHES, which they resemble in their habit of launching themselves from, and skittering along the surface of the water. They live mainly in warmer oceans, skimming along in pursuit of their prey, which they stab with their sharp beak or seize with their many needle-sharp teeth. Their speed also helps them to escape pursuit by larger fishes, although they often fall prey to the even speedier SWORDFISH and TUNA.

ORDER: Atheriniformes;
FAMILY: Belonidae.

Nests

A nest is a structure built by an animal to house its eggs, young and sometimes itself. Although birds are the most well-known nest builders, other vertebrates have developed this behaviour too. At one extreme, social insects such as TERMITES, ANTS and WASPS build complex nests to house while communities. In contrast, other animals such as the STICKLEBACK fish and small mammals such as the HARVEST MOUSE build solitary nests. RABBITS nest below ground in burrows. Amphibians and reptiles do not generally build nests, but certain frogs and the ALLIGATORS are exceptions.

Not all birds build nests, but most that do make simple bowl-shaped constructions of twigs, grass and leaves cemented together with saliva or mud. A nest may be anything from a PUFFIN'S hollow in the ground to an elaborate structure suspended from tree branches – a particular trademark of WEAVERBIRDS. WOODPECKERS drill nesting space in trees with their bills, and many OWLS make use of hollow trees and old buildings for their nests.

Above: The harvest mouse uses the shoots of corn to support its nest.

Above: The **swallow** builds an open nest of mud and straw.
Below: A **stickleback** at its nest.

Below: A wasps nests hanging from the branch of a tree in South America.

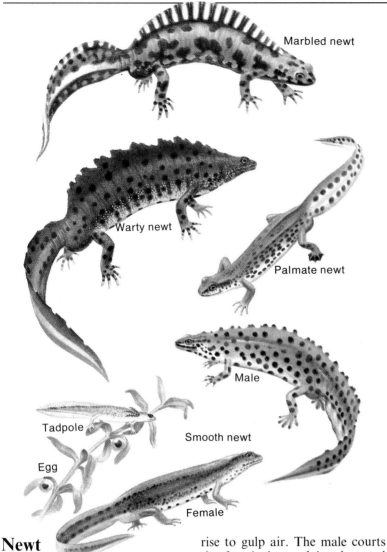

Marbled newt

Warty newt

Palmate newt

Male

Tadpole

Smooth newt

Egg

Female

the water and feed on slugs, worms and insects. Crested newts will eat smooth newts. In winter, newts hibernate, squeezing themselves into crevices.
ORDER: Caudata;
FAMILY: Salamandridae.

Night heron

Night herons are medium-sized birds with shorter legs and necks than other herons. They are mainly active in the evening. There are several species in the Americas and Asia. The most widely distributed is the black-crowned night heron, which breeds in southern Europe, but is also found in Africa, Asia and the Americas. In some parts of the United States, the black-crowned night heron is called the "qwauk" or "qwabird". Night herons catch small fish by standing motionless in shallow water and stabbing with their sharp beaks. They also eat small amphibians, shrimps, snails, crabs, worms and insects.
ORDER: Ciconiiformes;
FAMILY: Ardeidae;
SPECIES: *Nycticorax nycticorax* (black-crowned).

Newt

Newts are AMPHIBIANS, related to the SALAMANDERS. They have long, slim bodies like those of LIZARDS, but the tail is flattened from side to side. The largest European newt is the crested or warty newt, which grows up to 18 cm long and has blackish upper-parts and an orange belly. The male has a tall, toothed frill down its back and a crested tail. It also secretes a mild poison from its skin. The California newt has a far more potent poison. Less than one-hundredth of a gram can kill 7,000 mice.

Newts have a life history very similar to that of FROGS or TOADS. Adults spend most of their time on land but breed in still water where water plants grow. They swim by lashing their tails, but spend much time resting. Now and then they

rise to gulp air. The male courts the female by nudging her and vibrating his tail, which he bends double. Then he emits a package of sperm which she collects. After fertilization, her 200 to 300 eggs are usually laid singly on the leaves of water plants. The eggs hatch into tadpoles with gills and legs.

Newts have tiny teeth which they use to hold their slippery prey – CRUSTACEANS and insect *larvae* – in the water. In summer they leave

The **nightingale** is famous for its musical song.

Nightingale

The nightingale is a species of small perching bird noted for its song, especially at night. It is a shy bird, living in thick woodland undergrowth, scrub and damp, marshy spots where insects are plentiful. It feeds mainly on the ground, eating worms, spiders and insects. Fruit and berries are also taken. The female builds a bulky nest of dead leaves and lines it with grass and hair. Nightingales lay 4 to 5 eggs.
ORDER: Passeriformes;
FAMILY: Turdidae;
SPECIES: *Luscinia megarhynchos*.

Nightjar

There are 70 species of nightjar, spread throughout the world. The birds are nocturnal insect eaters,

Nightjars' bills open very widely to scoop up insects in flight.

and get their name from the jarring calls they make at night. The European nightjar breeds in North Africa and Asia as well as Europe, and winters in Africa as far south as the Cape. It is 25 cm long, and its brown-grey streaky plumage is typical of nightjars. These colours camouflage the bird very effectively as it roosts by day in trees or among plants on the ground.

ORDER: Caprimulgiformes;
FAMILY: Caprimulgidae;
SPECIES: *Caprimulgus europaeus* (European).

Nile fish

This strange-looking fish from the River Nile swims by waving a single long fin on its back, as its other fins are small or absent. The Nile fish sends out weak electric signals which it uses as a sort of radar to finds its way about in murky water. The pointed body of the Nile fish is about 15 cm long and is flattened from side to side. Its eyes are small and its broad mouth contains strong teeth for seizing small prey, which it may find with the aid of its electric signals.

ORDER: Mormyriformes
FAMILY: Gymnarchidae;
SPECIES: *Gymnarchus niloticus.*

Nile perch

The Nile perch was venerated by the ancient Egyptians, who placed its mummified body in their tombs. It is the largest freshwater fish of Africa, 2 metres or more long, and weighing up to 136 kg when fully grown. It ranges from Lake Mobutu to the Nile delta, but also lives in other African lakes and rivers. The Nile perch is a heavy-bodied fish with a rounded tail and prominent spiny fins, coloured brown or grey. mottled with silver. It has large eyes, perhaps to see better in the murky waters, and a large mouth for seizing the fish on which it preys. As the ancient Egyptians probably first discovered, the Nile perch itself tastes delicious.

ORDER: Perciformes;
FAMILY: Latidae;
SPECIES: *Lates niloticus.*

Nilgai

The nilgai is the largest Indian antelope. The bulls are 132 to 142 cm high and may weigh 270 kg. Only the males have horns, which average 20 cm in length. The males are blue-grey and the female and young are tawny. Nilgai browse or graze in hilly country with scattered trees, or among the long grass and scrub of the plains. They can go for long periods without drinking. The females and their young live in herds of 4 to 10 and always use the same places for resting and drinking within their home ranges. The adult bulls may be solitary or live in small groups. They usualy mate in March or April and the two young are born eight to nine months later.

ORDER: Artiodactyla;
FAMILY: Bovidae;
SPECIES: *Boselaphus tragocamelus.*

Noctuid moth

The noctuids, also known as owlet moths, are one of the largest groups of MOTHS, with over 25,000 known species. They are found all over the world, although most species live in the northern hemisphere. Most are medium sized moths with stout bodies and wings

Malachite moth

Herald moth

Orange sallow

Large yellow underwing

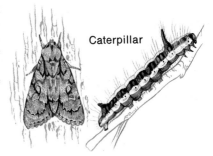

Caterpillar

Grey dagger

Red underwing

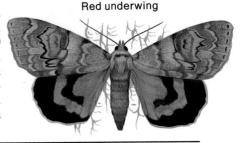

that are either held roof-like or folded flat over the body at rest. The front wings are generally grey or brown, and the insects are thus well camoufalaged when resting on tree trunks during the daytime. There are a few species with bright metallic markings, however, one of the best known being the burnished brass. The hind wings are generally drab, but some species, such as the red underwings and yellow underwings have brightly coloured hind wings. When disturbed, they fly off rapidly and flash the bright colours. They then drop quickly to the ground to conceal themselves, leaving the bird, or other enemy, searching for something brightly coloured. Noctuid caterpillars are fleshy and cylindrical, usually with only sparse hairs. They feed on all parts of plants and some are serious pests. The cotton BOLLWORM is an example. Many of the noctuid *larvae* are called cutworms be-

cause they tend to chew right through young shoots and cut them off at ground level. Others are called army worms because they exist in vast numbers and march to new feeding grounds when their food is exhausted in one place.
ORDER: Lepidoptera;
FAMILY: Noctuidae.

Noddy

The noddies, like other TERNS, are delicately-built seabirds. They are about 30 to 40 cm long, with slender wings, pointed bills and short legs. There are five species, living in most warm seas. The black noddy is 39 cm long, with dark plumage except for a pale cap on the head. The slightly larger

More usually, the slim-built **noddy** is seen resting on cliffs or flying rapidly across water.

brown noddy is similar. The other noddies have lighter plumages.
ORDER: Charadriiformes;
FAMILY: Laridae.

Numbat

The numbat is a voracious eater of TERMITES, consuming as many as seven million a year. It grows to about 30 cm long from nose to rump, and has a 18 cm bushy tail. It lives in open woodlands, often making its home in a fallen eucalyptus branch, hollowed out by termites. The numbat flicks out its cylindrical tongue about 10 cm to draw the termites into its mouth which has 52 sharp teeth. The animal generally rejects any ants that come its way so it is misleading to call it a banded anteater as some people do. Although a MARSUPIAL, it has no pouch.
ORDER: Marsupialia;
FAMILY: Myrmecobiidae;
SPECIES: *Myrmecobius fasciatus.*

Nutcracker

There are two species of nut-cracker. The European nutcracker ranges across central and northern Europe and, as a sub-species, across Asia. The North American or Clark's nutcracker is found in western parts of the United States. Nutcrackers are unusual members of the CROW family. They are at home in pine forests or mixed woodlands with numerous conifers. Their bills are specially adapted for cracking nuts. They eat mainly the seeds from pine, spruce, cedar and larch cones. Insects and the eggs of small birds are also taken.

ORDER: Passeriformes;
FAMILY: Corvidae;
SPECIES: *Nucifraga caryocatactes* (European); *Nucifraga columbianus* (North American).

Nuthatch

Nuthatches are small birds whose name is based on their habit of opening hazel nuts by hammering them with their beak on a tree trunk. Beechnuts, acorns and other seeds are opened in the same way. Nuthatches may also find insects in the crevices of tree bark. The commonest and most widely dstributed of the 31 species is the European nuthatch, which ranges across much of Europe and Asia. It lives in parks and woodlands and moves acrobatically over the trunks and branches of trees.

ORDER: Passeriformes;
FAMILY: Sittidae;
SPECIES: *Sitta europaea* (European).

Nyala

The true nyala of southern Africa, the mountain nyala of Ethiopia, and the sitatunga of West and Central Africa, belong to a group of ox-like ANTELOPES, which also includes the BUSHBUCK and KUDU. Male nyala have twisted horns with yellow tips. The true nyala stands 107 cm high and weighs 113

to 125 kg. It is slate-grey, with a red forehead. It has a fringe of dark hair on the throat and under-parts and about 14 white stripes on the body. The lower parts of the legs are bright tan. The female is bright chestnut, with a dark nose, about 11 body stripes and no throat fringe. She has no horns. The mountain nyala is larger and has a coarser, brown-grey coat and no body stripes. The sita-tunga, the smallest of the three species, has a coarse, grey to red-brown coat, with the same markings as the true nyala. It spends most of its time in swamps, often with just its head above water.

ORDER: Artiodactyla;
FAMILY: Bovidae.

Below: A group of **nyala** does at an African waterhole. The buck is larger, with swept-back horns.

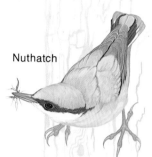

Nutcracker

Nuthatch

Top: The **nutcracker** lives in mountain forests.
Above: The **nuthatch** nests in a hole in a tree.

Oarfish

Sometimes also called the ribbon-fish, this large sea fish is an extra-ordinary and rare fish from deeper waters in many parts of the world. Up to 6 metres long or more, its body is about 30 cm deep but is so flattened that it is only about 5 cm wide. Along its back extends a fin which is coral red in colour, and which is raised into a remarkable, tall crest on its head. Its *pelvic fins* are long and slender, broadening at the tips to make two oar-like features that give the fish its name. Its long body ends in a point, with no tail fin. The oarfish's eyes are large and its mouth small. It feeds by sieving tiny shrimp-like creatures out from the water.
ORDER: Lampridiformes;
FAMILY: Regalecidae;
SPECIES: *Regalecus glesne*.

Ocean sunfish

Some species of ocean sunfish can grow up to 4 metres and weigh nearly a tonne. They look peculiar, with a shortened rear end, large head and small mouth. The teeth are fused into a single beak on each jaw. Gnashing their teeth makes a clicking sound, possibly used for communication. Their fins are high and pointed and very powerful. Ocean sunfish prey mainly on jellyfish, and occasionally crustacea and other fishes. They live in tropical and sub-tropical regions of the Atlantic, Indian and Pacific oceans, from the surface to a depth of 300 metres. A female *Mola mola* has been found to contain over 300,000,000 eggs.
ORDER: Tetradontiformes;
FAMILY: Molidae;
SPECIES: *Mola mola*.

Ocelot

The ocelot is a medium-sized member of the cat family. It is also one of the most beautiful. Its brown, grey or yellowish fur is blotched with large brown black-bordered spots, and there are black streaks around the head and neck. It grows up to 1.2 metres long and weighs up to 16 kg. Ocelots range from the south-western United States, south to Paraguay. They live in forests and hunt small animals by night and day. They often roam in pairs, mewing to keep in touch with one another. Although hunted for their coats; they seem to be in no danger of extinction.
ORDER: Carnivora;
FAMILY: Felidae;
SPECIES: *Felis pardalis*.

Octopus

Octopuses are eight-armed MOLLUSCS. Unlike the SQUIDS and CUTTLEFISHES, they have no internal shell, and the body is short and rounded instead of being stream-lined. The 150 species are found in all the world's seas, but they are especially numerous in warm, tropical waters. They range in size from 5 cm across, to the Pacific

The eye of the **octopus** is very remarkable in that it closely resembles the human eye.

Above: Each of the **octopus's** arms has two rows of suckers.

The **okapi** is a placid animal, and the giraffe's only living relative.

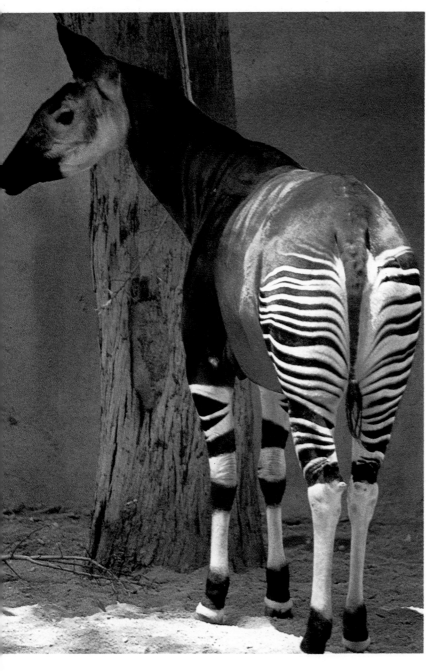

octopus, which has an arm span of up to 10 metres. Some species live in very deep water, but the best-known, the common octopus, lives among rocks in shallow water in the Mediterranean and on the tropical and sub-tropical Atlantic coasts. It usually swims backwards by blowing out water through a muscular tube, called the siphon. Octopuses eat small fish and crustaceans, which they trap in their sucker-covered arms and paralyse with poison.
ORDER: Octopoda;
FAMILY: Octopodidae;
SPECIES: *Octopus vulgaris* (common).

Oilbird

The oilbird is a nocturnal bird which lives in northern South America and the island of Trinidad. It is just over 30 cm long from bill to tail with a wingspan 90 cm, a curved, hawk-like beak and the large, ringed eyes of an owl.

Oilbirds feed at night but, unlike other nocturnal birds, they eat only fruit. They can see well in dim light but may be guided to their food by its scent. During the day they live in caves where there is no light at all. To find their way, they use echo location as bats do, sending out location sounds that resemble the clacking noise of a typewriter.

The young are raised on fruit brought to the caves by their parents, and grow very fat. Indians regularly kill the young birds and use them to make cooking oil.
ORDER: Caprimulgiformes;
FAMILY: Steatornithidae;
SPECIES: *Steatornis caripensis.*

Okapi

The okapi was one of the last big mammals to be discovered in Africa. It lives deep in the Zaire rain forests and, even now, little is known of its behaviour. The okapi is the GIRAFFE's only living relative. Its neck is shorter, but the general shape of the body is similar. It stands 165 cm at the shoulder and 185 cm to the top of the head and its back slopes slightly to the rump. It weighs about 250 kg. Females are usually slightly bigger than males. The coat is a deep, reddish or blackish-brown, becoming lighter with age. On the upper forelimbs, hind limbs and haunches, there are thick, irregular white stripes. The male has a pair of short horns on the forehead. After mating, the calf is born between 435 and 449 days later, which is similar to the gestation period of the giraffe.

ORDER: Artiodactyla;
FAMILY: Giraffidae;
SPECIES: *Okapia johnstoni.*

Olm

The olm is the only cave-dwelling AMPHIBIAN in Europe. It lives in the underground rivers and pools of limestone caves in Yugoslavia and Italy. Like many other cave-dwelling beasts, the olm is blind and white. It grows to 30 cm long. Its head is broad with a blunt snout, and red, feathery gills. Like the MUDPUPPY, it never becomes completely adult; it keeps its gills throughout its life. The eel-like body ends in a tail flattened from side to side and the legs are short and weak. Olms hide under boulders but can move fast, and catch crustaceans and small fish. Being blind, they find their prey by picking up the vibrations emitted when it moves.

ORDER: Caudata;
FAMILY: Proteidae;
SPECIES: *Proteus anguinus.*

Opossum

With the exception of the "rat" opossums, the opossums of the Americas are the only MARSUPIALS which live outside Australasia.

The best known of these is the Virginia opossum. This rat-like marsupial is 30 to 50 cm from nose to rump, and has an almost hairless tail as long as its body. The first toe on each hindfoot is clawless and is *opposable*, that is, it can touch the other toes to grasp, like the thumb of a human hand can grasp with the fingers. An opossum spends much of its life on the ground in wooded country, but will climb when threatened. It uses its tail as a fifth hand for extra support. The oppossum feeds mainly at night, eating insects, snails, toads, voles, snakes and small birds. When frightened, it may pretend to be dead.

Other Central and South American opossums look similar to the Virginia opossum, though some have a bushy tail. The water opossum has webbed feet and a water-proof pouch.

ORDER: Marsupialia;
FAMILY: Didelphidae;
SPECIES: *Didelphis marsupialis* (Virginia).

Opossum shrimp

Opossum shrimps are small, shrimp-like CRUSTACEANS whose females have a pouch to hold their young – rather like an opossum or other marsupial. There are about 650 species, all but 50 of which live in the sea. Most feed by filtering food particles from the water, but some species eat larger forms of food.

ORDER: Mysidacea;
FAMILY: Mysidae and others.

Orang utan

The orang utan is the only great ape in Asia. It lives in tropical forests in Borneo and Sumatra. It walks on all fours, with the hands either clenched or flat on the ground but spends most of its time swinging through the trees. It is a marvellous gymnast, holding branches equally well with feet and hands. In captivity, it often walks erect. But, to do this, it has to keep the knee locked and the leg straight.

Orang utans sleep in tree-top nests which they build each night. They do not live in large social groupings like CHIMPANZEES or GORILLAS. A female sometimes travels with other females for a while, and a male may join this group. But adult males are solitary most of the time. The young leave their mothers and form adolescent bands when they reach about four years of age.

The male orang utan stands about 135 cm high when upright and weighs as much as a man. The female weighs only half as much and is 117 cm high at the most. The arms are one and a half times as long as the legs. Coarse, dark grey skin shows through the sparse, reddish hair in many places. The male grows a moustache or beard, but the rest of the face is hairless. The Borneo race is maroon-tinted. The Sumatran race is lighter. Numbers of both races have been declining since World War II. Deforestation has affected the orang utan's distribution and so many have been shot or captured for private zoos that they may soon become extinct in the wild.

ORDER: Primates;
FAMILY: Pongidae;
SPECIES: *Pongo pygmaeus.*

Right: An adult male **orang utan**.

Omnivore

Although a great many animals feed only on flesh or only on plants, some creatures like a mixed diet. They are known as omnivores – animals that will eat anything. Omnivores have teeth that are adapted both for tearing meat and chewing plants.

BEARS, for instance, eat small animals and grubs, but like to vary their diet with plants. They are passionately fond of honey, and rip open bees' nests to get it. They cannot be stung because of their thick fur. BADGERS also like honey, though they feed mainly on insects and small animals such as mice and voles.

Orb spider

This is a collective name for the family of spiders that spin round or orb-shaped webs. Their bodies are large compared with their legs. The most numerous orb spider in Europe is the European garden spider, which has characteristic cross-shaped markings.

Generally, orb spiders spin their webs in open areas. Some species build a new web every night. The silk is secreted from silk glands and spun with specially adapted organs called spinnerets. Some tropical species spin webs 2.5 metres across, tough enough to be used as nets by local fishermen.

Orb spiders depend entirely on their webs for catching prey. They start with a rectangular outer scaffolding, then lay radial strands around a central hub, like the spokes of a wheel. This basic frame is made of non-sticky silk. The spider walks along this as it lays down a spiral of sticky snare threads. The result is a delicate but tough web which traps victims, from insects to small birds and even bats. These are quickly swathed in silk and injected with a paralyzing poison. This liquifies the body contents, which the spider then sucks out. Some spiders lay in wait for their prey at the centre of the web. Others attach a silk trapline to the centre then hide nearby, holding the trapline which vibrates when an unsuspecting insect lands on the web. The spider darts out and captures its meal.

ORDER: Araneae;
FAMILY: Argiopidae.

Oriole

The name given to a group of 30 birds in the Old World – the true orioles – and to the American orioles in a quite separate family. Best known of the Old World orioles is the golden oriole. This very striking bird breeds in most of Europe south of the Baltic. The

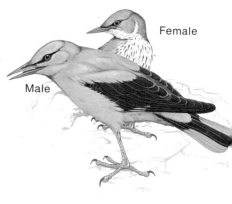

Female

Male

The **golden oriole** is about 25 cm long, with a sharply pointed beak.

male is golden-yellow with black wings and tail, the wing tips being yellow. Females are olive-green on the head and back, with lighter underparts, streaked with brown. The wings and tail are mostly brown. Orioles are forest birds. They eat insects in summer and fruit later in the season.

ORDER: Passeriformes;
FAMILY: Oriolidae;
SPECIES: *Oriolus oriolus* (golden).

Left: This **orb spider** is a typical arachnid, clearly displaying its four pairs of jointed legs.

Below: An **orb spider** web coated with frost shows up the delicate framework.

Oryx

Oryx are hardy ANTELOPES, white or fawn in colour, with long, backward-pointing, slender, ridged horns. There are three species, all living in desert regions of Africa and south-western Asia. The rare Arabian oryx is small and white. It is 107 cm high and has dark limbs. The scimitar oryx of the African Sahara is white, with reddish head markings and a red neck. The third species is divided into three races. The gemsbok of south-western Africa is 120 cm high. It is fawn-coloured, with white shanks and belly and black face markings. The beisa oryx of Somalia forms the northern race while, farther south, is the tufted oryx, which is redder. These wary animals live in herds of 6 to 12 or more. The female's gestation period is 260 to 300 days. In the rainy season, when the young are born (May to September in Arabia, and September to January in the Kalahari desert, where the true gemsbok is found), the small herds unite into larger groups of 24 to 60.

ORDER: Artiodactyla;
FAMILY: Bovidae.

Osprey

The osprey or fish-hawk is a bird the size of a small EAGLE. It is found in most parts of the world, migrating southwards to warmer regions in winter. The osprey feeds almost entirely on fish, and is usually found nesting by rivers, lakes and seashore. When hunting, it circles over the water, hovers for a moment to sight prey, then plunges into water, striking at the fish with its talons, which have rough spiny scales to help hold slippery prey. Sometimes the osprey vanishes completely under water before emerging and flying off with its meal.

ORDER: Falconiformes;
FAMILY: Pandionidae;
SPECIES: *Pandion haliaetus.*

Left: A young **osprey** tests out its wings on its nest. The drawing below shows the typical dark line on the head.

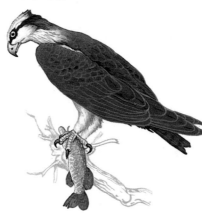

Ostrich

The ostrich is the world's largest living bird. The male may reach a height of 2.5 metres, of which nearly half is the long neck. Ostriches live on the plains, in the dry regions of Africa. They cannot fly, but their height enables them to see danger approaching and they can run to escape, reaching speeds of 60 km/h. Ostriches move about in search of food, often in large groups. They feed mainly on fruits, seeds, and leaves, and may get water from plants in arid areas. They also eat small animals, possibly even LIZARDS and TORTOISES.

Breeding may take place at any time of year, depending on the time of the rainy season. Ostriches are usually polygamous, a male having as many as five females in his harem. The females lay their eggs in a common nest – a large depression in the ground – which they guard together with the males, sitting on the eggs to shade them from the hot sun. The chicks can run about soon after they hatch, and form large bands when they leave the family group. They breed when they are four or five years old.

The plumage of the male ostrich is black with white plumes on the wings and tail. Demand for these plumes once caused a great reduction in numbers. Fortunately, ostrich plumes are no longer in fashion and the ostrich is not in danger. Ostriches have only two toes on each foot, compared to four in most birds. This helps them to run quickly.

ORDER: Struthioniformes;
FAMILY: Struthionidae;
SPECIES: *Struthio camelus.*

Otter

There are about 20 species of otter, found in all parts of the world except Australasia and Antarctica. They are long-bodied short-legged animals with a stout tail which is thick at the base and tapering towards the tip. The head is flat and broad and the ears are small. The sleek fur consists of a fawn, water-proof under-fur and an outer layer of stiff guard hairs, which are grey at the base and dark brown at the tip. The forefeet are small and the hindfeet are large and webbed. Otters sleep in burrows made in the banks of rivers and lakes and are mainly active by night. They spend much of their

A **sea otter** floats comfortably. Lying like this the animal will bash a shell against a stone laid on its chest until the shell is broken.

time in the water and are expert swimmers; their speed and manoeuvrability enables them to catch fish with ease. They also eat CRAYFISH, FROGS, BIRDS and small mammals. They have a great sense of fun which becomes apparent with such popular games as sliding down slippery banks into the water.

Except in the mating periods, otters are solitary, elusive creatures, always on the alert for danger. Mating takes place at any time of year, with a peak in spring and early summer. The 2 or 3 cubs remain in the burrow for eight weeks, after which their mother coaxes them into the water for their first swim.

Species include the European otter, the Canadian otter, the sea otter, and the Brazilian giant otter. Unfortunately, the fur of the giant otter is commercially valuable and it is now the most endangered species of Amazonian mammal.
ORDER: Carnivora;
FAMILY: Mustelidae.

Otter shrew

Three species of otter shrew inhabit fast-flowing or sluggish waters in western and central Africa. The largest species is the giant otter shrew. It grows to 36 cm long from nose to rump, and has a 30 cm tail. Its toes are not webbed so it swims by flattening its tail and using it like a vertical oar. The dwarf otter shrew does have webbed toes. Both species eat fish and crustaceans.
ORDER: Insectivora;
FAMILY: Potamogalidae.

Ovenbird

Ovenbirds form a large family of over 200 species. They live mainly in South America but occupy a wide range of habitats. They are named after the clay nests which some species build, but their habits are extremely varied. The rufus ovenbirds build domed clay nests in open country in Argentina and neighbouring areas. The miners and earthcreepers are also ground-living birds, while the shaketails live along watercourses. Some are even found along the shores of Chile, where they feed among the floating kelp; the only perching birds to take on a partially-marine way of life. Others are marsh birds, and many live in trees and forests. Most ovenbirds eat insects.
ORDER: Passeriformes;
FAMILY: Furnariidae.

Owl

The owls are birds of prey which, unlike hawks and falcons, are usually active at night. Because of their nocturnal habits, hooting calls and silent flight, owls have always been regarded as birds of mystery. They figure frequently in tales of witchcraft and the supernatural and were once thought to have the gift of prophecy and unusual intelligence.

Brown form

Tawny owl

Grey form

Owls fly almost noiselessly. The long flight feathers of an owl's wings are tipped with down. This deadens the noise of the owl's wing-beats so that their intended prey has no warning of attack. Owls have very keen sight, and the position of their eyes on the front of their rather flattened faces gives them excellent *binocular vision*. But experiments have shown that an owl can catch a mouse in a pitch-black room, relying only on its hearing. The owl has well developed ears, with flaps of skin forming "outer ears", hidden beneath the feathers. The "ear tufts" on the heads of many owls are, in fact, feathers.

Owls range in size from the North American elf owl, which is about 13 cm long, to the EAGLE OWL, which reaches a length of about 60 cm. Apart from the fairly common BARN OWL, other European owls include the tawny owl,

The face of this **owl**, with its large, acute eyes and hooked beak, shows clearly that the bird is a predator.

Pygmy owl

Little owl

Scops owl

Long-eared owl

Eagle owl

Dark-breasted form

Barn owl

the long-eared owl, the short-eared owl, and the little owl.

Most owls are woodland birds. Some live close to humans, nesting in church towers and old buildings. The BURROWING OWL of North America lives in burrows on the prairies. The SNOWY OWL, a large white bird, lives in the polar regions of the northern hemisphere. Owls feed on small mammals (particularly RODENTS such as mice, voles and rats) and insects, although some species are fish-eaters. Their prey is seized in the powerful talons, torn to pieces with the hooked beak, and swallowed in chunks. Fur, feathers, bones and other waste which the owl cannot digest, are later spat out in the form of small neatly wrapped pellets.
ORDER: Strigiformes.

Oxpecker

The name given to two species of birds which spend most of their time in close attendance on large mammals, from which they remove TICKS and bloodsucking flies. Oxpeckers, or tick-birds, are often seen perching on the backs of African game, particularly RHINOCEROSES, GIRAFFES, HIPPO-POTAMI and ELAND. The association helps both creatures. The hosts have their parasites removed and may even be warned of danger by the birds' alarm calls, and the oxpeckers obtain food. Oxpeckers nest in holes in trees, and rocks.
ORDER: Passeriformes;
FAMILY: Sturnidae;
SPECIES: *Buphagus*.

Oyster

The oysters used for food are *bivalve* MOLLUSCS. They also produce pearls, but the real pearl-producing species are in a different family. Pearl oysters are more like MUSSELS.

The right-hand side, or *valve*, of a true oyster shell is flat and the left-hand valve is rounded. Oysters anchor themselves to the sea bed by the rounded half of the shell, in which the body of the oyster rests with the flat valve acting as a lid. They draw in water at the rate of up to 11 litres an hour, and filter out food particles from it. If the oyster takes in too much non-edible sediment it expels it by a sudden "cough", clapping its valves shut. It can also close its shell slowly and keep it shut for long periods if danger threatens. An oyster may change sex many times during its lifetime.
CLASS: Bivalvia;
ORDER: Anisomyaria.

Oystercatcher

The oystercatcher is a large wading bird. It lives in Europe, South Africa, Asia, Australasia and the Americas. It is largely black above, with white underparts, a long, red bill and pink legs. It lives mainly on rocky shores, sandy beaches, mud-flats or sand dune areas, although it may breed inland. It eats mussels, cockles, winkles, crabs and worms, but it is unlikely that it eats oysters. Four

The **oystercatcher** averages about 40 cm in length. It can prize shellfish open with its chisel-like beak.

other species occur in the Americas and one is confined to Australia.
ORDER: Charadriiformes;
FAMILY: Haematopodidae;
SPECIES: *Haematopus ostralagus*.

A pearl **oyster** opened to reveal pearls. The oyster builds pearls by coating small foreign bodies such as particles of sand with layers of nacre (mother-of-pearl).

P

Paca

The paca is a large, rat-like RODENT with a very short tail. It is also called the spotted cavy, because its brown to black coat is marked with four rows of white spots running along its flanks. The paca, found from Mexico to Brazil, is about 76 cm long and can weigh up to 11 kg. The smaller mountain paca lives in the Andes forests. Both have large cheek bones which form the outer walls of huge cheek pouches.

Pacas usually live in swampy regions. They are strong swimmers and rugged fighters if cornered, using their large *incisor* teeth as weapons. They spend the day in burrows, coming out at dusk to feed on plants and fruit.

ORDER: Rodentia;
FAMILY: Cuniculidae;
SPECIES: *Cuniculus paca.*

Pack rat

The pack rat is in fact a VOLE. Its other names are wood rat and trader rat. A curious habit of this animal is that whenever it sees an interesting object, it will pick it up and carry it off. Whatever it takes, it replaces with something else from its hoard! Pack rats collect and hoard all sorts of objects, especially brightly-coloured metal ones.

There are 22 species of pack rat in North and Central America. The dusky-footed wood rat is a good example. It has typical vole features: blunt muzzle, small eyes, fairly large ears and a furry tail. Pack rats are nocturnal. They build nests of twigs and dried grasses, sometimes with several chambers, and they eat nuts, berries, leaves and roots. They are about 45 cm long from nose to tail, and dark brown to grey in colour.

ORDER: Rodentia;
FAMILY: Cricetidae.

Paddlefish

Like the STURGEON, the paddlefish is a member of an order that is the "missing link" between bony fishes and cartilaginous fishes such as SHARKS and SKATES. Although classified as bony fishes, these archaic creatures in fact have a skeleton made of cartilage, like that of a shark. Of the two species of paddlefish, the one found in Chinese rivers, is the larger, reputably up to 7 metres long. The other species is much smaller and lives in the Mississippi valley of the southern United States. Paddlefishes get their name from their long, paddle-shaped snout, which they use to detect the floating PLANKTON on which they live.

ORDER: Acipenseriformes;
FAMILY: Polyodontidae;
SPECIES: *Psephurus gladius* (Chinese); *Polyodon spathula* (Mississippi).

Pademelon

The four species of pademelon are MARSUPIALS found in areas of Australia, Tasmania and Papua New Guinea. They are sometimes called scrub wallabies. They grow up to 76 cm from nose to rump and have a long tail which is less hairy than the rest of the coat. Pademelons live in the dense undergrowth of forests and swamps, making tunnel-like runways through the long grass and ferns.

ORDER: Marsupialia;
FAMILY: Macropodidae.

Palm civet

Although similar to true CIVETS in appearance and habits, palm civets differ anatomically. For instance, their teeth are weaker and the scent glands less elaborate. There are six species in southern Asia and one in Africa. Best known is the Indian palm civet, found from India to the Philippines. Palm civets live mainly in trees. They leap and climb in search of fruits and seeds, birds and small mammals. Young palm civets take only three months to reach full size.

ORDER: Carnivora;
FAMILY: Viverridae.

Palm dove

The palm dove is an attractive pink, brown and blue bird, half the size of a pigeon. It lives in Africa and Asia and has been introduced to Australia. Palm doves are seed-eating birds that live in open country and forest clearings. They have become dependent on people for food in many places, and can be seen in towns, villages and gardens.

ORDER: Columbiformes;
FAMILY: Columbidae;
SPECIES: *Streptopelia senegalensis.*

Palm squirrel

Two kinds of palm squirrel are found in southern Asia and West Africa and a third kind, the oil-palm squirrel, comes from central and eastern Africa.

Palm squirrels resemble the tree squirrels of the northern hemisphere in their habits. They are at home in the trees but also feed on the ground, eating nuts, seeds, bark, and foliage as well as insects and their grubs. The Indian palm squirrels are striped much like CHIPMUNKS.

The Indian palm squirrels have the habit of "playing dead". On being shot at, one of these squirrels was seen to fall off a branch as if it had been hit. As the hunters went to retrieve it, it ran off.
ORDER: Rodentia;
FAMILY: Sciuridae.

Palolo worm

Palolo worms are segmented worms with a most remarkable life-cycle. They generally inhabit burrows in tropical coral reefs and among coral rocks in the Pacific and West Indies.

Each worm is about 40 cm long. Towards the breeding season the rear end changes. It becomes filled with either eggs or sperm, detaches itself and swims to the surface, guided by moonlight. It releases its contents and the dead skin floats away. The rest of the worm stays in its tube and regrows its rear end. All the worms release their rear sections at the same time, in a process known as swarming. This results in a "soup" of eggs and sperm, and ensure that as many eggs are fertilized as possible. Swarming is directly linked to the lunar cycle. With the Pacific species *Palolo viridis*, swarming takes place on a single night of the last quarter of the October–November moon. Samoan and Fijian islanders regard these worm sections as a great delicacy, and congregate on the predicted night to collect them in large quantities.
PHYLUM: Annelida;
CLASS: Polychaeta;
FAMILY: Eunicidae.

Panda

The panda is a bear-like animal found only in the damp, cold bamboo forests on the hillsides of eastern Tibet and Szechwan in South-West China. Its striking black and white colouring and

The **giant panda** is a solitary animal, except in the breeding season.

gentle appearance have captured the imaginations of people all over the world and it has become the symbol of the World Wildlife Fund, one of the leading conservation organizations. The name panda was originally applied to the red panda or cat bear. The panda usurped the name, but is frequently called the giant panda to avoid any confusion.

The first European to discover the panda was Père David in 1869. In 1937 the first live panda was seen outside China and there are now several in zoos all over the world.

The panda is about 1.8 metres long and weighs about 130 kg. Little is known of its habits in the wild. It is a secretive animal and its habitat is very inaccessible. Pandas appear to be solitary animals, except in the breeding season, which is believed to occur in spring. They live mostly on the ground and eat plant material, such as bamboo shoots, grasses, gentians, irises and crocuses, together with a few small rodents, birds and fish. It is not known how many wild specimens exist, but the panda is strictly protected and is not endangered.

The breeding habits of pandas are also unknown, despite the two attempts in Moscow and London to persuade their pandas An-an and Chi-chi to mate. It is believed that in the wild, pandas produce one or two cubs in January.
ORDER: Carnivora;
FAMILY: Procyonidae;
SPECIES: *Ailuropoda melanoleuca*.

The **pangolin** rolls up in a ball for safety.

Pangolin

Four species of pangolin, or scaly anteater, live in Africa, and three in southern Asia. Pangolins vary in length from 1 to 1.5 metres. They have a long tail which may be twice the length of the body. They have short legs and a long, rope-like tongue. The animals are toothless. Except for the underside of the body, pangolins are covered with large, overlapping, brown horny scales. They usually feed at night, using the powerful claws on their forefeet to rip open termites nests, and picking up the insects on their sticky tongues. Pangolins may also eat ants, although they seem to do this unintentionally. They have been known to take ant baths, allowing the ants to crawl under their scales, but they close their ear and nose openings to prevent entry. Swallowing a number of small pebbles helps to crush any ants in their stomach.

Most pangolins climb trees and use their tails to hang from branches. On the ground, they walk on the sides of their forefeet while they use their hind feet more conventionally. Sometimes they walk on hind legs only, with their tail stretched out behind to balance them.

ORDER: Pholidota;
FAMILY: Manidae.

Paradoxical frog

The paradoxical frog is found in tropical South America and spends most of its life in water. An extraordinary feature of this frog is that the tadpole is several times larger than the adult, being up to 27 cm long and decreasing in size as it matures. The froglets measure only 4 cm and, at first, scientists could not believe that the froglets and tadpoles both belonged to the same species. The adult frogs are about 7.5 cm long

ORDER: Salientia;
FAMILY: Pseudidae;
SPECIES: *Pseudis paradoxa.*

Paramecium

Paramecium is a tiny protozoan animal that lives in stagnant fresh water. There are about 10 species, all less than 0.3 mm long and all vaguely slipper-shaped. The animals are clothed with minute hairs, or *cilia*, which beat rhythmically to drive the animals through the water with a corkscrew motion. A groove on one side of the body leads to the mouth, and the cilia waft bacteria and other particles into it as the animal moves along. Being a single cell, Paramecium normally reproduces by splitting into two, just like amoeba, but it can also reproduce sexually. This usually happens when food is short, and two individuals come together and exchange genetic material from their nuclei. Each then swims away and produces four new individuals.

PHYLUM: Protozoa;
CLASS: Ciliata.

Parasite

A parasite is a plant or animal that lives in or on the body of another species, taking food from it but giving nothing in return. The attacked species is called the host and it is indispensable to the parasite. The fleas that live among the feathers of a bird are thus parasites, but the cat that catches the bird is not. FLEAS, TICKS, and other parasites that live on the outside of the host's body are called ectoparasites. Endoparasites live inside the bodies of their hosts, like the tapeworm which lives in the food canal of its host and absorbs some of the digested food. Surrounded by food, endoparasites do not need to search for it and as a result they have virtually no sense organs or means of movement. They devote themselves to absorbing food and producing eggs. The production of large quantities of eggs (or seeds in plants) is characteristic of most parasites because so many will inevitably fail to find a host. Those with the most eggs (or seeds) have the best change of success.

Parasites do not usually kill their hosts, because this would amount to committing suicide, although some do kill their hosts when they have finished with them. ICHNEUMON flies lay their eggs in or on caterpillars or other young insects, and the ichneumon grubs proceed to eat the host. They carefully avoid the essential parts at first, so the host remains alive and continues to provide fresh food. When the grubs are almost fully grown and have no further need of the host they destroy it.

Parental care

Without parental care few if any human babies could survive. The animal world can be divided into two groups. In one, the parents take no further notice of their offspring once they have given them life. In the other group the parents play an active part in caring for their young.

In the eat-and-be-eaten world of nature there is a great deal of wastage. But generally those creatures which take little or no care of their offspring produce huge quantities of them. The giant OCEAN SUNFISH, for example, lays up to 300 million eggs at a time. Other fish lay smaller but still huge numbers of eggs. Even if millions perish, enough survive to carry on the species. Fish, such as SEA-HORSES, that look after their young lay comparatively few eggs.

Animals that take great care of their offspring have only a few at a time. Monkeys, which are among the most devoted parents, have only one young at a time.

The amount of care that parents give to their offspring varies according to the speed with which the young animals mature and become able to look after themselves. One of the longest periods of care is needed for ELEPHANT calves. An elephant mother is helped by another female elephant, or "auntie", who keeps company with her for several months before the calf is born. The two adult elephants keep the calf between them while they graze. The calf starts to graze when it is three or four months old but continues to take milk from its mother for three to four years.

Hunting animals catch food for their young even after they are weaned because the infants are still too immature to catch their own food. If there are several young in the family, the stronger ones take more than their share of the food. As a result the weaker animals may die. But this does ensure that only the best and fittest animals survive, so that the species is kept at its best.

Birds are particularly industrious parents. After the female has laid her eggs, she sits on them to keep them warm until they hatch. In many species the cock also helps to hatch the eggs. Once the chicks have hatched both parents usually work to feed

Whenever a parent **robin** approaches the nest, the young respond by opening their beaks wide. The adult birds have to work hard to satisfy their offspring's appetite.

them, often flying many miles every day hunting for food. Some birds feed their chicks by regurgitation. The chicks tap the adult's beak, and this tapping triggers off a response that brings the food into the beak.

In most birds and mammals a curious process known as imprinting takes place during the first few minutes or days of life. The first thing the baby sees and hears is its mother and she becomes imprinted on its mind. It will then follow her everywhere and learn from her actions. This is most important if the youngster is to learn the proper behaviour for its species. Imprinting is so strong that geese hatched by humans will not swop their human "mothers" even for their real mothers.

Parrakeet

Parrakeet is a name given to many kinds of small PARROTS. Generally, parrakeets are small, brightly coloured parrots with long tails. The

Parrakeets are found in the Tropics around the world. They usually roost in trees, and the hanging parrakeets sleep head downwards like bats. Parrakeets live in groups. They are vegetarians and eat mainly seeds, fruit, leaves and flowers. They may be a menace to crops.

ORDER: Psittaciformes; FAMILY: Psittacidae.

Parrot

Parrots are among the most colourful creatures on Earth, and among the most endangered. The 317 remaining species live mainly in warm, topical forests in Australia and South America. Their bright plumage, long lifespan, agility and ability to "mimic" sounds make them popular cage birds. The family includes COCKATOOS, LORIES, MACAWS, and PARRAKEETS or small parrots such as BUDGERIGARS and LOVEBIRDS.

All members of the parrot family have large heads, short necks, strong hooked bills, short stout legs and "zygodactylous" feet. This means that two of the four toes point backwards, allowing the bird to grip firmly to branches and hold food with one foot, unlike most birds. The hooked bill conceals a strong fleshy tongue, used for manipulating food, obtaining nectar and for drinking. The bill is also used as an extra "foot" for climbing trees.

Their plumage is usually bold and bright, though some species are more colourful than others. The yellow-headed Amazon parrot, for example, is green with a yellow head and some blue and red on the wings. Others, such as the COCKATOOS, have crests which they erect during territorial or courtship displays.

A **St Vincent parrot** gnaws lichen from a tree with its powerful beak.

Parrots are essentially tropical forest 'dwellers, and do not migrate. They are gregarious, noisy creatures, twittering or uttering raucous shrieks as they travel about in flocks. They tend to build solitary nests, though some form loose colonies. Nests are usually in tree cavities, but some use burrows in the ground or crevices in rocks. A few Australian parrots dig holes in termite mounds. Pairs will mate for life, the female producing up to 12 eggs in a clutch and both parents generally sharing the tasks of incubating and feeding.

Parrots are threatened by destruction of tropical forests and trade in exotic species.

ORDER: Psittaciformes; FAMILY: Psittacidae.

A coral-chewer, the **parrotfish** Scarus.

Parrotfish

Parrotfishes are named after their "beak", which is formed by the joining together of their teeth, and which they use for grazing off corals and seaweeds. They live on coral reefs. These fishes are brilliantly coloured; some parrotfishes change their colour schemes as many as three times in their lives. Parrotfishes also range greatly in size, from about 30 cm to 4 metres in length. Some parrotfish have the unique habit of enveloping themselves in a mucus envelope as night falls to protect them from predators and to prevent their gills silting up while they "sleep".
ORDER: Perciformes;
FAMILY: Scaridae.

Partridge

The common partridge, or grey partridge is well-known as a game bird of farmland in Europe and south-western Asia. It is a plump bird, 30 cm long and brown in colour with grey and white markings. It is distinguished by a chestnut horseshoe-shaped marking on the pale grey lower breast, though this marking is smaller in the female than the male and may even be absent. The common partridge ranges across Europe into western Asia, and it has become acclimatized to the United States and Canada. The red-legged partridge is similar though slightly larger. It can be distinguished by its red legs and bill. It is a native of south-western Europe, but has been introduced into several more northerly countries in Europe. Partridges eat mainly plant food such as seeds and young shoots, which they find on the ground. In North America, the name "Partridge" is loosely applied to the bobwhite, the ruffed grouse and the Canada spruce grouse.
ORDER: Galliformes;
FAMILY: Phasianidae;
SPECIES: *Perdix perdix* (common).

Peafowl

The three species of peafowl belong to the PHEASANT family. The blue peafowl or Indian peafowl is best known as the peacock, though this name strictly refers to the male peafowl, the female being the peahen. The peacock is renowned for its beautiful train of eye-spot feathers that it raises to frame its glossy blue head and neck when it is courting the peahen, which is brown and lacks the train of the peacock. This species of peafowl lives in the wild in India and Sri Lanka. It feeds on the ground, and eats seeds, fruit and insects. The green peafowl lives farther east, from Burma to Java. Both sexes are green with bronze mottlings from the crest to the tail, and the wings are turquoise and black. The Congo peacock lives in the deep forests of Central Africa. The male is blue and green with a short broad tail, and the female is chestnut and green.
ORDER: Galliformes;
FAMILY: Phasianidae.

The rock **partridge** and red-legged partridge are similar, but the red-legged birds have black streaks below the breast band.

Male
Female
Partridge

The shimmering iridescence of a **peacock's** feathers (above and right) is partly caused by their cell structure.

Peccary

Peccaries are the South American equivalents of the Old World wild pigs which they superficially resemble. But peccaries are smaller than true pigs and scientists have placed them in a separate family. They have slim legs and small hooves. There are three toes on the hind feet, not four as in true pigs. The body is covered with thick, bristly hairs. When alarmed, the hairs on the spine are raised, exposing a scent gland on the lower back which gives out an unpleasant smell.

There are two species of peccary. The collared peccary is the smaller and stands 50 cm at the shoulder. This greyish-looking

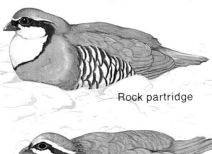

Rock partridge

Red-legged partridge

animal ranges from the southern United States to Argentina. The white-lipped peccary stands 60 cm at the shoulder and is dark reddish-brown to black. It lives in the tropical forests from Paraguay to Mexico.

ORDER: Artiodactyla;
FAMILY: Tayassuidae;
SPECIES: *Tayassu tajacu* (collared); *Tayassu pecari* (white-lipped).

Pelican

Although they look clumsy in captivity, pelicans are superb fliers and swimmers in the wild. They are sociable birds and nest in large colonies. Occasionally, they swim in a line, driving the fish into shallow water where they are easily scooped up. There are eight species: two are found in the New World, and six in the Old. They all live on coasts or inland waters in the warmer parts of the world, the

The **pelican** uses the pouch beneath its bill as a net to catch fish.

Below: A **collared peccary** wallows in mud.

White pelican

Dalmatian pelican

An ungainly bird on land, the **pelican** is graceful in flight.

species differing only in detail and both sexes being alike. Apart from the brown pelican, the plumage of the adults is mainly white. The primary (wing-tip) feathers are dark. The massive bodies are supported by short legs with strong webbed feet. They have long necks and small heads and are among the largest birds, measuring from 130 to 190 cm long. The enormous beak has a pouch which is used as a net for catching fish.
ORDER: Pelecaniformes;
FAMILY: Pelecanidae.

Penguin

Penguins are flightless seabirds. They are stout birds, with a layer of protective blubber around their bodies. The wings have evolved into powerful flippers which can propel the penguin through water like a torpedo, enabling it to catch fish and squid in its strong bill. The wings are almost featherless, but the body is protected by short, dense feathers without barbs, which make the body waterproof. On land, penguins strut or waddle around, lacking the grace that they show in water. The short legs are set far back on the body.

Penguins are found in the southern hemisphere, but they are not confined to the Antarctic region. Of the 17 species, only six breed in Antarctica. And only two of these six, the Adélie penguin and the emperor penguin are completely confined to the Antarctic. The other 11 species breed around the shores of Africa, Australia and New Zealand, and South America. One species actually breeds on the Equator in the Galápagos Islands. The Galápagos penguin survives there because the sea is chilled by a cold ocean current which sweeps up from the south.

Generally, adult penguins are black, with a white belly. But many penquins have distinctive colouring around the head, sometimes with plumes or crests of orange feathers. The largest species is the emperor penguin, which stands about 120 cm high and weighs up to 45 kg. Its collar of orange and yellow brightens its appearance.

Penguins nest in colonies on land. The one egg (2 or 3 in some species) is sometimes laid in a hole on the ground or in a nest of stones. The males usually help to incubate the eggs. Emperor penguins have interesting nesting habits. The female carries the single egg on her feet, covering it with a layer of skin. A few days after laying, the female leaves for the sea. The male is left to incubate the egg which he balances on his feet in the open for two months. During that time the male eats nothing. The female returns soon after the egg is hatched.

Newly hatched penguins are brooded by the parents. Later the chicks leave to gather in groups called crèches. Parents returning with food call to the chicks and feed them away from the crèches. The young penguins cannot forage for themselves until they are fully grown and feathered.

ORDER: Sphenisciformes; FAMILY: Spheniscidae.

Out of the water, **penguins** are ungainly birds. These are Magellanic penguins.

Speckled and black **peppered moths** on lichen-covered bark. The black moth stands out clearly.

Peppered moth

Populations of the peppered moth have undergone some remarkable changes during the 19th and 20th centuries and have enabled biologists to see evolution in action – gradual changes in form as a result of natural selection. The moth exists in two main forms: the normal form, which is speckled black and white, and the completely black form. The latter was very rare until the mid-19th century: any black moths resting on the tree trunks would have been quickly spotted and eaten by birds. As the Industrial Revolution progressed, however, pollution began to blacken tree trunks and the black peppered moths survived better. In fact, it was then the normal forms that were more easily seen and eaten. By the end of the 19th century, nearly all of the moths in industrial areas were black. Black forms have now spread beyond the industrial areas. Control of pollution in

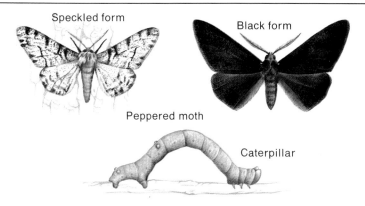

Speckled form

Black form

Peppered moth

Caterpillar

The **peppered moth** caterpillar resembles a twig.

recent decades has meant cleaner tree trunks, and the normal form of the moth is becoming more common again.
ORDER: Lepidoptera;
FAMILY: Geometridae;
SPECIES: *Biston betularia*.

The **perch** can be recognized by its spiny fins and the dark bars on its sides.

Perch

The largest and most successful order of fishes, the Perciformes, was originally named after the European perch, one of several species of perches common in the rivers of Europe. This species has a rather streamlined body, 30 cm or more long, yellow-green in colour and patterned with darker bars. Its under-surface is silvery and its under-fins tinged with red. However, the fish vary in colour and pattern from one place to another.

A similar species, the yellow perch, is common in eastern North America. Other members of the family include the pikeperches and the darters. Perches are shoal fishes, but when hunting they lurk among the stems of water plants, dashing out to seize their prey in their mouth, which opens into a

wide gape. They live as long as 10 years.
ORDER: Perciformes;
FAMILY: Percidae;
SPECIES: *Perca fluviatilis* (European); *Perca flavescens* (yellow).

Père David's deer

Père David's deer was discovered by the French missionary Père Armand David in 1865 in the Chinese Emperor's hunting park

Père David's deer in a nature park. These unusual deer are extinct in the wild.

near Peking. It has long been extinct in the wild, but several hundred survive in zoos and in Woburn Park, England. This strange deer resembles a donkey with long antlers. The front prong of the antlers is forked, but the hind prong is usually straight and slender. Unlike those of other deer, the antlers are sometimes shed twice a year. Père David's deer stands about 114 cm at the shoulder. The coat is reddish-tawny, mixed with grey.
ORDER: Artiodactyla;
FAMILY: Cervidae;
SPECIES: *Elaphurus davidianus*.

Peregrine

The peregrine is a large falcon, between 35 and 45 cm long. The upper parts are grey-blue, striped with darker bars. The under parts are white and also barred. Peregrines are found on every continent except Antarctica, usually near sea cliffs or in rocky mountain country. Northern peregrines fly south in winter to warmer

The **peregrine** (left and above) is the speediest of all the falcons. It hunts by diving steeply at great speed, wings drawn back, mainly after birds, especially pigeons.

The **common periwinkle** (below left) browses on seaweeds on rocks at around low-tide level. The **flat periwinkle** (below right) browses on rocks of the middle shore.

regions. The European peregrine is much less common than formerly, because of the harmful effects of agricultural insecticides.

The peregrine is the supreme hunter among birds of prey and highly prized by falconers. It usually hunts birds, such as PIGEONS, GULLS, DUCKS, or even HERONS, but also eats small mammals, reptiles and even insects. Its "stoop" or dive, with wings nearly closed, is an amazing demonstration of streamlined strength and accuracy; the peregrine's speed as it dives to strike its prey may well exceed 400 km/h.
ORDER: Falconiformes;
FAMILY: Falconidae;
SPECIES: *Falco peregrinus*.

Periwinkle

This name is given to several species of sea snails. There are four important species around the coasts of Europe, and they prob-

ably represent four stages in the gradual colonization of the land from the sea.

The largest and best known species is the edible or common periwinkle. It has a black shell, up to 4 cm high, and lives on all kinds of shores below the high water mark of neap tides. The flat periwinkle, with yellow or brown shell, lives among the brown seaweeds on the middle shore. The rough periwinkle lives between mean tide level and high water mark, and so is exposed for much of the time. Its shell is yellow or white, more pointed than the flat periwinkle. The small periwinkle lives mainly in the splash zone – that part of the shore above extreme high tide that is wetted by spray only during high spring tides. It is a dark, reddish-brown colour, in a conical shape.

The common and flat periwinkles breathe with gills in the normal way, but the other two species have reduced gills and can

fill their mantle cavities with air so that they act like lungs. The small periwinkle is really a land animal, although its young live in water. It feeds on lichens, while the other species eat seaweeds.
ORDER: Mesogastropoda;
FAMILY: Littorinidae;
SPECIES: *Littorina littorea* (common).

Phalanger

There are about 46 species in the Phalanger family. It is the largest and most widespread of Australian MARSUPIAL families. The name comes from a Greek word meaning "a web", and refers to the web of skin that joins the second and third toes on the phalangers' feet. Phalangers are tree-living animals. They feed on leaves, flowers and fruit, though a few are insect eaters. The animals are commonly called possums.

Phalangers as a group have many shapes. Some have bushy

tails, and some have pen-shaped tails or feather-like tails. The scaly-tailed possum has a *prehensile* tip to its tail. In other members of the family, such as the greater gliding possum, a flying membrane has evolved along the sides of the body. Their breeding and life history are much the same as those of kangaroos.
ORDER: Marsupialia;
FAMILY: Phalangeridae.

Phalarope

Phalaropes are dainty water birds, ranging in length 16 to 25 cm. Although classified as wading birds, they swim in shallow water, often turning in rapid circles perhaps to stir up food from the bottom. Phalaropes breed in northern Asia, Europe and America. As they take on a more colourful breeding plumage, the females become brighter than the males. The breeding roles are reversed. The female courts the male, and the male tends the eggs and raises the young. They fly to the south for the winter, and then their plumage becomes drab.
ORDER; Charadriiformes;
FAMILY: Phalaropodidae.

Pheasant

The birds of the pheasant family include a selection of colourful birds that include the JUNGLE FOWL, PARTRIDGE and PEAFOWL. They are ground birds, mainly of eastern Asia. Most are large and beautiful birds with long tails, the males being more showy than the females.

The best-known pheasant is known as the common or ringed pheasant. The male is up to 90 cm long, over half of which is tail; and the female is smaller. The male pheasant is a coppery colour, with a dark green head and neck and red wattles around the eye. There

A handsome cock **pheasant**, with the hen in the background.

Right: The **phalaropes** are unusual birds. The female courts the male and the male buillds the nest and sits on the eggs.

The front end of the **common piddock's** shell is used to drill burrows in rock.

may be a white ring on the neck. The female is brown. The pheasant is a native of Asia, but has been introduced to many other parts of the world as a game bird.

Other beautiful pheasants include the golden pheasant of China with its exquisite mane of golden plumes, and the argus pheasant of South-East Asia.
ORDER: Galliformes;
FAMILY: Phasianidae;
SPECIES: *Phasianus colchicus* (common).

Piddock

The popular name for several species of marine bivalves which

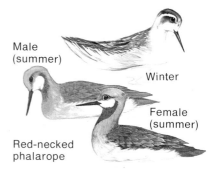

Male
(summer)

Winter

Female
(summer)

Red-necked
phalarope

bore into rock with a remarkable rotary action. In North America they are are commonly known as rock-borers, rock-boring clams or pholas. The two halves of the piddock's shell can move on each other in a see-saw movement, so that the shell, with its toothed outer surface, can scrape at rock or other objects. As it bores deeper, the piddock grows and makes a wider tunnel, so escape back along the narrow tunnel is impossible. It therefore becomes entombed in the hole it has bored, but its siphons protrude from the end for filter feeding.
CLASS: Bivalvia;
ORDER: Adapedonta.

Pig

Pigs are *ungulates* with relatively short legs and heavy bodies. They

are poor runners compared with most of the other hoofed mammals. There are four toes on each foot, although only two toes reach the ground. The animals are scavenging OMNIVORES, eating a wide variety of plant and animal material. They have more teeth than the other ungulates and the *canines* form large tusks which often protrude from the mouth for defence and also for digging up tubers and other underground food. The animals do not chew the cud.

The domestic pig has been derived from the WILD BOAR. We do not know when domestication began, but it was probably about 6,500 years ago, when man was settling down to an agricultural life. Even in prehistoric times there seem to have been several types of domestic pigs – probably derived from the various races of wild boar scattered through Europe and Asia. Today, there are many distinct breeds. One of the main changes brought about in recent times has been the shifting of the weight from the front to the hind quarters, where the best meat is produced. This has been brought about by careful selection of the animals with the best features and by breeding only from these individuals.

ORDER: Artiodactyla;
FAMILY: Suidae.

Pika

Pikas are related to RABBITS and HARES. There are 12 species in Asia and two in North America, with a variety of names, such as rock rabbit, mousehare, whistling hare and rock coney. Pikas look like rabbits with short, rounded ears and no tails. They are mountain dwellers and one species lives on Mount Everest at heights of up to 5500 metres.

Pikas do not hibernate. Instead they cut vegetation, dry it in the sun and store it for winter fodder beneath an overhanging rock or fallen tree. First discovered in Asia

by Peter Pallas in 1769, the pika is easily kept and so has become a popular laboratory animal.

ORDER: Lagomorpha;
FAMILY: Ochotonidae.

Pike

This long-bodied, long-jawed fish is sometimes called the freshwater shark because of its ferocity. The pike or northern pike and several closely related species, live in rivers and lakes of the northern hemisphere. The pike grows up to 1.5 metres long and can weigh as much as 24 kg. It attacks fish even as large as itself, holding the prey fast in its clamped jaws and swallowing it whole. Between such large catches a pike will remain motionless among the weeds, digesting its meal for a week or more. Then it will dart out with lightning rapidity to seize another passing victim. Pike have few enemies except fishermen – and themselves, cannibalism being common.

ORDER: Salmoniformes;
FAMILY: Esocidae;
SPECIES: *Esox lucius* (northern).

Pilchard

When young, this sea fish is called a sardine. Like its close relative the HERRING, the pilchard is an important source of human food. There are extensive canning industries in France, Portugal and Spain, and the canned fish are exported to many other countries. The pilchard is a silvery, streamlined fish up to 25 cm long. It swims in shoals, all the members of which are about the same size, that is, they are either sardines or pilchards which is very convenient

The powerful **pike** has large teeth in the lower jaw only.

for canneries! These shoals, which contain enormous numbers of fishes, swim at different depths during the day and night, as they follow the rise and fall of the floating PLANKTON on which they feed.

ORDER: Clupeiformes;
FAMILY: Clupeidae;
SPECIES: *Sardina pilchardus.*

Pilot fish

This fish is so called because it swims close to other larger fishes, as though it were guiding or piloting them. This, however, is almost certainly not the case. The pilot fish may travel in this way because it gets a "free ride" in the layer of water surrounding the larger fish. Pilot fishes accompanying a large shark may be travelling much faster than they could swim by themselves, being dragged along by the shark's boundary water layer. Pilot fishes grow up to about 60 cm long and have black-and-white striped bodies. Until the young pilot fishes are large enough to begin their life as "pilots" they shelter among the stinging tentacles of jellyfishes.

ORDER: Perciformes;
FAMILY: Carangidae;
SPECIES: *Naucrates ductor.*

Pilot whale

The pilot whales are large DOLPHINS, up to 9 metres long, with a curious bulbous head. Pilot whales live in large schools numbering hundreds or even thousands, and appear to follow one another blindly. If one whale becomes stranded in shallow water, the rest will follow it until the whole school is stranded. Pilot whales are found in many parts of the world, although not in polar waters. They migrate long distances, usually to warmer waters in

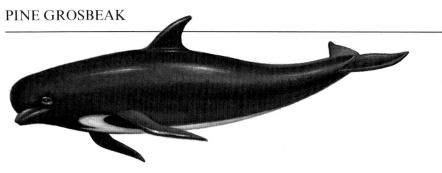

The **long-finned pilot whale** is about 8.5 metres long.

the winter. Pilot whales are still hunted in the Faroe Islands, as they have been for centuries.
ORDER: Cetacea;
FAMILY: Delphinidae;
SPECIES: *Globicephala melaena.*

Pine grosbeak

The pine grosbeak is one of a number of species of FINCH-like birds. It lives in both pine forests and mixed woodland throughout northern Europe, across northern Asia, and in North America down as far as the western United States. It is larger than most other grosbeaks, growing to over 20 cm in length. The male has a red head, breast and rump with brown wings and tail; the female lacks the red colouring. Pine grosbeaks have stout, conical beaks, and eat berries, small seeds, buds and some insects. They nest in conifers.
ORDER: Passeriformes;
FAMILY: Fringillidae;
SPECIES: *Pinicola enucleator.*

Right: The **pintail** is a large, slim dabbling duck.

Pintail

The pintail is a common freshwater DUCK distributed throughout the northern hemisphere. It is so named because of its long, pointed tail feathers. The male has a dark brown head and neck; a white line runs down both sides of the neck to join the white breast. The back is patterned black, white and buff. The female is a mottled grey-brown.

Pintails feed in shallow water on water plants and small animals. They breed in the far north and migrate south for the winter. In the courtship display, a female is pursued by several males. The eggs are incubated in a down-lined hollow on the ground.
ORDER: Anseriformes;
FAMILY: Anatidae;
SPECIES: *Anas acuta.*

Male

Pintail

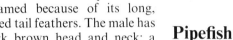

Female

Pipefish

Pipefishes are long, thin fishes that live in coastal areas of temperate and tropical seas. The 150 or so species live mainly among weeds in shallow water. Their greenish or olive-coloured bodies are concealed as they swim in a vertical position among the weed stems. Pipefishes are closely related to SEAHORSES, and like them their bodies are covered with a series of bony rings and their snouts are drawn into a long tube. They feed by sucking in small PLANKTON animals. Pipefishes are also similar to the seahorses in their breeding

The **pine grosbeak** gets its name from its heavy bill.

Male

Female

Right: **Worm pipefishes** hiding among the long thin leaves of eelgrass in shallow water.

behaviour. The males carry the fertilized eggs until they hatch.
ORDER: Gasterosteiformes;
FAMILY: Syngnathidae.

Pipistrelle

The pipistrelle is the smallest of the European bats. It is up to 5 cm long and has a wingspan of 20 to 23 cm and, although small, is of robust build. Its flight is erratic, but it is effective in hunting insects on the wing. Gnats are its staple diet, although it also takes many other insects. There are about 40 closely related species distributed throughout most other parts of the world.
ORDER: Chiroptera;
FAMILY: Vespertilionidae.

Pipit

The name given to a group of more than 50 species of birds which are related to WAGTAILS. Although similar in colour to house SPARROWS, pipits have a

Common pipistrelle

Summer Winter Rock pipit Meadow pipit

Water pipit Tree pipit

The **pipits** can be recognized by their narrow beaks and slender bodies.

Below: A swim in the Amazon might not be a good idea with a shoal of **red piranha** about.

more elaborate pattern of light and dark. The birds resemble LARKS in appearance and habit. They live on the ground in open country and some sing in flight. They eat mostly insects. Pipits are found all over the world. Several species, such as the meadow pipit, tree pipit and rock pipit range over large areas of the northern hemisphere. Only one species lives on Antarctica.
ORDER: Passeriformes;
FAMILY: Motacillidae.

Piranha

Notorious for their attacks on animals and humans, these fishes of South and Central American rivers have strong jaws with razor-sharp teeth, with which they bite out whole chunks of flesh from their victims. Actually, only 4 of the 18 species of piranha are thought to be dangerous to man, but these aggressive fishes can be so numerous that a river can be impossible to enter without risk of life. Piranhas have deep, short

bodies 10 to 46 cm long and are usually dark coloured. The tail is slender and muscular, operating a broad tail fin that drives the body through the water with speed and force. Piranha hunt in shoals of several thousand fishes. These shoals are attracted towards almost any unusual object in the water, which is immediately attacked if it provides food. A large animal such as a horse can be reduced to a skeleton in a matter of minutes.
ORDER: Cypriniformes;
FAMILY: Characidae.

Pitta

Pittas, also called jewel THRUSHES, are brightly coloured songbirds, most of the 50 species of which live in South-East Asia. Some are found as far east as Japan and Australia. Pittas live in forests, jungle or tropical scrub, feeding mainly on land snails. They are about the size of a thrush, with long legs, large feet and very short tails, giving them a "front-heavy" look. Their plumage is varied: greens, reds, yellows and blues are common. The Indian pitta sets up choruses of whistlings, particularly at sunrise.
ORDER: Passeriformes;
FAMILY: Pittidae.

Pit viper

The 60 species of pit vipers include some of the most venomous snakes. The pit vipers are distinguished from the true vipers in having two sensory pits, one on each side of the head between the eyes and the nostril. A thin membrane near the base of each pit is crammed with temperature receptors which enable the snake to detect the presence of warm blooded prey. Pit vipers are nocturnal in habit. Most species live on small mammals, but some feed on birds, amphibians, lizards and even insects. Most pit vipers bear live young, but a few are egg layers.

Pit vipers occur in Asia and the Americas. Asian kinds include the Himalayan pit viper, found high in the mountains. American pit vipers include the BUSHMASTER and FER DE LANCE in the south, and the RATTLESNAKE group in North America.
ORDER: Squamata;
FAMILY: Crotalidae.

Plaice

The plaice is an inhabitant of the sea floor of northern oceans, and is one of the most important flatfishes to be used as human food.

A green **Wagler's pit viper** twines itself around a vine.

Like its close relatives the DAB, FLOUNDER and SOLE, it swims by undulating its flattened body which is marked with red spots on the upper side, and virtually colourless underneath. It has a sideways-twisted mouth and both its eyes lie on the same side of its head, these being adaptations for a life spent mostly lying on the seabed. The plaice is an artist in self-concealment. It disturbs sand so that this covers its fins and so breaks up its outline on the sea

Left: The **plaice** is recognized by its bright orange spots.

Left: The **plaice** is recognized by its bright orange spots.

Right: The seas teem with tiny floating plants and animals – the **plankton**.

Below is a much enlarged head of the larva of a hermit crab.

floor. Its body then changes its colour pattern until this closely matches the pebbles and sand on which it lies. When active, plaice feed on cockles and mussels and other small sea animals. Plaice can grow to almost 80 cm long, but is usually somewhat smaller.
ORDER: Pleuronectiformes;
FAMILY: Pleuronectidae;
SPECIES: *Pleuronectes platessa*.

Plankton

All animal life depends ultimately on plants, which can produce their own food from water and chemicals, by a process called *photosynthesis*. In the sea these plants exist as countless millions of minute organisms, many too small to see without a microscope. They float around in the upper layers of the great oceans. Floating with them and feeding on them are millions of tiny animals. All this floating life is called the plankton, from a Greek work meaning "to drift". The plants are called phytoplankton and the animals zooplankton.

The main animals of the zoo-

plankton are CRUSTACEANS – little shrimp-like animals. Few are bigger than a grain of rice; many are much smaller. There are also miniature snails, jellyfish, worms and other forms, together with a great variety of PROTOZOANS, one-celled animals. In addition, there are the eggs and other young stages of larger sea animals. Among the larger animals of the plankton are KRILL. The zooplankton become the food of larger animals.

The phytoplankton stay in the upper layers of the sea, where sunlight can reach them. The zooplankton on the other hand, migrate towards the surface at night, and sink down, sometimes as far as 90 metres by day. This migration has the value to the animals of taking them down into currents of water that may be moving in a different direction from the surface. In this way the zooplankton can move to fresh feeding grounds, and so exercise some control over their drifting existence.

Plant hopper

Plant hoppers are sap-sucking BUGS belonging to several different families. They range from 2 mm to more than 60 mm in length, and most have strong back legs with which they can leap into the air. Some are also strong fliers. Greens and browns are the main colours, although some of the insects are brilliantly coloured. Some are serious crop pests, often carrying diseases as well as simply taking large quantities of sap.

One of the best known species is the common frog-hopper, a small brown insect looking vaguely like a miniature frog. It spends its early life in a mass of froth on a plant stem. This froth, abundant in early summer is often called cuckoo spit. One group of hoppers, known as tree-hoppers, have tough and often very ornate shields on their backs, often combined with spiky outgrowths at the

A **platypus** wallows in the mud of its native creek.

front. Some of these insects look remarkably like thorns when they sit on the twigs of their food plants, and they are very difficult to pick out.
ORDER: Hemiptera-Homoptera.

Platypus

The platypus is one of Australia's two egg-laying mammals. It is about 75 cm long, including the beaver-like tail. It is often called a duckbill because of its long flattened snout.

Its appearance may be strange, but the platypus is well adapted to its semi-aquatic environment. Its feet are webbed. On the front feet, the webbing extends beyond the toes, but is folded back on land to free the claws for digging and walking. The eye and the opening to the inner ear lie in a furrow on each side of the head. These can be closed as the animal submerges, making it blind and deaf when under water. It relies on its sensitive bill to hunt for worms, shellfish, and aquatic insects in the water. Adult platypuses are toothless. The males have hollow spurs on the hindfeet connected to poison glands. These spurs are used to scratch and poison the enemy.

The female digs a long, winding burrow in a river bank, and lays her eggs in a nesting chamber at the far end. There are usually two white, soft-shelled eggs, about 1.3 cm in diameter. The eggs hatch in 7 to 10 days, and the young are born naked and blind. The mother has no teats; milk exudes from the mammary glands in her abdomen and is lapped up by the young.
ORDER: Monotremata;
FAMILY: Ornithorhynchidae;
SPECIES: *Ornithorhynchus anatinus*.

Plover

Plovers belong to a large family of wading birds that also includes the SANDPIPERS. They range in size from 15 to 30 cm. Plovers live on shores or in open country, usually

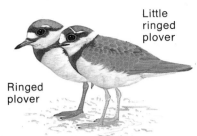

Little
ringed
plover

Ringed
plover

Left, above and below: **Plovers** can be told apart from almost all other wading birds by their short beaks. They probe for worms, grubs and shellfish.

Grey
plover

Winter   Summer

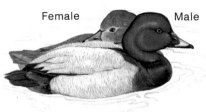

Female   Male

Pochard

The female **pochard** has a brown head with a light stripe through the eye.

Pochard

Pochards are diving ducks. Because their legs are placed well back on the body, they walk with difficulty and spend most of their time on the water. Pochards breed in freshwater ponds and lakes and spend the winter in salt or brackish water. They migrate in V-formation, and sometimes the whole flock plunges spectacularly from a great height into the water.
ORDER: Anseriformes;
FAMILY: Anatidae.

Pocket gopher

Pocket gophers, of which there are about 30 species, are small HAMSTER-like RODENTS found only in North America. Their name is derived from the two external fur-lined cheek pouches, which run from face to shoulder. They are burrowing animals, with thickset bodies and short, powerful legs. They dig with their clawed forelegs and use their sensitive tails as

near water. Outside the breeding season, they gather in flocks to feed at estuaries and shores. Plovers eat mainly small animals such as insects, worms and shellfish. The four species of golden plover are distinguished by spangled black and gold backs. They live mostly in North America, Europe and Asia. The sand plovers are brown or grey and white with black bands, and live in all continents.
ORDER: Charadriiformes;
FAMILY: Charadriidae.

Plume moth

The plume moths are so-called because their wings are each broken up into a number of feather-like plumes. There are about 600 species, found in most parts of the world. Best known of the several European species is the white plume moth, which often comes to lighted windows at night. Its caterpillar feeds on bindweed. A common species found in the United States is the grapevine plume moth, which attacks the young leaves of vines. Most plume moths are brown.
ORDER: Lepidoptera;
FAMILIES: Pterophoridae, Alucitidae.

A ghostly **plume moth** clings to a twig.

antennae to feel their way backwards below ground.

Pocket gophers live alone, except during the breeding season. They rarely come to the surface, keeping to the safety of their burrow systems where they feed on tubers, bulbs and roots. At night they may venture out to snatch a meal of farm crops. Gophers never seem to drink, and little is known about their breeding habits. In some areas, their burrowing habits make them a pest, but on the credit side, the gophers' digging helps to improve the soil.

ORDER: Rodentia;
FAMILY: Geomyidae.

Pocket mouse

Pocket mice are related to KANGAROO RATS. But instead of hopping, they run around on all four legs. There are a number of genera, found from North to Central America, including the spiny pocket mice and the forest spiny pocket mice, which are the largest pocket mice, being 15 cm long with a tail longer than the body. Unlike the others, they live in woodland. In general, pocket mice live in dry country where the vegetation is scanty. They live in burrows, coming out at night to feed on seeds and leaves. Like many rodents, pocket mice cram food into cheek pouches. These pouches can be turned inside out for cleaning.

ORDER: Rodentia;
FAMILY: Heteromyidae.

Polar bear

The polar bear is one of the largest land CARNIVORES in the world. Males average 2 to 2.5 metres in length and weigh 295 to 790 kg. Females are smaller. Polar bears are found only around the North Pole, along the southern edge of the Arctic pack ice. They are carried south by the ice in spring and return northwards when the ice breaks up.

A polar bear survives the cold because of its thick coat, which consists of a dense under-fur beneath the visible long guard hairs, and the thick layer of fat under the skin. The undersides of the broad feet are hairy, enabling it to walk on the ice without slipping. Polar bears are strong swimmers, but generally avoid large areas of water. Males range over vast areas.

Polar bears prey on SEALS, particularly ringed seals. They also eat fish, seabirds and, in spring and early summer, large quantities of plant material, such as grass, lichen, seaweed and berries. They can kill young WALRUSES, but an adult walrus will usually defeat a polar bear by goring it with its tusks. Humans are the polar bear's only other enemy. The bears were formerly hunted for their skins, but are now protected by international agreement.

A **polar** bear on the Arctic ice searches for seals.

Mating occurs in April or May and the cubs are born in December or January. There are generally two cubs, weighing about 0.7 kg, and they remain with their mother for up to two years, when she is ready to mate again.

ORDER: Carnivora;
FAMILY: Ursidae;
SPECIES: *Thalarctos maritimus.*

Polecat

The polecat is a large relative of the WEASEL. Its almost cylindrical body is about 50 cm long and it weighs up to 1.4 kg. The long, coarse fur is dark brown, with dense yellowish under-fur which shows through; the face has white patches. Ferrets are semi-tame albino polecats.

Polecats are common in Europe and Asia. They prefer woods but can adapt to a wide variety of habitats and make their dens in any suitable hole. In the wild, an unpleasant-smelling discharge is used to mark their territories. They feed on rabbits, small rod-

The wary and smelly **polecat** is often killed as a pest.

ents, birds, lizards and snakes, and also prey on poultry.
ORDER: Carnivora;
FAMILY: Mustelidae;
SPECIES: *Mustela putorius*.

Pond skater

The common pond skater is a slender WATER BUG that skates over the surface of still and slow-moving water. Tufts of water-repellent hairs on its feet prevent it from breaking through the surface film. The long middle legs "row" the insect over the surface. The hind legs act as rudders, and the front legs are free to grasp prey – usually other small insects that fall onto the water surface. Many pond skaters have poorly developed wings, but others have good wings and fly well, often wintering far from the water. There are many similar species.
ORDER: Hemiptera-Heteroptera;
FAMILY: Gerridae;
SPECIES: *Gerris lacustris* (common).

Pond snail

Pond snails are a group of freshwater snails that have pointed

spires to their shells and more or less oval openings in them. Some pond snails surface at intervals to renew the air in their lung, but they can also absorb oxygen from the water through the skin surface. Most pond snails feed mainly on scum-like algae and other plant material. Others eat small animals as well.
CLASS: Gastropoda;
ORDER: Basommatophora;
FAMILY: Lymnaeidae.

Above: The **great pond snail** grows to a length of 6 cm.

Left: The common **pond skater** lives on the surface of still water.

Poor-will

The poor-will is a species of NIGHT-JAR found in western North America from southern Canada to Mexico. It lives in woodlands, prairies and arid country, and feeds on flying insects that it hunts by night. The poor-will is very unusual because it is the only bird that is known to hibernate. Most birds that cannot get food in winter migrate to warmer places, but the poor-will lowers its body temperature and goes to sleep in a rock crevice.
ORDER: Caprimulgiformes;
FAMILY: Caprimulgidae;
SPECIES: *Phalaenoptilus nuttallii.*

Porbeagle

Among the more dangerous of its family of mackerel sharks, the porbeagle roams the Atlantic Ocean in search of the fish it preys upon. A fast, deep-bodied shark usually not more than 2 metres long, it has a pointed nose, a large, crescent-shaped mouth and a large tail fin at the sharply-narrowed end of its body. Like its larger but more slender relative the mako shark, the porbeagle has a bad reputation for attacking human beings. The several species of these two sharks are also notorious for attacking small boats, something that most other sharks will not do.
ORDER: Lamniformes;
FAMILY: Isuridae.

Porcupine

Porcupines are small to large rodents, up to 70 cm long and 27 kg in weight. There are two families: *Old World* and *New World*. Their long, curved claws are ideal for burrowing but make them clumsy runners. To make up for lost speed, they are covered in quills to deter predators.

The **porcupine** can rattle its quills to warn off enemies. This is the North African crested porcupine, with quills 40 cm long.

The **porcupine fish** inflates like a balloon and erects its spikes when it senses danger.

Old World or terrestrial porcupines live in the forests and savannas of warm countries such as Ethiopia and Australia. They are herbivorous and nocturnal, spending their days in burrows or rock crevices, and feeding by night on bulbs, roots, fruit and berries. New World or arboreal porcupines live in South America, are generally smaller, and can climb trees to feed. They spend days in hollow trees or leaf nests.
ORDER: Rodentia;
FAMILY: Hystricidae (Old World); Erethizontidae (New World).

Porcupine fish

The several species of porcupine fishes which inhabit tropical seas are famous for their ability to blow themselves up into a spiny ball.

They are particularly well known around CORAL reefs, where they feed on coral and shellfish, crushing this hard food with their plate-like teeth. Apart from their many spines, porcupine fishes normally have a fairly ordinary appearance, but when disturbed or alarmed they draw in water to inflate themselves. If lifted out of the water, they swell from an intake of air. In either case the porcupine fish becomes a hard, spiky ball, difficult to handle and, in the case of an underwater predator, very difficult to swallow.
ORDER: Tetraodontiformes;
FAMILY: Diodontidae.

Right: A **Portuguese man-o'-war** dangles its long tentacles, which include dangerously painful stingers.

Porifera

These animals are the SPONGES – strange, sedentary creatures which live in water. Although they consist of numerous cells, there are only three types of cell and they have no sense organs or nervous systems. The cells are arranged on a simple skeleton, which may be horny, glassy, or chalky. There are about 2500 species, most of them living in the sea.

Porpoise

The porpoise is less streamlined than its cousin, the dolphin, and has a blunt snout. Most species, such as the common porpoise, live in coastal waters, travelling in pairs or in schools of up to 100. Porpoises fall prey to sharks and killer whales and at times are hunted by man for their flesh and blubber. Like dolphins, they will swim in the bow waves of fast-moving ships, much as a surf rider rides a wave. The common porpoise is found around Europe and North America. Other species live in South American waters and around southern and eastern Asia.
ORDER: Cetacea;
FAMILY: Phocaenidae;
SPECIES: *Phocaena phocaena* (common).

Port Jackson shark

This primitive shark lives in seas off the south coasts of Australia. Up to 2 metres long, it has a large, blunt head with prominent, widely-spaced nostrils. Its mouth is unusual for a shark, being placed far forward and not just underneath the head. It is filled with small teeth suitable for seizing and crushing the shellfish on which it feeds. This and nine other related species of sharks, all inhabitants of warmer seas, have another unusual and primitive feature. Their two *dorsal fins* each bears a poison spine, similar to spines possessed by fossil sharks that lived 150 million years ago.
ORDER: Heterodontiformes;
FAMILY: Heterodontidae;
SPECIES: *Heterodontus phillipi.*

Portuguese man-o'-war

This colourful name belongs to a COELENTERATE which has a sting almost as powerful as a COBRA's venom. The name comes from the animal's fancied resemblance to an eighteenth century warship. Each Portuguese man-o'-war is a colony composed of four different kinds of *polyp*. The main polyp is a bladder-like, gas-filled float, up to 30 cm long. It has a high crest which serves as a sail to catch the wind. The colour ranges from blue through purple to scarlet. Hanging beneath the float in the water are many other polyps. Some are concerned with feeding, others with reproduction. There are trailing tentacles, up to 12 metres long, armed with stinging cells. These are used for catching prey which consists of fish and other sea animals. The sting can kill a man, but one small fish, *Nomeus albula*, is immune and shelters among the tentacles. Although often called a JELLYFISH, the Portuguese man-o'-war is actually more closely related to the SEA FIRS. It is found in warm seas throughout the world.
CLASS: Hydrozoa;
ORDER: Siphonophora;
GENUS: *Physalia*

Potoo

The five species of potoos are nocturnal birds related to NIGHT-JARS. Like nightjars, they have streaky dark brown plumage that camouflages them as they hide away to sleep by day. Potoos live in Central and South America and the West Indies. They are fairly large, reaching 50 cm in size. They are birds of woodlands, and hunt flying insects by night. Potoos hunt from their perches, keeping still until an insect flies by and then swooping out in pursuit. They can open their mouths very wide and may catch large insects.
ORDER: Caprimulgiformes;
FAMILY: Nyctibiidae.

Potto

A close relative of the LORIS, the potto lives in African rain forests from Guinea to east-central Africa, north of the Zaire river. It is a small, fairly aggressive animal 36 to 40 cm long, with a short tail and weighing about 1.4 kg. The potto has thick, normally dark brown, woolly fur, round ears and big, round eyes.
ORDER: Primates;
FAMILY: Lorisidae;
SPECIES: *Perodicticus potto.*

Prairie chicken

The two species of prairie chickens belong to the GROUSE family. They live on the prairies of the eastern and central United States. The greater prairie chicken is 43 cm long and pale brown with black barring. The male has an orange crown, large orange airsacs and an epaulette of stiff, pointed feathers. The airsacs are inflated and the epaulette raised during the courtship dances. The lesser prairie chicken is slightly smaller and has violet airsacs. Agriculture has restricted the bird's range.
ORDER: Galliformes;
FAMILY: Tetraonidae;
SPECIES: *Tympanuchus cupido* (greater); *Tympanuchus pallidicinctus* (lesser).

Prairie dog

The prairie dog, also known as the prairie marmot, is a small North American GROUND SQUIRREL, which gets its name from its barking alarm call. There are five species. The prairie dog is about 30 cm long, with a short tail, small ears and a yellowish brown coat. It lives on the plains, feeding on grasses and other prairie plants. Prairie dogs are social animals.

They live together in vast "towns", though these are smaller now than in the past when as many as 400 million prairie dogs might be found in a single colony. Each family in the town defends its own burrow and territory. Each burrow entrance is surrounded by a volcano-like cone of soil, which makes an ideal vantage point from which the prairie dog can keep watch for enemies.

ORDER: Rodentia;
FAMILY: Sciuridae.

Prawn

The name prawn is given to many small, long-bodied CRUSTACEANS, although originally it referred to just one species which lives around the coasts of Europe. This prawn is a SHRIMP-like crustacean, about 6 cm long, excluding is *antennae*. Prawns live close inshore, walking on the sandy sea bed on three of

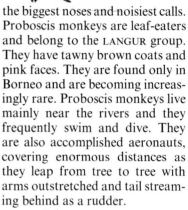

The **prawn** can be recognized by the saw-like shield at the front.

their five pairs of limbs. They can also swim, using other limbs. Prawns are scavengers, eating any small pieces of dead fish they can find.

ORDER: Decapoda;
FAMILY: Palaemonidae;
SPECIES: *Palaemon serratus* (original).

Proboscis monkey

The proboscis monkey gets its name because the males develop enormous noses which may be up to 20 cm long. The nose is used as an amplifier to magnify the monkey's territorial calls, and it is also used in courtship displays. The females prefer the males with

A **prairie dog** town is a network of family burrows, each with a cone-shaped mound at its entrance.

the biggest noses and noisiest calls. Proboscis monkeys are leaf-eaters and belong to the LANGUR group. They have tawny brown coats and pink faces. They are found only in Borneo and are becoming increasingly rare. Proboscis monkeys live mainly near the rivers and they frequently swim and dive. They are also accomplished aeronauts, covering enormous distances as they leap from tree to tree with arms outstretched and tail streaming behind as a rudder.

ORDER: Primates;
FAMILY: Colobidae;
SPECIES: *Nasalis larvatus*.

Male

Pine processionary moth

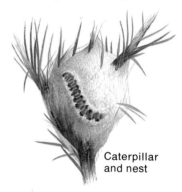

Caterpillar and nest

The caterpillar of the **pine processionary moth** lives communally in a large silken nest among pine twigs.

Processionary moth

The processionary moths, of which there are several species, get their name from the remarkable behaviour of their caterpillars. Best known is the pine processionary which inhabits pine trees in southern Europe. The caterpillars spend the daytime in a ball of silk spun among the branches, and they troop out to feed at night. They move in single file, each one nudging the one in front, and the procession may contain up to 300 caterpillars. They lay strands of silk as they go, and follow the track back to the nest when they have finished feeding. The insects often strip all the leaves from small trees.

ORDER: Lepidoptera;
FAMILY: Thaumetopoeidae;
SPECIES: *Thaumetopoea pityocampa* (pine).

Pronghorn

The pronghorn, although commonly called the pronghorn antelope, is not a true antelope. It is the only living representative of an ancient animal family that arose and developed in North America. It lives in deserts and grasslands in western Canada, the western United States and northern Mexico.

The agile pronghorn is probably the fastest mammal of North America and can reach a speed of 80 km/h over a short distance. It stands 100 cm at the shoulder; it is reddish-brown, with white underparts, white cheeks and rump, and has two white bands on the throat. It has a short dark mane and long curving horns. The animal depends on its keen eyesight to detect its natural enemy, the COYOTE. Pronghorns are extremely curious and will investigate any moving object, a habit once exploited by hunters. Millions of pronghorns once roamed the land, but hunting reduced their numbers drastically by 1925. Today they are a protected species.

ORDER: Artiodactyla;
FAMILY: Antilocapridae;
SPECIES: *Antilocapra americana.*

Ptarmigan

The three species of ptarmigans range across northern Europe, Asia, Canada and Greenland. They belong to the GROUSE family, but live at higher altitudes than other grouse. They feed on shoots, leaves, seeds, berries and insects. The wings and underside are white, but the rest of the plumage changes with the seasons. In summer, the head, neck and upper parts become mottled brown to match the low summer vegetation. In autumn, the brown goes grey as the plants die, and in winter, ptarmigans are white all over to match the snow.

ORDER: Galliformes;
FAMILY: Tetraonidae.

Pudu

The pudu are the smallest of all DEER and they live in South

Protozoa

The very simplest animals consist of single cells. They are called protozoa, which means "first animals", and the earliest forms of animal life must have been of this kind. Scientists do not know how many species of protozoa there are. At least 30,000 have been identified, and several times as many have not yet been classified. It is quite impossible to estimate how many individuals there are — millions upon millions, far more than any other kind of animal life.

Scientists do not agree on how to classify these tiny creatures. But there are four basic kinds, grouped according to how they move about. Almost all live in water.

Flagellates have long whip-like threads that thrash about to drive them through the water.

Sarcodines are creatures that move by putting out a part of the cell wall to form what is called a pseudopod. The rest of the cell then moves into it. Sporozoans are very tiny parasites with no particular locomotion.

Ciliates have fine hair-like structures, or cilia, which they use to move with and to capture their food.

Magnified tiny shells belonging to the **protozoa**. Countless billions of these shells form deep layers on the ocean floor.

Below: The **ptarmigan** changes colour with the seasons.

Above: A **willow ptarmigan** is revealed against the sparse spring vegetation of its Yukon homeland.

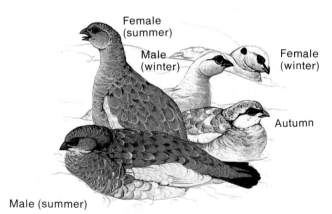

Female (summer)

Male (winter)

Female (winter)

Autumn

Male (summer)

America. The animal ranges from central Chile almost to the southern tip of the continent. It is very shy, but easily tamed when young. It is up to 80 cm long, and weighs 9 kg. It has short, spike-like antlers.
ORDER: Artiodactyla;
FAMILY: Cervidae;
SPECIES: *Pudu pudu.*

Puff adder

Puff adders, of which there are eight species, are stout-bodied, venomous snakes with short tails. They range in size from the 180 cm long Gaboon viper down to the Peringuey's desert adder, which is only 30 cm long. Puff adders are found in Africa and they are divided into two groups: those which live in tropical forests, such as the brightly coloured Gaboon viper; and the more drably coloured savanna and desert species. The common puff adder belongs to the second category and is found in Arabia as well as Africa.

Puff adders have a loud warning hiss which sounds something like a horse puffing air through its lips. They bite to disable their prey or in self defence and their fangs may inject 15 drops of venom. As few as four drops are fatal to humans, though fortunately these snakes will bite only after extreme provocation.
ORDER: Squamata;
FAMILY: Viperidae;
SPECIES: *Bitis arietans.*

Puffer

Like their relatives the PORCUPINE FISHES, puffers are found mainly near tropical reefs, and are able to inflate their bodies to twice or more their usual size. This makes them more difficult for predators to swallow, especially since puffers, again like porcupine fishes, have spiny skins. Puffers have the bright colours typical of inhabitants of coral reefs. They have large eyes and beak-like mouths with crushing teeth, suitable for eating coral and other hard foods. Puffers include dangerously poisonous fishes which have killed many people who ate them.
ORDER: Tetraodontiformes;
FAMILY: Tetraodontidae.

Puffin

Puffins are small auks, about 30 cm long. The bills are massive,

Summer

Winter

The **puffin's** triangular beak is bright red and yellow in summer.

triangular-shaped and coloured by red, yellow and blue stripes, with a thick yellow skin in the corners of the mouth. The bills give these seabirds a comic appearance. The plumage is black above and white underneath, with the black extending around the neck as a collar. The legs are bright orange. The Atlantic puffin breeds from Greenland to the Gulf of St Lawrence in the west and from Spitzbergen to northern France in the east. Some spread as far south as the Mediterranean. Puffins swim underwater using their wings while searching for food. They are able to hold as many as 30 small fishes in their beak.

ORDER: Charadriiformes;
FAMILY: Alcidae.

Puma

The puma looks like a lioness. It is one of the two big cats of the Americas. Both sexes have a coat of short, close, yellowish-brown fur. The largest known puma was a male, 2.4 metres long from head to tail and weighing 118 kg. At the other extreme are individuals less than half as long and one-sixth as heavy. The females are usually smaller than the males. They live on mountains, plains and deserts, and in forests, ranging from western Canada to Patagonia in southern South America.

Puma, cougar and mountain lion are three names for this large American cat.

The puma is known for its great strength and stamina. It can cover 6 metres in one bound, and leap upward to a height of 4.6 metres. Like most cats, it leads a solitary life and a puma may travel up to 80 km when hunting. Its main prey is deer but it sometimes attacks sheep, goats and even ponies. It also takes small mammals. A puma stalks large prey and lands on the animals back with a powerful leap, usually killing by biting into its throat. One puma has been known to drag a carcass three times its own weight over the snow.

Pumas breed all the year round. A litter consists of 1 to 4 cubs, born blind and with spotted fur. They stay with the mother for up to 2 years. A puma's life span is up to 18 years. Apart from humans, this cat has few enemies. But JAGUARS and WOLVERINES and sometimes even grizzly bears will fight pumas.

ORDER: Carnivora;
FAMILY: Felidae;
SPECIES: *Felis concolor*.

Purple emperor

The purple emperor is one of Europe's largest and most handsome butterflies. It also occurs right across temperate Asia to Japan. The wings of the male span 6 cm and have a beautiful purple sheen when seen from certain angles. Otherwise, they are brown and white. The female is somewhat larger and never has a purple sheen. Male butterflies spend much of their time flying around tall oak trees, where they feed largely on honeydew from APHIDS, but they occasionally come down to drink at muddy pools and even visit dung and carrion. The females are less attracted to oaks and they lay their eggs on sallow bushes. The larvae resemble green slugs and are very hard to see among the sallow leaves.
ORDER: Lepidoptera;
FAMILY: Nymphalidae;
SPECIES: *Apatura iris*.

Purple sea snail

The purple sea snail floats around the oceans upside down, attached to a raft of bubbles. The snail is shaped like a garden snail. It has a purple body, and its very thin shell is coloured in shades varying from blue to purple. The shell may be up to 6 cm across, but is usually smaller. The snail makes its raft by secreting a mucus, which traps bubbles of air and then hardens. It feeds on CRUSTACEANS and JELLY-FISHES, and sheds a violet dye into the water which apparently anaesthetizes its victims.
ORDER: Mesogastropoda;
FAMILY: Ianthinidae;
GENUS: Ianthina.

Puss moth

The adult puss moth is a fairly bulky grey insect with no startling features, but its caterpillar is a fascinating creature with several lines of defence. It is mainly green, but a dark brown "saddle" breaks up its outline and makes it very difficult to see among the sallow and poplar leaves. If disturbed, the caterpillar pulls its head back into the front end of its body, which then rears up and sways in a menacing fashion. The effect is

Above: A **purple emperor** caterpillar feeding on sallow leaves.

Below: **Purple emperor** butterflies can usually be seen flying around the upper branches of oak trees.

Male

Purple emperor

Male

Female

Below: The **puss moth** caterpillar, when disturbed, rears up and displays a threatening "face".

The **puss moth** is large and furry.

enhanced by a face-like pattern which scares birds away. At the same time, the caterpillar waves two slender tails, and if it is further molested it squirts formic acid at its attacker.

ORDER: Lepidoptera;
FAMILY: Notodontidae;
SPECIES: *Cerura vinula*.

Python

Pythons inhabit the Old World and are related to the New World BOAS. Like the boas they have small spurs. These are vestigial hind limbs, reminders that snakes evolved from legged reptiles. At up to 10 metres, the beautifully patterned reticulated python of South-East Asia may be the world's longest snake. The African python prefers open country, but other large pythons live in tropical forest, where they climb trees.

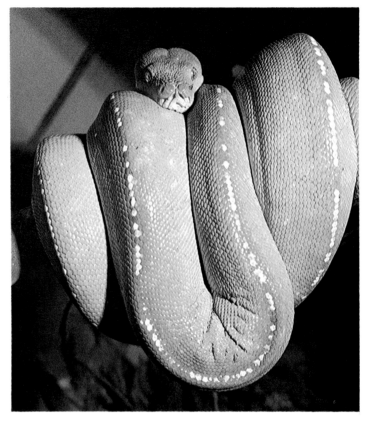

Prey such as HARES, RATS and ANTELOPE is caught by ambush. The snake lies in wait, then springs out, knocking the victim with its head and getting a grip with the jaws. Next it wraps its body around its prey and suffocates it. Big pythons can kill a person, and at least one has swallowed a LEOPARD. A large animal will last a

A green tree **python** coiled around a branch.

python for weeks.

Three or four months after mating, each female lays up to 100 eggs, which she broods until they hatch.

ORDER: Squamata;
FAMILY: Boidae.

Q

Quail

Quails, of which there are nearly 100 species, are small plump birds belonging to the PHEASANT family. The common quail of Europe, Asia and North Africa is 18 cm long, and mottled brown in colour. It lives in fields and pastures, keeping to the ground unless forced to fly. Quails form small family groups. They eat seeds, grain, insects, small snails and other small *invertebrates*. Related

The **quail** is a solitary bird but may be seen in small flocks during migration.

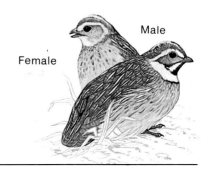

Male

Female

quails of similar build but brighter colours live in Africa, South-East Asia, Australia and New Zealand. American quails such as the bob-white and the crested quails are more colourful and slightly larger.
ORDER: Galliformes;
FAMILY: Phasianidae;
SPECIES: *Coturnix coturnix.*

Quelea

A member of the WEAVERBIRD family, the quelea is an agricultural pest. The three species of quelea live in Africa south of the Sahara. The red-billed quelea is a sparrow-sized bird with a stout red beak. Queleas breed in tropical Africa and migrate south in such large numbers that they have been compared to swarms of locusts. They cause great damage to crops such as rice, wheat and guinea corn, and all sorts of measures have been tried in an effort to control them. Nests are packed closely together, several hundred often woven in one tree.
ORDER: Passeriformes;
FAMILY: Ploceidae.

Quetzal

The quetzal lives in the forests of Central America from southern Mexico to Panama. It is one of the most beautiful birds known. The head, neck and chest are a golden green and the breast and lower belly are crimson, while the wings and tail are adorned with shimmering green plumes up to 60 cm long. Quetzals feed in the canopy of the forest, plucking berries from the trees while in flight.
ORDER: Trogoniformes;
FAMILY: Trogonidae;
SPECIES: *Pharomachrus mocinno.*

Quokka

The quokka looks like a large rat. It is a small species of WALLABY, about 90 cm long, one-third of which is tail. Its fur is short and coarse with a reddish tinge around

Above: The **quetzel** is one of the most beautiful of all birds. The breast is crimson.

Below: **Queleas** are so numerous in Africa that they can be extremely destructive.

its chest and head. Like kangaroos, it hops through the dense grass of its habitat but, unlike other wallabies, does not use its tail as a prop when moving slowly. The quokka feeds mainly at night, on grasses and plants.

Quokkas mate only in winter.

The *gestation period* is 27 days and the single joey remains in its mother's pouch for about six months. The animal matures at two years.
ORDER: Marsupialia;
FAMILY: Macropodidae;
SPECIES: *Setonix brachyurus.*

R

Rabbit

The European rabbit was originally a native of south-western Europe and north-western Africa. Once carefully kept in warrens for its meat and fur, the wild rabbit is now a worldwide species, and in many places has become a pest.

Rabbits have long ears, prominent eyes, and strong hind legs which provide the main force in running. The wild rabbit has greyish-brown fur. The short tail, upturned at the tip, is white below and is a form of signal coloration. When a rabbit flees from danger, the bobbing white tail warns other rabbits to do the same. Domesticated rabbits show a wide range of colour and the fur of some breeds is much longer and silkier than that of the wild rabbit.

Rabbits live mainly in grassland or open woodlands where they dig extensive burrows. They generally come out to feed on grass and other plants at dusk, but in areas where they are not disturbed they often come out during the day as well. One buck mates with several does. The young are born in a burrow lined with hay and fur, and the nursery chamber is blocked by the doe to keep the young safe from predators and also from the bucks, which might otherwise kill

The **rabbit** feeds mainly on grass, but can destroy cereal crops, roots and young trees.

The common **rabbit**, snug and plump in a grassy hide.

them. The babies are blind and naked when born.

During the 1950s, a disease, myxomatosis, made the wild rabbit a rare animal in Europe, although its numbers have since increased again.

ORDER: Lagomorpha;
FAMILY: Leporidae;
SPECIES: *Oryctolagus cuniculus.*

Raccoon

The raccoon, or coon, of which there are seven species, belongs to the same family as the PANDA. The body length is 40 to 60 cm, with a tail measuring 20 to 40 cm. The fur is greyish with black patches round the eyes and black rings on the tail. The most widespread species is the North American raccoon, which is also found in Central America.

Raccoons are solitary, largely nocturnal animals. They live in woods or open country and spend most of the day in dens in hollow trees or rock crevices. At night they feed on earthworms, insects and frogs, as well as searching in water for crayfish and shellfish.

The **raccoon** is about the size of a cat. It is mainly a nocturnal animal.

The strange habit of washing food seen in captive raccoons is probably a substitute for actually finding food in water.

Mating occurs in January or February, each male mating with several females. The 3 to 4 cubs remain with their mother for about a year.

ORDER: Carnivora;
FAMILY: Procyonidae;
SPECIES: *Procyon lotor* (North American).

Racer

Racers are slim, streamlined snakes with rather large heads. They are not poisonous and catch their prey by pinning it to the ground with their bodies. True racers occur from Guatemala to Canada. The largest kind is the black racer, which may be over 1 metre long. Racers can move faster than many snakes, yet no quicker than a man walking briskly.

ORDER: Squamata;
FAMILY: Colubridae.

Rail

Several different kinds of birds belong to the rail family. They include the COOT, CORNCRAKE, GALLINULE and MOORHEN. The birds that are called rails are secretive birds, usually confined to marshes. They have narrow bodies that enable them to slip easily through the reeds, and long toes that support them on floating plants. The plumage of mixed black, brown and grey feathers effectively camouflages these birds in their natural habitat.

Rails are found throughout the world. The most common species in Europe and Asia is the water rail. The king rail and the Virginia rail are two of several species found in North America.

ORDER: Gruiformes;
FAMILY: Rallidae.

Rain frog

This short-headed, fat-bodied frog, gets the name rain frog because it appears in numbers at the onset of rain. In spite of this habit, the frog cannot swim and may drown if it falls into water. It spends all but three months a year hibernating underground. It even lays its eggs in damp soil where they hatch into tadpoles. Rain frogs live in southern Africa.

ORDER: Salientia;
FAMILY: Microphylidae;
SPECIES: *Breviceps adspersus*.

Rat

So disliked are these rodents that the name "rat" is a widespread term of abuse. The two most common rats found in Europe are the black ship rat and the brown rat. Both may in fact be blackish-brown in colour, but the black rat is more slimly built and, with a body length, including its scaly tail, of about 46 cm, it is the smaller of the two.

The black rat probably originated in south-western Asia and was brought to Europe in ships returning from the Holy Land during the Crusades. The Black Death, the bubonic plague which swept through Europe in the 14th century, was carried by fleas living in the black rat's fur. The black rat is a world-wide traveller, often found on ships and in docks and warehouses. The brown rat seems to have reached Europe much later, about the 18th century. It is now the more common of the two species in Europe, found in nearly every town and country area where people have settled.

Rats will eat almost anything. Strong, agile and intelligent they do much damage to food stores, both by eating grain and contaminating it with their droppings. Breeding occurs throughout the year, the females making nests of rags, paper and straw. Its prolific breeding makes the rat an ideal laboratory animal. By living close to people, the rat has assured itself of food, despite the human efforts to combat it.

ORDER: Rodentia;
FAMILY: Muridae;
SPECIES: *Rattus rattus* (black); *Rattus norvegicus* (brown).

Water rail

The **common rat** will eat almost anything. It is a pest of stored produce, often polluting more than it eats, and is notorious as a disease carrier.

Rat kangaroo

Rat kangaroos are small members of the kangaroo family. Their habitats vary from desert to rain forest in Australia. They look a little like a rat, but with longer hindlegs. The rufous rat kangaroo is largest of the nine species. It is 90 cm long, including the tail. Some species have prehensile tails which they use to carry bundles of nesting materials.
ORDER: Marsupialia;
FAMILY: Macropodidae.

Rat snake

Rat snakes are non-venomous snakes named after their habit of eating rodents. They are found in America, Europe and Asia. The largest American species is the black rat snake which measures up to 2.5 metres long; about the same as the Eurasian four-lined snake. Rat snakes have stout bodies, square heads and flat bellies with slight keels that help in tree climbing. They kill by constricting their prey, which include rodents, birds, frogs, and lizards. The snakes defend themselves by emitting a foul smelling fluid and will strike at their attackers if cornered.
ORDER: Squamata;
FAMILY: Colubridae.

Rat-tail

Rat-tails are fishes that occur in great numbers in the deepest waters of the oceans. They vary in length from 15 cm to 90 cm. They have a large head from which the body tapers to a pointed tail. Some rat-tails have very large eyes and some species have very small ones. Most have luminous organs which probably help them recognize other members of the same species and perhaps play a part in courtship. The rest of the rat-tail's body is dark brown or black, providing good camouflage from their enemies in the murky water. Rat-tails have a curiously shaped

snout, either blunt or sharp, with the mouth placed on the underside. They feed largely on worms and other small animals of the bottom ooze.
ORDER: Gadiformes;
FAMILY: Macrouridae.

Rattlesnake

These highly poisonous snakes are renowned for the rattle on the end of their tails, from which they get their name. If disturbed, the snake vibrates its tail and the loud rattling noise acts as a warning. The rattle consists of several loose scales, each of which originally covered the tip of the tail. At each moult except the first the scale is not shed, and every moult adds a new one. So the rattle grows larger and louder – eight scales gives the loudest noise, though more than this deadens the sound.

Twenty-nine species of rattlesnake live in North America, ranging from Canada to Mexico, and one in South America. There are two main groups. Pygmy rattlesnakes never exceed 60 cm. They have short, slim tails and tiny

A **rattlesnake** vibrating its tail rattle, warning that it is about to strike.

rattles. Rattlesnakes proper are longer, and the Eastern diamondback has a record length of 2.4 metres. Rattlesnakes of the same species from one part of the range may be more venomous than those from another part, and older snakes are more venomous than young ones.

Like other snakes in the PIT VIPER group, rattlesnakes prey on warm-blooded creatures, especially rodents and rabbits. All rattlesnakes give birth to live young. A litter usually numbers 10 to 20, but may be as many as 60. Few of them will survive the first year, however, for hawks, skunks and other snakes prey on them.
ORDER: Squamata;
FAMILY: Crotalidae.

Raven

The raven is an all black bird, with a heavy bill and a wedge-shaped tail. At about 60 cm long, it is the largest member of the CROW family. The raven is found

The **raven** is easily identified on the wing by its size and its deep call of "corronk".

throughout the northern hemisphere, although it is now restricted to the wilder, more inaccessible parts of its range where it is safe from human persecution.

Ravens live in pairs or small groups but roost in large numbers. The birds build their nests on cliffs and on tree tops. They are playful and often acrobatic in flight. Their diet is mainly carrion but they will eat anything edible.
ORDER: Passeriformes;
FAMILY: Corvidae;
SPECIES: *Corvus corvus.*

Ray

Many fishes with flattened bodies are called rays. In all species the body is flattened from top to bottom and is further widened by the large *pectoral fins*, which extend from the head to the start of the tail, and may be flapped like wings when swimming. Other rays swim with a wave-like movement

The **thornback ray** lives in mud, sand and shingle in shallow water.

of their pectoral fins. Rays and their relatives, the SKATES, are mostly bottom-living fishes which feed on shellfish, which they are able to crack open with their broad teeth. Many rays have long, whip-like tails, which in the STINGRAYS bear a poison spine. SAWFISHES are ray-like fishes having a long, double-toothed projection from the snout. The ELECTRIC RAYS, or torpedoes, can produce a powerful electric shock. All rays, like their SHARK relatives, lack bone, their skeletons being formed of hard cartilage.
ORDER: Rajiformes.

Razorbill

The razorbill or the razorbilled auk is well-named because the edges of its deep, PUFFIN-like bill are very sharp. It is restricted to the North Atlantic and has suffered in recent years from oil slicks. It spends much of the year

well out to sea and only moves inshore in winter to breed. On land it has an upright stance, like a GUILLEMOT, and is about 40 cm long. The plumage is black and white. In summer the head and neck are black, but in winter, white extends from the breast to the throat, chin and the sides of the feet.
ORDER: Charadriiformes;
FAMILY: Alcidae;
SPECIES: *Alca torda.*

Razorshell

Razorshells are *bivalve* MOLLUSCS with narrow, open-ended shells, and are usually about 15 cm long. The shape is admirably suited to burrowing in sand. Razorshells live on the shore, resting just below

Razorbills spend the winter out at sea, although storms may force them back to shore.

the surface of the sand with their short *siphons* showing. When the tide is out, the razorshells usually hide below the surface of the sand. If alarmed they can retreat to a depth of almost a metre and, if necessary, can swim.

CLASS: Bivalvia;
ORDER: Adapedonta.

Razorshells are so called because their shape is like that of an old-fashioned razor.

Rearfanged snake

Also called backfanged snakes, rearfanged snakes have grooved teeth or fangs at the rear of the upper jaw. These fangs carry poison from the salivary glands into prey held in the mouth. Except for the BOOMSLANG, most rearfanged snakes are not harmful to humans. They cannot open ther mouths wide enough to dig the rear fangs into a large animal. The group includes twig-thin, tree-climbing species such as the green vine snake of tropical America. Rearfanged snakes mainly eat lizards, but sometimes also birds, frogs and smaller snakes.

ORDER: Squamata;
FAMILY: Colubridae.

Red deer

The red deer of Europe also occurs in parts of western Asia. It is found in North-West Africa where it is called the Barbary stag. Its range is even wider if we include the two Asian deer, the hangul and the shou, as sub-species of the red deer. Red deer have also been introduced into Australia, New Zealand and South America.

The red deer is sometimes called the wapiti, but this name really applies to a closely related deer in eastern Asia and North America. Another name for red deer, used in North America, is the elk. But this is confusing because the Eurasian elk is the same as the North American MOOSE.

For most of the year the red deer stags and the hinds, or females, live in separate herds, each occupying a well-defined territory. The stags shed their antlers between February and April. New antlers soon start to sprout and are fully grown by late September. In October the stags round up the hinds and mate with them. A master stag guards his group of hinds by roaring at, or fighting with, any other stag which comes too close. The *gestation period* is 225 to 270 days. The calves are born in May and June, usually just one to each hind.

The adult red deer is reddish-brown, with light under-parts and a white patch under the tail. In

The **red deer's** habitat is dense forest, but it has adapted to live in moorland.

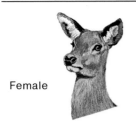

Female

Only the male **red deer** carries antlers.

The **red fox** has a bushy tail, usually with a white tip.

winter it is brownish-grey. The size of red deer depends on where they live. The red deer that live on moorlands in Britain are smaller than other European red deer that live in forests. This is because the moorland animals have to graze on relatively poor food while the forest animals browse on nutritious tree leaves. Generally, a stag stands up to 135 cm at the shoulder and is up to 240 cm long in the head and body. The hind is somewhat smaller. The stags have antlers up to 110 cm long.
ORDER: Artiodactyla;
FAMILY: Cervidae;
SPECIES: *Cervus elaphus*.

Red fox

The red fox is a handsome but wily and sometimes vicious member of the dog family. Red foxes are found all over Europe, Asia and North America and although they prefer woody country they have also become urban dwellers, living off rats and mice and scavenging in dustbins.

An adult dog fox stands about 36 cm at the shoulder. The head and body measure just over 60 cm and the tail, or brush, can be 40 cm long. A vixen is slightly smaller. The fur is sandy or red-brown above and white underneath. Colouring varies however, according to locality and there are several *mutant* strains, such as the silver fox and the cross fox, which has a black band across the shoulders.

Red foxes mostly live on the ground although they are known

to climb trees on occasions. They are largely nocturnal, but do venture out in the daytime. They feed mainly on rodents, although birds, frogs and some plant materials are also eaten. Sometimes they take poultry and small lambs, but few foxes become regular poultry-killers.

Mating occurs between December and February. In about April the 3 to 8 cubs are born and remain in the nest, or earth, until nearly a month old. The dog fox supplies his family with food. Later, the cubs are taught to hunt for themselves and they leave their parents after about three months.
ORDER: Carnivora;
FAMILY: Canidae;
SPECIES: *Vulpes vulpes*.

The sharp muzzle, erect ears and quick eye movements give the **fox** an alert appearance.

Red panda

The red panda is a cat-like relative of the giant panda. It is also known as the cat-bear, fox-cat, fire-fox and Himalayan raccoon. Its head and body measure up to 66 cm and its tail may be 50 cm long. Its woolly fur is a rich chestnut colour, with white patches on the face and dark rings on the tail.

Red pandas live high in the mountain forests of Nepal, Sikkim Yunnan, Szehwan and Upper Burma. They spend most of their time in the trees, where they display great agility. On the ground they move slowly. They sleep during the day and feed in the early morning and evening, eating mainly leaves and fruit, much of which they gather on the ground. They are said to eat eggs and are reputed to steal milk and butter in Nepalese villages.

Mating occurs in winter and the young are born in spring. They remain helpless until shortly before the next litter is born.
ORDER: Carnivora;
FAMILY: Procyonidae;
SPECIES: *Ailurus fulgens.*

Redpoll

The name given to two species of small finch, the lesser redpoll and the Arctic redpoll. Looking rather like a sparrow, the redpoll has a crimson forehead and a black chin. Races of the lesser redpoll are found throughout the cold and sub-tropical parts of the northern hemisphere. Redpolls feed on seeds and small insects. They live in small flocks outside the breeding season.
ORDER: Passeriformes;
FAMILY: Fringillidae;
SPECIES: *Carduelis flammea* (lesser); *Carduelis hornemanni* (Arctic).

Redstart

The several species of redstarts are small active birds, most of which are found in Asia. The Old World

A **redpoll** shows the scarlet head patch that gives it its name. The bird's main diet is small seeds.

Male

Female

The male **redstart** has a black throat and orange breast. These birds constantly flick their tails up and down.

Female, summer

Male, summer

The **reindeer** is the only deer in which the females carry antlers.

redstarts are related to THRUSHES and European ROBINS. The common redstart is found throughout Europe and central Asia. The male has a black face and throat, and an orange breast. The female is grey-brown above and buff below. The tail is reddish in both sexes. The black redstart is slightly darker and has a more southerly range.

The New World redstarts are wood warblers unrelated to the European species. There are two species: the American redstart and the painted redstart.
ORDER: Passeriformes;
FAMILY: Turdidae (Old World); Parulidae (New World).

Reedbuck

Reedbuck are small African antelope. The common reedbuck, stands 76 to 90 cm at the shoulder. It lives in savanna country south of the Equator and is mainly solitary. It is light grey-fawn, tawny on the neck and white below. The mountain reedbuck inhabits uplands in three separate places: South Africa and Mozambique; part of East Africa; and in Cameroon. It stands 70 to 80 cm at the shoulder. Its horns are shorter than the head and they are only slightly hooked forward at the tips. The coat varies from grey-

fawn to bright red. The Bohor reedbuck ranges from Senegal to Ethiopia and Tanzania. It is the same height as the mountain reedbuck, but its horns are strongly hooked forward at the tips and longer than the head. The coat is a yellowish colour.
ORDER: Artiodactyla;
FAMILY: Bovidae;
SPECIES: *Redunca arundinum* (common).

The **reed buck** is closely related to the waterbuck, kob and lechwe.

Reed frog

More than 200 species of these tiny frogs live in Africa. Most are about 2.5 cm long. Many sunbathe on reeds and dive into water if scared. In the dry season they hide in cracks in the ground. Their colours vary greatly. The arum frogs are ivory, but the painted reed frogs may be black and white, black and green, black and yellow, or brown and yellow.
ORDER: Salientia;
FAMILY: Rhacophoridae.

Reindeer

The reindeer belongs to the same species as the CARIBOU. Unlike the caribou, the reindeer of Arctic Europe and Asia are domesticated or semi-domesticated. Reindeer may be 110 cm high at the shoulder and adult bulls can weigh 100 kg. Reindeer are very important to the nomadic Lapps of northern Europe, because they provide almost everything the Lapps need.
ORDER: Artiodactyla;
FAMILY: Cervidae;
SPECIES: *Rangifer tarandus*.

Remora

Remora are fishes which hitch rides on larger sea creatures. They attach themselves to their hosts by means of a large, ridged sucker on the top of their head. This sucker, oval in outline, is really a highly-adapted *dorsal fin*. Its hold is so strong that remoras are used by fishermen of many countries to catch turtles, the remora's body being secured to a rope with a ring, after which the fish is thrown into the water to search for a captive. There are eight species of remora, and they live mainly in tropical seas. They range in size from 18 to 90 cm, the largest and best known being the striped remora. It seems that they hitch rides mainly in order to travel more widely than they could otherwise do.

ORDER: Perciformes;
FAMILY: Echeneidae.

Reptiles

The reptiles belong to the Class Reptilia, and the living species, totalling about 6000, fall into four orders. These are the CROCODILES and ALLIGATORS, the TORTOISES and TURTLES, the LIZARDS and SNAKES, and the Rhynchocephalia, represented only by the TUATARA of New Zealand. Reptiles evolved from AMPHIBIANS more than 350 million years ago.

Today's lizards and snakes are a very successful group, but the other three orders are only relics from long ago. Lizards and snakes are quite closely related. The lizards include both *carnivorous* and *herbivorous* species, but the snakes are entirely carnivorous.

Rhea

Rheas are flightless birds of South America. They resemble the ostrich, and are the largest American birds, standing about 150 cm high. Rheas live in open country on the pampas and highland plateaus, roaming in flocks of 20 to 30 birds.

They escape danger by running, or by crouching if there is enough cover. Rheas are OMNIVOROUS, eating both plants and animals. There are two species. The common rhea, *Rhea americana*, ranges from north-eastern Brazil to central Argentina. Darwin's rhea, *Pterocnemia pennata*, ranges from southern Peru to southern Argentina.

ORDER: Rheiformes;
FAMILY: Rheidae;
SPECIES: *Rhea americana* (common); *Pterocnemia pennata* (Darwin's).

Rhesus monkey

The rhesus monkey is one of the best known of the MACAQUES. It is 46 to 60 cm long, with a tail of less than 25 cm. This long-haired monkey is brown, with much brighter, more reddish hind parts. Its face is pink. Rhesus monkeys are Old World monkeys found in northern India, South-East Asia and northern China. They live in troops of 10 to 25 and, where protected, in troops of up to 60. They are captured and used in great numbers for scientific research.

ORDER: Primates;
FAMILY: Cercopithecidae;
SPECIES: *Macaca mulatta*.

Rhesus monkeys bathing. The macaque monkeys of Japan are most famous for their swimming habits.

The **white rhino** is really grey. It has been exterminated in many places.

Rhinoceros

Rhinos are bulky animals with one or two horns on the snout. These horns are made of fibres cemented together and contain no bone. Like their relatives the HORSE and the TAPIR, rhinos bear the weight of each leg on a single central toe. There are, however, two subsidiary toes on each foot. The thick skin is naked or sparsely-haired. All rhinos are short-sighted, but their senses of smell and hearing are acute. These animals are now seriously threatened with extinction, because of hunting.

There are five species. The Asian species are the Indian rhino, the Javan rhino, and the Sumatran rhino. They have a short horn (or horns) and long, tusk-like lower

canine teeth. Their skin is folded and looks rather like armour plating. The African species, the black rhino and the white rhino, have two long horns. They lack front teeth, and their skin is much less folded.

The Indian rhino grows up to 193 cm high and weighs up to 4 tonnes. It has a deeply folded skin which is studded with raised knobs, and one horn. It lives in tall elephant grass through which it makes well-worn tunnels. It can run at 40 km/h. Considerably less than 1000 now survive in reserves in India and Nepal.

The Javan rhino stands 135 to 170 cm at the shoulder. Its skin is less heavily folded, but it is broken by a network of cracks. It has. one short horn. Less than 30 survive in Java.

The Sumatran rhino is found in South-East Asia. It is up to 137 cm high and weighs 340 to 900 kg. It

Oxpeckers removing ticks from the hide of an African **rhinoceros**. This species is almost entirely hairless.

has two short horns. Only the front half of the body has folded skin, and it is distinctly hairy. It is estimated that fewer than 100 animals remain.

The black rhino which is really grey, grows up to 170 cm high. It has rough skin, with marked grooves over the ribs, and a mobile, pointed lip. It is a nervous creature, and when annoyed it may charge and strike with its horns, reaching speeds of 56 km/h. The estimated population is now between 11,000 and 13,500.

The white rhino, which is also grey, is much rarer. It feeds entirely on grass, unlike the black rhino which is a browser. It is found in small pockets in Zululand (South Africa), and in Sudan, Uganda and Zaire. It grows up to

190 cm high. Its skin is smoother than the black rhino's; there are no rib grooves, and the mouth is wide and square. Its name has nothing to do with colour and is a corruption of the Afrikaans word *wijt*, meaning "wide". The white rhino is an unwary animal, and so was quickly exterminated in many areas.

ORDER: Perissodactyla;
FAMILY: Rhinocerotidae.

Ribbon worm

Ribbon worm is an apt name for these long, thin, flattened animals. There are nearly 650 species, varying considerably in length, though most are less than 20 cm. Each ribbon worm has a long muscular *proboscis* which it can shoot out at prey – usually some other kind of worm. The proboscis may be more than twice the body length. Most

ribbon worms live in the sea, a few in fresh water and some on land.
PHYLUM: Nemertea.

Right whale

The Greenland right whale or bowhead, one of five species of right whale, was hunted during the Middle Ages and almost became extinct in the 19th century. However, it is now a protected species. It is so called because in the early days of whaling it was the "right" whale to catch, being a slow swimmer and because, when killed, it is kept afloat by its very thick blubber. Right whales are baleen whales (see WHALE). They have much longer baleen plates in their mouths than their cousins, the RORQUALS, and grow to about 18 metres. They feed by swimming with their mouths open so the baleen plates can act as a sieve to trap KRILL and other small animals.
ORDER: Cetacea;
FAMILY: Balaenidae;
SPECIES: *Balaena mysticetus.*

Roach

The roach is a freshwater member of the CARP family, and is a common fish of rivers and lakes from Europe to northern Asia. It is closely related to the freshwater BREAM and the RUDD, a fact which is shown by the readiness with which these fishes interbreed. Roach are shaped rather like GOLDFISH but their bodies are silvery-green on the back and greenish-gold on the flanks. They reach lengths of up to 46 cm and usually weigh about 0.5 kg. Roach live in shoals and sometimes surface to eat insects.
ORDER: Cypriniformes;
FAMILY: Cyprinidae;
SPECIES: *Rutilus rutilus.*

Roach

Roadrunner

Roadrunners are members of the CUCKOO family, though they do not lay their eggs in the nests of other birds as cuckoos do. They live in the deserts of the United States and Central America, feeding on a variety of small animals, from insects to lizards and snakes. Roadrunners can run well, and got their name from their habit of running alongside vehicles. They are streaky brown in appearance, and measure about 60 cm long. There are two species, the greater roadrunner of the United States, and the lesser roadrunner of Central America.
ORDER: Cuculiformes;
FAMILY: Cuculidae;
SPECIES: *Geococcyx californianus* (greater); *Geococcyx velox* (lesser).

Robber crab

The robber crab is a land-living crab with two unusual characteristics: it drowns in water; and it frequently climbs trees. The females lay their eggs in the sea. The eggs hatch as *larvae*, and later change form and migrate onto land. An adult robber crab may be 45 cm long and weigh up to 2.7 kg. Robber crabs feed on dead animal matter and on coconut pulp, but contrary to popular belief, they do not climb trees in order to pick coconuts, nor can they open the nuts. Nobody yet knows exactly why the crabs climb, but they may do so to pick soft fruit. The crabs often drop to the ground as the easiest way of getting down.
ORDER: Decapoda;
SPECIES: *Birgus latro.*

Robber-fly

The various species of robber-flies are rather bristly flies with slender, but strongly-built bodies and powerful legs. They feed on a variety of other insects, which they capture in mid-air. A stout beak drains the juices from the prey, and dense bristles around the face protect the eyes from the struggling prey. Robber-fly grubs feed on decaying matter.
ORDER: Diptera;
FAMILY: Asilidae.

Robin

The European robin also called the redbreast, is a small plump bird about 14 cm long. It is easily identified by its rusty-red face and breast, olive brown upper-parts and white abdomen. It is found throughout Europe, western Asia and north-western Africa. The robin is a woodland bird but is now often seen in parks and gardens. It spends much time hopping on the ground, looking for insects, worms and other small *invertebrates*. It also eats berries and some soft fruit. The bird sings a melodious song almost all the year round. The nest is in holes in walls, banks, trees and the like. Usually 5 to 6 eggs are laid.

The American robin is more closely related to the European BLACKBIRD than to the European robin. It is also about twice as large. It has a brick red breast, brownish-grey upper-parts, black and white speckled throat and white rings around the eyes. It lives in North America from Alaska to Georgia and may fly south to Mexico in winter.
ORDER: Passeriformes;
FAMILY: Turdidae;
SPECIES: *Erithacus rubecula* (European); *Turdus migratorius* (American).

Rock dove

The rock dove is the wild ancestor of all domestic pigeons and feral pigeons, which are domestic pigeons that have reverted to the wild. Feral pigeons are very common in city centres. The truly wild bird, the rock dove, lives in

Right: The **robin** is friendly towards human beings but very aggressive towards its own kind.

The wild **rock dove** has a white rump and two black wing stripes.

open country, usually nesting on rocky outcrops or cliffs. It feeds mainly on seed, but also takes worms and snails. It is 33 cm long and has blue-grey plumage with no white on the wings, but with two very distinct black wing bars and a white rump. Domestic pigeons and feral pigeons exist in a wide variety of forms.
ORDER: Columbiformes;
FAMILY: Columbidae;
SPECIES: *Columba livia.*

Rocky Mountain goat

The Rocky Mountain goat is related to the CHAMOIS, both members of the family that includes cattle, antelope, goats and sheep. It lives above the *tree line* from Alaska to Oregon in the United States, feeding on stunted plants, mosses and lichens. The dense white coat, thick undercoat and layers of fat all help it to endure the extreme cold. Being quite small, about 100 cm in length, with short stocky legs and small hoofs, the Rocky Mountain goat is able to clamber up apparently vertical rock faces. The male has a full beard. The horns rise straight up from the head and curve backwards. Males lead solitary lives except in the mating season, whereas females form small herds. Predators such as wolves seldom reach their high habitat, where avalanches are a greater threat. In some areas the animal has been over-hunted and is becoming rare.
ORDER: Artiodactyla;
FAMILY: Bovidae;
SPECIES: *Oreamnos americanus.*

Rodents

The word "rodent" comes from a Latin word meaning to gnaw – and gnawing is what the life of rodents is all about. Their four front teeth are specially made for gnawing. They are constantly growing, like fingernails, to make up for the wear. The order Rodentia is divided into four sub-orders containing about 1800 species.

Rodents live in all parts of the world, and in all conditions of climate, from deserts to swamps, and valleys to mountains. They are among the fastest breeding of all animals – a pair of rats, for example, can have almost a hundred offspring in one year. Females can be fertile at 6 weeks old.

The grey squirrel is a serious pest of forestry but an attractive animal in our parks. This **rodent** can kill trees by stripping bark for food, but its main diet is nuts.

Roe deer

The roe deer of Europe and Asia is widely distributed and has recently been increasing in numbers, but it is seldom seen. This is because it is active mainly at night, and because it can skulk noiselessly through dense cover. It lives mostly in woodland, sparsely wooded valleys and the lower slopes of mountains.

A buck stands 76 cm at the shoulder, weighs up to 32 kg, and seldom exceeds 120 cm in length. In summer, the coat is red-brown, with white underparts and a white chin. In winter, the coat grows longer and turns a dark greyish-fawn. The antlers, which are knobbed at the base, are only 20 to 23 cm long. They are shed in November or December. The new antlers are fully grown around the start of May. Mating occurs in July and August. The one or two and, rarely, three, spotted kids are born in May or June. Roes live in family groups, which break up at the end of winter, but the adult buck and doe live together for much of the year.

ORDER: Artiodactyla;
FAMILY: Cervidae;
SPECIES: *Capreolus capreolus.*

Roller

Rollers are colourful birds related to BEE-EATERS and KINGFISHERS.

A pair of **rooks** at their nest.

They range from 23 to 33 cm in length, and are confined to the Old World, most of them living in Africa. Rollers are usually solitary and can be seen perching on exposed places such as bare boughs and buildings. They feed mainly on large insects caught in mid-air or on the ground. Rollers nest in holes in trees or banks, or in crevices in rocks or walls. During courtship, they indulge in a spectacular tumbling and rolling flight that gives the birds their name. These antics display the birds' vivid colours, and at the same time they scream loudly. The European roller breeds in North Africa, western Asia and Europe, migrat-

ing to tropical and southern Africa for the winter. It was once fairly common farther north, but wet summers have resulted in a decline there.

ORDER: Coraciiformes;
FAMILY: Coraciidae;
SPECIES: *Coracias garrulus* (European).

Roman snail

This name is sometimes given to the edible snail because it was a favourite food of the ancient Romans. The snail has a shell about 4 cm across. It lives in open woodland and on grassy downland, and flourishes best on chalky soil. In France it is often found in vineyards. It spends the cold weather in HIBERNATION, and also hides away during very dry weather. It feeds on fungi and vegetable matter.

CLASS: Gastropoda;
ORDER: Stylommatophora;
SPECIES: *Helix pomatia.*

Rook

The rook is the most common Eurasian member of the CROW

Roe deer have small upright antlers with only three points.

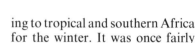

The **roller** gets its name from the way it rolls over in flight to attract a mate.

The **rook** has a grey patch at the base of the beak.

family. The adult bird is about 46 cm long and differs from the other members of its family in having a patch of grey skin at the base of the pointed beak. There is also a purple sheen to its plumage. The upper-parts of the legs are feathered and look rather like baggy trousers.

Rooks are lowland birds found especially where the land has been ploughed. They feed in large flocks and gather in communal roosts at night. Their main food is grain, earthworms and insects.
ORDER: Passeriformes;
SPECIES: *Corvus frugilegus*.

Rorqual

Rorquals or finback whales are baleen whales (see WHALES), related to the BLUE WHALE, and are among the kinds most affected by commercial whaling. There are four species. The largest, second in size only to the blue whale, is the fin whale, which can grow to as much as 24 metres in length and is thought to live for up to 80 years. In the past, a school of fin whales could contain several hundred individuals, but now, due to excessive hunting by humans, the schools are much smaller.
ORDER: Cetacea;
FAMILY: Balaenopteridae.

Rotifer

These very small creatures, also called wheel animalcules, are among the most abundant animals in freshwater ponds. They vary in length from 0.05 to 2 mm. The animals get their name from the arrangement of *cilia* on the front end, which often looks like a rotating wheel. There are many different shapes among the 1500 or so known species. Some swim freely, while others anchor themselves to the bottom. Males are usually much smaller than the females.
PHYLUM: Rotifera.

Roundworm

These slender worms are found in every possible habitat. They attack almost all kinds of plants and animals and many of the 10,000 species are PARASITES. Roundworms range in size from 4 metres long to tiny parasites too small to see except under a microscope. They live in the soil, the sea and fresh water. Some are found high up mountains, others deep in the oceans; some live in the Tropics, and others in Arctic lands. They exist in enormous quantities: 90,000 were once counted inside one rotting apple, and an acre of farmland may hold several billion. Some species of roundworms live for 15 years or more.

Roundworms are shaped like tiny cylinders, with tapering ends. Most species reproduce by laying eggs, but some, including the vinegar eel, produce live young. Vinegar eels live in the sediment of vinegar, but are harmless. Many parasitic roundworms live in the intestines of animals, including humans. Some cause serious diseases, including anaemia and elephantiasis, while others are apparently harmless.
PHYLUM: Nematoda.

Rove beetle

The rove beetles are a large group of elongated beetles whose *elytra* are mostly very short and square, leaving much of the abdomen exposed. There are about 27,000 species ranging from little more than 1 mm to more than 30 mm in length. Most are black and brown, but there are a few brightly coloured species in the family. Despite the short elytra, most species have well developed hind wings and fly very well. Rove beetles are normally found on the ground, and in all kinds of decaying plant and animal material. Some actually feed on the decaying matter, but most are CARNIVOROUS insects feeding on other small animals which themselves eat the rotting material.
ORDER: Coleoptera;
FAMILY: Staphylinidae.

Rudd

The rudd is a member of the CARP family that is native to fresh waters from Europe to northern Asia. Rudds grow up to 46 cm in length and 1.5 kg in weight. They are similar in size and general appearance to the ROACH, but can be distinguished from roaches by the *dorsal fin*, which is set back farther on the body. However, the rudd and the roach are known to interbreed. To complete the confusion, rudd introduced into American fresh waters are known as pearl roach.
ORDER: Cypriniformes;
FAMILY: Cyprinidae;
SPECIES: *Scardinius erythrophthalmus*.

Ruff

The ruff is a species of SANDPIPER named for the ornate ruff of colourful feathers that adorns the male bird at breeding time. The male is about 30 cm long, and the ruff can vary in colour. The males court the smaller females, or reeves, in groups, displaying their ruffs before them. Ruffs breed across northern Europe and Asia, and migrate to South Africa, southern Asia and Australia for the winter. Then the males lose their ruffs and resemble the females. They feed mainly on insects

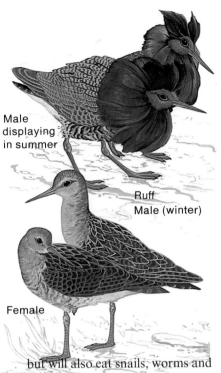

Male displaying in summer

Ruff
Male (winter)

Female

S

but will also eat snails, worms and crustaceans.
ORDER: Charadriiformes;
FAMILY: Scolopacidae;
SPECIES: *Philomachus pugnax.*

Ruminants

Most of the hoofed animals with even numbers of toes – two or four – belong to the group known as the ruminants – the cud-chewers. They have evolved a complex digestive system to cope with their diet of grass and other hard-to-digest vegetation.

A typical ruminant such as a cow has a four-part stomach. All the grass it bites off is mixed with saliva and swallowed whole to be stored in stomach No. 1. There the food is heated up so that bacterial action can take place to break down the most indigestible part of the grass, the cellulose. Then the food passes to stomach No. 2, where it is moulded into pellets or cuds. When the cow has finished grazing, it lies down and regurgitates the cuds into its mouth, where it chews solidly away for hours to break down the food. The food then goes to the third and fourth stomach for further digestion.

Sable antelope

The sable antelope is one of the most handsome and aggressive of antelopes, with its long, backward-curving horns. It is found in south-central Africa, but is now rather rare.

Sable antelopes live in herds of 8 to 40, consisting of one bull, several females and the young. The bull fiercely guards the females at all times and there is no fixed mating season. The animal has few predators except man. Sable antelopes stand up to 145 cm at the shoulder. Bulls may weigh 230 kg. Males are black or nearly black and females vary from golden-brown to nearly black. A race of extra large animals, known as giant sable antelopes, is found in Angola. These animals have horns up to 180 cm long, while those of the typical race are only about 135 cm long. Females' horns are always shorter than those of the males.
ORDER: Artiodactyla;
FAMILY: Bovidae;
SPECIES: *Hippotragus niger.*

Saiga

The saiga inhabits the Russian steppes. It has a very large nose which probably warms the air as it is breathed in. This is a useful adaptation as the saiga lives in cold, dry regions. It stands up to 80 cm high and weighs about 45 kg. Only the male has horns, which are slightly lyre-shaped, strongly ringed, and about 30 cm long. The woolly coat is buff in summer and white in winter.

Saiga mate in December, when the rams fight for the ewes, and the young are born in April. Sudden panics set them running in a pack at speeds of up to 80 km/h. Their mobile and down-pointing nostrils help keep out the dust. Once hunted almost to extinction, the animal is now protected by law and quite common again.
ORDER: Artiodactyla;
FAMILY: Bovidae;
SPECIES: *Saiga tatarica.*

Sailfish

The single species of sailfish lives in tropical seas. It swims at high speed at the surface in pursuit of its prey, which include flying fishes. With its close relatives the MARLINS, and the slightly less closely related SWORDFISH, the sailfish is a sprint champion of the oceans, reaching speeds of more than 80 km/h in short bursts. Its cruising speed is nearer 40 km/h. The sailfish is named after its sail-like *dorsal fin.* Like its relatives, it has a long beak produced by an extension of the upper jaw, with which it often spears its prey. A sailfish can grow up to 6 metres long and weigh 450 kg, although most sailfishes are smaller than this. The powerful, streamlined body is blue-black above and silvery below, with a large tail fin and two long thin "keels" extending backwards below its head. At full speed, the large sailfin is folded down into a groove on the back.
ORDER: Perciformes;
FAMILY: Istiophoridae;
SPECIES: *Istiophorus platypterus.*

The **sailfish** is perhaps the fastest of all fish.

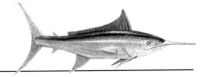

Salamander

There are 300 species of salamander. They are AMPHIBIANS, but their long bodies and tails sometimes cause them to be mistaken for LIZARDS. Unlike lizards, they have rounded heads, moist skins without scales, and no claws on their toes. Most have short limbs and wriggle along when in a hurry. They breathe with a regular gulping movement, and also breathe through the skin. Those in one family are without lungs and

A **salamander** slithers snakelike through wet mosses. This small amphibian has even thinner and weaker legs than the average newt.

The **fire salamander** (below) is recognized by its yellow markings. **Spectacled salamanders** are bright red under the tail and legs.

Fire salamander

Spectacled salamander

The **salmon** is narrow just in front of the tail fin.

The **alpine salamander** is usually black all over.

breathe entirely through the skin, which is kept moist by special glands. Other glands produce poisons that discourage attack by predators. From time to time, salamanders shed their skins in one piece.

Salamanders tend to live in wet or moist places. Some live entirely in water, for instance the hellbender, the MUD-PUPPY and the OLM. Others live on land and return to water to breed. This applies to most species of NEWT and to the fire salamander, a glossy yellow and black salamander widespread in Europe.

Most salamanders rely largely on scent and sight to find food. Those hunting on land eat only moving prey, such as worms and slugs.

The male salamanders court females with a special display, then deposit packets of sperm which the females collect. Most salamanders lay eggs that hatch into *larvae* with gills. The AXOLOTL, mudpuppy and some other aquatic salamanders keep their gills throughout life.
ORDER: Caudata.

Salmon

The Atlantic salmon is a silvery, streamlined fish up to 1.5 metres long, closely related to the European trout. As a young fish it makes its own way down river to the Atlantic Ocean, where it grows to the adult stage. Then it migrates back to its home river to spawn. The parent fishes, now reddish or blackish in colour, may repeat this double migration, or they may die, exhausted from spawning, on their way back to the sea. The salmon is greatly prized as a food fish, being caught generally by river fisher-men when on its way back to its spawning grounds. However, severe over-fishing and pollution have made the Atlantic salmon rare or completely absent from many rivers.

The Pacific salmon, which has six species, has a similar life history. The young fishes migrate

A young **salmon** lurks among river weed before continuing its journey to the sea.

down river to the Pacific Ocean, then return up their home rivers as adults to spawn. Unlike the Atlantic salmon, however, the parent Pacific salmon always die after spawning. Another point of difference is that their bodies become more brilliantly coloured before spawning.

ORDER: Salmoniformes;
FAMILY: Salmonidae;
SPECIES: *Salmo salar* (Atlantic).

Sand dollar

These flat-shelled sea animals are closely related to SEA URCHINS. Also known as cake urchins or sea biscuits, they live on sandy shores, mainly in the warm waters of the world, and bury themselves in the sand below the low-tide mark. A sand dollar is covered with short spines, about 2 mm long, and these spines are covered with *cilia*, minute beating hairs. Under water, the sand dollar stands on edge with about two-thirds of its shell projecting above the sand. The movement of the cilia draws in food particles from the water, and these particles become trapped in mucus secreted by the spines. This flows down grooves to the mouth.

CLASS: Echinoidea;
ORDER: Clypeasteroidea.

Sand-fly

The sand-flies are tiny flies whose wings are clothed with long hairs. They live in a variety of habitats, not just sandy places, and suck the blood of numerous VERTEBRATE animals, including humans. They carry several serious human and animal diseases. The *larvae* live mainly in damp soil. There are many species.

ORDER: Diptera;
FAMILY: Psychodidae.

Sandgrouse

The 16 species of sandgrouse are related to pigeons. They range in size from 23 to 41 cm, and live in the dry regions of Africa, Madagascar, central and southern Asia and southern Europe. They are found in desert and steppe country, and are brown to grey with black, white and orange markings that serve to CAMOUFLAGE them against the sand or scanty vegetation. Sandgrouse feed on seeds and, to obtain water, they may fly as far as 60 km to a waterhole every day. They lay their eggs in a depression in the ground, and often make use of the footprints of large animals such as camels.

ORDER: Columbiformes;
FAMILY: Pteroclididae.

Sandpiper

Sandpipers are wading birds. They are similar to PLOVERS, though the bill is longer and may be straight or curved. They feed on CRUSTACEANS, insects, worms and shellfish. It has been estimated that a single purple sandpiper can consume 4600 PERIWINKLES per day. Sandpipers are famous for their long migrations, for instance the wandering tatler nests in Alaska and flies south for the winter, occasionally reaching as far as New Zealand, a distance of about 12,000 km.

ORDER: Charadriiformes;
FAMILY: Scolopacidae.

Wood sandpiper

Common sandpiper

Sapsucker

Sapsuckers are WOODPECKERS known for their habit of drilling into tree tunks to feed on the sap that oozes out. There are two species, both brightly-coloured black, white, red and yellow. They are 20 cm long. The yellow-bellied sapsucker breeds in southern Canada and the northern United States, migrating to the rest of Canada and the United States and to Central America. Williamson's sapsucker is less common and confined to the western side of the continent north to the Canadian border. It migrates to the south-western United States.

ORDER: Piciformes;
FAMILY: Picidae.

Sawfish

The six species of sawfishes are close relatives of the RAYS and live in the coastal waters of warm seas. They have less flattened bodies than other rays, and their *pectoral fins*, although large and wing-like, are not joined for their whole length to the side of the head. Also, the rear half of their body, with its high back fins and large tail, is more like a shark's than a ray's. But the sawfishes' unique feature is their long, saw-like snout, with its double row of teeth. With sideways lunges of its head, a sawfish uses this weapon to kill and stun other fishes. It also employs its saw to search in the bottom mud for shellfish, which it then grinds up with its blunt teeth. Sawfishes can be very large indeed, a few growing to be monsters 10 metres in length and 2 tonnes in weight.

SUB-ORDER: Rajiformes;
FAMILY: Pristidae.

The usual place to see **sandpipers** is on the shore or in marshes.

Green sandpiper

The **hawthorn sawfly** is a fast-flying insect.

Sawfly

The sawflies belong to the same group of insects as the BEES and WASPS, but they lack the narrow waists of these insects. They get their name from the delicate, saw-like *ovipositor* with which most females cut slits in plants in which to lay their eggs. Some sawflies, such as the horntail or wood wasp, have a drill-like ovipositor with which they bore into wood. Most species are rather drab in colour, but some are boldly marked and they mimic various wasps. Adults may nibble pollen from flowers, and some eat other small insects, but they do not feed much. Most sawfly *larvae* feed freely on leaves and are often mistaken for the caterpillars of butterflies and moths. They can be distinguished because they always have at least six pairs of fleshy legs towards the back. Butterfly and moth caterpillars never have more than five pairs. Some sawfly larvae tunnel inside stems, and some cause the formation of *galls*.
ORDER: Hymenoptera.

Scale insect

Scale insects are small, sap-sucking BUGS in which many of the females are covered with a waxy or horny scale. Others, known as mealy bugs, are covered with masses of waxy threads. The adult

An open **scallop** showing the eyes at the edge of the mantle.

females plunge their beaks into their host plants and rarely move after that. They are all wingless and some are legless as well. Male scale insects look like tiny midges, but they are rare. Like the APHIDS, the scale insects reproduce mainly by *parthenogenesis* and they can build up immense populations. Each female can produce 1000 eggs, which she protects under her scale or her body until they hatch and the young *nymphs* crawl away. The insects often completely cover leaves, stems, and fruits and they do immense damage to crops. The Californian citrus industry, for example, was almost destroyed by the cottony cushion scale.
ORDER: Hemiptera-Homoptera.

Scallop

Most of the 300 species of this *bivalve* MOLLUSC live close to the shore, from just below low-tide

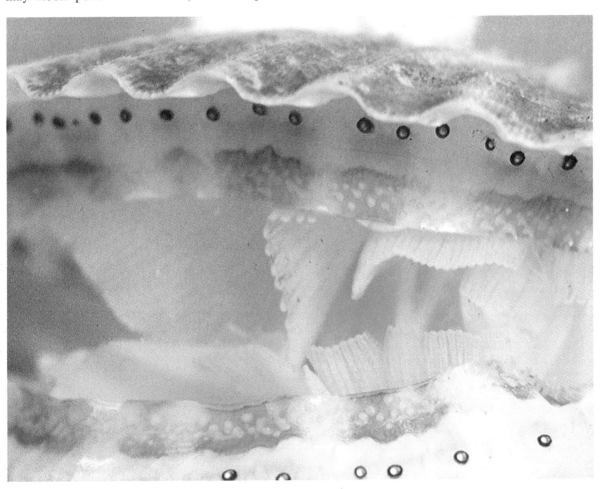

mark to about 90 metres deep. A few live in the great ocean depths. They are almost circular in outline, with wavy edges to their *valves*. Most have one flat valve and one rounded one. Scallops normally lie free on the sea-bed, and swim away if a predator comes near. Some species attach themselves to rock by a bunch of horny threads. The southern scallop can also push itself along with its foot. Scallops swim by opening and shutting their valves, producing a form of jet propulsion. Normally, they lie on the sea-bed with their valves slightly agape, revealing a large number of tentacles and more than 100 blue eyes around the edge of the mantle. Like all bivalves, the scallops filter food particles from the water. Their main enemies are STARFISHES and OCTOPUSES.

CLASS: Bivalvia;
ORDER: Anisomyaria.

Scarab beetle

The scarab beetles, known as tumblebugs in America, are DUNG BEETLES which actually make balls of dung and roll them along until they find a suitable place in which to bury them. The beetles often work in pairs, and having buried the dung by digging the soil from under it, they eat it at their leisure. At breeding time, males and females pair up to roll and bury extra large balls in which the female lays her eggs. The balls are cleverly pushed along by the hind legs, with the beetle moving backwards, and the insect can negotiate remarkably steep banks in this way.

ORDER: Coleoptera;
FAMILY: Scarabaeidae.

The most famous **scarab beetle** is the sacred scarab of the ancient Egyptians, who thought the insect represented the Sun. The beetle shown here is a South African scarab.

Scavengers

Some animals feed on dead decaying matter. These are the scavengers and they play a very important role in nature's economy. By consuming dead matter, they ensure that the goodness is rapidly returned to the soil, and also that the ground is not littered with slowly decomposing bodies. VULTURES, renowned for their ability to spot dead and dying animals from immense distances, soon reduce corpses to skin and bone – and some species even dispose of the bones by carrying them up in the air and dropping them until they break open. JACKALS and HYENAS are other well known scavengers.

Less spectacular,. but even more important are the myriads of FLY maggots and BEETLES that eat decaying flesh.

The sexton or BURYING BEETLES feed on the bodies of small animals such as VOLES, and actually bury them in the ground by digging the soil out from underneath them. The beetles can then feed undisturbed. Animal dung is also eaten by many beetles, including the SCARABS or tumblebugs. These beetles usually work in pairs to trundle a ball of dung along the ground until they find a suitable place to bury it. The female then lays one or more eggs in the ball, and the *larvae* feed in it as they grow up.

Scorpion

About 650 species of scorpions are found in the warm regions of the world. They are particularly abundant in deserts. Like all arachnids, scorpions have eight legs. They have powerful pincers like the claws of a lobster, and a long thin "tail" is carried arched over the back. At its tip is a sharp, hollow spine through which poison is squeezed.

Scorpions range in size from .5 cm to the 20 cm of one African species. They hunt by night their prey consisting almost entirely of insects and spiders. Only if the victim offers resistance will the scorpion use its sting. The prey is then slowly eaten.

The ferocity of scorpions has been much exaggerated. They will not use their sting against humans unless provoked. The main danger lies in their coming into houses and getting into shoes and clothing. The sting of the more dangerous species can be fatal.
ORDER: Scorpiones.

Scorpionfish

There are at least 300 of these sea fishes. They get their name from their many sharp spines which can be poisonous, inflicting dangerous wounds. These very poisonous species tend to live in shallower waters and are often brightly coloured, although the most poisonous of all, the STONEFISH, has a mottled colour which helps camouflage it. Scorpionfishes of deeper water tend to be less brightly patterned and less venomous. A few species have some importance as food fishes, although they make their appearance on the table disguised in the form of fish fingers.
ORDER: Scorpaeniformes;
FAMILY: Scorpaenidae.

Screamer

The three species of screamers are birds related to DUCKS, GEESE and SWANS. They resemble these birds

A **brown scorpion** from South Africa scuttles across stony ground.

in their behaviour, but do not look like them. They are heavy-bodied with long legs and thick, column-like necks. The feet have only small webs between the toes, and the bill is hooked. The wings bear two sharp spurs. Screamers live in South America, and are found in marshes, lagoons and damp grassland. They mainly eat plants, but may also catch insects. Screamers get their name from their loud two-note trumpeting calls.
ORDER: Anseriformes;
FAMILY: Anhimidae.

Scrub-bird

There are two species of scrub-bird, both rather wren-like in appearance, but probably related to the LYREBIRDS. The western or noisy scrub-bird is 20 cm long with a long tail and short, rounded wings. It has a dull plumage, mottled brown with black above and a whitish throat and abdomen. Discovered only in the mid-19th century, it was then thought to be extinct until it was rediscovered in 1961. The rufous scrubbird is almost as rare. Both species live in Australia.
ORDER: Passeriformes;
FAMILY: Atrichornithidae;
SPECIES: *Atrichornis clamosus* (western); *Atrichornis rufescens* (rufous).

Sculpin

Sculpins are rather grotesque, bottom-living fishes related to the BULLHEADS. They have big heads, on which the eyes are placed high up, and wide mouths with which they catch and eat a variety of seabed life. Their bodies are either scaleless or have very small scales, but they have sharp spines, some on the fins and others in front of the gill covers. Sculpins are fairly

A **dahlia sea anemone** viewed from above. Its mouth is in the centre, surrounded by stinging tentacles.

common fishes around the coasts of North America. One of the larger sculpins, the crab-eating cabezon, is a fish about 76 cm long. It is a tasty food, despite the fact that its roe is poisonous and its flesh is green.

ORDER: Scorpaeniformes;
FAMILY: Cottidae.

Sea anemone

The best known of the so-called "flower animals", the sea anemones are found in all the oceans of the world. They are closely related to CORALS. Their most outstanding feature is the variety of their colours and, in many species, the beauty of the patterns these colours make. They are most abundant in warm seas, where they can reach to almost 1 metre in diameter. The smallest are little more than the size of a pin's head, though such small individuals may, however, be starving. Sea anemones can exist for some time without food, which causes them to shrink in size. This ability may be one of the secrets of their long life span.

Most species of sea anemones spend their lives attached by their bases to weeds or rocks, but the animals are by no means sedentary. Some glide along the rock; others somersault by bending over to take hold of adjacent rock with their tentacles and then letting go at the base and flipping over to a new holding place. Some species burrow, while a few simply release their hold on the rock surface and float freely in the water. A few live with HERMIT CRABS. The crabs place them on their shells where the sea anemones' stinging cells may serve as a defence for both animals.

A sea anemone is cylindrical, with a mouth on the upper surface surrounded by a ring of tentacles. The tentacles armed with stinging cells, catch food – small fish and other sea animals – and carry it to the mouth. Most sea anemones are either male or female, but some contain organs of both sexes.

PHYLUM: Coelenterata.
CLASS: Anthozoa. .

Sea butterfly

The name sea butterfly is given to two groups of semi-transparent sea snails which swim by means of wing-like extensions of the foot. There are 100 species. The thecosomes have shells, the largest being up to 5 cm across, and eat microscopic organisms. All the gymnosomes are shell-less and mostly bear various kinds of armamemt for capturing larger prey. Sea butterflies are more abundant in tropical waters than in temperate seas, and they are sometimes found swimming in large numbers near the surface. They are so numerous in some parts that 1,295,000 km² of sea-bed are covered with their empty shells.

CLASS: Gastropoda;
ORDER: Thecosomata, Gymnosomata.

Sea cow

Sea cows are aquatic MAMMALS which are rather SEAL-like in appearance. Unlike seals they never come ashore but live permanently in the water. There are only four living representatives: the dugong, and three manatees. A much larger relation of these animals was the 6-metre-long Steller's sea cow, which became extinct in 1768, less than 30 years after its discovery in the Bering Sea.

The 3-metre-long dugong lives in the tropical waters of the Pacific and Indian oceans. It lives in shallow water, browsing on seaweeds. Female dugongs are very affectionate to their single young and will float to the surface, embracing the baby while suckling it. Despite their split lips and hairy, creased faces, this sight may well have given rise to the sailors' legend of the mermaid.

The manatee lives in rivers and estuaries, rarely venturing out to sea. There are three species, found in West Africa, the Caribbean and South America. The manatee lacks the whale-like tail of the dugong. Instead its tail is a broad flattened paddle. It is also larger than the dugong, up to 4 metres, but, like its relative, is a harmless and rather timid plant-eater.
ORDER: Sirenia;
FAMILIES: Trichechidae, Dugongidae.

Sea cucumber

Sea cucumbers are related to STARFISHES and SEA URCHINS. As the name suggests, many of the 1000 species look like cucumbers, though they come in a variety of shapes and sizes, and some look more like pressed holly leaves. The mouth is at the front end and usually surrounded by branching tube-feet. The animals creep about on the sea bed by means of the many tube-feet on their bodies, sweeping their tentacles in front of them to pick up particles of edible matter. A few species burrow into the sea bed, leaving the mouth with its ring of tentacles exposed for catching the debris that rains down from above. A few species feed on PLANKTON.
PHYLUM: Echinodermata;
CLASS: Holothuroidea.

Sea fir

Hydroids, as sea firs are commonly called, look like small, delicate seaweeds. They are, in fact, colonies of minute animals, related to HYDRAS and SEA ANEMONES. There are more than 2000

The **seahorse** swims upright and is cased in rings of bony armour. It holds on to seaweeds by its tail.

species, ranging from the smallest at 3 mm high to a few deep-sea specimens which reach a height of 1.8 metres. Sea firs have many-branched bodies. Some have a horizontal network of branching "roots" from which vertical stems arise. The stems have a zig-zag shape with a horny cup at each angle of the zig-zag. Each cup contains an animal known as a *polyp* and there may be several different kinds of polyp in a colony.
CLASS: Hydrozoa.

Sea hare

Sea hares are soft-bodied MOLLUSCS, halfway between SEA SLUGS and sea snails. Their popular name is due to a resemblance to a crouch-

ing hare. The sea hare has a slender body with a small, thin shell. Most species are about 8 cm long, but a few Pacific kinds may reach 30 cm. There are two pairs of tentacles on the head. They lay their eggs on beaches in strings of yellowish jelly.
CLASS: Gastropoda;
ORDER: Anaspidea.

Seahorse

Seahorses are among the oddest-looking of all fishes. They are closely related to the PIPEFISHES, and, like them, they live widespread in coastal waters among eelgrass and other weeds. There are 20 species of seahorses. They bear a strong resemblance to the chessboard knight, all the more so because they swim in the upright position, cruising steadily forward under the power of their *dorsal fin*,

The **sea cucumber** below can grow to a length of 30 cm. It is an echinoderm, like the starfish.

The **sea hare** browses on seaweed below low-tide level.

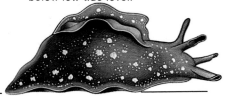

which beats so rapidly that it looks like a small propeller. They are able to turn their heads from side to side and to curl their long, tapering tails around any convenient support. They feed by sucking tiny planktonic animals into their small, bone-ringed mouths. Their eyes, each mounted in a little bony turret, are able to swivel independently. The male seahorse carries the babies. The female lays her eggs into a pouch on his abdomen, from which he gives birth to young seahorses when the eggs hatch, about $4\frac{1}{2}$ weeks later.

ORDER: Gasterosteiformes;
FAMILY: Syngnathidae.

Although they spend most of their lives in the sea, **seals** must come ashore to breed. A few species live in fresh water.

Seal

Seals are aquatic MAMMALS. Unlike the FUR SEALS and SEA LIONS, which belong to a different family, the true seals have no external ears and little hair on their bodies. Their hind flippers cannot be swung forwards, and progress on the land is laborious because the animals can only drag themselves on their bellies.

In the water, however, seals are powerful swimmers. The paddle-like hind flippers are used to provide the power, the front flippers for steering, and the body is streamlined to reduce drag when swimming. To prevent water from entering their lungs, seals are able to close their nostrils under water while searching for food.

The common seal also known as the harbour seal, lives around the coasts of the northern oceans and rarely goes far out to sea. Adults range up to about 2 metres in length, with males being a little larger than females. Their short, coarse hair varies from silvery grey to dark brown or even black. Common seals feed mainly on the seabed, where they catch various kinds of flatfishes, sand eels, and assorted CRUSTACEANS and MOLLUSCS. The pups are born in sheltered coves and estuaries in May and June and they can swim almost immediately. The females spend no more than an hour or two on land for the birth, and the pups swim off with them when the tide returns. The pups grow rapidly and are weaned within four weeks.

The most ferocious of the seals is the LEOPARD SEAL, which preys on penguins, and the largest species is the huge ELEPHANT SEAL, which weighs up to 4 tonne. Some seals spend their lives near the coast, living together in colonies

Common seal

Pup

Head profile

Pup

Grey seal

Head profile

Pup

Monk seal

on the shore during the mating season. Others such as the harp seal live in the open seas and make long, regular migrations in the breeding season.

Most seals live in cool or polar seas, although some are found in warm waters, and one species, the Baikal seal, lives in fresh water. Hence, the seal has a thick layer of blubber beneath the skin. This has made it a target for hunters. So too has the attractive baby fur of the young of some species, and the annual seal culls in parts of the world have created international controversy.

ORDER: Pinnipedia;
FAMILY: Phocidae.

Sea lily

Sea lilies are sea animals which look like plants. They belong to a group known as *crinoids*. Sea lilies have existed for 600 million years,

A **Weddel seal** pup meets its mother as she bobs up in a breathing hole in the ice.

and at one time it was thought that they were extinct. Now it is known that they are abundant deep in the ocean. A sea lily's body is at the end of a long stalk. It has five arms, each of which branches, often several times, and serves to catch food particles in the water. The sea lily is almost 90 per cent limestone, and there is only a small amount of living tissue.

PHYLUM: Echinodermata;
CLASS: Crinoidea;
ORDER: Articulata.

Sea lion

There are five species of sea lion but the most familiar, and the one seen most often in zoos and circuses, is the Californian sea lion. This and Steller's sea lion live in the Northern hemisphere; the others inhabit southern oceans,

living close to the South American and Australasian coasts.

Along with the FUR SEALS, they are often referred to as eared seals due to their small ears, a feature lacking in true seals. They are expert swimmers and divers, catching fish under water. They apparently use their long, sensitive whiskers to help detect prey. On land, they can move with surprising speed, bounding along on their flippers and leaping over rocks and down cliff-sides, their blubber and soft gristly ribs protecting them from harm. Naturally playful, sea lions can be trained to perform simple tricks.

Sea lions, like most seals, breed in colonies on beaches, each bull staking out his own territory and herding a group of females around him. The single young is carefully guarded by the mother until able to take to the sea and fend for itself. Sea lions are unpopular with fishermen, who blame them for damaging fish stocks. Californian sea lions seem to prefer SQUID to fish, while the Australian sea lion preys on PENGUINS

ORDER: Pinnipedia;
FAMILY: Otariidae;
SPECIES: *Zalophus californianus* (Californian).

Sea otter

The sea otter is the largest of the OTTERS. It is up to 1.2 metres long and may weigh 36 kg. Unlike other

There are many species of **sea slug**, in all shapes and sizes. The common grey sea slug can be up to 8cm long.

sea MAMMALS it has no layer of fat under its skin, but relies on air trapped in its thick fur to keep it warm. Overhunting the otter for its fur brought it near to extinction in the early 1900s, but there are now several colonies on the northern Pacific coasts of North America and the USSR.

Sea otters seldom venture onto land, and may even give birth at sea, resting on "rafts" of seaweed. They spend their time in shallow water particularly among the kelp which they wrap around their bodies to prevent themselves drifting while asleep. There they feed on SEA URCHINS, CRABS, MUSSELS and ABALONES. Sea otters are one of the few animals to use tools – a flat stone with which they smash open shells while lying on their backs in the water.

ORDER: Carnivora;
FAMILY: Mustelidae;
SPECIES: *Enhydra lutris.*

Sea pen

These "flower animals" are relatives of SEA ANEMONES and SEA FIRS. They get their popular name from the resemblance some bear to old-fashioned quill pens. They vary in size, the largest being 1.8 metres tall, and consist of a central stem with numerous *polyps* springing from the sides. They live on the seabed but can move from one place to another by pumping water in and out of their bodies. Sea pens are mostly yellow, orange, red or brown, and when disturbed, they give off coloured lights.

CLASS: Anthozoa;
ORDER: Pennatulacea.

There are about 45 families of **sea slugs** in all shapes, sizes and colours.

Sea slug

Like land SLUGS, these are really snails without shells. There are many species generally described as sea slugs, the most common being in the class Nudibranchia. These animals have naked gills on their outer surface. Well-known species include the sea lemon, with a tough yellow body covered with purple "warts", and the common grey sea-slug. They creep around the lower shore and shallow water, and produce a slime to tackle even poisonous prey.

CLASS: Gastropoda;
ORDER: Nudibranchia;
SPECIES: *Aeolidia papillosa* (common grey).

Sea snake

Sea snakes live in tropical coastal waters of the Indian and Pacific Oceans. They are well adapted to a life spent in water, having a paddle-shaped tail which acts as a scull, and valved nostrils on the top of the snout. But they breathe air and will drown if held under water too long. The body is flattened from side to side and may reach 1.5 metres or more in length. Sea snakes usually hunt at night, using their poisoned fangs to kill prey such as eels or small fish. They may collect in the water in huge numbers and there is one report of a gathering seen in the Malacca Strait which formed a writhing belt of snakes 3 metres wide and 100 km long. A sea snake's bite is almost painless and slow-acting in humans but can nevertheless be fatal, for the venom is very poisonous. Some primitive species of sea snake lay their eggs on land, while other species give birth to live young in the sea.

ORDER: Squamata;
FAMILY: Hydrophiidae.

Sea spider

There are 500 species of sea spider, most of them living in deep water. They are not closely related to true spiders. These sea animals have small bodies and 4 to 6 pairs of extremely long legs. The largest, living in the deepest seas, have a leg-span of 60 cm. They live on other sea animals, piercing the skin with their fangs and sucking out the body fluids. The female lays eggs and the male carries them around until they hatch.

CLASS: Pycnogonida.

Sea squirt

Sea squirts are so called because they squirt out jets of water when disturbed. They are sea animals which are distantly related to the VERTEBRATES. The body is sac-shaped and enclosed in a firm, jelly-like coat or tunic. There are two spout-like openings, the upper

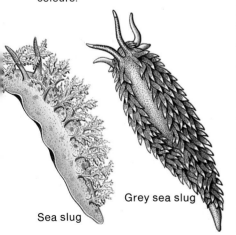

Sea slug

Grey sea slug

Part of a colony of **gooseberry sea squirts**.

Above: Ciona is a more elongated form of **sea squirt**.

one of which is the mouth. Water is drawn in through the mouth and filtered through gill slits before passing out of the other spout. Food particles are strained out by the gills, and oxygen is also taken in by them. Most sea squirts are attached to the sea bed, down to depths of 5000 metres, but there are some free-swimming species in the PLANKTON.

The typical sea squirt is an *hermaphrodite* animal, producing both eggs and sperm. Fertilization takes place in the water and leads to the development of a tadpole-like *larva* about 6 mm long.
PHYLUM: Chordata;
CLASS: Ascidiacea.

Sea urchin

The 800 species of sea urchin are relatives of the STARFISHES, BRITTLESTARS and SEA CUCUMBERS. They are round, spiky creatures, sometimes called sea hedgehogs. Most species walk on tube feet,

Below: **Rock urchins** resting in hollows they have made in soft limestone.

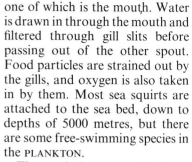

Edible sea urchin

Test of violet heart urchin

Left: **Violet heart urchins** showing their dense fur-like spines. They live under the sand.

which are pushed out through little holes, though some species walk on their spines. The mouth is underneath in the middle, and has five teeth with which the animal chews seaweed.

The spines are both tough and sharp, and some sea urchins use them for burrowing in sand and even in rock. Bathers treading on them can sustain painful wounds. Some sea urchins have poisonous spines.

PHYLUM: Echinodermata;
CLASS: Echinoidea.

Secretary bird

The secretary bird is a bird of prey, having the hooked bill of an EAGLE. However, it looks more like a CRANE, being long-legged and standing about 120 cm high. It is mainly grey and black, and has a crest of black-tipped feathers that

A **secretary bird** coming down to roost at night in the African bush.

hangs down behind the head, in the same way that clerks once carried their quills stuck into their wigs. This is how the secretary bird got its unusual name. They live in Africa south of the Sahara, and inhabit grasslands and open bush, feeding on snakes and other animals.

ORDER: Falconiformes;
FAMILY: Sagittariidae;
SPECIES: *Sagittarius serpentarius*.

Serow

Serow are good climbers and live in rocky places. They are "goat-antelopes". The maned serow is found in the Himalayas, southern China and South-East Asia. It stands up to 107 cm high and weighs 68 to 90 kg. Its rough coat is grizzled black to red. Serow are solitary animals; four or five will divide up a hillside and stick to their own territory. At the first

sign of danger, they dash away with a whistling snort.

ORDER: Artiodactyla;
FAMILY: Bovidae;
SPECIES: *Capricornis sumatraensis* (maned).

Serval

The serval is a slender cat found in most of Africa south of the Sahara. It is beautifully marked with stripes and spots, and has large erect ears, a fairly short tail, and long legs. Servals stand up to 50 cm high and are up to 1 metre long. They prefer open country to the fringes of forests, spend the day curled up in a nest of grass, and hunt at night. Their long legs enable them to run very fast over short distances. They travel through high grass with long, high leaps and can climb fast and swim well. Servals live mostly on rodents and birds. MOLE RATS are common prey, and it is thought that the

serval's large ears help it to hear these rodents burrowing in the ground. Like many cats, the serval adopts the slink-run to stalk certain of its prey and can kill with a sharp blow of the outspread forepaw. There are 2 to 3 kittens in each litter.

ORDER: Carnivora;
FAMILY: Felidae;
SPECIES: *Felis serval.*

Shad

A deeper-bodied relative of the HERRING, the shad was once an important food fish in Europe until overfishing reduced its numbers. The European species now swim singly or in small shoals, but their close relatives in the waters of North American and Far Eastern seas still occur in vast shoals. The European shad are up to 60 cm long, with silvery-blue bodies tinged with yellow. They feed on plankton.

ORDER: Clupeiformes;
FAMILY: Clupeidae.

Shark

The most generally feared fishes of the sea, sharks are an ancient group with a history going back 500 million years. Their skeleton, like that of their relatives the RAYS, SKATES and CHIMAERAS, is formed, not of bone, but of hard *cartilage.* Their skin is covered with tooth-like scales: in fact, the terrifying array of sharp teeth in a man-eater's jaws is really just so many enlarged scales. Unlike bony fishes, all sharks lack a *swim bladder,* so that their bodies are not buoyed up in the water. To stop itself from sinking a shark must swim continuously. Its tail fin has a longer upper lobe and a shorter lower lobe. Together with its large, wing-like *pectoral fins,* this helps to keep the shark's body on an even keel as it swims along.

Sharks range greatly in size, from small DOG-FISHES to the WHALE SHARK, greatest of all fishes. But this giant and the huge BASKING SHARK are inoffensive beasts which cruise along near the surface, sieving out their food from the small floating creatures of the PLANKTON. Some bottom-living sharks are also fairly harmless, feeding on shellfish which they grind up with their blunt teeth. More notorious are sharks such as the PORBEAGLE, mako, sand shark, tiger shark and GREAT WHITE SHARK, all fast swimmers with crescent-shaped mouths gaping wickedly on the undersides of their snout. They are able to chop large chunks from the bodies of their prey. A shark hunts by scent – indeed, most of its brain is concerned with the sense of smell. Its eyes probably help it to aim for the final kill.

CLASS: Selachii;
ORDER: Lamniformes.

Below left: A **grey shark** glides through shallows on its long, outstretched pectoral fins.

Below: **Shearwaters** normally come ashore only to breed. They may then be seen in large colonies.

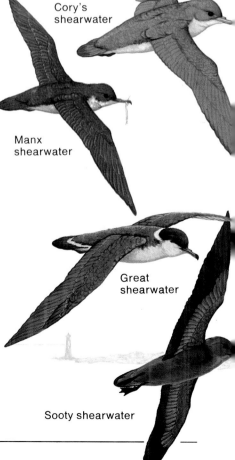

Cory's shearwater

Manx shearwater

Great shearwater

Sooty shearwater

Shearwater

Shearwaters belong to the same family as petrels and fulmars, and are related to ALBATROSSES though generally smaller. Their plumage is dull, usually black or brown above and whitish underneath. They earn their name because of their ability to "shear" or skim low over the water, like albatrosses, scooping out a diet of surface marine life such as fish, squid and crustaceans.

Excellent gliders, these birds range great distances out to sea over many parts of the world. They usually breed on islands in large colonies, and form tight pair bonds. Both partners look after the single egg, nested in a burrow in the ground. The chicks are covered with long down and become very fat, and in this condition are considered good eating in parts of the world. Because of this, certain species such as the short-tailed shearwater of Australia are known as "mutton-birds".
ORDER: Procellariiformes;
FAMILY: Procellariidae.

Sheathbill

The only land bird to breed on the icy continent of Antarctica. This white, pigeon-like bird is 40 cm long, with short, sturdy legs and a conical bill. The sheathbill is named after the greenish, horny sheath which covers the base of its bill. Two very similar-looking species are the white sheathbill and the lesser sheathbill.
ORDER: Charadriiformes;
FAMILY: Chionididae.

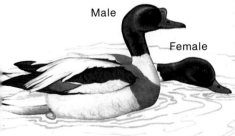

Male

Female

Sheep

The sheep was probably first domesticated by man as long as 12,000 years ago. It is still not certain what its wild ancestors were but it is most likely that the domestic sheep we see today is derived from the MOUFLON and the urial.

There are now over 400 breeds of domestic sheep, providing a huge variation in size, shape, colour and types of fleece. The Merino sheep, farmed in Australia, the United States, the USSR, South Africa, Argentina, France and Germany, provides the best wool, while sheep originating in the British Isles are often bred to supply both meat and wool. There are some sheep, however, such as the East Friesian and the La Razza Sarda of Sardinia, which are bred especially for their milk.
ORDER: Artiodactyla;
FAMILY: Bovidae;
SPECIES: *Ovis aries*.

Sheetweb spider

Sheetweb spiders, sometimes called tunnel-web spiders, spin horizontal webs in all kinds of corners, including those in houses and hollow trees. The most familiar in Europe are those of the genus *Tegenaria*, whose long-legged species are often found in the bath. Other sheetweb spiders spin among heathers and other low-growing shrubs. Unlike the web of the ORB SPIDER the sheetweb is not sticky. It is intended to trap crawling insects which blunder into a tangle of trip-wires. The spider responds to a pull on the trip-wires and runs out quickly from its tunnel shelter which is in one corner of the web. Sheetwebs were formerly pressed onto wounds to stop bleeding.
ORDER: Araneae;
FAMILY: Agelenidae.

The female **shelduck** looks like the male, except that there is no knob over the bill.

Shelduck

The common shelduck is a goose-like duck. It is found in estuaries and on coasts and feeds on small mud-dwelling animals. The plumage is white with bold patterns of chestnut and black. It breeds all over Europe and Asia and in July the entire population of north-western Europe migrates to the Heligoland Bight, off north-western Germany, to moult.
ORDER: Anseriformes;
FAMILY: Anatidae;
SPECIES: *Tadorna tadorna*.

Shield bug

Shield bugs are mostly sap-sucking bugs which get their name because most of them have distinctly shield-shaped bodies. There are many hundreds of species in several families, and most live in tropical regions. Shield bugs are also called stink bugs because many of the species produce pungent odours to deter predators. Many also display warning colours.
ORDER: Hemiptera-Heteroptera.

Two of the many **shield bugs**, so-called for their shape.

Hawthorn shield bug

Pied shield bug

Shipworm

The shipworms are marine *bivalves* which bore into wood, causing severe damage to ships and the supports of piers. Boring starts early in a shipworm's life when the *larva* grows a pair of valves, often within two days. It holds on to a piece of wood with its sucker-like foot and bores into the timber with the sharp edges of the valves. As the shipworm grows larger it bores a wider hole, but it cannot then

leave by the small hole through which it entered. It pushes a *siphon* out of the hole to bring in water and PLANKTON to supplement its diet of wood.
CLASS: Bivalvia;
ORDER: Adapedonta.

Shoebill

The shoebill or shoebill stork is a strange-looking bird with its huge, broad bill, the upper part of which is concave and ends in a hook. The lower part of the bill is convex. The eyes are unusually large and the plumage is slate-grey with a greenish gloss. Shoebills stand about 90 cm high and have a wing-span of 2.6 metres. They live in papyrus marshes and swamps in east-central Africa where they may stand motionless, sometimes on one leg, for hours. They eat frogs and fish. When frightened, they fly off with slow wing-beats.
ORDER: Ciconiiformes;
FAMILY: Balaenicipitidae;
SPECIES: *Balaeniceps rex*.

Shrew

Shrews are mouse-like MAMMALS found in most parts of the world except Australasia and the Polar regions. The Etruscan shrew of southern Europe is the world's smallest mammal. It weighs as little as 2 grams and measures about 4 cm from nose to rump. It has a tail of up to 3 cm. Shrews have weak sight, their eyes are small and, in some species, partly hidden in fur. But their hearing and smell are highly developed. Most of the 200 or so species of shrew are land animals, but some are aquatic.

The greater white-toothed **shrew** has whiskers on its tail.

Shrews mainly eat insects and worms, but also include in their diet nut kernels, seeds and other vegetable material. Young shrews are born in nests of leaves and litter. They are blind and naked at birth. It takes about four weeks to wean them. A shrew's life-span is about one year.
ORDER: Insectivora;
FAMILY: Soricidae.

Above: The **water shrew** has a body 70 to 90 mm long. Its back is nearly black.

Below: A common **tree shrew** of Asian forests.

Shrikes are like small birds of prey. Insects are their main prey, but larger shrikes will catch lizards and rodents.

Great grey shrike

Lesser grey shrike

Female

Male

Male

Female

Woodchat shrike

Red-backed shrike

As the **sidewinder** moves, only two points of the snake's body touch the hot desert sand at any one time.

Shrike

Shrikes are small perching birds named after their piercing calls. They have the habit of sticking their food on thorns or wedging it in clefts. For this reason they are also known as butcherbirds. The true shrikes live in Europe, Africa, Asia, as far south as New Guinea, and North America. They are 15 to 25 cm long and have strong legs, sharp claws and a hooked bill. Best known is the great grey shrike, called the northern shrike in North America. Like other shrikes, it is a hunter. It swoops after small animals, striking them with its feet. Nests are built in bushes, hedges and brambles.
ORDER: Passeriformes;
FAMILY: Laniidae.

Shrimp

The name shrimp is often given to a great many kinds of smaller CRUSTACEAN. The common European shrimp, to which the name was originally applied, is up to 7.6 cm long. It has two pairs of *antennae*, the outer pair being as long as the body. It is slightly shorter than the common PRAWN, with which it is frequently con-

fused, and does not have a saw-like shield over the head. By day the common shrimp buries itself in sand or mud, coming out after dark to walk along the sea bottom or swim close to it. Shrimps eat various small sea animals including CRUSTACEANS and MOLLUSCS, and they also eat seaweed.
ORDER: Decapoda;
SPECIES: *Crangon vulgaris* (common European).

Sidewinder

Also called the horned rattlesnake, the sidewinder is a small, squat RATTLESNAKE, about 75 cm long. Sidewinders cross loose sand with an unusual sideways looping movement of the body that leaves a set of tracks rather like the rungs of a ladder. The snakes spend the hot daytime hours in mouseholes or buried in sand. Their mottled

The common **shrimp** is abundant in coastal waters.

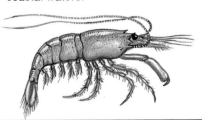

brown colour makes half-buried individuals difficult to see. In the late evening they emerge and hunt rodents. Side-winders are found in the deserts of the south-western United States and north-western Mexico.
ORDER: Squamata;
FAMILY: Crotalidae;
SPECIES: *Crotalus cerastes*.

Sika

The sika is closely related to the RED DEER. This hardy animal formerly lived in many forested re-

The **sika deer** grazes and browses on young tree and shrub shoots.

gions of eastern Asia, but it has become rare there. However, it was introduced into Europe as a park animal. Many sika escaped and there are now many wild herds descended from them. The sika stands about 120 cm at the shoulder. The faint, spotted coat is buff-brown, becoming darker in winter.

ORDER: Artiodactyla;
FAMILY: Cervidae;
SPECIES: *Cervus nippon.*

Silk moth

Many moth *larvae* surround themselves with silken cocoons before turning into *pupae*, and several different species provide silk on a commercial basis in India, China, and Japan. Most belong to the same family as the ATLAS MOTH, but the great bulk of today's silk comes from *the* silk moth, *Bombyx mori.* Domesticated for centuries, the species is now unknown in the wild and the moths have lost the ability to fly. The sturdy cream caterpillar is fed on mulberry leaves, and when fully grown it spins a *cocoon* which may contain 900 metres of unbroken silk.

ORDER: Lepidoptera;
FAMILY: Bombycidae.

Silverfish

The silverfish is a BRISTLETAIL – a wingless insect with three slender "tails" at the hind end. Its carrot-shaped body is about 1 cm long and covered with silvery scales, which come off very easily if the insect is touched. It lives in houses and feeds on starchy materials such as spilled flour and the glue of cartons and book-bindings. The young have no scales, but are otherwise just like the adults and hardly change as they grow up.

ORDER: Thysanura;
FAMILY: Lepismatidae.

Silverfish

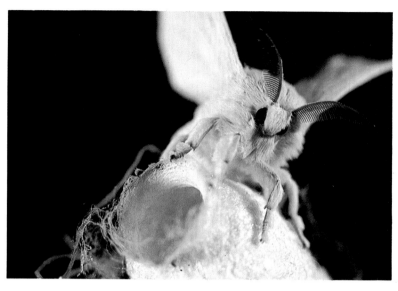
Above: A **silk moth** newly emerged from its cocoon.

Siskin

The siskin is a small FINCH, found in much of Europe, and parts of Asia – even breeding in western Siberia. A similar bird, the pine siskin, lives in North America, and can be regarded as representative of siskins throughout the cold, temperate and sub-tropical parts of the northern hemisphere. The siskin spends the summer in pine-woods and the winter among the alders along the riverside.

ORDER: Passeriformes;
FAMILY: Fringillidae;
SPECIES: *Carduelis spinus.*

Skate

The common skate is a bottom-living flatfish of European waters, and a useful food fish. As the Latin name of this fish suggests, it can also be called a RAY – the names skate and ray are interchangeable. Like other rays, the skates have bodies flattened from above to below, and large, wing-like *pectoral fins* which extend along the head and body, and ripple when the skate is swimming. The tail is long and slim with small tail fins. Common skates grow to about 2 metres in length. Their egg-cases

Below: The male **siskin** is yellow-green with a black crown and chin.

Male
Female

are familiar objects on European beaches, where they are known as mermaids' purses.

ORDER: Rajiformes;
FAMILY: Rajidea;
SPECIES: *Raia batis* (common).

Skink

There are over 600 species of skink, making up one of the lar-

A **skink** with its eggs. Note the very small legs.

gest LIZARD families. Many are smooth-scaled with small limbs. Some have no limbs at all. Such features help the skink to burrow in the sand and some species such as the Greek legless lizard, spend most of their lives underground. Other species have well developed legs and live above ground. The giant skink has a *prehensile* tail that adapts it for climbing. This is

the largest skink, up to 60 cm long. Most skinks eat insects though a few are vegetarian. Skinks live in most continents outside Antarctica and are active mainly by day.
ORDER: Squamata;
FAMILY: Scincidae.

Skipper butterfly

The skippers are mostly fairly small BUTTERFLIES with a rapid, darting flight. In many ways, they are intermediate between butterflies and moths, although they have clubbed *antennae* and almost

all of them fly by day. There is usually a little point beyond the club of each antenna. Skippers are mostly brown or orange, although some tropical species have metallic blues and greens on their wings. The wings may be held above the body at rest, as in most other butterflies, but some species rest with their wings partly or fully open. The caterpillars feed mainly on grasses and spin flimsy *cocoons* around themselves before pupating. There are hundreds of species.
ORDER: Lepidoptera;
FAMILY: Hesperiidae.

Skipper butterflies are mostly small with a broad head and body.

Grizzled skipper

Dingy skipper

Large chequered skipper

Small skipper

Silver-spotted skipper

Male

Male

Male

Caterpillar

Large skipper

Male

Male

Skua

Aggressive seabirds related to GULLS and TERNS. Skuas are fish-eaters, but they also waylay other birds and force them, by continual buffeting, to disgorge their food. The great skua also preys on such birds as KITTIWAKES and PUFFINS and, in Antarctica, on the eggs and chicks of PENGUINS. The great skua is about 60 cm long. From a distance, the plumage appears dark brown, but is, in fact, streaked with brown and white. Skuas breed in the northern and southern hemispheres and vigorously defend their nests against predators, repeatedly swooping on intruders, including humans. In North America, skuas are known as jaegers.
ORDER: Charadriiformes;
FAMILY: Stercorariidae.

Skuas are aggressive fast-flying sea birds with hooked beaks.

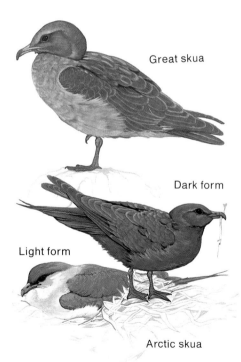

Great skua

Dark form

Light form

Arctic skua

Skunk

All members of the WEASEL family have *musk* glands at the base of the tail, but the most notorious are the skunks. They can squirt a foul-smelling liquid from their glands a distance of 3.7 metres. This pungent spray often causes temporary blindness. The striking black and white colour pattern of the fur acts as a warning to all potential predators.

Most skunks grow up to about 76 cm long, including the tail. The commonest species is the striped skunk which is found from southern Canada southwards to Mexico.

Skunks live in burrows in a variety of habitats, including woods, plains and desert areas. They feed mainly on insects, but also on mice, frogs, small birds and eggs.

Mating occurs in spring and the 4 to 5 kittens are born after about 50 days. They remain with their mother until autumn.
ORDER: Carnivora;
FAMILY: Mustelidae;
SPECIES: *Mephitis mephitis (striped)*.

Skylark

A small, dark brown LARK noted for its song while flying. It sings continuously for up to five minutes as it makes a vertical ascent into the sky. The skylark breeds in most of Europe, except the extreme north of Scandinavia, in North Africa and across Asia to Japan. Because of its popularity it has been introduced to many other parts of the world. It lives in open country, in pastures, moors and marshes, but not near trees. The small nest is built on the ground among grass and the eggs are well camouflaged.
ORDER: Passeriformes;
FAMILY: Alaudidae;
SPECIES: *Alauda arvensis*.

The **skylark** has white edges to its tail and a slight crest. It is found in all kinds of open country.

The **sea slater** scavenges on the shore at night.

Slater

The slater is a semi-aquatic form of WOODLOUSE which spends its life close to the sea. It lives mostly just above high-tide level, hiding in crevices by day – or even in bright moonlight – and coming out to hunt for food in the dark. The slater is drably coloured, with two large black eyes and two pairs of *antennae*. Slaters are large compared with land woodlice and females are up to 5 cm long. They are able to run very fast. They are general scavengers of animal and vegetable matter, although their preferred food is seaweed.
CLASS: Crustacea;
ORDER: Isopoda.

Sloth

Despite belonging to the order Edentata – meaning without teeth – the sloth has teeth in its cheeks, nine on each side. Its movements are very slow indeed. The sloth spends most of its life hanging upside down from branches. For this it uses its long curved claws, which look like hooks. The hands and feet serve no other purpose than to anchor the claws, so a fold of skin has grown over them joining the fingers and toes. The sloth can turn its head through 270 degrees so that it can hold it almost upright, even when upside down.

Its hair lies in the opposite direction to that of other mammals, so rain water can run off it. Each hair is grooved and often infested with algae that make the

The **two-toed sloth** takes its rest in a South American forest.

animal look green. This camouflages it in the forests of South America where it lives. Sloths have a diet of leaves and fruit. The seven kinds of sloth include two-toed and three-toed species.
ORDER: Edentata;
FAMILY: Bradypodidae.

Sloth bear

The sloth bear, or Indian bear, does not look like a bear. It has a long shaggy coat coloured black or blackish brown, with a white or brown U-shaped mark on the chest. Its long muzzle is off-white. The sloth bear grows up to 1.8 metres in length and can weigh up to 113 kg. It is found in India and Sri Lanka and is extremely dangerous, particularly when frightened.

Sloth bears live in low country, both in dry and jungle areas. They are active mostly at dusk and dawn. They eat a wide variety of food, including insects, carrion, eggs and fruit. They are par-

ticularly fond of TERMITES, which they suck up through a tube they form with their loose lips.

Mating occurs in June in India and at any time of year in Sri Lanka. The cubs are born after 7 months and remain with their mother for 2 to 3 years.
ORDER: Carnivora;
FAMILY: Ursidae;
SPECIES: *Melursus ursinus.*

Slow-worm

The snake-like slow-worm is a legless LIZARD found in Europe, south-western Asia and North Africa. Adults measure about 30 cm and have a smooth "enamelled" body, brownish above and darker beneath. Slow-worms live in open woodlands, grasslands, and heaths, especially where conditions are slightly damp. They bask in spring and autumn. Otherwise they burrow or hide under logs or stones by day. After sunset or after rain they come out and feed on slugs and other small creatures.

Slugs have a small saddle-like mantle, usually near the front.

The **slow-worm** is very smooth and shiny; grey to coppery in colour.

If disturbed, slow-worms move away slowly. If attacked they may shed the tail. They are long-lived; Copenhagen Zoological Museum kept one for 54 years.
ORDER: Squamata;
FAMILY: Anguidae;
SPECIES: *Anguis fragilis.*

Slug

Slugs are essentially snails which have lost or almost lost their shells. The internal organs which are housed in the snail's shell are all packed into the body of the slug, and the *mantle* is reduced to a small saddle on the back (see SNAIL). The space between the

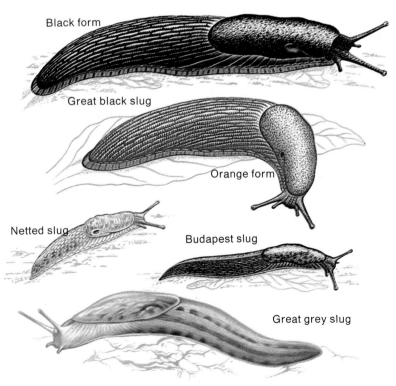

Black form

Great black slug

Orange form

Netted slug

Budapest slug

Great grey slug

Large **slugs** can be up to 15 cm long. They can be very destructive of garden and farm crops.

mantle and the body forms the lung. There are three main groups of land slugs in temperate regions, probably derived from three quite separate groups of snails. They are the keeled slugs, the round-backed slugs and the shelled slugs. The keeled slugs have a fairly prominent ridge, or keel, running forward from the tail end on the upper surface. Round-backed slugs lack such a keel, although they may have strongly ribbed backs, and shelled slugs are easily recognised by the little ear-shaped shell perched on the hind end.

Slugs vary in size from 6 to 200 mm. They live in damp places and some species spend most of their lives underground. They are most active at night or after a daytime shower. Most feed near ground level, but some are good climbers and ascend trees to heights of more than 9 metres. Slugs are *hermaphrodite*, and a two-way exchange of sperm is usual between mating pairs. Each slug lays eggs soon afterwards, under a stone or in some similar damp recess. The eggs are soft, round and pearly white and up to 5 mm in diameter. They hatch within about a month. Most slugs eat decaying vegetation, but some like the leaves or underground parts of growing plants. Some eat nothing but fungi, while the shel-led slugs eat earthworms and other slugs.

PHYLUM: Mollusca;
CLASS: Gastropoda.

Smelt

The European smelt is a small, silvery fish which lives in large shoals in coastal waters as far east as the Baltic Sea. It reaches a maximum length of 20 cm. A similar species lives off the Atlantic coast of North America. The other eleven species of smelt live mainly in the North Pacific Ocean. Smelts have a slim body with a pointed head and a jutting lower jaw. Teeth in the jaw and on the tongue serve to capture small planktonic animals and worms. Smelts are themselves much preyed upon by larger fishes, and sometimes are useful food fishes for humans. The European smelt is said to have a flavour of cucumber.

ORDER: Salmoniformes;
FAMILY: Osmeridae;
SPECIES: *Osmerus eperlanus* (European).

Snail

Snails are MOLLUSCS with coiled or conical shells. There are more than 80,000 species, widely distributed in the sea, in fresh water and on land. The snail's soft body has a muscular foot on which it creeps along, and the front end of the foot merges into the head. The head carries one or two pairs of tentacles, eyes – frequently at the tips of the longer tentacles – and a mouth armed with teeth on a horny tongue known as the *radula*. That part of the body that remains inside the shell is covered with a cloak of thick skin called the *mantle*. The shell is actually formed by certain parts of the mantle. When necessary, the whole body can be withdrawn into the shell for safety.

There are about 55,000 species of sea snail, living in all parts of the ocean from the shore to the deeps. They normally breathe with gills, which are feathery structures situated in the mantle cavity. This is a space between the mantle and the body. Water is pumped in and out and the gills absorb oxygen from it The sea snails include *carnivores*, *herbivores* and scavengers, as well as a few parasitic species. The hind end of the foot carries a horny disc called an *operculum*. This forms a door to close the shell when the snail retires.

There are about 5000 species of freshwater snail. Some have gills like marine snails, but many have lost their gills and the mantle cavity acts as a lung. The snails

Most land **snails** have two pairs of tentacles, usually with eyes at the tips of the longer ones. Most water-snails have only one pair of tentacles, with eyes at the base.

Garden snail

Roman snail

Strawberry snail

Two-toothed door snail

Kentish snail

Brown-lipped snail

Garlic glass snail

Round-mouth snail

Great ram's horn (a water snail)

must then come to the surface every now and then to take in air, although they can absorb a certain amount of oxygen direct from the water through their skins. Only some freshwater snails carry an operculum.

Land snails tend to flourish on soils with a good supply of calcium, which they need for their shells. They are less successful on sandy soils. The group contains herbivorous and carnivorous species, one of the best-known herbivores being the garden snail, whose mottled brown shell is up to 4 cm across. In dry weather and in winter the land snails spend much of their time coiled inside their shells. Some species have an operculum, but most close their shells with layers of slime which harden to form a waterproof disc.
CLASS: Gastropoda.

Snake

Snakes, of which there are 2300 species, are long legless reptiles. Unlike LIZARDS, they lack shoulder girdles, moveable eyelids or visible ears. Snakes have long,

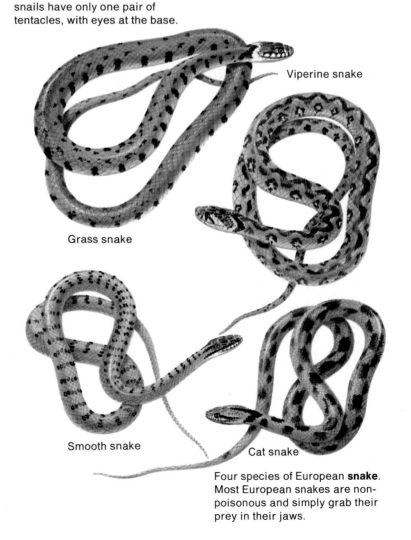

Viperine snake

Grass snake

Smooth snake

Cat snake

Four species of European **snake**. Most European snakes are non-poisonous and simply grab their prey in their jaws.

Horseshoe whip snake

Western whip snake

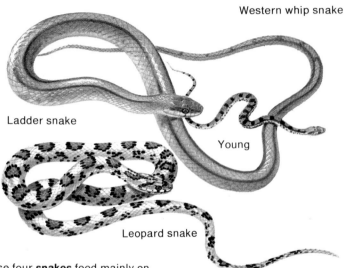

Ladder snake

Young

Leopard snake

These four **snakes** feed mainly on small mammals. The **western whip snake** is very fast. The **ladder snake** gets its name from the ladder-like pattern of its young.

deeply forked tongues with which they can "taste" their surroundings, and follow scent trails. All are carnivorous and rarely eat anything that they have not caught themselves. When they swallow large prey, snakes can "unhinge" their jaws and work their victims into the throat by means of a see-saw movement. In this way a snake can swallow a victim more than twice the diameter of its own head.

Most snakes travel by side-to-side movements of the body, gliding forward as their sides press against any roughness in the ground. Big snakes, such as the BOA and PYTHON species proceed by the "caterpillar crawl", thrusting back with the exposed edges of their overlapping belly scales. The SIDEWINDER uses its own special type of propulsion.

Only about 300 species of snake are dangerous to people. These are the venomous snakes. The venom is not carried in the quick darting tongue, which the snake uses as a sensing organ, but in some of the teeth which are hollow and are known as poison fangs.

Snakes live in all continents but Antarctica. Some species are adapted to a burrowing life, many others live on the ground and some climb trees or swim in fresh or salt water. Most kinds lay eggs, but some give birth to live young.
ORDER: Squamata.

Snapper

Snappers are fishes which get their name from their perilous habit, when landed by a fisherman, of suddenly snapping their jaws. They live in the coastal waters of warm seas. Snappers are often very colourful, their deep bodies being streaked or spotted a bright yellow colour, or tinted delicately in rose or red. There are more than 250 species of snapper, the largest being about 60 cm in length. They have large jaws and teeth, and eat almost anything.
ORDER: Perciformes;
FAMILY: Lutjanidae.

Snapping turtle

These large American freshwater turtles are well named; they can badly maul a person's hand. The common snapping turtle has a shell up to 38 cm long and can weigh 23 kg. The alligator snapper is far larger and weighs up to 90 kg. Both species live in muddy ponds, lakes and rivers. The common snapper occurs from Canada to Ecuador and hunts MUSKRATS and other prey. The alligator snapper lives in the south-eastern United States. It lures the fish on which it preys by wriggling its tongue's two worm-like tips.
ORDER: Chelonia;
FAMILY: Chelydridae;
SPECIES: *Chelydra serpentina* (common); *Macroclemys temmincki* (alligator).

Snipe

Snipe are wading birds. They have the same general form as other waders, but the legs are not very long and the neck is short. The bill is long and straight, and the eyes are set well back on the head. Their plumage is generally dark brown, mottled and barred. Snipe are found in all continents, the common snipe itself having a worldwide distribution. It is 27 cm long. Snipe live in open country, usually in wet places such as marshes, damp meadows and moors, where

A mother **snowy owl** forms a soft feathery cave for her young chicks.

they blend in with the low vegetation. They probe the mud or damp ground for worms and insects.
ORDER: Charadriiformes;
FAMILY: Scolopacidae;
SPECIES: *Gallinago gallinago* (common).

Snowy owl

The barren frozen tundra of the polar north is the home of the snowy owl. A large owl some 50 cm long, its plumage is white, barred and spotted with black. Snowy owls prey on LEMMINGS, mice, rabbits, seabirds and fish. They often hunt by day, gliding slowly above the ground. Their eggs are laid in a hollow in the ground and, unusually, the chicks

are fed with pellets regurgitated by the mother. Unlike other Arctic creatures, the snowy owl keeps its white plumage all year round.
ORDER: Strigiformes;
FAMILY: Strigidae;
SPECIES: *Nyctea scandiaca*.

Sole

There are about 40 species of sole forming a family of flatfishes.

The **snipe** can be recognized by its long straight beak and the dark stripes along its head.

Most live in warm shallow waters, though the common Dover sole is found as far north as the Faeroes. This species averages about 30 cm in length and is a popular food fish, thought by some to be the tastiest of all fishes. The common American sole, also known as the hogchocker, is found along the eastern coast of North America and occasionally enters fresh waters.

Soles have rather tongue-shaped bodies with a long *dorsal fin* extending from head to tail They spend most of their lives on the sea-bed, half covered by sand and fully camouflaged by their sandy colour. Like their fellow flatfishes, the PLAICE and DAB, soles have both eyes on the side of the head that lies uppermost, one eye having migrated around the head during early life. The mouth, although twisted to one side like those of the other flatfishes, lies mostly underneath the head, which suits the sole's more exclusively sand-grubbing way of feeding.

ORDER: Pleuronectiformes;
FAMILY: Soleidae;
SPECIES: *Solea solea* (common).

Solifugid

These animals are often called sun spiders, camel spiders or wind scorpions, according to species and habits. They look like hairy spiders. There are about 800 species, varying in body side from 1 to 5 cm, with proportionately long legs and large heads. They live in hot climates, many of them in deserts. Solifugids have four pairs of walking legs, plus a pair with suckers on the end which are used in climbing. They have huge, toothed jaws and are voracious carnivores, eating insects, birds and lizards.

CLASS: Arachnida;
ORDER: Solifugae.

Sparrow

This name is given to various small perching birds found in many parts of the world – wherever there are humans, there will probably be sparrows too! They are generally brown or grey, sometimes with black and white patterning, and with short conical bills.

Best known are house sparrows, regular visitors to birdtables and gardens. They feed on grain, seeds, buds, fruit and insects. Their continual cheeping and chirruping

House sparrows (right and below) have lived alongside people for thousands of years and so, quite naturally, followed them into cities.

Female
House sparrow
Male
Italian sparrow (male)

keeps large flocks together. In these tight-knit flocks they feed, dust-bathe and roost together. In the breeding season, away from buildings and gardens, sparrows will occasionally build free-standing, domed grass nests in bushes, like weaverbirds.

ORDER: Passeriformes;
FAMILY: Passeridae, Emberizidae;
SPECIES: *Passer domesticus* (house sparrow).

Sparrowhawk

The sparrowhawk is one of the best known birds of prey. It is found throughout Europe, Africa and Asia. As in other hawks, the female is much larger than the male – up to 38 cm long. The sparrowhawk has brownish upper plumage, a white breast barred with brown, and long legs. It prefers woods and forests, catching its prey by swooping on it from cover. Often a sparrowhawk will fly along a hedgerow, surprising small birds such as SPARROWS and FINCHES, and seizing them in its sharp claws. WOOD PIGEONS are also taken, and so are insects and small mammals.

ORDER: Falconiformes;
FAMILY: Accipitridae;
SPECIES: *Accipiter nisus*.

Spectacled bear

The spectacled or Andean bear is the only South American bear. It

Female

Male

Above: The female **sparrowhawk** is larger than the male. Below: A sparrowhawk stands keen-eyed on is nest of twigs.

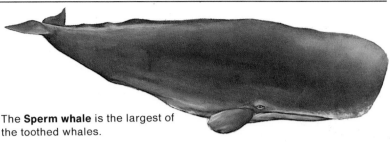

The **Sperm whale** is the largest of the toothed whales.

is one of the smaller bears, 1.5 to 1.8 metres in length and weighing up to 136 kg. Its shaggy coat is black or dark brown with white chest markings. Many have white circles or partial circles round the eyes – hence the common name.

Spectacled bears live in tropical forests in the foothills of the Andes up to an altitude of 3000 metres and as far south as Bolivia. Little is known of their habits. They are expert tree climbers and feed largely on leaves, fruits and roots. However, it is possible that they occasionally prey on DEER, guanaco and VICUNA. They are said to make large nests of twigs in trees and this is quite possible, as other small bears do the same.

ORDER: Carnivora;
FAMILY: Ursidae;
SPECIES: *Tremarctos ornatus.*

Sperm whale

The main feature of the sperm whale is its enormous head, making up a third of its total length, which may be over 18 metres. Sperm whales are found in all the oceans, but are most common in warm seas. Apart from the main species, there are two species of pygmy sperm whales. These grow to only 3.7 metres and look more like DOLPHINS than their massive relatives.

Sperm whales feed on SQUID and CUTTLEFISH, which they capture in their enormous toothed jaws. They can dive for up to an hour at a time, reaching depths of well over 1000 metres. Sperm whales are hunted for spermaceti, a clear oil found in the head of the whale, and for ambergris, a substance from the animal's stomach. Both substances are used in making medicines and cosmetics, but ambergris is most valuable as a base for expensive perfumes. The slaughter of the sperm whale has caused its numbers to be greatly diminished.

ORDER: Cetacea;.
FAMILY: Physeteridae;
SPECIES: *Physeter catodon.*

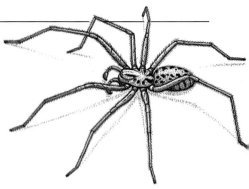

Above: The **house spider** is the creature that commonly scuttles across the floor in the evening.

Left: A **garden spider** sits in its beautifully constructed web. Notice the trapped fly bound with silk.

Below: Three **orb-web spiders** – creatures that, like the garden spider, spin beautiful circular webs.

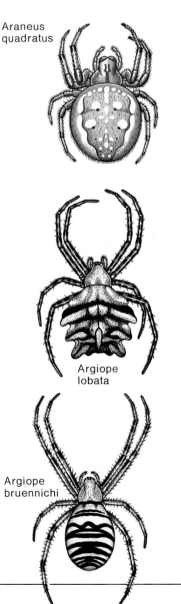

Araneus quadratus

Argiope lobata

Argiope bruennichi

Spider

Spiders are eight-legged ARTHRO-PODS which spin silk. At least 32,000 species have been identified, and there are probably many more to be found. Spider populations are huge – there may be as many as 2,500,000 spiders in 5000 square metres of grassy meadowland. In the course of a year the world's spiders eat an incredible quantity and weight of insects. Without them the earth would be overrun with insects.

Spiders vary in size from less than 0.5 mm to the huge BIRD-EATING SPIDERS, monkey spiders and TARANTULAS which have a body length of 9 cm and an even greater leg span. They all have fangs for seizing their prey, and most spiders have poison glands to subdue insects before killing and eating them. Only a few spiders are poisonous to humans, among them the BLACK WIDOW.

Spiders live in all kinds of habitat, from hot and dry to cold and damp. One species has been found near the top of Mount Everest, and spiders are among the 50 species of small animals that contrive to exist on the bleak continent of Antarctica.

All spiders produce silk, which they spin from organs at the end of the abdomen, called *spinnerets*. Most spiders can make more than one kind of silk. Different species use silk in various ways. Many make webs in which to trap insects. The bolas spider spins a thread with a sticky blob on the end, and with one of its legs it swings the blob at a passing insect to catch it. Almost all spiders lay out a line of silk as they move about, anchoring it at intervals. It serves much the same purpose as a mountaineer's safety line. Silk can also be used to truss up a victim. Some young spiders let the wind catch their silk threads, and in this way travel as if by balloon.

Female spiders lay anything from 1 to 2000 eggs, which they hide in a bag made of silk until they hatch.

CLASS: Arachnida;
ORDER: Araneae.

Spider crab

Spider crabs have very long limbs in relation to their bodies. Many of the 600 species are tiny, such as the long-beaked spider crab of Europe, which has a shell less than half an inch (1 cm) across. The

The **spider monkey's** tail is effectively a ''fifth hand'' used for grasping.

largest recorded spider crab was a specimen of the giant crab of Japan, which had a claw-span of 3.7 metres.
ORDER: Decapoda;
FAMILY: Majidae.

Spider monkey

Spider monkeys are slender *primates* found in Central and South America. They have remarkable tails which can wrap round and cling to branches. They live in troops high up in trees and eat only fruit. There are two species. The common spider monkey has coarse, wiry hair. The colour varies: one race is black and buff, another is black, while a third is black with a red face. The head and body length is 40 to 60 cm, with a tail of 60 to 90 cm. The woolly spider monkey occurs only in the forests of south-eastern Brazil. It is yellowish or greyish-brown and its woolly hair is thicker than that of the common species. It is about the same length as its relative but is somewhat heavier.
ORDER: Primates;
FAMILY: Cebidae.

Spiny anteater

The five species of spiny anteater, also called echidnas, are egg-laying MAMMALS found in Australasia. The Australian or short-nosed spiny anteater grows to 46 cm long and may weigh over 4.5 kg. It has a squat body, covered with sharp spines over 5 cm long. These are interspersed with coarse brown hair. The animal has no spines on its underparts. Its eyes are at the base of its long, tapering snout, from which it shoots out a long sticky tongue to gather its food. It has no teeth.

The spiny anteaters are said to be able to fast for a month, but they eat ants and termites with relish. When afraid, they dig rapidly into the earth, and if the ground is unsuitable, can run swiftly to escape an enemy. When the female produces her egg, she rolls it into her pouch where it stays until it hatches. The young echidna laps the milk secreted from slits inside its mother's pouch. When its spines are sufficiently developed for safety, the mother puts her offspring in a burrow. She visits it every day or two with food until it is weaned about three months later.
ORDER: Monotremata;
FAMILY: Tachyglossidae.

Spiny lobster

Also known as the crawfish, the spiny lobster is a relative of the true LOBSTER but it lacks the large claws. It defends itself with its large, powerful *antennae*, and is also protected by a dense coating of spines at the front end. The animal may grow up to 50 cm – about as long as the lobster – but it is usually little more than half this length, especially in cooler waters. It lives on the sea-bed in rocky areas around the Mediterranean and Atlantic coasts of Europe and also in the English Channel. It can shoot itself backwards with a quick flick of the tail fan, but it cannot really swim. Like the other lobsters, it is a scavenger, feeding on a variety of living and dead animal matter. A popular food in southern Europe, the spiny lobster is often seen in fish tanks outside restaurants around the Mediterranean.
ORDER: Decapoda;
FAMILY: Palinuridae;
SPECIES: *Palinurus vulgaris.*

Spiny mouse

Spiny mice are found in Africa, Asia and Central and South America. They are of interest because of the way in which their hair has evolved into a prickly coat, presumably for self defence. Spiny mice live in rocky country. In the desert they will sometimes take over GERBIL burrows. They normally eat seeds and other plant food but, like house mice, will eat almost anything . Other so-called spiny mice found in Central and South America are related to VOLES and POCKET MICE and belong to different families from the true spiny mice.
ORDER: Rodentia;
FAMILY: Muridae.

Sponge

Sponges are the most primitive of multi-celled animals. There are about 3000 species, and they nearly all live in the sea. About 150 species are found in fresh water. Sponges are always fixed to some solid object, such as a rock, and look more like plants. It was not until 1765 that scientists realized that they were in fact animals.

A sponge consists of a large group of cells clustered together. The shape varies from species to species: some are thin and flat, others are round, vase-shaped, or branched like a twig. Their popular names generally describe their shape, such as elephant-ear, breadcrumb sponge, purse sponge, or Venus's flower basket.

The body of a sponge is built up around a skeleton, which may be made of limestone, silica, or horny fibres. The skeletons of some sponges are used as the familiar bath sponges. A sponge feeds by filtering food particles out of the water in which it lives. The water is

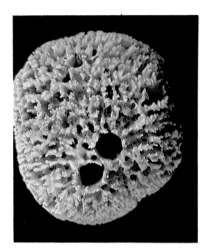

Right: A bath **sponge**, the skeleton of a sponge widely distributed in the Mediterranean and various oceans.

Below: **Tube sponges** from the Caribbean.

Above: The delicate filigree skeleton of a **Venus flower basket sponge**.

drawn in through small pores all over the body and passed out through the large opening at the top.

PHYLUM: Porifera.

Spoonbill

Spoonbills are wading birds related to IBISES. They have most peculiar bills, which are long and flat, broadening out into a flattened spoon shape at the end. They live mainly near shallow water or in marshes. They feed by swinging the end of their bills through water, taking in anything that is edible. The six species of spoonbills are up to 76 cm long. They have long legs and an almost wholly white plumage, with the exception of the roseate spoonbill of America which has a pink tinge to its plumage. It also has pink legs and a yellow bill, in contrast to the European spoonbill, which has black legs and a black bill tipped with yellow.

ORDER: Ciconiiformes;
FAMILY: Threskiornithidae;
SPECIES: *Ajaia ajaja* (roseate); *Platalea leucorodia* (European).

The **roseate spoonbill** is an attractively coloured if odd-looking bird.

Sprat

Several small HERRING-like fishes are called sprats, but more specifically this name belongs to an important food fish which lives in vast shoals along the Atlantic coasts of Europe. Rarely more than 13 cm long, the sprat is among the smallest of the herring family. Like the PILCHARD and sardine it is often preserved by canning, the largest sprat canneries being in Norway.

ORDER: Clupeiformes;
FAMILY: Clupeidae;
SPECIES: *Clupea sprattus.*

Springbok

The common springbok is a GAZELLE which lives in the Kalahari region of south-western Africa. A somewhat larger race, the Angolan springbok, lives to the north. This beautiful and lively animal is known for its habit of leaping up to 4 metres into the air. With the legs stiff and close together, and the head held low, the spingbok gives the impression that it is bouncing. Leaping may be done in play or when the animal is alarmed.

The springbok stands 76 to

90 cm at the shoulder and weighs 32 kg. The coat is reddish-fawn, with a black stripe on the flanks and white underneath. The lyre-shaped horns are ringed. Between the middle of the back and the rump is a pouch containing white hairs. When alarmed, the pouch is turned outwards, showing the white hairs as a warning signal. Springboks were once very common in South Africa, but their numbers have been greatly reduced through hunting and competition from farmers.
ORDER: Artiodactyla;
FAMILY: Bovidae;
SPECIES: *Antidorcas marsupialis* (common).

Springhare

The springhare looks like a miniature kangaroo. It is about 40 cm long, with a bushy tail of about the

The **springbok** is an accomplished jumper. It can leap vertically to a height of 4 metres.

same length, large ears and long hind legs. It lives in Africa, south of the Sahara, and is a shy, nocturnal animal, remaining underground in its burrow by day. It eats roots, bulbs and grain. When chased, the springhare escapes in a series of leaps, dodging from side to side to evade its pursuer.
ORDER: Rodentia;
FAMILY: Pedetidae;
SPECIES: *Pedetes capensis.*

Springtail

Springtails are small and rather primitive wingless insects that live mainly in leaf litter and other rotting vegetable matter. They get their name from a tiny, forked "spring" at the hind end. This is

normally folded forward and clipped up under the body, but when the insect is disturbed the spring is released. It flicks downwards and backwards, hitting the ground and shooting the insect forward through the air. A few of the 2000 or so species feed on living plants.
ORDER: Collembola.

Squat lobster

There are four species of squat lobsters and although they look like small, bristly lobsters they are more closely related to HERMIT CRABS. The body is broader and flatter than a true lobster's and the broad abdomen is carried tucked

Right: The small, silvery creatures on this crowded water surface are **springtails** – primitive wingless insects.

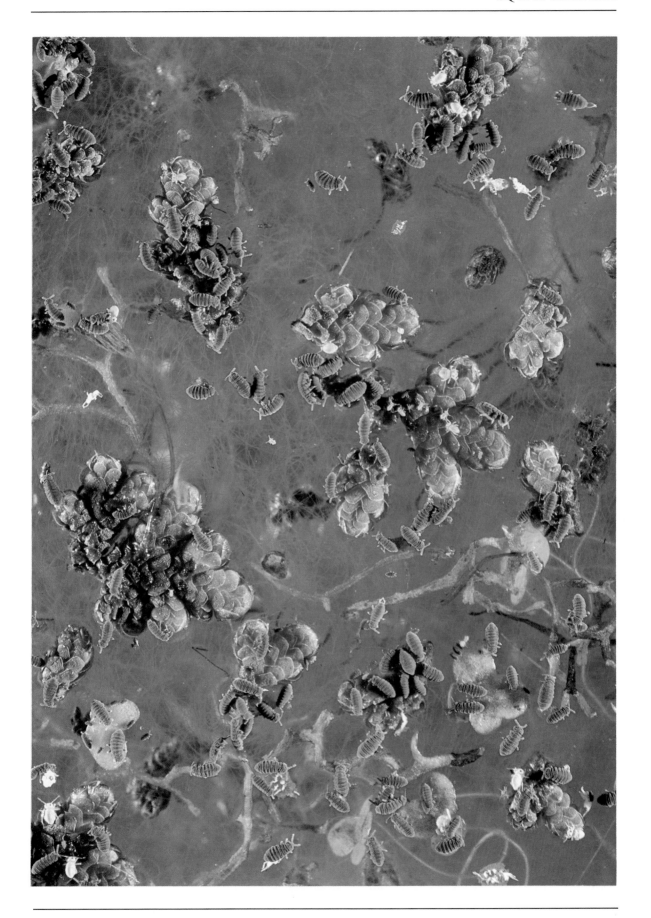

up beneath it. Squat lobsters can swim, but generally crawl around the sea-bed close to shore, feeding on scraps of animal matter floating in the water. If alarmed, they try to crawl under rocks or large pebbles.

CLASS: Crustacea;
ORDER: Decapoda;
FAMILY: Galatheidae.

Squids

Squids are MOLLUSCS related to the OCTOPUSES and CUTTLEFISHES. There are about 350 species, ranging in size from less than 2.5 cm to nearly 18 metres. They have streamlined, torpedo-shaped bodies supported by an internal horny plate. The head has two well-developed eyes, remarkably like those of humans. There are eight arms, similar to those of an octopus, plus two longer tentacles. A squid has blue blood. The animal continually draws in water and pushes it out through a funnel behind the head. It can shoot the water out to give it jet propulsion, and can swivel the funnel to direct the jet forward or backwards.

Squids tend to move about in shoals which often consist of only one sex. They can swim well, and usually travel backwards. They can change their colour to match their background. Many squids have organs that produce light. Fish and crustaceans are their main food. They seize their prey with their arms and tentacles and paralyze it by venom produced in the salivary glands. Like other *cephalopods*, they can emit a cloud of ink as a decoy when danger threatens. Some species can leap out of the water and glide through the air to escape.

CLASS: Cephalopoda;
ORDER: Decapoda.

Squirrel

Squirrels are medium-sized, lively RODENTS found almost world-wide. Typically, a squirrel has a rather rat-like appearance, with a bushy tail, and the habit of

Above: The **common squid** has a slender body with a diamond-shaped stabilizing tail fin. There are several similar species.

The **grey squirrel** (right) has a reddish tinge to its coat in summer. The tail has light-coloured fringes and there are no ear tufts. It is a North American species that has become a pest in Britain and other countries. The **red squirrel's** summer coat is usually a rich red, with a darker mid-back area. The winter coat is greyish. During winter, dark ear tufts are prominent, but these are lost in the spring. The **flying squirrel** glides from tree to tree by using a furred membrane extended between the fore and hind limbs.

Red squirrel

Grey squirrel

Flying squirrel

grasping food in its front paws as it feeds. Squirrels are usually grouped into three categories: FLYING SQUIRRELS, GROUND SQUIRRELS and TREE SQUIRRELS – although many species are equally at home on the ground or in trees.
ORDER: Rodentia;
FAMILY: Sciuridae.

Squirrel monkey

The squirrel monkey is found near the edges of forests in Central and South America. It is a small, slender monkey, with a small, white face, large, dark eyes and a slightly protruding black muzzle. Its long hind legs are thin, and its arms rather shorter. The body measures only 25 cm, but the long tail is up to 40 cm in length. It has short, usually greenish-grey fur, with blue-black on the top of the head.

Squirrel monkeys live in large bands kept together by the females, with the males keeping more to the edges of the troop. Their food consists of fruit, birds and insects, with little or no leaf matter.
ORDER: Primates;
FAMILY: Cebidae.
SPECIES: *Saimiri sciurea.*

Stag beetle

The stag beetles are large black or reddish-brown insects which get their name because the jaws of the males are greatly enlarged and often branched in the manner of a stag's antlers. In spite of their size, however, these jaws are not powerful weapons, for they do not have powerful muscles to work them. The smaller jaws of the females can give a much more powerful nip. The males display their antlers to each other as a threat when they are disputing ownership of the females, and they may even grapple with each other like stags. Strong fliers, the stag beetles live in wooded areas and the adults get what little food they take by lapping the sap oozing from trees. The fleshy white grubs

A five-armed **starfish**, the vermilion star.

feed in decaying logs and tree stumps. They take three years to reach maturity. There are several species, some reaching 90 mm in length, including the antlers.
ORDER: Coleoptera;
FAMILY: Lucanidae.

Starfish

Starfishes are related to SEA URCHINS. A typical starfish has five arms radiating out from a central disc, though some have as few as three and others have larger numbers, up to 50. The smallest starfishes are less than 1 cm across

It is obvious why the **stag beetle** got its name, but its "antlers" are really large jaws or mandibles.

and the largest are 1 metre. The most common colours are yellow, orange, pink and red. There are 1600 species, most of which live in shallow seas.

Starfishes move about by means of water-filled tube feet arranged in rows along the underside of each arm. Each tube foot ends in a sucker which can take a grip on stones and other objects and pull the animal along. The surface of each arm is coverd with many minute pincer-like parts which are used for seizing small organisms and cleaning the surface. The mouth is on the underside of the central disc. Starfishes are generally carnivorous, feeding on MOLLUSCS, WORMS, fish, CRUSTACEANS and other sea animals. Some prey on SCALLOPS and other *bivalves*, which they open by pulling on the *valves* with their tube feet. When the valves part a little the starfish pushes its stomach into the scallop, secretes digestive juices into it and digests the resulting solution. Starfishes can grow new limbs if they lose them, and one kind can regrow an entire animal from 1 cm of arm.
PHYLUM: Echinodermata;
CLASS: Asteroidea.

Stargazer

These fishes get their name from their wide-set, bulging eyes which gaze permanently upwards. The 20 species of stargazer spend most of their time buried in the mud or sand in warm seas, with only their eyes and snouts showing. The large jaws of a stargazer point upwards like those of a bulldog. On the lower lip is a fleshy lure which attracts unsuspecting fishes close enough to get snapped up.

Stargazers are small fishes, usually not more than 30 cm long, but they are well protected against larger predators. Behind each of their eyes is an electric organ which can give a considerable shock, and as if this was not enough, their *pectoral fins* bear poisonous spines.
ORDER: Perciformes;
FAMILY: Uranoscopidae.

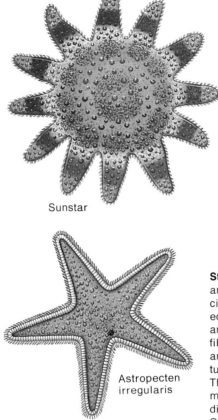

Sunstar

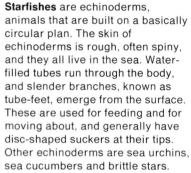

Cushion star

Common starfish

Astropecten
irregularis

Starling

This name is given to a large group of medium-sized perching birds, which includes MYNAHS and OXPECKERS. Best known is the common starling, found almost everywhere in the *Old World*. Starlings have spread throughout North America since their introduction, and are close neighbours to humans in many parts of the world.

Common starlings tend to live in flocks outside the breeding season. During the day the flock spreads out for feeding, but in the later afternoon individuals begin to congregate for roosting. By evening thousands of noisy starlings are gathered together – a common feature in cities. They eat insect grubs and adult insects, soft fruit and berries. They usually nest in holes in trees, but can be a nuisance in buildings.
ORDER: Passeriformes;
FAMILY: Sturnidae;
SPECIES: *Sturnus vulgaris* (common starling).

Starfishes are echinoderms, animals that are built on a basically circular plan. The skin of echinoderms is rough, often spiny, and they all live in the sea. Water-filled tubes run through the body, and slender branches, known as tube-feet, emerge from the surface. These are used for feeding and for moving about, and generally have disc-shaped suckers at their tips. Other echinoderms are sea urchins, sea cucumbers and brittle stars.

Stick insect

The stick insects, of which there are about 2000 species, include the world's longest insects. Some species reach lengths of 36 cm. They are usually very slender, however, and their bodies are often so twig-like that they are almost impossible to see as they sit on the trees and bushes. They hold their legs and bodies in just the right positions to resemble the twigs. The insects are basically green or brown, and many species

In summer, **starlings** are a slightly speckled glossy black. In winter they are black with white spots.

Winter

Summer

exist in two distinct colour forms. Some can actually change colour to some extent to match different backgrounds. There are winged and wingless species. Quite often the male is fully winged and able to fly, while the female, usually a good deal larger than her mate, has poorly developed wings. Many species are *parthogenetic*, meaning that the females can lay eggs without mating, Males, in fact, are very rare or even unknown in some species. Most stick insects are tropical, but about half a dozen species – all wingless – occur in southern Europe, often living undetected in long grass. In the United States stick insects are commonly known as walking sticks.
ORDER: Phasmida.

Stickleback

These little fishes are named after the sharp spines of their fins. The various species are named after the number of these spines. The 3-spined stickleback or common tiddler is most widespread in streams of the northern hemisphere. The 10- or 9-spined stickle-

Nine-spined stickleback

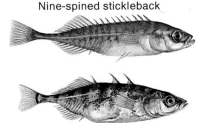

Three-spined stickleback

The **nine-spined stickleback** has 8 to 10 short spines on its back and a long, narrow tail. The **three-spined stickleback** has 2 or 3 long spines.

back is more likely to be found in more stagnant waters. The 4-spined stickleback is a sea fish.

The 3-spined stickleback has been of great interest to students of animal behaviour. The male fish builds a nest and entices the female to it by a courtship dance. He guards and aerates the eggs until they hatch, then protects his small progeny until they leave the nest. At all times the male stickleback is ready to defend his territory and he will attack any rival male, or even a piece of wood of his own size, if this is painted the red colour of his own throat.
ORDER: Gasterosteiformes;
FAMILY: Gasterosteidae.

Stilt

The stilt is a wading bird which belongs to the same family as the AVOCET. It has proportionately longer legs than any other wader and the head and body length is about 40 cm. There are several races of this black and white bird. The black-winged stilt breeds in Africa, southern Europe and Asia. The American race, the black-necked stilt, has a continuous black band from the crown to the back. Other races are found in Australasia. Stilts live around shallow lakes, slow rivers and marshes, picking up food with their straight bills.
ORDER: Charadriiformes;
FAMILY: Recurvirostridae;
SPECIES: *Himantopus himantopus.*

Stingray

The stingrays are relatives of the SHARKS, and have very flattened bodies. They are dangerous fishes because of their sting, or poison spine, borne on a whip-like tail. This spine is up to 35 cm long and can inflict severe lacerations, which sometimes prove fatal because of the poison injected by the spine. Stingrays are inhabitants of shallow seas, feeding on the bottom on shellfish and molluscs. They range greatly in size, from 30 cm to 4.5 metres across the full stretch of their wing-like *pectoral fins.*
ORDER: Rajiformes;
FAMILY: Dasyatidae.

Stoat

The stoat, a close relative of the WEASEL, has a long slender body up to 43 cm in length. Its fur is reddish-brown with white underparts and the tail is tipped with black. In northern regions the fur turns white in the winter, at which

A **stingray** rests on the seabed. Its spinelike tail not only injects poison but also cuts the flesh of anyone unlucky enough to step on it.

time it is known as ermine and is highly prized by the fur trade.

Stoats are found all over Europe and Asia, and also in North America where they are known as short-tailed weasels. They live in all types of country, hunting wherever there is the chance of food. They can swim well and climb trees. They usually hunt at night, preying on rabbits, hares, rodents, reptiles, birds and fish.

Mating occurs in March or in June and July. However, owing to a delay in the *gestation* process the young are not born until the following spring. After they are weaned, the 4 to 5 young hunt with their parents in a family party and sometimes two or more families may join up together.
ORDER: Carnivora;
FAMILY: Mustelidae;
SPECIES: *Mustela erminea*.

Stone curlew

Stone curlews are waders, although most of them live well away from water. They range in size from 36 to 53 cm long. The bill is usually short and thick, yellow and green with a black tip. The plumage is dull grey, with streaks of brown or black. The European stone curlew lives in Europe, in Africa south to Kenya, and in Asia.
ORDER: Charadriiformes.
FAMILY: Burhinidae.

The **stone curlew** gets its name because it is often found in stony places, and because its call is like that of a curlew.

Stonefish

Of the many poisonous fishes in the sea, the three species of

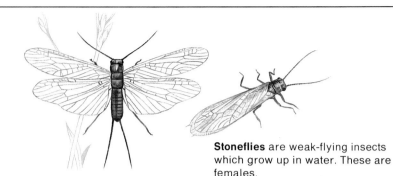

Stoneflies are weak-flying insects which grow up in water. These are females.

stonefish are certainly the most deadly. They live in warm coastal seas in the areas of north-east Africa, northern Australia and the Indian Ocean. Their squat, ugly bodies are well camouflaged against the coral or mud on which they lie quite still, waiting for small fishes or other prey to come within reach of their large jaws. The poison spines are never used for catching food, only in self-defence. Any bather or fisherman who steps on a stonefish will most likely receive a dose of venom that can lead to prolonged agony, followed in some cases by death.
ORDER: Scorpaeniformes;
FAMILY: Scorpaenidae.

Stonefly

The stoneflies are rather drab brownish or yellowish insects of the waterside. They do not fly much, and spend most of their time sitting on stones and vegetation with their wings folded tightly down on the body. Many only drink and do not feed, while others scrape algae from stones and tree trunks. The young grow up in the water and most of them prefer fast-flowing streams. They crawl out of the water when fully grown, and the adults break out of the nymphal skins. There are about 3000 species.
ORDER: Plecoptera.

Stork

Storks are related to HERONS and IBISES. True storks include the MARABOU, but not the stork-like SHOEBILL, which is a member of another family. Storks have long

necks, bills and legs, and the plumage is usually black and white. Most storks live near water. Many nests in trees, but some nest on cliffs or on roof-tops. The nests are usually large platforms made of sticks.

The most familiar stork is the white stork. It stands 90 cm high and has a white plumage, with black flight feathers and a red bill and legs. It breeds from the Netherlands eastwards into central Asia, and in Spain and Turkey. There are also isolated populations in southern Africa. Like some other storks, white storks go on long migrations. Others species of stork are found in Africa, Asia, Australia and the Americas, the two American species being the jabiru and the maguari stork. The four species of wood ibises are also true storks.
ORDER: Ciconiiformes;
FAMILY: Ciconiidae;
SPECIES: *Ciconia ciconia* (white).

Storm petrel

Storm petrels are seabirds which spend much of their lives at sea. They were so named because sailors once thought that a storm was near whenever they appeared. There are 20 or more species. They are 13 to 25 cm long and are mostly dark, but some have white under-parts and rumps. Three species are grey. Storm petrels of the southern hemisphere have rounded wings, square tails, slender bills and long legs. Those of the

Right: The chimney of this European house has been specially prepared to accommodate a **stork's** nest.

Storm petrels nest in crevices in rocks or stone walls on islands.

northern hemisphere have shorter legs, longer, pointed wings and forked tails. Most of the species are found in the Pacific Ocean. They are also called Mother Carey's chickens, possibly after Mata Cara, meaning Virgin Mary.
ORDER: Procellariiformes;
FAMILY: Hydrobatidae.

Sturgeon

Sturgeons are river dwellers that show some of the characteristics of bony fishes and some of SHARKS. For example, like bony fishes they have a *swim bladder*, but the general shape of their body, and more particularly the tail strongly resembles that of a shark. Their skeleton is formed of a mixture of bone and *cartilage*. The two dozen species of sturgeon occur in waters of the northern hemisphere, where they grub in the mud for food. They range greatly in size, the largest being the BELUGA of Russian rivers (not to be confused with the white whale of the same name). This fish grows to over 2 metres in length – and can yield a quarter of a tonne of caviare – the fish's roe.
ORDER: Acipenseriformes;
FAMILY: Acipenseridae.

Sun bear

The Malayan sun bear is the smallest of the bears, growing to 1.2 metres and weighing about

The **sturgeon** is a long-living fish. One specimen was known to be 75 years old.

50 kg. Its smooth, sleek coat of short, coarse fur is black with a yellow, crescent-shaped mark on the chest – from which the bear gets its name.

The sun bear is found in the tropical forests of South-East Asia, including Borneo and Sumatra. It is an expert climber and spends most of its time in the trees. During the day it sleeps high up in a nest of branches and twigs. At night it feeds on rodents, birds, lizards, insects, fruit and the soft cores of palm trees. It will dig out termite nests, inserting its forepaws and licking the insects off. It is also fond of honey and is an expert at getting bees' nests out of trees.
ORDER: Carnivora;
FAMILY: Ursidae;
SPECIES: *Helarctos malayanus.*

Sunbird

Sunbirds are similar to the American HUMMINGBIRDS, although they are not related and are found only in the *Old World*. Their flight is not as rapid, but they share the habit of feeding on small insects and nectar which they can get at by using their special tongues. The male's plumage is usually brilliant. There are 100 species, all less than 20 cm in length. They are found over most of the warmer forested areas of the *Old World*, half the species living in Africa. Their nests are bag-like masses of woven roots and grasses.
ORDER: Passeriformes;
FAMILY: Nectariniidae.

Sunfish

Freshwater fishes with this name are natives of North American rivers and are quite different from the OCEAN SUNFISHES. Freshwater sunfishes are PERCH-like and generally small, although one or

two can grow up to a weight of about 12 kg. They get their name from the way in which their activity is affected by the sun. On a cloudy day they become inactive, due perhaps to a fall in water temperature, and on a sunny day a shadow from a passing cloud will make them stop all activity. The male freshwater sunfish shows elaborate nesting and courtship behaviour which resembles that of the stickleback.
ORDER: Perciformes;
FAMILY: Centrarchidae.

Suni

The suni and its relatives are the smallest of the ANTELOPES. These slender, dainty creatures stand 33 to 38 cm high. The males have strongly-ridged horns in line with the face. The horns are between 6 and 16 cm long. The females do not bear horns. The coat is reddish- to greyish-brown and lightly speckled, and the underside is white. Suni are found in eastern Africa, from South Africa to Kenya. Little is known of their behaviour, but they live in dense, dry scrub. They generally live alone and it is rare to see more than two individuals together.
ORDER: Artiodactyla;
FAMILY: Bovidae;
SPECIES: *Neotragus moschatus.*

Surgeon-fish

Colourful inhabitants of coral reefs, surgeon-fish are named after the two sharp, bony lancets projecting from each side of their tail fin. By thrashing their tail from side to side surgeon-fish use their lancets to defend themselves, and can inflict nasty wounds. The 200 species of surgeon-fish have deep bodies up to 60 cm long. They feed by nibbling small animals and seaweeds from their home reefs, and many species have long, tubular snouts for poking into coral crevices.
ORDER: Perciformes;
FAMILY: Acanthuridae.

Suricate

One of the smallest MONGOOSES, the suricate or meerkat has the unusual habit of "sun-worshipping". It basks, not only lying down but also sitting upright on its haunches facing the sun. This slim, sharp-featured animal has a pale coat with reddish under-fur and dark patches round the eyes. It measures up to 60 cm in length, including its long, narrow tail. Suricates live in colonies in burrows dug in dry, sandy plains. They mainly eat insects, spiders, centipedes and bulbs. When it exhausts the local food supply, the colony migrates elsewhere.

ORDER: Carnivora;
FAMILY: Viverridae;
SPECIES: *Suricata suricatta.*

Surinam toad

The Surinam toad is both tongueless and toothless, and is more accurately called a tongueless frog, along with other members of the family. This strange creature has a slippery, flat body covered with tiny warts and a small triangular head. It lives in ponds and streams in Brazil, French Guiana, Guyana and Surinam. It swims strongly with its powerful,

Surgeon fish live in shoals on and around coral reefs.

webbed hind legs. When mating takes place, the male helps to press the female's eggs into the spongy skin on her back. The skin swells until each egg sits in its own small hole, covered by a lid. The young develop in these pockets. After 3 to 4 months, the lids opens and dozens of the young frogs emerge and swim away.

ORDER: Salientia;
FAMILY: Pipidae;
SPECIES: *Pipa pipa.*

Swallow

Swallows are members of the family which also includes the MARTINS. They are small perching

A frontal view of the flat bodies of a mating pair of **Surinam toads**.

birds with long, pointed wings and forked tails. The common swallow (known in America as the barn swallow), has the widest distribution, breeding in Europe, Asia and North America. It winters as far south as northern Australia, Sri Lanka and South Africa.

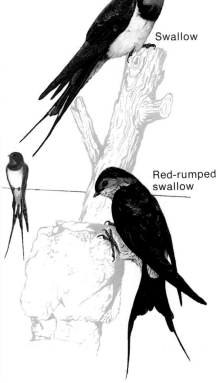

Swallow

Red-rumped swallow

A **swallow** takes a drink as it swoops across a stream.

About 19 cm long, it is blue on the upper parts, it has a red forehead and throat and white underside. The barn swallow has pinkish or buff under-parts.

Swallows spend much of the daytime on the wing. They catch insects in their wide gaping mouths, and come to the ground almost solely to collect mud for nest building. The nest is usually a shallow cup made of pellets of mud reinforced with pieces of dried grass. The eggs, 3 to 7 in a

There are over 500 species of **swallowtail butterfly**. Most of them have tailed hind wings.

clutch, are white, plain or speckled, according to species. Swallows return unerringly from South Africa to the same nesting site in Europe each year.

ORDER: Passeriformes;
FAMILY: Hirundinidae.
SPECIES: *Hirundo rustica* (common).

Swallowtail butterfly

The swallowtails are a large group of butterflies which get their name from the slender, tail-like projections from the back of the hind wings. They belong to the same family as the APOLLO and BIRD-WING butterflies. Swallowtails of one kind or another can be found nearly all over the world, but most

of the species are tropical. All swallowtail caterpillars have a strange Y-shaped organ which can be pushed out from the neck when the insect is disturbed. It releases a strong scent, which is believed to ward off parasitic insects such as ICHNEUMON flies.

ORDER: Lepidoptera;
FAMILY: Papilionidae.

Swan

Swans, of which there are six species, are closely related to geese. Most of them have long slim necks.

The most familiar species is the mute swan. Its name is a misnomer, for it has a variety of calls and if disturbed will hiss violently

at its attacker. It originally bred in Europe and Asia, but it has been introduced into many parts of the world. The mute swan is 1.5 metres long and weighs about 16 kg. Its plumage is all white and the bill is orange with a prominent black knob at the base.

Swans are strong fliers, although because of their weight they need long stretches of water to land and take off. They feed mainly on plants. On land they graze grass and and on water they feed by lowering their necks underwater. Mute swans pair for life. In the breeding season the males set up territories which they defend vigorously from other males. They use the same territories each year and build large nests of reeds and twigs near the water. Occasionally, mute swans nest in colonies, indeed some colonies have existed for centuries. The 5 to 7 eggs are incubated by the pen (female), while the cob (male) stands guard. The cygnets remain with their parents for 4 to 5 months.

ORDER: Anseriformes;
FAMILY: Anatidae;
SPECIES: *Cygnus olor* (mute).

Water droplets gleam on the neck and head of this **black-necked swan**, a native of South America.

Mute swan

Whooper swan

Bewick's swan

Swift

Swifts are birds designed for high-speed flight, having long and narrow wings. Their legs are weak, so that they find it difficult to take off from the ground. Usually, they cling to vertical surfaces when they land. However, swifts spend most of their lives in the air and come down only to nest. They feed on the wing, gathering flying insects

and other aerial life, such as drifting spiders. They drink and bathe by making quick dips into water from the air, and they collect nest material while in flight. Swifts even sleep in the air, spending the night wheeling high aloft and presumably sleeping in short "cat-naps". All swifts have dark plumage and are similar in appearance. They live mainly in the Tropics, where flying insects are common at all times. In temperate zones, swifts migrate for the winter. When food is scarce, they can become torpid to save energy.
ORDER: Apodiformes;
FAMILY: Apodidae.

Swordfish

The swordfish, together with the MARLINS and the SAILFISH, is a speed champion of the oceans. When chasing its prey, the swordfish can attain speeds of more than 80 km/h, its high, elegant *dorsal fin* and tail fin cutting smoothly through the water surface. Its powerful, streamlined body can be up to 5 metres long and weigh as much as half a tonne. Its sword, which it has been known to drive into ship's timbers, is up to 1.5 metres long. The swordfish is an inhabitant of tropical seas but sometimes wanders into temperate waters in summer months.
ORDER: Perciformes;
FAMILY: Xiphiidae;
SPECIES: *Xiphius gladius*.

Swordtail

The swordtail is one of the most popular aquarium fishes and gets its name from a long, sword-like extension of the tail fin which sticks out backwards in the male. Not counting his sword, the male is smaller than the female, which reaches a maximum length of about 13 cm. Swordtails have been bred in many colour variations, the body colour being yellowish-green or orange-red, with streaks

The **swifts** are masters of the air. They may spend weeks in the air without coming down.

of carmine, purple and other dark colours. The male's sword is edged in black. The swordtail's natural habitat lies in the fresh waters of Central America. Swordtails are OMNIVOROUS feeders. They are interesting but aggressive fishes, spending a lot of time bullying each other.
ORDER: Cypriniformes;
FAMILY: Cyprinodontidae;
SPECIES: *Xiphophorus helleri*.

Symbiosis

Animals of the same species often live together in groups. These range in size from a family unit to insect colonies of many thousands. But very often animals of different species also find it advantageous to team up. Strange partnerships of this kind are known as symbiosis.

In some partnerships both animals benefit. African OX-PECKERS perch on the backs of buffaloes and other large mammals and rid them of TICKS and insects. The mammals are freed from irritation and the birds have a source of food Cattle egrets also stay with big game animals, eating the insects stirred up by their hooves. PLOVERS and thick-knees are believed to pick parasites from the skin and mouths of Nile CROCODILES.

In the sea, some tiny creatures live by eating the parasites on larger ones and small fish perform the same service for larger ones. The cleaner WRASSE sets up shop in an easily identifiable place and then displays his colours to attract customers. Other fish queue up for the benefit of his cleaning service. The wrasse works over the bigger fish, removing harmful para-sites, bacteria and dead tissue. The host fish remains perfectly still while it is being cleaned. Even a predatory SHARK will allow a cleaner wrasse to enter its mouth unharmed. HERMIT CRABS, which live in borrowed shells, carry hydroids and sea anem-ones on them. The crabs are provided with camouflage and their guests with free trans-port and access to food.

There are many partner-ships in the insect world. ANTS, for example, keep APHIDS in much the same way that we keep cows. They "milk" the aphids of their honeydew and, in return, protect them from their enemies. Certain kinds of BEETLES live in the nests of TERMITES and ANTS, apparently as valued guests. Probably they assist their hosts by their scavenging activities. A ter-mite has one important guest it is probably unaware of: trichonympha, a kind of one-celled creature that lives in the termite's digestive sys-tem. Termites feed on wood and the trichonymphae help to break down the cellulose which the termite cannot digest. Without the trichonym-phae, the termite would prob-ably starve to death.

T

Tailor-bird

Tailor-birds are members of the WARBLER family and are so-called because of their extraordinary nesting habits. Nests are made from leaves by stitching them together to form a pouch. After punching holes through adjacent leaves, the tailor-bird draws them together and secures them by threading strands of fibres or spider's web through and teasing the ends to form knots. The Asian tailor-birds arrange the leaves so that one arches over the top to form a canopy.
ORDER: Passeriformes;
FAMILY: Sylviidae.

Taipan

The taipan is one of the world's deadliest snakes. It comes from the tropical forests and grasslands of New Guinea and northern Australia. It attains a length of 3.4 metres and has a brown or blackish back. Reptiles and small mammals are its normal prey. Usually timid, the taipan responds to provocation by attacking. Its large fangs deliver one of the deadliest-known venoms. The venom paralyzes the nerve centres controlling the victim's heart and lungs. Anyone bitten is unlikely to live unless given the right antidote quickly.
ORDER: Squamata;
FAMILY: Elapidae;
SPECIES: *Oxyuranus scutellatus.*

Takahe

The takahe is a flightless bird of the RAIL family, found only in a remote region of New Zealand. It is about the size of a small turkey and is brightly coloured, being blue and green with a pink beak surmounted by a scarlet shield, and rose-coloured legs and feet. The takahe feeds and nests among snow grass, large clumps of grass that grow on marshy land in a high valley in the South Island. The takahe was thought to have been extinct for 50 years when it was dramatically rediscovered in 1948. It is now rigorously protected.
ORDER: Gruiformes;
FAMILY: Rallidae;
SPECIES: *Notornis mantelli.*

Tamarin

Tamarins are rather primitive MONKEYS that are included in the same family as the MARMOSETS. There are 13 species. They are usually 15 to 25 cm long, with a tail of 25 to 40 cm. They live at all levels in the trees of South American forests, and are very agile. Most species seem to live in pairs with their young. They make high-pitched calls, some of them too high to be heard by the human ear. The coats vary greatly in colour from species to species, and also within species. They eat leaves, fruit, buds and insects.
ORDER: Primates;
FAMILY: Callithricidae.

Tanager

Tanagers are members of a large group of mostly brilliantly-coloured, medium-sized birds found mainly in tropical America. Five of the over 200 species live in North America. Tanagers live in forests, usually in the treetops or in bushy areas and clearings. Despite their bright colouring they

The **cotton-top tamarin**, one of many little marmoset-like monkeys of South American jungles.

are not easy to see. In most species the males and females look alike. Tanagers are mostly fruit-eaters, but they all take insects. The North American summer tanager hunts on the wing for flying insects.
ORDER: Passeriformes;
FAMILY: Emberizidae.

Tapeworm

Tapeworms are parasitic FLAT-WORMS which live as adults in the intestines of VERTEBRATES, including humans, sometimes causing illness. Tapeworms are ribbon-shaped, and are divided into short sections. The number of sections varies from species to species, but ranges from 3 to 3000. Some worms are exceptionally long, reaching up to 18 metres. The head end of the tapeworm carries suckers or hooks, sometimes both, with which the parasite anchors itself to the intestine wall. New sections form just behind the head, and at the other end the old sections containing the eggs break off and pass out of the host. Some eggs hatch in water; others are swallowed by a new host before they hatch. Many tapeworm species require two or more host species to complete their life cycles. Some of the species that infect man use fish, dogs, and pigs as their other hosts.

PHYLUM: Platyhelminthes.
CLASS: Cestoda.

Tapir

Tapirs are related both to the RHINOCEROS and to HORSES and ZEBRAS. They live in wet, tropical forests near water, in which they spend much of their time. About the size of a donkey, but with shorter legs, the tapir is about 180 cm long, stands 106 cm at the shoulder and weighs up to 320 kg. The snout is prolonged to form a highly mobile proboscis. Short,

One of the brightly-coloured species of **tanager**.

bristly hairs cover the body. There are four species. The Malayan tapir has black limbs and foreparts, while the rest of the body is white. This unusual colouring provides surprisingly good camouflage by breaking up the outline of the body, especially at night. The three South American species are dark brown to reddish above. All species browse on water plants and on low-growing vegetation on land.

ORDER: Perissodactyla;
FAMILY: Tapiridae.

Tarantula

The name "tarantula" has been applied to a great many different kinds of spiders. It is now commonly given to the large spiders variously called bird spiders or monkey spiders, and to the TRAP-DOOR SPIDERS, but the true tarantulas are fast-running hunting

This is the famous **tarantula** of southern Europe – a wolf spider whose bite was supposed to be fatal.

spiders. There are about 12 species, all of which live in short burrows in the ground, and run down their prey rather than build webs. They kill by injecting a poison, which is instantly fatal to the small insects they eat. Most tarantulas have long, hairy legs, large bodies and beady eyes.

The original tarantula was a WOLF SPIDER, living near the town of Taranto in southern Italy. Legend has it that its bite was fatal unless the person bitten danced

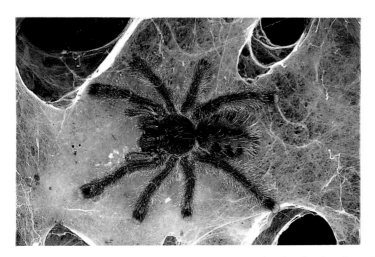

The orange-kneed **tarantula** of Mexico is capable of catching small birds.

until exhausted to sweat the poison our of the system. Males of this species do a courtship dance, which may have prompted the legend.

ORDER: Araneae;
FAMILY: Lycosidae (true tarantulas)

Tarpon

This game fish of the warm waters of the Atlantic Ocean is notable for the spirited fight it puts up when hooked. But to zoologists its main interest is as a primitive representative of the most advanced bony fishes, the teleosts. It is a large fish, growing up to 2.4 metres long and weighing up to 154 kg. Some primitive characteristics include its covering of large scales and its *swim bladder* connecting with the throat, with which it gulps down air at the water's surface.

ORDER: Elopiformes;
FAMILY: Elopidae;
SPECIES: *Megalops atlantica*.

Tarsier

Tarsiers are the only *primates* which are wholly *carnivorous*. They eat grubs, insects, frogs and small birds. These tiny animals weigh between 85 and 110 grams. They have thick, woolly fur and a long, almost naked tail. Being nocturnal animals, they have large eyes and mobile ears. They are always on the alert to escape such predators as owls, and they can turn their head through almost 360°. Their long hind limbs enable them to make great leaps among the branches of their tree homes. There are three species. Horsefield's tarsier lives in Borneo, Sumatra and two smaller islands that lie between. It is dark reddish brown in colour and up to 15 cm long, with a tail almost twice that length. The Philippine tarsier is the same size but greyish in colour. The Celebes tarsier is about 13 cm long with a dark greyish coat.

ORDER: Primates;
FAMILY: Tarsiidae.

The **Tasmanian devil** now lives only in Tasmania.

Tasmanian devil

The Tasmanian devil now lives only in Tasmania. It was once widespread on the mainland of Australia. This carnivorous MARSUPIAL has a reputation for ferocity which is probably exaggerated, although fights with its own kind can be noisy and impressive. The animal is a scavenger, eating bones and fur as well as meat. Stockily built, it measures up to 90 cm long, including its long tail, and has a wide mouth with sharp teeth. The female is smaller than the male. The animal searches for food at night, and likes to bask in the sun during the day. Tasmanian devils live about seven or eight years.

ORDER: Marsupialia;
FAMILY: Dasyuridae;
SPECIES: *Sarcophilus harrisii*.

Tasmanian wolf

The Tasmanian wolf or thylacine is a MARSUPIAL. It has a dog-like head because its carnivorous way of life is similar to that of the WOLF, but its hind quarters are distinctly kangaroo-like. It is about 1 metre long and its fur is light brown, with dark bands across the back. It is nocturnal and hunts alone or in pairs, preying on WALLABIES, rats and birds.

Tasmanian wolves were for-

merly numerous in Australia, but were probably wiped out by the introduction of the DINGO, with which they could not compete. In Tasmania they were relentlessly hunted by humans, because they attacked sheep and poultry. The Tasmanian wolf is now thought by many to be extinct, but a few paw marks have been seen and it may exist in some remote areas of Tasmania.

ORDER: Marsupialia;
FAMILY: Dasyuridae;
SPECIES: *Thylacinus cynocephalus*.

Teal

A number of species of this bird are found all over the world. In Europe, Asia and North America the teal is the northern green-winged teal, which is a small DUCK with colourful plumage. The male is greyish, with a brown, speckled breast and a chestnut and green head. Teal are closely related to the MALLARD and are similar in behaviour and migratory habits. They feed in shallow water, where they can upend. The Laysan teal, which is almost flightless, came close to extinction in 1911 when Japanese feather hunters reduced their numbers to 3 pairs. Happily they recovered and today over 600 exist.

ORDER: Anseriformes;
FAMILY: Anatidae.

Tench

A freshwater fish of Europe and northern Asia, the tench, *Tinca tinca*, is a member of the CARP family. Its plump body bears prominent, rounded fins and is

The **tench** is about 70 cm in length, with rounded fins and a deep tail.

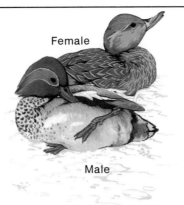

The **teal** is a dabbling duck. The male is brown with a green head; the female is smaller.

covered with small greenish or golden-yellow scales. Its head and eyes are large, and it has two barbels or feelers on its lower jaw, which help it to find food on the bottom mud. The tench lives in weedy pools, where it is a popular fish with anglers. A large specimen can weigh up to 3.6 kg or sometimes more, and tench is counted one of the tastiest of freshwater carp.

ORDER: Cypriniformes;
FAMILY: Cyprinidae.

The black, armoured head of this **termite** soldier has a pointed snout which squirts a poisonous liquid to deter enemies.

Tenrec

The 20 species of tenrec are found only in Madagascar. Some look like HEDGEHOGS, others like SHREWS or MOLES. They can be considered in two groups. Of the hedgehog kind, the common tenrec is 38 cm long and is the largest of the tenrecs. The second group includes the rice tenrec, which is only 13 cm long, and is mole-like. The tenrecs behave much like the animals they resemble. The common tenrec may be the most prolific of all mammals. The females have 12 to 16 babies in a litter, but sometimes produce as many as 25 at a time.

ORDER: Insectivora;
FAMILY: Tenrecidae.

Termite

The termites are social insects, living in colonies containing anything from a few dozen to more than a million individuals. They are often called white ants, although they belong to a very different group of insects. Most of the 200 or so known species live in the Tropics, but several occur in the United States. Only two species are found in southern

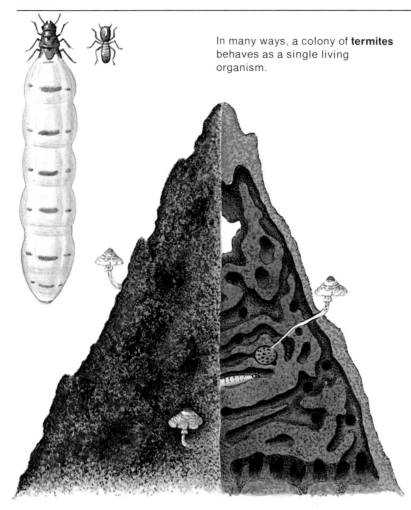

In many ways, a colony of **termites** behaves as a single living organism.

Europe. Each colony is ruled by a king and a queen, which live 15 years or more in some species. There are a number of large-jawed soldiers to defend the colony, and the bulk of the population consists of the workers.

Termites are all vegetarians. Some species, including the European ones, live in and feed on dead wood. Others live in underground nests or in huge mounds, which they stock with grasses and seeds. Some of the most advanced termites feed on fungi, which they actually grow on beds of chewed leaves in their nests. New males and females periodically swarm from the nests to mate and start new colonies.

ORDER: Isoptera.

Tern

Terns are seabirds closely related to GULLS. There are about 30 species of these birds, which are characterized by a fluttering flight. All terns migrate, and the Arctic

Termites' nests several metres high rise from the undergrowth in Zaire.

tern is one of the greatest bird wanderers. It nests in the Arctic, within 8° of the North Pole. In autumn it migrates across the Equator and flies to the Antarctic returning again in spring. The round journey may be as much as 37,800 km.

Terns are usually smaller than gulls, but they have similar habits. The wings are tapering and the tail is forked: as a result, terns are also called sea-swallows. The bill is narrow and pointed and the legs are short. Most terns have a white plumage with light grey wings and back, and a dark crown. Terns are widely distributed. Most species occur in the Tropics, but two species breed in the Arctic and live in the southern ocean.
ORDER: Charadriiformes;
FAMILY: Laridae.

Tetra

There are 34 species of this brilliantly-coloured little fish, many of which are popular in home aquaria. Nearly all of them live in the great rivers of Amazonia, although one species is native to the Zaire river. Most tetras are under 5 cm in length, an exception being the glass tetra, which reaches 25 cm. Their colours are as varied as the rainbow, and in the case of the neon tetra, they have a glowing iridescence.
ORDER: Cypriniformes;
FAMILY: Characidae.

Thresher

The common thresher is an Atlantic SHARK which gets its name from its long, scythe-shaped tail fin. The common thresher, and three related species in the Pacific and Atlantic oceans, use their long tails to herd shoals of prey into a tight mass, which they then stun by charging into them. The only fish that seems not to be afraid of its tail is the PILOT FISH, which is often seen escorting the thresher.

With its tail, the thresher reaches a length of more than 6 metres,

Common tern

Sandwich tern

Arctic tern

Terns have slender wings and forked tails that often point downwards during flight.

and may weigh 450 kg. It is not known to attack human beings.
ORDER: Lamniformes;
FAMILY: Alopiidae;
SPECIES: *Alopius vulpinus*.

Thrips

Thrips are tiny, slender, dark-bodied insects. They usually come to our notice on still summer days, when they swarm everywhere on their tiny feathery wings and get in our hair and eyes. Most of the 3000 or so species feed by scraping and sucking material from plant leaves and from flowers. Those that annoy us in summer have usually grown up on wheat and other cereals. They are considered pests by farmers. Many species hibernate indoors.
ORDER: Thysanoptera.

Thrush

A member of a large family of birds including the songthrush, mistlethrush, American robin, ROBIN, BLACKBIRD and REDSTART. Small to medium-sized birds, thrushes are closely related to the *Old World* FLY-CATCHERS. They are mainly insect-eating, but many eat fruit. Thrushes are found throughout the world with the exception of New Zealand and Antarctica. Most species live in scrub or woodland.

The songthrush is a common garden bird. Like the mistlethrush, it is noted for its fine song. These two species feed mainly on snails, worms and insects. The songthrush is famous for its habit of breaking snails open on stones, a stone being called a thrush's "anvil". It builds its nest in bushes or low trees. The female usually lays 4 eggs. Like the songthrush, the wood thrush of North America is brown above and white below, with a spotted breast. It is also a fine songster.
ORDER: Passeriformes;
FAMILY: Turdidae.

The **songthrush** and **mistlethrush** are similar, but the songthrush is smaller with a more lightly spotted breast.

Songthrush

Mistlethrush

A hedgehog **tick** gorges itself with blood from its host animal.

Tick

Ticks are oval-shaped parasites, closely related to MITES, the largest being about 2.5 cm long. Their colour is generally dull yellow or brown, and they live by sucking the blood of mammals. A typical tick's life is very simple. The female lays up to 8000 eggs on the ground. *Larvae* hatch and climb up plant stems, where they wait until an animal brushes past. They cling to the animal and drink its blood. Each larva falls off, *moults*, and repeats the performance twice more until it becomes an adult. Ticks attack many domestic animals, including dogs, cats, sheep and cattle, and they carry several serious diseases. They also attack humans.

CLASS: Arachnida;
ORDER: Acari.

Tiger

The tiger is the largest member of the cat family. Its sinuous grace, splendid carriage and beautifully patterned coat make this one of the most magnificent of all animals. A large male averages about 2.7 metres in length including a 1-metre tail, stands 1 metre at the shoulder and weighs 180 to 230 kg. Females are slightly smaller. The various races of tigers differ greatly in size from the small Bali Island tiger, recently declared extinct, to the outsized tiger from Manchuria which may reach a total length of up to 3.6 metres. The ground colour of the coat is fawn to rufous red, overlaid with black or blackish-brown transverse stripes. These contrasting colours provide splendid camouflage in forests and tall grasses. The under-parts of the coat are white. Tigers that inhabit cold Siberia and Manchuria have thick, shaggy coats. The hair around the face is longer than that on the rest of the body, and adult males have a distinct "ruff". In India there have been rare cases of white tigers.

Tigers live in South, South-East, and East Asia, with perhaps a few surviving in Iran. They prefer thick cover, but have adapted to life in rocky mountainous regions. They inhabit the reeds of the Caspian and islands such as Java. Tigers dislike great heat. At the hottest time of day they rest in long grass, caves or shallow water. They are splendid swimmers, but unlike most cats they are poor climbers. Tigers depend mainly on their keen hearing to help them stalk their prey. When they attack or are disturbed they give a full-throated roar.

A tiger will prey on deer, antelopes, wild pig and smaller beasts like porcupines and monkeys. It takes fish and turtles in times of flood. Sometimes it may attack larger animals such as wild bull buffaloes. Old or injured tigers seek easy prey, including humans.

Male and female tigers meet only to mate. Each litter has 3 or 4 cubs (sometimes up to 6). At seven months they can kill for themselves, but stay with their mother until they are two, during which time she teaches them to hunt. They are fully grown at three. Humans are the tiger's main enemy. Hunting and deforestation have greatly reduced its numbers.

ORDER: Carnivora;
FAMILY: Felidae;
SPECIES: *Panthera tigris.*

Tiger moth

The tiger moths are fairly large, stout-bodied, and hairy moths with bright colours and bold patterns which do not always resemble tiger markings. The colours warn birds that the moths are unpleasant or poisonous to eat. They possess poison glands, which can even irritate human skin. The caterpillars are very hairy, and are often called "woolly bears". Best known of many species in the northern hemisphere is the gaudy garden tiger.

ORDER: Lepidoptera;
FAMILY: Arctiidae.

Right: A noble Indian **tiger**.
Below: A garden **tiger moth** displays its striking coloration.

Tilapia

The 100 species of tilapias are freshwater fishes of the CICHLID family. Some of these are important food fishes in the Tropics. They occur in large numbers in the lakes and rivers of Africa. In some places they are the only source of food containing animal protein. Tilapias have been reared in many other countries. They are excellent candidates for fish farming because they eat almost any vegetable or small animal food, and waste very little of it. Tilapias are large-headed, deep-bodied fish usually 30 cm or less in length, dark in colour but with a metallic sheen. Like some other cichlids they are mouth breeders; one or other (or both) of the parents allow the eggs to hatch in their mouths. They take the young fry back into their mouths whenever danger threatens.

ORDER: Perciformes;
FAMILY: Cichlidae.

Tit

Tits are members of a family of some 60 species of small birds. They are found in wooded country in North America, Europe, Asia and Africa. In North America they are known as chicadees and titmice. There are three groups of tit; the true tits; the long-tailed tits and bush tits; and the penduline tits. The name is also given to unrelated birds such as the bearded tit, the shrike-tits, wren-tits, tit-babblers, tit-larks and others. Tits are usually colourful birds.

The best known species are the blue tit and great tit. The great tit, one of the most closely studied birds, is 14 cm long, greenish-blue above, yellow below with black on the head and under-side and white on the cheeks. The blue tit 11 cm long, has a bright blue crown, wings and tail, yellow under-parts

A **blue tit** carrying a beakful of insects.

and white cheeks. The best known of the American tits is the black-capped chickadee, which is about the same size as the blue tit. It is a pale grey with a black head and throat and white cheeks. The tits attract attention by their acrobatics when feeding, often hanging upside down as they search for insects and seeds. In northern regions tits store surplus food in the autumn. All true tits nest in holes. A few, such as the willow tit, dig holes in rotten timber. A cup-shaped nest of moss, lined with hair and feathers is built in the hole.

ORDER: Passeriformes;
FAMILY: Paridae.

Toad

The name toad is loosely applied to any tailless AMPHIBIANS that have a warty skin or live in places which are drier than those of the true FROGS. But the "true toads" are restricted to the family

Bufonidae. They have short, squat heads and bodies, and their warts contain poison glands which help deter predators. Their hinds legs are shorter than those of frogs. This limits them to hopping or walking rather than leaping.

The common toad lives in nearly all parts of Europe and temperate Asia. The colour is usually brown, but it ranges from brick red to grey or green and it is usually more uniform than that of the common frog, with which the toad is sometimes confused. The colour tends to match that of the ground on which the animal lives. The toad can reach lengths of

A **mountain toad** displays its vivid warning colours.

15 cm, especially in the southern parts of its range, but most are less than 8 cm long.

Toads hibernate on land – among the leaves in ditches, under stones, and even under the floors of damp buildings. In the spring, they make their way to their breeding grounds, often covering large distances to get back to favoured ponds where large numbers of toads congregate. These migrations usually take place at night. The mating habits are similar to those of the frog,

although the male toads tend to sing mainly at night. They have no external vocal sacs. The eggs are laid in strings rather than in masses.

ORDER: Salientia;
FAMILY: Bufonidae.

Toadfish

Toadfishes are bottom-dwellers in shallow seas, and get their name from their ugly, toad-like heads. They are remarkable fishes for several other reasons, the most famous of which is their ability to make loud noises, often like that of a foghorn, with the aid of their *swim bladder*. These sounds can be deafening underwater. They seem to be a type of territorial advertisement, like birdsong. Toadfishes are dangerous to bathers and fishermen because of the poison spines they bear on their *dorsal fin* and gill covers. A few of the 30 or so species are deep-sea fishes with luminous organs like glowing buttons.

ORDER: Batrachoidiformes;
FAMILY: Batrachoididae.

Topshell

That once-popular children's toy, the whip-top, gave topshells their popular name. They are cone-shaped sea snails ranging in size from 1 mm to 15 cm across the base of the shell, and many of the hundreds of species are beautifully coloured. They are found on rocks or coral rather than on sand or mud, because sand tends to clog their gills. The animals feed on various kinds of seaweeds.

CLASS: Gastropoda;
ORDER: Archaeogastropoda.

Toucan

The 37 species of toucans make up a family of birds with large, coloured bills. They are up to 60 cm long, and their plumage is also brightly coloured. Toucans live in the forests of Central and South America, ranging from Mexico to Argentina. They feed

Tortoises and turtles

Tortoises and turtles are reptiles whose bodies are protected by a shell, or *carapace*. In many species this is hard and rigid, acting as a castle into which the animal can pull its head, legs and tail. The lower shell also consists of bony plates. The protection afforded by this bony home has worked well, helping to shield the animals from their enemies, and so assisting their survival since the group evolved 200 million years ago. In fact, land tortoises today still look much like their early ancestors which were already plodding around when the Age of Dinosaurs was still young.

Most tortoises and turtles live in warm parts of the world. They rely on the sun's heat to hatch their round, white eggs, laid in soil or sand. These reptiles form three main groups: land tortoises, freshwater turtles and marine turtles.

Land tortoises tend to have high domed shells, scaly legs, and toes with claws. Each day they warm up by basking, then feed on leaves, flowers or fruits. They travel slowly but can sometimes manage normal human walking speed. When the sun becomes too hot, tortoises seek the shade. Those from temperate climates HIBERNATE in winter, burying themselves in soft earth or dead leaves. European tortoises include the spur-thighed tortoise and Hermann's tortoise. At about 20 cm long, both are dwarfed by the giant tortoises of some remote oceanic islands. Galápagos GIANT TORTOISES have reached nearly 1.5 metres long and a weight of 136 kg. Whether large or small, land tortoises rank among the longest-lived of all animals. One individual given to the King of Tonga in 1773 reputedly lived 200 years, and died in 1966.

Fresh water turtles tend to have flatter shells than land tortoises, and largely live and feed in water. Unlike land tortoises, most freshwater turtles eat fish, water snails, or other animals, alive or dead. Many species bask at the water's edge, and dive in if disturbed. Some species hibernate beneath the water. Many freshwater species are called terrapins, especially in America.

Marine turtles have a flattish *carapace*, and limbs which have evolved as flippers. The LEATHERY TURTLE is the largest living member of the tortoise group. Marine turtles roam warm seas and oceans. The GREEN TURTLE feeds on water plants, but other species are CARNIVOROUS. Breeding females flop clumsily up sandy beaches to lay eggs. When these hatch, the baby turtles scamper down into the sea. But crabs, gulls, dogs and other predators kill and eat all but a few of them.

ORDER: Chelonia.

Tortoises and turtles have existed almost unchanged for over 200 million years. This is a **Hermann's tortoise**, about 20 cm long.

The large bill of this **red-billed toucan** is, in fact, very light.

mainly on fruit, the long bill being useful for reaching out to pluck the fruit and berries from trees. The food is held in the tip of the bill, and then passed into the mouth with a flick of the head. Toucans may also eat insects, termites, spiders, lizards and young birds.

Toucans nest in holes, raising their young in tree holes high above the ground. They live in small flocks of about a dozen birds. The colours of the bill may vary from one individual bird to another, and could function as an attraction in courtship displays.
ORDER: Piciformes;
FAMILY: Ramphastidae.

Trapdoor spider

Trapdoor spiders dig a shaft in the ground, which may be as much as 30 cm deep and 4 cm in diameter. They line the shaft with silk and make a trapdoor or lid for the shaft out of soil and silk. The spider camouflages the outside of the trapdoor with moss or other suitable material so that it is very hard to see. The lid is hinged at one side with silk. The spider usually sits with the door just ajar, looking out for prey. When an insect walks by, it opens its trap, leaps out, grabs its victim and retreats inside again, all so quickly that the eye can hardly follow its movements. The burrow with its lid serves not only as an ambush, but also as a protection against enemies and bad weather. The spider some-

times leaves its burrow to go hunting. Like almost all spiders, it has a poisonous bite.
ORDER: Araneae;
FAMILY: Ctenizidae.

Treecreeper

The name given to birds from several groups which have the habit of creeping or hopping jerkily over the branches and up the trunks of trees. Treecreepers, or creepers as they are called in North America, are sparrow-sized birds with brown, streaked plumage on the back and lighter under-parts. They have slender, pointed bills and long curved claws. The tail looks tattered, as it is made up of stiff pointed feathers. The common treecreeper ranges from the British Isles to Japan, and in North America from Alaska to Nicaragua.
ORDER: Passeriformes;
FAMILY: Certhiidae.

Tree duck

The tree ducks, or whistling ducks, so-called because of the sound they make while eating, are goose-like waterbirds related to the SWANS. There are eight species found in the tropical and sub-tropical parts of Central and South America and Africa. The plumage is generally chestnut with black and white markings.

Tree ducks are mainly vegetarians. On land they feed at night on grass seeds; they also feed on plants in shallow water. Most of the year is spent on rivers, swamps and pools. Some species, such as the black-billed tree duck often perch in trees.
ORDER: Anseriformes;
FAMILY: Anatidae.

Tree frog

Several families of frogs include species which are expert climbers. They are found in all continents except Antarctica. There are more than 400 species. The largest species is the Cuban tree frog, 14 cm long. The smallest tree frog is a mere 2.5 cm. Tree frogs tend to have slim waists, long limbs and toes that end in disc-shaped suckers. These help them to grip vertical surfaces, including shiny leaves. The frogs often capture insects in mid air, leaping many times their body length and landing safely on a twig or leaf. Most return to water to breed.

ORDER: Salientia;
FAMILY: Hylidae.

Tree kangaroo

The seven species of tree kangaroos live in rain forests, and are seldom seen. They are related to WALLABIES but differ from them in appearance. They are 50 to 76 cm from nose to rump and have a tail of 40 to 90 cm. They have short, rounded ears, and their feet have large, cushioned pads. These, and the strong nails on the forefeet, help them to climb well. Tree kangaroos feed mainly on fruit and leaves, probably gaining most of their water requirement from these foods.

ORDER: Marsupialia;
FAMILY: Macropodidae.

Tree shrew

The 15 to 25 species of tree shrew range from India to South-East Asia and south-western China. They resemble squirrels, except for their pointed, shrew-like snouts which lack prominent whiskers. Most species have bushy tails, which make up half their 20 to 40 cm length. Although they spend much of their life in trees, as their name implies, tree shrews do descend to the ground, and some species even forage there. There are usually 1 to 3 babies in a litter, and the mother suckles them every two days until they are weaned.

These inconspicuous animals have been the centre of a classification controversy for some time. Some zoologists consider them insectivores, while others classify them with the primates. It is likely that the very early mammals were similar to these creatures.

ORDER: Tupaioidea;
FAMILY: Tupaiidae.

Tree squirrel

There are some 55 species of tree squirrels, found throughout Europe and most of America and Asia. Tree squirrels have bushier tails than the ground squirrels and flying squirrels. The tail is used to help the squirrel keep its balance as it runs nimbly about the trees. Squirrels are excellent climbers and can make leaps of up to 4 metres from branch to branch.

The two best known tree squirrels are the grey squirrel of North America, and the red squirrel of Europe and Asia. The red was formerly the most widespread species in Britain, but its numbers have been in decline for some time The grey squirrel, introduced in the 19th century, has replaced the red over much of its old range in Britain.

Squirrels eat nuts, berries, soft fruits and some fungi, but will also take bird's eggs, nestlings and carrion. They do not hoard food in the true sense, but will bury single acorns and berries. Their fondness for gnawing bark has made squirrels (particularly the grey) unpopular with foresters. A squirrel's nest is called a drey. It is a bulky cup-shaped or domed structure made from twigs, bark, leaves and moss, but sometimes an old bird's nest is taken over for nesting. Squirrels are often found living in wooded parks and gardens. Their most deadly predator is the pine marten, which matches the squirrel's agility. Other enemies include horned owls, hawks and foxes.

ORDER: Rodentia;
FAMILY: Sciuridae;
SPECIES: *Sciurus carolinensis* (grey); *Sciurus vulgaris* (red).

Trogon

The 35 or more species of trogons make up a family of brightly coloured tropical birds. They are usually green, blue or brown, with red, orange or yellow beneath. Included among them is the QUETZAL. Trogons range in size from 23 to 33 cm. They are found mainly in tropical forests, from America through Africa, India and southern China, to the East Indies and Philippines. They eat insects, which they pluck from leaves and twigs while hovering in the air. Other small animals such as snails, tree frogs and lizards may be captured in the same way, and fruit is picked while they are flying.

ORDER: Trogoniformes;
FAMILY: Trogonidae.

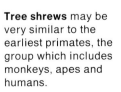
Tree shrews may be very similar to the earliest primates, the group which includes monkeys, apes and humans.

A **Narina trogon** – harmony of pink and gold. The 35 or so species of trogon are all tropical birds with beautifully coloured plumage.

Trout

The name given to fishes which are close relatives of the European SALMON. The European trout exists in a rather confusing number of races or varieties. The brown trout is small with a dark spotted body and is an inhabitant of rivers and streams. The lake trout is rather larger and paler, and the sea trout is larger still and looks very like a silvery salmon. All three belong to the same species. Other species of trout include the rainbow trout, cut-throat trout and brook trout, or CHAR, of North America.

In general, trout are very active fishes with a need for clear, aerated water. Sometimes they are the only large forms of life in fast, cold, mountain streams. The tastiness of their flesh needs no emphasising, and trout are fav-ourites for fish farming.

ORDER: Salmoniformes;
FAMILY: Salmonidae.

Trumpeter

Trumpeters, of which there are three species, are odd-looking birds of the Amazon region of South America. They are 70 cm long, and look rather like dumpy, hunch-backed CRANES. The tail is so short that it is hidden under the rump feathers. Trumpeters are mainly black. They are forest birds and prefer to run or even swim, rather than fly, to evade capture. They feed on fallen fruits, berries and insects. Trumpeters live in flocks of up to 200 birds. They get their name from the trumpeting calls they make to threaten other birds and can be used as watch-dogs.

ORDER: Gruiformes;
FAMILY: Psophiidae.

Tsetse fly

The tsetse flies are blood-sucking insects living in various parts of Africa. They are carriers of sleeping sickness, and of a cattle disease called nagana. There are about 20 species, each with a different habitat. The main carrier of human sleeping sickness prefers the dense forests around lakes and rivers. A little larger than a HOUSE-FLY, it feeds on crocodiles and antelopes as well as on humans.

Unlike MOSQUITOES and HORSE-FLIES, both male and female tsetse flies suck blood. The female does not lay eggs: a single egg develops in her body, and the *larva* hatches while still inside the mother. It remains there, feeding on secre-tions from her body, until it is fully grown, the larva is then "born", and it immediately pupates in the ground. A female will produce about 12 young during her life.

ORDER: Diptera;
FAMILY: Muscidae.

Tuatara

The tuatara is the sole survivor of an ancient order of reptiles with beak-like upper jaws which flourished 100 to 200 million years ago. At up to 60 cm long, the tuatara resembles a large LIZARD. But the skull and backbone are different and its teeth are fused to

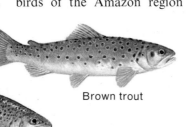

Brown trout

Rainbow trout

the jawbone instead of set in sockets. Also the young have a prominent "third eye" – the remains of a light-sensitive organ, perhaps important in the tuatara's ancestors. Tuataras were once common on the New Zealand mainland. Now they live only on a few small offshore islands. They spend the day in burrows, coming out at night to hunt for insects. They may move around in temperatures as low as 7°C – the lowest temperature recorded for any reptile activity.

ORDER: Rhynchocephalia;
FAMILY: Sphenodontidae;
SPECIES: *Sphenodon punctatus.*

Tuna

Giant relatives of the MACKEREL, the tuna or tunnies have very similar streamlined bodies, although tuna are plumper. This is due to the greater proportion of muscle in their fast-moving bodies. Some can be very large fishes indeed: the bluefin tunny of the Mediterranean can reach a length of more than 4.25 metres and a weight of 820 kg. Smaller tuna include the bigeye, yellowfin, albacore and bleeker.

Tuna are shoal fish, especially the smaller species, and chase prey fishes near the surface. They are strangely migratory, their movement being linked with those fishes on which they feed, and on the temperature of the water. Although they migrate to northern waters in summer, they return to warmer seas in autumn. Tuna are the only fishes that have a body temperature higher than that of the surrounding sea.

ORDER: Perciformes;
FAMILY: Scombridae.

Turaco

Turacos are tree-living birds of Africa, south of the Sahara. There are about 18 species, most of them about 45 cm long. They live both in forests and dry savanna where there are scattered trees and

The **white-cheeked turaco** lives in forests from Ethiopia to South Africa.

bushes. The forest dwellers tend to be green whereas the birds of more open country are grey or brown. Almost all turacos have striking crests of feathers. Their main food is fruit, and they are usually solitary. Turacos have harsh cries. Some are known as "go-away" birds, in imitation of their calls.

ORDER: Cuculiformes;
FAMILY: Musophagidae.

Turbot

A larger relative of the FLOUNDER, PLAICE and DAB, the turbot is a flatfish even more prized as food. It lives in shallow water in the North Atlantic and Mediterranean oceans, lying on the bottom for a good part of the time. Occasionally it swims by rippling movements of its whole body. It can put on a spurt fast enough to catch SPRATS and other small fishes which are its main prey. Like its flatfish relatives, the turbot has an asymmetrical head with both eyes on the upward-facing side, and it can change the colour of its scaleless body to match that of the background on which it lies.

ORDER: Pleuronectiformes;
FAMILY: Bothidae.

Turkey

Turkeys live in the wild in the southern United States, Mexico and Guatemala. They are found in open woodland, moving over the ground in small flocks and roosting in the trees. They eat mainly insects, seeds and berries. The wild birds are 120 cm long and a metallic green, bronze and copper in colour, the head and neck being blue and red. Domestic turkeys are descended from the common turkey. They were first tamed by the Aztecs, long before they were brought to Europe in 1500.

ORDER: Galliformes
FAMILY: Meleagrididae;
SPECIES: *Meleagris gallopavo.*

Turnstone

Turnstones are so-called because of their habit of turning over stones when hunting for food. They are small waders about 23 cm long, with rather short legs. There are two species. The ruddy turnstone lives in the Arctic. In summer it has a "tortoiseshell" appearance on its upper parts, with rusty red on the back. The head, neck and underparts are white and the legs are orange. In winter the head, breast and back turn a dark brown but the throat stays white. The black turnstone breeds only in Alaska. Turnstones migrate long distances every year.

ORDER: Charadriiformes;
FAMILY: Scolopacidae;
SPECIES: *Arenaria interpres* (ruddy); *Arenaria melanocephala* (black).

Summer and winter plumage of the **turnstone**.

Winter

Summer

Turtle dove

The turtle dove is one of the smaller members of the pigeon family, being 25 cm long. It breeds in North Africa, south-western Asia and Europe, and migrates to tropical Africa for winter. It frequents open woodland and areas with scattered trees and bushes, often near cultivated ground. Turtle doves feed mainly on small grains and grass seeds. Each pair of doves raises 2 to 3 broods in a season. The soft cooing note of the dove is often heard in spring.

ORDER: Columbiformes;
FAMILY: Colombidae
SPECIES: *Streptopelia turtur*.

Tussock moth

The tussock moths and their allies form a family of about 2500 species which are found mainly in the *Old World* Tropics. The moths are generally rather furry and of moderate or large size. The tongue is very small or absent and the adults do not feed. The males have very feathery *antennae*. The females, which often have dense tufts of hair at the hind end of the body, are usually larger than the males, although the females of some species, such as the vapourer moth are wingless. These females rarely move far from their *cocoons* before mating and laying their eggs. The name of the group comes mainly from the very hairy nature of the caterpillars. Many of these bear dense tufts of hair on various parts of their bodies, and there are individual bristles as well. The hairs are easily detached, and they can cause severe irritation if the caterpillars are handled. The *larvae* feed on various trees and shrubs, often causing damage in forests and orchards. Among the destructive species are the gipsy moth, which is a forest pest, and the brown-tail. The latter is a serious orchard pest, especially in the United States.

ORDER: Lepidoptera;
FAMILY: Lymantriidae.

Above: The **turtle dove** lives in low trees and bushes and is well known for its soft, murmuring calls.

Below: The **tussock moths** are a family of fairly stout, hairy insects. Even the caterpillars are hairy.

Male
Pale tussock
Caterpillar
Gold ta
Female
Gipsy moth
Male
Vapourer
Female
Male
Caterpillar

u v

Uakari

The uakari is the only South American monkey whose tail, which is about 18 cm long, is shorter than the head and body (46 cm). The animal has a shaggy coat which hides a lean muscular body. There is virtually no hair on the head and face. The two species live around the upper reaches of the Amazon river. The black-headed uakari is chestnut-brown with a black face. The bald uakari may have a white or silvery coat or a red or pink coat. The face is red or pink.

ORDER: Primates;
FAMILY: Cebidae.
SPECIES: *Cacajao melanocephalus* (black-headed); *Cacajao calvus* (bald).

Ungulates

Mammals with hoofs are known as ungulates – from a Latin word, *ungula*, meaning hoof. Ungulates are divided into two main groups: those with an odd number of toes on each foot, and those with an even number. Odd-toed ungulates are HORSES, RHINO-CEROSES and TAPIRS. The more numerous even-toed ungulates include the CATTLE, PIGS, HIPPOS, ANTELOPES, DEER, CAMELS and the GIRAFFE. Smaller groups of hoofed mammals include the ELEPHANTS and HYRAXES.

Vampire bat

All three genera of vampire bats are native to Central and South America. They are small bats, no more than 6 to 9 cm long and weighing 14 to 48 grams. Their upper *incisor* teeth are large and razor-edged, well-adapted for making a small wound from which they can lap up the blood which is their diet. The vampire's saliva contains substances that prevent the victim's blood from clotting, and the bat's digestion is specialized for its liquid diet.

The common vampire is now one of the most widespread mammals in Mexico. It attacks large animals, such as horses, cattle and sometimes humans, often transmitting diseases such as rabies. Little is known of its breeding habits, but females bear single young, perhaps more than once a year.

ORDER: Chiroptera;
FAMILY: Desmodontidae.

Vanessid butterfly

The vanessids are a group of medium- and large-sized butterflies related to the FRITILLARY BUTTERFLIES. Several species are widely distributed in Europe and North America and they include some of the commonest and most colourful visitors to our gardens. Most of them hibernate for the winter, and their rather drab under-sides provide excellent camouflage in the caves and hollow trees in which they go to sleep. Attics and out-houses are also frequently chosen as hibernation sites. One of the best known species is the peacock butterfly, found from Western Europe to Japan. Its wings are deep reddish brown on the upper surface, and each wing bears a large bluish eye-spot. The under-

Small tortoiseshell

Caterpillar

Painted lady

Comma

Large tortoiseshell

side is almost black. The caterpillar is black and spiky and feeds on stinging nettle. This plant is also the food of the larvae of the small tortoiseshell, the commonest of the European vanessids. Orange and black on the upper side and mottled brown beneath, it can be found on garden flowers from early spring until late in the autumn. The large tortoiseshell is similar, but has less black on the hind wings. Its caterpillar feeds on elms and various other trees and the species is much rarer than its smaller cousin. The painted lady is another orange and black species, although the orange is paler than in the tortoiseshells. It is a strongly migratory species and is found all over the world. The red admiral is another migrant found on both sides of the Atlantic. It is velvety black, with red bands and white spots. It hibernates in the southern parts of its range and flies north for the summer The adults are very fond of ripe fruit, while the larvae feed on stinging nettles. Other vanessids include the commas and the Camberwell beauty. The latter is known as the mourning cloak in North America because of its sombre brown colouring with a cream border on both surfaces. With a wing-span of more than 60 mm, it is one of the largest vanessids. Its larvae feed on sallows and other trees. The commas get their name from the white comma-shaped mark on the hind wing. They are also easily identified by their jagged wing margins. They hibernate in the open among dead leaves and twigs and are remarkably well camouflaged. Their larvae feed on nettles, hops, and various other plants.
ORDER: Lepidoptera;
FAMILY: Nymphalidae.

Velvet ant

Only distantly related to the true ants, velvet ants are actually parasitic WASPS. The females are wingless and ant-like, although they are clothed with dense, short hairs which give them a velvety appearance. Males are winged and look very much like other solitary wasps. Armed with a powerful sting, the female velvet ant enters the nest of a bumble bee or another solitary wasp and lays her eggs there. Her youngsters feed on the bee or wasp grubs. There are about 3000 species of velvet ant, living mainly in hot dry regions.
ORDER: Hymenoptera;
FAMILY: Mutillidae.

Vervet monkey

The vervet, or green monkey is the most common of the African *primates*. It is a colourful monkey of the GUENON group. Its coat is yellowish-brown with an olive tinge, and it has a black face, a white throat and white whiskers. It lives in open *savanna* in much of Africa south of the Sahara. All vervet monkeys live in groups which average 12 in number. The range of a group contains trees or clumps of bushes at its centre. Here the monkeys sleep and feed, eating mostly leaves, with some fruit and flowers. During the day, they move on to open ground.
ORDER: Primates;
FAMILY: Cercopithecidae;
SPECIES: *Cercopithecus aethiops*.

Vicuna

The vicuna is the smallest member of the CAMEL family in South America. It can stand 90 cm at the shoulder and weighs 35 to 45 kg. Its range extends from northern Peru to northern Chile and it is seldom found less than 4000 metres above sea-level. The vicuna is wild and lives in herds of a few females and their young, with one male. However, bachelor herds may be large. The coat is light brown with a yellowish-red bib.

Vertebrates

The vertebrates – animals with backbones – are the most advanced animals alive. There are seven living classes of vertebrates: lampreys and hagfish, cartilaginous fish, bony fish, amphibians, reptiles, birds and mammals. All vertebrates have a spinal cord enclosed in the backbone. They have an internal skeleton, and are always bilaterally symmetrical – the left and right sides of their bodies are mirror images. All but the most primitive have a cranium (brain case) and land-dwelling vertebrates generally have two pairs of limbs. Some, such as the snakes, have lost their limbs during evolution. Vertebrates can grow much larger than invertebrates, because the internal skeleton gives the animal support while it is growing. The first vertebrates, small fish-like creatures without jaws or paired fins, appeared about 480 million years ago.

A herd of **vicuna**, a smaller, daintier cousin of the llama.

The wool is prized and the vicuna has been greatly reduced in numbers, although it is now protected.
ORDER: Artiodactyla;
FAMILY: Camelidae;
SPECIES: *Lama vicugna*.

Viperfish

These odd, deep-sea fishes get their name from their long, fang-like teeth which project on either side of the jaws. The tips of these teeth are barbed, which helps in the capture of prey such as large PRAWNS and small fishes. The viperfish itself, although fearsome in appearance, is only 15 to 25 cm long. In the black, mid-deep waters, viperfish attract their prey with a luminous lure, formed from a long flexible fin spine, which dangles invitingly in front of the predator's mouth. Other luminous organs on the viperfish's body, besides attracting prey, may also serve as recognition signals between the sexes.
ORDER: Salmoniformes;
FAMILY: Chauliodontidae.

The **viscacha** is a South American rodent related to the chinchilla.

Viscacha

The Viscacha is a South American RODENT closely related to the CHINCHILLA. There are two kinds: the plains viscacha and the mountain viscacha. The plains viscacha is up to 80 cm long, including the short tail, and has fairly long fur and short ears. The much slighter mountain viscacha has long, rabbit-like ears and a much smaller head.

Viscacha are social animals and live in colonies. The plains viscacha lives on the pampas where it digs extensive burrows. The excavated earth is piled up at the burrow entrance, and the viscacha, being a great collector, adorns these mounds with various small objects, such as bones or twigs, which are gathered from the surrounding area. Because plains viscachas compete with livestock for grazing, and their earth mounds can be a hazard to horsemen, these animals are regarded as pests by farmers and ranchers alike.

The mountain viscachas do not burrow but live in rock crevices. They are hunted by humans for food and for their hair which is mixed with wool for yarn.
ORDER: Rodentia;
FAMILY: Chinchillidae;
SPECIES: *Lagostomus maximus* (plains); *Lagidium peruanum* (mountain).

The **vole** can cause serious damage to crops and grassland pastures. It is active day and night.

Vole

Voles are commonly mistaken for rats and mice, but have blunter snouts and smaller eyes and ears. The water vole is about the same size as the brown rat. It makes its home in a burrow dug into the bankside, and although its feet are not webbed, it swims and dives well. In much of Europe, the water vole is replaced by another species which looks very similar but which does not enter the water.

The smaller short-tailed or field vole is more mouse-like in appearance but has a relatively short tail This vole lives in pastures, orchards and gardens, and being a voracious feeder can do some damage to crops. Voles have many enemies for they are the favourite food of a variety of predators, including foxes, weasels, hawks and owls. The field vole relies on alertness and concealment for protection, but a family of water voles will sometimes unite to fight off a would-be predator.

Meadow voles are the most common species in North America. As their name suggests, these voles live in fields and feed on grass and seeds.

ORDER: Rodentia;
FAMILY: Cricetidae.

Vulture

Vultures are the best known SCAVENGERS of the bird world. They are found in the Old World and in the New. Most vultures are large, heavily-built birds with dark brown or black plumage. The head, and sometimes the neck too, is naked. Vultures feed on carrion, thrusting their long necks inside carcasses, so this lack of feathers is a necessary hygienic adaptation. Unlike other birds of prey, vultures rarely hunt live food. Their beaks are not strong enough to tear open a carcass until it has rotted, and their relatively weak feet are adapted for running rather than for seizing prey.

Vultures are ungainly on the ground, and after a heavy meal become so gorged that they can

hardly fly. Once aloft, however, they soar effortlessly for hours on their long, broad wings. They find food by sight, detecting carrion from vast distances by watching the behaviour of other vultures and carrion-eaters. Vultures are usually found in dry, open country. But the hooded vulture is a forest-dweller and also scavenges around towns and villages in Africa. The Egyptian vulture is one of the few birds seen to use tools; it will throw rocks at ostrich eggs to crack the shells. The griffon vulture and other species live in flocks, nesting in trees or on cliffs. The larger vultures, such as the hooded vulture and the palm-nut vulture nest singly.

ORDER: Falconiformes;
FAMILY: Accipitridae (Old World); Cathartidae (New World).

If these three vultures arrive at a carcass together, the **black vulture** feeds first, then the **griffon vulture** and finally the **Egyptian vulture**.

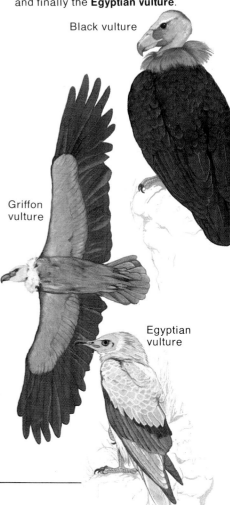

Black vulture

Griffon vulture

Egyptian vulture

W

Wagtail

Wagtails are small insect-eating birds. They are closely related to PIPITS, but are more brightly coloured and have longer tails which continually "wag" up and down. The bill is needle-like, typical of insect-eaters, and the feet are well developed with long toes. The tail is nearly as long as the head and body, making a total length of around 15 cm. There are about eight species of wagtail. They live in the Old World but are not found in Australia. Wagtails usually live in open country but there is a forest wagtail. The pied and grey wagtails are often found near water.
ORDER: Passeriformes;
FAMILY: Motacillidae.

Wallaby

There are more than 20 species of these kangaroo-like MARSUPIALS. The hare wallabies, like their namesakes, have a habit of lying in a "form" or shallow trench. They

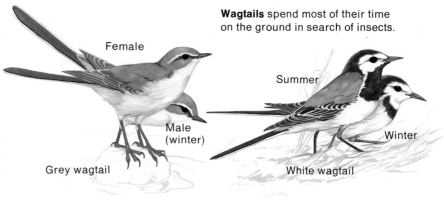

Female
Male (winter)
Grey wagtail

Wagtails spend most of their time on the ground in search of insects.

Summer
Winter
White wagtail

are nocturnal and solitary animals. The nail-tail wallabies are fast runners, and have the strange habit of swinging their forelegs in a rotary action to the sides of their bodies. This earns them the local name of "organ-grinders". The purpose of the spur or nail at the tip of the tail is unknown.

Scrub wallabies are nocturnal feeders but are occasionally seen on the fringes of scrub in daylight. They thump the ground with their feed when alarmed, possibly as a signal to their companions. The little rock wallaby is the smallest of

the wallabies, no more than 40 cm from nose to tail.
ORDER: Marsupialia;
FAMILY: Macropodidae.

Walrus

The large walrus seems to fall between the true SEALS and the eared seals (fur seals and SEA LIONS). It is an aquatic mammal found in the northern waters of both the Atlantic and Pacific oceans. The Pacific walrus is slightly larger than the Atlantic walrus. Walrus bulls are much larger than the cows. A large Pacific bull may reach 4 metres in length and weigh 1700 kg.

Walruses live together in groups or colonies, the adult bulls remaining apart except during the breeding season. They lie on beaches and ice floes, diving to depths of up to 100 metres to grub up clams from the sea bed with their long curving tusks. The tusks are also used as weapons and as grapnels to help the walrus haul its bulky body out onto the ice. In

Many of these **Bennett's wallabies** now live wild in Europe.

spite of its clumsy appearance, the walrus can move overland as fast as a man can run. Normally timid, walruses will fight to protect their young. Apart from humans, their only enemies are polar bears and killer whales. Strict conservation measures have saved the Pacific walrus from extinction, but the Atlantic species is still in danger after years of over-hunting.
ORDER: Pinnipedia;
FAMILY: Odobenidae;
SPECIES: *Odobenus rosmarus divergens* (Pacific); *Odobenus rosmarus rosmarus* (Atlantic).

Reed warbler

Warble-fly

The warble-flies are rather hairy, yellowish flies about the size of honeybees, and they are serious pests of cattle. The female fly normally lays her eggs on the legs of the cattle, and the resulting grubs bore their way into the flesh. They move right through the body and, after about two months, they take up position just under the skin of the back. They feed there for a further two months, causing great irritation to the host and severe damage to the skin, which swells up around the grubs to form "warbles". When fully grown, the warble-fly grub drops out and pupates in the ground.
ORDER: Diptera;
FAMILY: Oestridae.

Sedge warbler

Warbler

A name given to two families of birds: the *Old World* warblers and the *New World* warblers. The New World warblers are also known as wood warblers or American warblers. Although similar in appearance, there are major differences between the two families. One of the main differences is in the number of primary flight feathers. The Old World warblers have ten, the New World variety only nine.

There are about 400 species of Old World warblers, named after their melodious song. They are small, usually 10 to 13 cm long, with fine, pointed bills for eating insects. They are usually drably coloured green, brown or grey, and are therefore very difficult to tell apart. Old World Warblers are found from Western Europe to Australia, and about half the species are African. Some are migratory, while others spend their lives in one area. The willow warbler travels up to 11,000 km from eastern Siberia to East

Marsh warbler

Dartford warbler

Willow warbler

Bonelli's warbler

Wood warbler

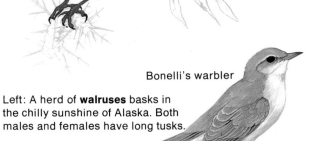

Left: A herd of **walruses** basks in the chilly sunshine of Alaska. Both males and females have long tusks.

Africa, and the Arctic warbler may travel even farther.

Nests are built near the ground among bushes, reeds and grasses, and the 3 to 12 eggs are usually speckled.

ORDER: Passeriformes;
FAMILY: Sylviidae (Old World); Parulidae (New World).

Warthog

The warthog is a member of the pig family. It is found in most open country in Africa south of the Sahara. It has an oddly proportioned, flat and almost shovel-shaped head, armed with tusks. In the male, two lumps or "warts" appear on either side. The curled upper tusks, 30 cm or more in length, are longer than the lower. The male is up to 150 cm long, standing up to 70 cm at the shoulder, and weighs about 90 kg. The female is somewhat smaller. The skin is slate- or clay-coloured. Warthogs can inflict severe wounds with their tusks, but are basically inoffensive animals. The lion is their main enemy.

ORDER: Artiodactyla;
FAMILY: Suidae;
SPECIES: *Phacochoerus aethiopicus.*

Wasp

Wasp is the name given to the many different kinds of stinging insect which belong to the same group as the BEES and ANTS. As among the bees, there are both

The **warthog** must be one of the world's most unattractive animals.

A **bee-killer wasp** with its victim tucked securely under its body.

social and solitary species, belonging to several different families, but they all provide their offspring with some kind of animal food. Solitary wasps range from minute black insects, through a variety of black and yellow, or black and red species, to giants nearly 8 cm long. Most of them dig nest-tunnels in the ground or in rotten wood, but some actually build nests with clay. The potter wasp builds a beautiful little clay vase. Wasps stock their nests with prey which they have paralysed with their sting, and lay their eggs. Because the prey is only paralysed, and not dead, it does not rot, and the wasp grubs can feed on it until they are fully grown. The type of prey provided by these solitary or hunting wasps depends on the species. Some use APHIDS, some use FLIES, some stock up with caterpillars, and others use SPIDERS. The mother wasp does not usually live to see her offspring.

Common wasp

Paper-wasp

The social wasps are typified by the HORNETS and the numerous black and yellow species that plague us in late summer. The common wasp, the German wasp, and the American yellowjackets, form annual colonies in temperate climates. Their social organization is very similar to that of the BUMBLE BEE. The queen wasps *hibernate*, and begin their nests in spring. The nests are actually made of paper, which the wasps produce by scraping fence posts and other dead wood with their jaws and chewing the wood to pulp. Nests are sometimes found in hollow trees or hanging freely from branches, but most are built below the ground or under the roofs of buildings. The queen builds some six-sided paper cells for her first few eggs. Then she feeds the first batch of larvae with chewed insects and other meat. The queen usually catches prey with her jaws and does not use her sting other than for defence. She herself feeds on nectar.

As with the bumble bees, the first grubs grow into workers, which enlarge the nest and feed the later grubs. They also feed the queen, who busies herself with more egg-laying. Males and new queens appear in later summer, and egg-laying then falls off. With less work to do the worker wasps turn their attention to fruit and other sweet things. They can be a real nuisance, although they do not normally sting unless provoked. They all die in autumn, leaving just the newly mated queens to carry on the race.

ORDER: Hymenoptera;

Water beetle

Many families of beetles have taken to life in the water and there are over 2000 species of water beetle. Some crawl slowly over water plants, but most swim freely with the aid of broad, fringed legs. Although some species can absorb oxygen direct from the water, most have to get their oxygen from the surface. They come up periodically, some head-up and some head-down, and hang from the surface while they draw air into the space between the body and *elytra*. Air can pass from this bubble straight into the breathing pores, just as it does in land-living beetles, and the water beetle can stay down for quite a long time. There are both *herbivores* and CARNIVORES among the water beetles, the best known of the carnivores being the great diving beetle. This deep green insect is 3 cm long and is one of the most powerful of the water beetles. It regularly attacks frogs and fishes with its great jaws. Its *larva*, known as the water tiger, looks quite delicate as it picks its way over the bottom, but it is equally murderous. Its massive jaws are like hypodermic needles, and when they have impaled prey the insect injects digestive juices. The resulting fluids are then sucked up, leaving little more than the prey's empty skin. Most water beetles can fly, and often move to new ponds at night.

ORDER: Coleoptera.

Waterbuck

The waterbuck is a large ANTELOPE which roams savanna country in Africa, south of the Sahara. It stays near rivers, but lives on drier ground than its name might suggest. Males hold territories along rivers, while females move about in groups. The males try to attract females into their terri-

The **great diving beetles** are ferocious hunters. They propel themselves at speed with their oar-like legs.

tories. The waterbuck is 120 to 135 cm high and weighs between 200 and 230 kg. It has a coarse, brown coat with blackish feet. The common waterbuck has a white ring around the rump, whereas another species, the defassa waterbuck, has an entirely white rump. Only the male waterbuck has horns.

ORDER: Artiodactyla;
FAMILY: Bovidae;
SPECIES: *Kobus ellipsiprymnus.*

Water bug

Several different families of bugs have adopted an aquatic life. Some, such as the POND SKATER, live on the surface. With the exception of the true water boatmen, which feed mainly on alga and other plant debris, the water bugs are CARNIVOROUS. Some of the larger species, such as the backswimmers, feed on tadpoles and fishes; and their powerful beaks can easily draw blood from a human finger if the insects are handled. The water scorpion crawls slowly over mud or water plants, but most other water bugs swim by means of broad, feathery legs. The backswimmers actually swim upside down, and can move their bullet-shaped bodies very

rapidly. A few bugs can absorb oxygen directly from the water, but most have to get oxygen from the surface. The water scorpion has a long tube at the hind end, and pushes it to the surface to draw in air. Most other species float to the surface and hang there while renewing their air supplies. They carry bubbles of air under their wing cases, or trapped between dense hair on their bodies. Many water bugs fly well and can easily move from pond to pond.

ORDER: Hemiptera-Heteroptera.

Water flea

In spite of its name, the water flea is not a flea at all, but a tiny freshwater CRUSTACEAN. There are several species, the largest of which is only 5 mm long. They are often seen as a cloud of dancing specks in a pond, or as surface scum. Water fleas spend much of their time bobbing up and down in the water, heads uppermost. They actually swim by "rowing" with their long *antennae*. The water flea feeds on bacteria and single-celled

Daphnia, the **water flea**, jigs along in pond water, carrying her brood of eggs in an internal pouch.

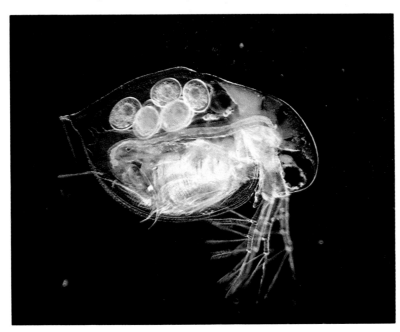

algae, which it filters out of the water. Some water flea eggs can survive drying and freezing to hatch out months or even years later. These resting eggs, as they are called, carry the population over the winter.

ORDER: Cladocera;
FAMILY: Daphniidae;
GENUS: *Daphnia.*

Water spider

The water spider lives under water nearly all the time. It is an ordinary-looking small-bodied, long-legged spider. One unusual feature is that the female is usually smaller than the male, whereas the reverse is true in most spiders. Like all other spiders, it breathes air, but is able to live submerged by constructing a diving bell out of silk which it attaches to the stems and leaves of water plants. The spider swims to the surface, traps a bubble of air between its hind legs and dives down to the bell with it, repeating the process until the bell is full. The spider lurks in the bell, and when a small water animal, such as an insect or its *larva* swims near, it darts out and seizes it.

ORDER: Araneae;
FAMILY: Agelenidae;
SPECIES: *Argyroneta aquatica.*

Wattlebird

The name wattlebird is applied to a small family of extremely rare New Zealand birds. Of the three species, one is now extinct. Wattlebirds have rounded wings, long tails, strong legs, long hind claws and wattles, usually orange, at the corner of the mouth. The kokako, or wattled crow, is jay-like with a stout curved bill; the other smaller species is the tieke.

ORDER: Passeriformes;
FAMILY: Callaeidae.

Waxbill

Waxbills form a group of small, colourful finch-like birds. They are about 10 cm long and many have

finely barred upper-parts. The birds like to gather in swampy country, where they feed on seeds, particularly those of grasses. The common waxbill has a bright red patch around each eye, and the cheeks and throat are white. It is found in many parts of Africa but most waxbills live south of the Sahara. The AVADAVAT is Asian and the Sydney waxbill Australian.
ORDER: Passeriformes;
FAMILY: Estrildidae.

Waxwing

Waxwings are starling-sized, crested birds whose flight feathers are tipped with red. The plumage is generally brownish or greyish with some black around the eyes. There are three species: the cedar waxwing of North America, the Bohemian waxwing of the colder parts of the northern hemisphere, and the Japanese waxwing.

Except when nesting, **waxwings** continually wander about in flocks.

Waxwings feed mainly on berries throughout the year, but they are also fond of insects. They usually nest in coniferous and birch forests. The 3 to 7 bluish, dark-spotted eggs are incubated for 2 weeks.
ORDER: Passeriformes.
FAMILY: Bombycillidae.

Weasel

Weasels are short-legged, slender animals with reddish-brown fur and white under-parts. Closely related to the STOAT, their appearance is quite similar, though they are smaller, being about 20 cm long, and they do not have black-tipped tails. Like the stoats, some

Below: A short-tailed **weasel** in its winter coat.

weasels turn white in winter in northern regions.

The common weasel is found all over Europe, Asia and North Africa. It is a ferocious killer found in almost every kind of habitat, including woods, scrubland, hedgerows, rocky country and even towns. It is a good climber and moves swiftly on the ground. It hunts mainly at night and preys on small birds and RODENTS – even rats two or three times its own size.

Mating usually occurs in April or May. Unlike other members of the family, there is no delay in the gestation process and the kittens are born six weeks later. A female usually bears two litters in a season.

In North America there are two species. The long tailed weasel is about 30 cm in length and cannot climb. The least weasel, as its name suggests, is the smallest, being only 10 cm long. However, some scientists consider the least weasel as a sub-species of the common weasel.
ORDER: Carnivora;
FAMILY: Mustelidae.

Weaver ant

The weaver ANTS live in trees and bushes and get their name from their habit of making a nest of several living leaves fixed together to make a pouch. The leaves are not actually woven together, but fixed by sticky strands produced by the *grubs*. While some adults hold the edges of the leaves together, others move along the junctions carrying grubs. They squeeze the grubs gently to force out the silk, which is laid in zig-zag fashion across the join. If the nest is broken open, the ants rush out and attack the invader with their large jaws. They also spray formic acid, which produces a painful, burning sensation. Other workers get busy to bring the broken edges together again. If the gap is too large for one ant to bridge, two or more ants link up across the gap and gradually pull the edges

A male **red-headed weaverbird** sits in its partly-constructed nest.

together. Weaver ants are mainly carnivorous and can be found throughout the Tropics of the *Old World*.
ORDER: Hymenoptera;
FAMILY: Formicidae;
GENUS: *Oecophylla*.

Weaverbird

Weavers are small, sparrow-like birds that live in Africa and Asia.

Like all seed-eating birds they have conical bills. The males of many weavers have bright plumage during the breeding season but revert to their drab, streaky plumage afterwards. Weavers are found in a variety of habitats, but always where there are trees for nesting and roosting. Weavers are

named after the elaborate flask-shaped nests which the male makes from strands of grass or palm fronds. Each nest is separate, but a single large tree may contain hundreds of nests.
ORDER: Passeriformes;
FAMILY: Ploceidae.

Web spinner

Web spinners are slender brownish insects that live under logs and stones in the warmer parts of the world. Several species live in southern Europe and in the United States. They spin narrow silken tunnels, in which they can move backwards and forwards with equal ease. Females are always wingless, but males sometimes have wings. They eat various small soil dwelling creatures and vegetable matter.
ORDER: Embioptera.

Weever

Weevers are sea fishes that are widespread form Norway to West Africa. They are greatly feared because of their poisonous spines. Weevers spend much of their time half-buried in sand or gravel, where they are difficult to see. Frequently a bather steps on one and is poisoned by its *dorsal* spine, which causes great pain.

The greater weever, about 45 cm long, is so abundant in the Mediterranean that it is fished for food. The eyes and mouth of weevers both point upwards enabling them to see and feed when buried in the sand.
ORDER: Perciformes;
FAMILY: Trachinidae.

Weevil

The weevils are a group of plant-feeding BEETLES in which the head is drawn out to form a prominent snout, or trunk, sometimes as long as the rest of the body. The jaws are at the end of the snout, and the sharply-elbowed *antennae* are at-tached about half way along. Some tropical weevils reach lengths of 7 cm, but most of the 50,000 or so species are less than 4 cm long. They rarely fly, and many species lack hind wings. The *elytra* are often covered with fine scales and are sometimes brilliantly coloured. Most adult weevils nibble leaves and buds, but the legless grubs live inside the plants. The adult female uses her snout to drill a hole in a stem, bud or fruit in which she lays her eggs. Many weevil grubs live in fruit and seeds. They are serious pests, both in the

An **acorn weevil** on an oak leaf. All weevils are plant-feeders, both as larvae and adults.

field and in stores. Examples include the grain weevil, which destroys huge amounts of stored grain each year, and the cotton boll weevil, which costs the American cotton industry millions of dollars.
ORDER: Coleoptera.

Whale

Whales are aquatic MAMMALS. They evolved over 100 million years ago from land mammals, and their nearest living relatives are the UNGULATES or hoofed mammals. Instead of hair, they have a thick insulating layer of

blubber beneath their skins to keep them warm in the cold waters in which they live. The whale's skeleton has traces of hind limbs, relics of its distant ancestry. The front limbs have become flippers, used mainly for balance and steering, while the power for swimming comes from the broad-fluked tail. The nostrils have migrated to the top of the head where they form the blow-hole. After a dive, a whale "spouts" to expel the used air from its lungs before taking another breath.

Whales have been able to grow to great sizes, far larger than any living land animal, because the water supports the weight of their

A southern **right whale** breaching, or leaping out of the water. This whale is about 16 metres long.

bodies. Yet, despite the vast size of some species, most whales are inoffensive creatures. Indeed, the largest eat only tiny creatures, some 5 cm long, called krill.

There are two main groups of whales: the whale-bone or baleen whales (which include the BLUE, HUMPBACK, RIGHT and RORQUAL whales); and the toothed whales. The latter (which include the KILLER and SPERM WHALES, DOL-PHINS, NARWHALS and PORPOISES) feed mostly on fish and squid, although the killer, the most

ferocious of all whales, preys on seals, penguins and other whales. The baleen whales eat only krill. Instead of teeth, they have two sets of whalebone or baleen plates which are made from modified hair. The whales use these plates as seives to catch the krill on which they feed.

ORDER: Cetacea.

Whale shark

Not only the largest SHARK, but also the greatest of all fishes, the whale shark can grow up to 21 metres long and can weigh as much as 70 tonnes. The gape of its

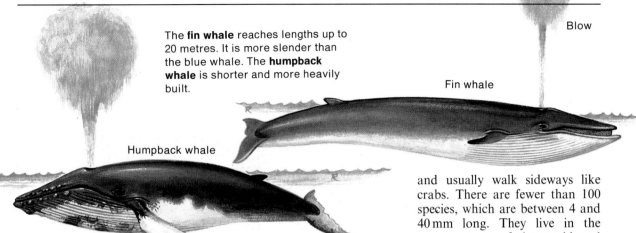

The **fin whale** reaches lengths up to 20 metres. It is more slender than the blue whale. The **humpback whale** is shorter and more heavily built.

Blow

Fin whale

Humpback whale

wide mouth is enough to allow two or three full-grown persons to crouch inside it. Yet this enormous creature is completely inoffensive, using its cavern-like mouth as a scoop for gathering small creatures such as PLANKTON on which it feeds. The whale shark cruises along near the surface at about 6 km/h. It steers itself with its powerful tail and its long, sickle-shaped *pectoral fins*. It can be recognized even at a distance by its covering of white or yellow spots.

ORDER: Lamniformes;
FAMILY: Rhincodontidae;
SPECIES: *Rhincodon typus.*

Whelk

Whelks are carnivorous sea snails with pointed shells. They feed on a variety of living and dead animals, often using their horny teeth to rasp holes in *bivalve* shells to get at the flesh. They are themselves eaten by fishes such as COD. There are several hundred species, the best known being the common whelk of European and North American coasts. It has a shell up to 15 cm long.

CLASS: Gastropoda;
ORDER: Neogastropoda;
SPECIES: *Buccinum undatum* (common).

Whip scorpion

Whip scorpions used to go under the general name of pedipalpi. This name comes from the well-developed pair of pincer-like appendages, the pedipalps, which the animals use for seizing their prey.

The "whip" of the main group of whip scorpions is a long, thin tail at the end of the abdomen. The 700 species live in tropical and semi tropical places, and range in size from tiny forms about 2 mm long, up to an American species which is 65 mm long. They feed on insects such as cockroaches and grasshoppers, plus slugs, worms and even small frogs and toads.

The Amblypygi are often called tailless whip scorpions. Their first pair of legs are long and look like whips. They have flattened bodies,

The common **whelk**, a predatory sea snail.

and usually walk sideways like crabs. There are fewer than 100 species, which are between 4 and 40 mm long. They live in the warmer parts of the world and hunt by night.

The Palpigradi are often called micro-whip scorpions because they are less than 5 mm long and have a whip-like tail similar to that of the true whip scorpions. They live in warm, humid places and hunt at night.

CLASS: Arachnida;
ORDERS: Uropygi, Amblypigi, Palpigradi.

Whip snake

This name describes snakes in two separate families. Australian whip snakes are venomous. Whip snakes found around the Mediterranean are non-venomous. They are relatives of the RACER group of snakes and have slim bodies and long, tapering tails. At up to 2.5 metres long, the dark green whip snake is among the largest European snakes. Mediterranean whip

snakes live mainly on the ground in dry places among shrubs and stones. They generally feed on small reptiles such as lizards, which they chase and swallow alive. They move with remarkable speed, and are very difficult to capture.

ORDER: Squamata;
FAMILIES: Colubridae (Mediterranean) and Elapidae (Australian).

Whirligig beetle

The whirligig beetles are small, shiny beetles that spin round rapidly on the surface of still and slow-moving water. Their oval bodies are rarely more than 8 mm long, and they are shiny blue-black or bronze. They skate round on the surface with the aid of their very short, broad second and third pair of legs, and they capture other small insects that fall onto the water surface. Each eye is divided into two parts – one looking out over the surface and one looking down into the water. The insects usually dive when they are disturbed, and they can also fly well. There are several hundred species.

ORDER: Coleoptera;
FAMILY: Gyrinidae.

White butterfly

In the broadest sense of the term, the white butterflies incude all the members of the family Pieridae. Some tropical species are brightly coloured, but the main colours are white and yellow, especially in the temperate regions. There are well over 100 species, most of them of medium size. The best known are the CABBAGE WHITE butterflies, whose caterpillars ravage our cabbages and cauliflowers. Familiar yellow members of the group include the sulphurs or clouded yellows, which have prominent black borders to their wings, and the European brimstone. The latter has brilliant yellow wings in the male, while the female is very

pale green. The undersides of both sexes are very leaf-like and conceal the insects while they are hibernating in evergreen shrubs. Other well known members of the family include the orange-tips, the Bath white and the black-veined white. Many of these species are strong migrants, some of them flying from the Mediterranean region to northern Europe each summer. Their caterpillars feed on a wide variety of plants and their *pupae* are always attached in a vertical position by means of a silken girdle. Most of the species inhabit light woodland and open grassland, including high mountain tops and the Arctic tundra.

ORDER: Lepidoptera;
FAMILY: Pieridae.

White-tailed deer

The white-tailed deer is so named because the under-side of its tail is white. This can be seen when the animal is running and the tail is raised. It is closely related to the MULE DEER. The various races stand up to 120 cm at the shoulder, and weigh up to 140 kg. They live in woodlands from southern Canada, through the United

States and Central America, into northern South America. They live in groups of about six animals, the males and females usually being separate. Overhunting once reduced their numbers, but they are now abundant in many areas.

ORDER: Artiodactyla;
FAMILY: Cervidae;
SPECIES: *Odocoileus virginianus*

Whiting

A member of the cod family about 70 cm long, the whiting is also an important food fish. It lives in great abundance in the North Sea and is also found in the Mediterranean and the Black Sea. Similar in general appearance to the COD and HADDOCK, the whiting can be recognized by its smaller size, silvery sides and more pointed head. Also it lacks a *barbel*, or has only a very small one, on its chin. Whiting feed on smaller fishes and shellfish.

ORDER: Gadiformes;
FAMILY: Gadidae;
SPECIES: *Merlangus merlangus*.

Male **white butterflies** usually differ slightly from the females in colour pattern.

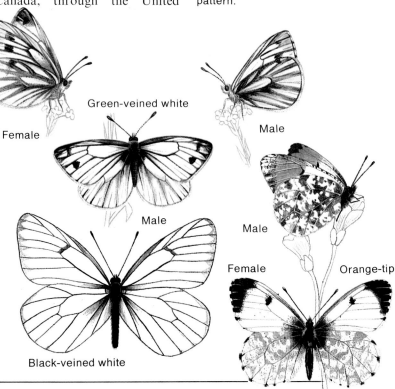

Green-veined white

Female

Male

Male

Male

Female

Orange-tip

Black-veined white

Whydah

The whydahs are a group of sparrow-like, seed-eating birds which lay their eggs in the nests of weaver finches. There are about 11 species, all of which live in Africa, and like CUCKOOS they are parasites. The females are drab throughout the year but in the breeding season the males have a special plumage which is usually shiny black, sometimes with very long tail feathers. The male pin-tailed whydah, which is found throughout most of Africa south of the Sahara, measures 38 cm of which about 25 cm is tail. The breeding plumage is black and white. It performs dispay flights ascending 30 to 60 metres, before slowly fluttering down with its long tail waving.

Each species of whydah usually lays its eggs in the nest of a particular species of weaver finch. One egg is laid in each nest and the host's eggs are not destroyed.
ORDER: Passeriformes;
FAMILY: Ploceidae.

Wild boar

The European wild boar is one of the species from which the domestic pig was derived. The Chinese wild pig and the Indian wild boar are closely related to it. The three animals may, in fact, be one species, and are sometimes referred to as the Eurasian wild boar. They range across Europe and Asia as far as the East Indies, as well as North Africa. Wild boar are pale grey to brown or black in colour. The body hairs are sparse bristles, with some finer hairs. The tail has only short hairs. Some individuals, however, have longer hairs on the cheeks, or a slight mane, or both. The wild boar's disk-like snout is used for rooting.

The boar usually grows to 150 cm long including the tail, and weighs up to 180 kg. The sow is

The **wild boar** lives in family parties in open woodland.

smaller. The tusks may be 30 cm long. These animals live in small, family parties in open woodland, but they sometimes come together to form bands of up to 50. Most of the old males remain solitary.
ORDER: Artiodactyla;
FAMILY: Suidae;
SPECIES: *Sus scrofa.*

Wild cat

At first glance, the wild cat of Europe and Asia resembles the domestic tabby. But its body is longer and stouter than a domestic cat's, and the thick bushy tail is shorter and is ringed, ending in a black tip. The legs, too, are longer than those of a domestic cat. Average body length is 84 cm, including the tail. Males average 5 kg, but the record is almost three times greater.

Wild cats live on lonely mountainsides or in wooded places. By day they hide among rocks and by night they hunt alone or in pairs. The home range is 60 to 70 hectares. Mountain hares, grouse, rabbits, and small rodents provide the main food, but wild cats will also attack poultry and lambs. In May and August an adult female gives birth to a litter of 4 or 5 kittens. While these remain in their nest the female is very fierce and attacks any intruder. The kittens are weaned at 4 months and independent at 5 months.
ORDER: Carnivora;
FAMILY: Felidae;
SPECIES: *Felis sylvestris.*

Wobbegong

Wobbegongs are very unusual sharks that live around the coasts of Australia and other far-eastern countries. They are also called carpet sharks from their broad, fringed head and carpet-like patterning. The patterning and the fringe that grows around the jaws are really a camouflage which disguises the wobbegong as it lies on the bottom among rocks and seaweeds, waiting for any unwary

A fine example of camouflage – a **wobbegong**, seen head-on.

fish to swim close enough to be snapped up. The largest wobbegongs reach a length of more than 3 metres, and with their multiple rows of stiletto-like teeth they can be very dangerous. But normally wobbegongs are not aggressive towards human beings and a diver is unlikely to be harmed unless he unwittingly treads on one.
ORDER: Lamniformes;
FAMILY: Oroctolobidae.

Wolf

Wolves are doglike animals found in Europe, Asia and North America. The grey or timber wolf was formerly widespread in these regions, but is now restricted mainly to the more northerly and uninhabited areas. The red wolf is confined to a small area of the southern United States.

The grey wolf is the larger of the

A family party of **grey wolves**.

two species, being up to 1.5 metres long and weighing up to 70 kg. Its colour varies considerably but is usually grey sprinkled with black, with yellowish-white under-parts and legs. The red wolf is more slender and the average weight is 15 kg. Its coat is tawny, and small individuals may resemble COYOTES.

Wolves live in open country and forests, hunting by day and hiding by night under fallen trees, among rocks or in holes dug in the ground. They usually hunt in family parties or in packs of 20 to 40 individuals. A single wolf can bring down a medium-sized deer, but a pack can tackle a MOOSE or an elk. Wolves have great powers of endurance and can usually outrun their prey. They are good swimmers when necessary, and will pursue deer into water. Because they resort to killing livestock when food is scarce, their chief enemy is man. In the United States the grey wolf has been almost completely exterminated.

Mating occurs from January to March and 5 to 14 cubs are born about 60 days later. Both parents teach the cubs to hunt and the family may remain together for some time.
ORDER: Carnivora;
FAMILY: Canidae;
SPECIES: *Canis lupus* (grey); *Canis niger* (red).

Wolf spider

The wolf spiders get their name because, like wolves, they run their prey down instead of snaring them like so many other spiders. There are a great many species.

Wolf spiders are small to medium sized, the largest having bodies no more than 2.5 cm long, with legs of the same length. They are particularly active and numerous among leaf litter. Most are active by night, but some can be seen sunbathing in bright sunlight. They rest in small burrows dug in soft earth, and some line the burrow with silk. Wolf spiders eat

The **wolverine**, often known as the glutton, is the largest of the weasel family.

small insects, which they chew to a pulp and suck through their small mouths. They have keen sight. The females carry their eggs about with them, wrapped in a ball of silk and held either in the jaws or attached to the spinnerets.
ORDER: Araneae;
FAMILIES: Lycosidae, Pisauridae.

Wolverine

The wolverine, or glutton, is the largest member of the WEASEL family. Up to 1.2 metres in length and 27 kg in weight, it resembles a small BEAR or a large BADGER. Its shaggy coat of short, dense fur is dark brown, with a pale band on each side, and its tail is thick and bushy.

Wolverines are found in the coniferous forests of Europe, Asia and North America. They prey on small mammals and birds, and eat carrion, often driving other predators from their kills. Being powerful and formidable animals, they can drive bears from their food. They are reputed to kill even REINDEER, and because of this, and their reputation for destructiveness, the wolverine is persecuted by humans. The animal is also said to eat more than any other carnivore, hence the name glutton.

However, this reputation is probably exaggerated.
ORDER: Carnivora;
FAMILY: Mustelidae;
SPECIES: *Gulo gulo*.

Wombat

The wombat is a MARSUPIAL, well adapted for burrowing. It has a compact body, about 75 cm long, a short neck and a large, flat head. The legs are short and powerful and the toes have sharp nails. Unlike other marsupials, wombats have continuously growing *incisor* teeth. They eat grasses, tree roots and the tender bark of shrubs. They are nocturnal animals and sleep during the day in extensive burrows with grass-lined nest chambers. They are solitary animals, pairing only for mating. A female gives birth to one young which it carries at first in a rear-facing pouch.

Wombats are divided into two groups: hairy-nosed, and smoothed-nosed or common wombats. Hairy-nosed wombats are found in small areas of central and southern Australia. They have silky soft grey fur and larger ears. Smooth-nosed or common wombats live in south-eastern Australia and Tasmania. They have a coarser, blackish-brown coat, short ears and naked muzzle.
ORDER: Diprotodontia;
FAMILY: Vombatidae.

The **woodcock** is recognized by its long beak and the dark stripes across its head.

Woodcock

Woodcock are plump-bodied, long-billed birds belonging to the SANDPIPER family. There are two species. The Eurasian woodcock is found in most of Europe and across Asia to Japan. It is about 28 cm long with a brown plumage, mottled and barred with black. The American woodcock, found in the eastern United States, is a smaller bird with lighter colouring.

Woodcock live in woodland and more open country with a preference for damp places. During the day they hide among vegetation, relying on their plumage to conceal them. They feed at dawn and dusk, probing the soil for earthworms and ground-living insects.

ORDER: Charadriiformes;
FAMILY: Scolopacidae.

Woodlouse

Woodlice are the only CRUSTACEANS that spend all their lives on land. They are small, never more than 2 cm long, with oval bodies, flat or hollow underneath and rounded on top. The *thorax* is composed of seven hard, overlapping plates, and there are seven pairs of legs. Woodlice hide by day in dark, damp places: they must keep moist to survive. They come out at night to scavenge for food – usually decaying plant material. The pill woodlouse rolls up into a ball when touched, its horny plates providing protection from attack. One species of small, blind, colourless woodlouse lives in ants' nests.

ORDER: Isopoda.

Left: A **great spotted woodpecker** outside the hole it has made for its brood.

Woodpecker

There are about 200 species of woodpecker, and they are found in woodlands around the world, except in Australasia, Madagascar and certain oceanic islands. They grow as long as 60 cm, and are usually brightly coloured, with patterns of black, white, green or red. A few woodpeckers have crests. The bill is straight and pointed. The legs are short, and the feet usually have two toes facing forwards and two backwards. Woodpeckers are tree-living birds, and the arrangement of toes enables them to get a good grip on the bark. However, some woodpeckers have only three toes. The tail is made up of stiff feathers, and is used to prop up the woodpecker as it clings to a tree trunk.

Woodpeckers are solitary birds, and spend most of their time climbing trees in search of insects. They use their bills to prize their prey from the bark or drill into the wood for them. The pointed bill makes an excellent chisel, and the skull is strengthened to withstand repeated hammering. Woodpeckers also have long tongues that can extract insects from the holes drilled in the wood. With the exception of ground woodpeckers that burrow in the ground, woodpeckers drill nesting holes in trees.

ORDER: Piciformes;
FAMILY: Picidae.

Wood pigeon

The wood pigeon is found throughout Europe, except in the far north, and extends into Russia and North Africa. It is 40 cm long, and can be recognized by the white patch on the side of its neck and broad white band across the wing.

The wood pigeon is primarily a woodland bird but since the spread of agriculture it has taken to feeding on cultivated land and is now regarded as a pest. It is also a familiar bird of city parks and suburban gardens, and is often found on downs and on coasts, some way from woodland. From autumn to spring, and sometimes also in summer, it congregates in large flocks to feed, though single birds and small groups may also be seen. In woods, the wood pigeon feeds on seeds, nuts, leaves and berries, as well as worms and other small animals. On cultivated land, it takes cereal grains and vegetables.

ORDER: Columbiformes;
FAMILY: Columbidae;
SPECIES: *Columba palumbus*.

Woolly monkey

The woolly monkey of South America is common in zoos, but little is known of its habits in the wild. The animals have been seen in troops of 15 to 50 in the upper parts of trees, where their grasping tails serve as a fifth limb. The woolly monkey is 40 to 56 cm long in head and body, with a tail of 56 to 70 cm. It has close, woolly fur, a black face and a high, rounded forehead. There are two species. The most common is Humboldt's woolly monkey. It varies in colour from grey to pale brown or nearly

Humboldt's **woolly monkey**, seen, rather unusually, on the ground.

black. The very rare Hendee's woolly monkey is a deep mahogany colour. Only a few of these monkeys survive on the eastern slopes of the Andes mountains.
ORDER: Primates;
FAMILY: Cebidae.

Worm

A worm is a legless animal with a long, usually cylindrical, body. It has no hard outer shell or casing although some species build tubes in which to live. The term worm is applied to a great many different kinds of small animal, which fall into a number of totally unrelated phyla.

FLATWORMS, FLUKES and TAPE-WORMS, are mostly parasites in larger animals. RIBBONWORMS, mostly live in the sea. ROUND-WORMS and the EELWORMS are extremely abundant and include many important parasites. Threadworms are long and thin, as their name suggests.

The thorny-headed worms, comprise about 500 species of cylindrical parasites, ranging in length from 2 to 500 mm. They live mostly in the digestive organs of fishes, birds and mammals.

Sipunculoids are small sea animals, often called peanut worms. The 350 species vary in length from 2 to 700 mm. They live on the sea bed, either buried in the sand or mud, or in rock and coral crevices, empty shells, and other protective places. Some bore holes into soft limestone.

ANNELIDS are the segmented worms, and the most important worm phylum of all. Their bodies are muscular and cylindrical, and arranged in a series of segments. The blood, digestive and nervous systems run through all segments. There are three classes: the BRISTLEWORMS, most of which live in the sea; the EARTHWORMS; and the LEECHES. Included in this phylum are the FANWORM, LUG-WORM and PALOLO WORM.

Pogonophores are thread-like, deep-water worms living in stiff

tubes on the sea bed, mostly between 2000 and 10,000 metres deep. They were unknown until 1900, when the first specimen was found off Indonesia. They are often called beard worms.

ARROW WORMS, are some of the most abundant creatures living in PLANKTON.
ACORN WORMS belong to the phylum *Hemicordata*, which has links with both the *echinoderms* and the back-boned animals.

In addition, there are some worm-like creatures among the ARTHROPODS, the huge phylum which includes insects and spiders. These are the velvet worms, which are rather like annelid worms with legs.

The **cuckoo wrasse** is about 35 cm long, with a long dorsal fin.

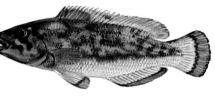

A **lyretail wrasse** hovers over the surface of a tropical reef.

Wrasse

The 600 species of wrasse are brightly coloured fishes that live around rocky coasts and reefs in many parts of the world. A typical example is the cuckoo wrasse, a heavy-bodied fish 1 metre or more in length, with large eyes, large mouth and teeth, and thick lips. The sexes are differently coloured, the male fish being particularly brilliant in its striped patterning of red, green and yellow. Wrasses tend to be solitary fishes and haunt rock crevices in search of crabs and sea snails which they prize open with their prominent, fang-like teeth. But they will probably eat any animal food they can find.
ORDER: Perciformes;
FAMILY: Labridae.

Wren

Wrens are small, drab-coloured, insect-eating birds. Most of the

The tiny **wren** is recognized by its upturned tail.

170 species live in the *New World*; only one species is found in the *Old World*. The common European wren is also found in North America, where it is known as the winter wren. It is about 9.5 cm long, brown with lighter underparts, and dark bars on the rounded wings and upturned tail The house wren of North America is similar in appearance but bigger.

Wrens can be found in many different habitats. The European wren and the house wren will often use nest boxes and are commonly seen around houses, in gardens and in woodlands. The cactus wren prefers rocky desert country, whereas the shortbilled marsh wren lives in marshes.

Wrens feed mainly on insects such as caterpillars, beetles and bugs, although the European wren has been known to catch fish. Most wrens build domed nests and the eggs are incubated by the female alone for about two weeks. There is more than one brood a year.
ORDER: Passeriformes;
FAMILY: Troglodytidae.

Wryneck

The wryneck is a small woodpecker about 15 cm long. It has mottled grey-brown plumage and, since it lacks the pointed bill and stiff tail of woodpeckers, it cannot chisel into tree trunks. However, like other woodpeckers, it does climb trees to search for insects in the bark, although it also feeds on the ground. The name wryneck comes from its habit of twisting its neck round when frightened. The wryneck ranges across Europe and Asia from Britain to Japan, and extends into North Africa.
ORDER: Piciformes;
FAMILY: Picidae;
SPECIES: *Jynx torquilla.*

XYZ

X-ray fish

Although by no means the only fish with a transparent body, the X-ray fish is the best-known fish to have this peculiarity. A favourite in home aquaria, it is a member of the CHARACIN family, native to rivers of South and Central America. Its body, about 5 cm long, is so transparent that its *swim bladder* and much of its skeleton can be clearly seen. X-ray fishes swim about in a jerky manner, in search of small animal prey. Although so vulnerable-looking, they are CARNIVORES that count among their nearest relatives the dreaded PIRANHA.
ORDER: Cypriniformes;
FAMILY: Characidae;
SPECIES: *Pristella riddlei.*

Yak

The wild yak lives on the bleak Tibetan plateau, where tempera-

A **yak** in the upper Langtang valley, Nepal.

tures in winter may plummet to $-40°$C. Its long, thick black coat protects it even at these temperatures. Bulls are said to stand over 200 cm high and weigh three-quarters of a tonne. Its horns are up to 90 cm long and point straight out sideways before turning up. The tips turn back and inwards.

The cows and calves spend most of the year in herds of 20 to 200. Adult bulls are either solitary or they live in herds of up to five.

Herds split up during the mating season, which takes place in June or July. The young are born in April or May. The domesticated yak is the chief beast of burden and milk-producer of the people of Central Asia. It is sure-footed on the mountain slopes and has great powers of endurance. It is smaller than the wild yak and its coat varies from black to piebald or white. Domestic yak have been much crossed with domestic cattle.

ORDER: Artiodactyla;
FAMILY: Bovidae;
SPECIES: *Bos mutus* (wild); *Bos mutus grunniens* (domesticated).

Yellowhammer

The yellowhammer is a brightly-coloured bunting. It has a yellow head and underparts, chestnut back and rump, and a thick seed-eating bill. The bird prefers wooded habitats, especially the edges and clearings of broad-leaved and coniferous forests. It is also found near cultivated land.

ORDER: Passeriformes;
FAMILY: Emberizidae.
SPECIES: *Emberiza citrinella.*

The male **yellowhammer** has a yellow head and underparts. The female has a streaky pale yellow head and a chestnut rump.

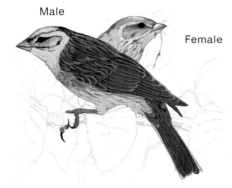

Male

Female

Zambezi shark

This large and aggressive shark is chiefly notable for spending most or all of its life in fresh waters. The same species is found in many widely-separated inland waters, including the Zambezi River of

A **yellowhammer** in flight.

Africa and Lake Nicaragua in Central America, where it grows to its full length of 3 metres and lives out its life without ever entering the sea. It is a heavy-bodied shark weighing up to 180 kg, with a large mouth containing a battery of saw-edged teeth. Its eyes are small for a shark's but probably fairly acute. The Zambezi shark normally cruises along but will accelerate suddenly to attack any prey-like object, which can include small boats. It is also likely to attack other large animals in the water, including human beings.

ORDER: Lamniformes;
FAMILY: Carcharhinidae;
SPECIES: *Carcharhinus leucas.*

Zander

A favourite sport fish of anglers in rivers of Central Europe, the zander can weigh as much as 6 kg and makes very good eating. It is one of a group of fishes called pike perches, from their close relationship to PERCHES and their resemblance to PIKES. A close relative of the zander is a pike perch of North American rivers called the walleye. However, the name of pike perch is not altogether appropriate for these lively fishes because they make much better angling sport than any pike.

ORDER: Perciformes;
FAMILY: Percidae;
SPECIES: *Stizostedion lucioperca.*

Zebra

The most obvious difference between zebras, horses and asses lies in the zebra's striped coat. Other differences include the fact that wart-like knobs, called chestnuts, occur only on the forelegs of zebras, not on the hind legs as in horses. There are also differences in the skull and teeth. Zebra live as long as horses, the record being 29 years. The zebra's chief predator is the lion. There are three species of zebra: Burchell's zebra, the mountain zebra and Grevy's zebra.

Burchell's zebra are the most common. They range between Zululand and Namibia in the south to Somalia and Sudan in the north. The stripes of these zebra reach under the belly. On the flanks, they broaden and bend backwards towards the rump, forming a Y-shaped pattern.

Right: Two **Burchell's zebras** drink peacefully at an African waterhole.

There are several races of Burchell's zebra, because features vary from south to north.

The mountain zebra, the smallest of the species, lives to the south and south-west of the range of Burchell's zebra. There is a prominent dewlap, or fold of skin, under the throat and the stripes always stop short of the belly.

Grevy's zebra, in Somalia, eastern Ethiopia and northern Kenya, is the tallest zebra, standing 135 cm at the shoulder. It has an unstriped belly and the stripes on the rest of its body are narrower and closer together than in Burchell's zebra. It has very large ears.

ORDER: Perissodactyla;
FAMILY: Equidae.

Zebu

The zebu or Brahman cattle originated in southern Asia and is now found throughout Africa, where it is better adapted to hot climates than western cattle. The Zebu has a prominent hump on its shoulder which is an enlarged muscle, rather than a store of fat as is usually claimed. There is also a large dewlap under the throat. The coat is usually grey, but may be white, black or brown. The legs are slender and the horns are more upright than those of aurochs, the wild ancestors of western cattle. The wild ancestor of the zebu is unknown.

ORDER: Artiodactyla;
FAMILY: Bovidae;
SPECIES: *Bos indicus.*

Zorille

The zorille, with its black and white fur, strongly resembles the SKUNKS of North America. Like them, it can project an evil-smelling fluid with deadly accuracy. However, it is only distantly related and is found in Africa, where it is very common. It is small and slender, with a head and body length of 30 to 40 cm.

The zorille lives in a variety of habitats, but seems to prefer dry areas. During the day it shelters among rocks or in a burrow dug with its strong claws. At night it hunts rodents, small reptiles, birds and large insects.

ORDER: Carnivora;
FAMILY: Mustelidae;
SPECIES: *Ictonyx striatus.*

GLOSSARY

Note: Words in bold type indicate a separate glossary entry.

Abdomen The hind part of an animal's body, generally between the **thorax** and pelvis in vertebrates, containing the stomach, intestines and other organs. In mammals it is separated from the thorax by the diaphragm. In arthropods it is the section behind the thorax.

Albino An animal that lacks colouring or pigment. It often has pale or white skin, hair or fur, and pink eyes. Albinism is caused by a factor passed down in the animal's genes.

Anal fin In fishes, the fin that lies along the underside of the body just behind the anus. The anal fin works with the fish's other fins in swimming, turning and balancing (see **Dorsal fin**; **Pectoral fin**; **Pelvic fin**)

Antenna Either of a pair of long, thin movable sense organs on the head of an insect or crustacean. Antennae are sometimes called "feelers" and are used for locating and identifying the animal's surroundings.

Barbel A thread-like organ of touch that grows from the lips or jaws of some fishes. In general, barbels serve the same purpose as **antennae**.

Binocular vision A kind of vision in which both eyes are used at the same time and move in the same direction.

Bivalve A mollusc, such as an oyster, cockle, mussel or clam, that has two hinged *valves*, or shells, each usually the mirror image of the other. When the valves are shut the body of the animal is completely enclosed. Under water, a bivalve opens its valves to feed. When it is stranded above the water line at low tide the valves close to prevent the animal's body from drying out.

Canine teeth In carnivorous mammals, the pair of teeth in the upper and lower jaw, behind the **incisors**. Canine teeth generally are long and pointed and are used for seizing hold of and piercing the prey.

Carapace Any skeletal shield on an animal's back. It can be the hard **chitinous** covering of some insects or crustaceans, the heavy structures of armadillos, or the bony structures of turtles and tortoises. These are covered with a horn-like material which gives the "shell" its pattern and colour.

Cartilage Sometimes called "gristle", cartilage forms the skeleton of the embryos of **vertebrates** and of the adults of a few groups such as sharks and rays. Cartilage, which is firm but flexible, also covers the joints between limb bones in most adult vertebrates and forms the discs between vertebrae in the spine.

Casque A bony shield on the upper surface of the head. In birds it may form the base of the bill, and give the apparance of a helmet on some species.

Cephalopod A member of one of the three largest classes of mollusc. Squids, octopuses and cuttlefishes are all cephalopods, a word meaning "head-foot'. Most cephalopods have a head with a sharp, horny beak and muscular tentacles around the mouth. Cephalopods are the only invertebrates to have an eye like that of vertebrates.

Chitin A tough, fibrous material present in **cuticle** which forms the **exoskeleton** of insects and crustaceans. It performs a similar role to bone in vertebrates, making the body rigid and protecting the internal organs.

Chordate A member of the phylum Chordata, which includes all the vertebrates. All chordates at some stage of their development have gill slits, a **notochord**, and a spinal nerve cord.

Chrysalis In the life cycle of butterflies and moths, the stage that occurs between the last larval stage and the adult. In the chrysalis stage the insect goes through a complicated **metamorphosis** before emerging as an adult. The term **pupa** is used to refer to the similar stage in flies, ants, bees, wasps and beetles.

Cilia Hair-like projections that cover the surfaces of certain animal cells. Their main function is to move fluids over the cell surface, which they do by moving together with a rhythmical beating motion in a constant direction. Single-cell animals called protozoa use cilia for swimming. Epithelial cells which line the nose and wind pipe use cilia to move fluid (mucus) that carries dust and germs away from the lungs.

Cocoon A silky or fibrous case which the larvae of certain insects spin round themselves to shelter them during the **pupa** stage. The cocoons of spiders, earthworms and leeches are produced to protect their eggs.

Cornicle A small, horn-like projection, as in the horns, or tentacles, on the head of a snail. Cornicles are used as sensory organs. Many land snails have two pairs of cornicles, with their eyes at the tips of the top pair.

Crinoid A word meaning "lily-shaped", used to refer to members of the class Crinoidea of sea animals, such as the sea lily and feather star, which resemble flowers.

Cuticle The tough outer covering of the bodies of many invertebrates such as insects and crustaceans. The cuticle is secreted by the epidermis underneath and may be coated with wax to prevent water loss.

Dorsal fin In fishes, the fin that lies along the spine on the upper side of the body. The dorsal fin works with the fish's other fins in swimming, turning and balancing. (See **Anal fin**; **Pectoral fin**; **Pelvic fin**)

Elytra The front pair of tough, thickened wings in beetles which act as a protective covering for the more delicate rear wings.

Exoskeleton The hard supporting structure on the outside of the body of an invertebrate. Its function is similar to that of the bone or cartilage *endoskeleton* inside a vertebrate. The material from which the exoskeleton is formed is secreted from the animal's body.

Flagella The tiny, whip-like parts of some bacteria and protozoans that are used to propel these organisms through their fluid surroundings. The word is also used to describe the thin, lash-like tips of the antennae in many insects.

Frenulum A tiny, stiff, bristle-like structure on the hind wing of some moths that locks into hooks on the front wing to link the wings together during flight.

Fry Newly-hatched young fish. Fry also sometimes refers to small adult fish, especially when they are in large groups.

Gall A thick swelling or tumour, produced by a plant in response to the presence of an insect or other creature on its tissues. The plant is not seriously harmed and the invading animal lives and feeds quite happily in the swelling until fully grown. Gall wasps are the best known of the gall causers.

Gestation period The period from conception to birth in mammals, which varies from a few weeks in animals such as mice to 22 months in the elephant, the longest gestation period of any animal.

Gizzard A part of the digestive tract, especially in birds, that is specialized for breaking down food. The walls of the gizzard are thick and muscular and the food is ground up for digestion by small stones and grit swallowed by the bird.

Grub The short, fat **larva** of some insects, especially beetles.

Herbivore The opposite of carnivore – that is, any animal that eats only plant material rather than flesh. Grazing animals such as horses, sheep and cattle are all herbivores. Animals that eat both plants and meat are called omnivores.

Hermaphrodite An animal with the sexual organs of both male and female. Some hermaphrodites, such as certain earthworms, can function as male and female at the same time, though they must mate with another individual. Others, such as prawns and limpets, are male at a certan stage in their lives and female at another (see **Intersexes**).

Hormone A chemical messenger produced in one part of the body, such as in the thyroid, adrenal and pituitary glands, which is transported to another part to stimulate activity, growth or reproduction or to regulate metabolism.

Hybrid An animal or plant that is the result of a cross-breeding between two distinct species. A mule, for example, is the result of a cross between a donkey (jackass) and a horse (mare). A mule, like most other animal hybrids, is sterile – that is, it cannot reproduce.

Incisor Any of the wide, chisel-like teeth between the **canines** in carnivores that are used for cutting rather than tearing or grinding. Herbivores such as rodents have especially large incisors for gnawing. Because they wear down quickly, rodents' incisors grow continuously from the roots.

Intersexes Certain species of animal that undergo sex reversal to change from male to female or vice versa. The sex of some frogs and crustaceans can be altered by changing the temperature of their surroundings. The European flat oyster can reverse its sex several times.

Invertebrate Any of the large group of animals without backbones. Of the million or more species of animal only about 42,000 are **vertebrates** (back-boned animals) – the rest are invertebrates. Sponges, jellyfish, worms, insects, crustaceans and molluscs are all invertebrates.

Keratin A tough, fibrous protein that forms the major part of hair, nails or claws, and horn in animals.

Larva A pre-adult stage in the development of many animals, especially insects. The larvae of animals look completely different from the adult and may go through several stages before reaching adulthood. For example, caterpillars are the larvae of moths and butterflies, maggots are the larvae of flies, and grubs are the larvae of certain beetles. In the same way a tadpole is the larval stage of a frog. Unlike the adults, the larval stages of the frog, mosquito and caddis fly live entirely in the water. Insect larvae go through a complete **metamorphosis** to become an adult (see **pupa**).

Mandible The lower jaw of vertebrates, or one of a pair of arthropod mouthparts.

Mantle The soft flap or folds of the body wall of a mollusc such as a mussel or clam. The mantle usually secretes the fluid from which the shell is formed.

Metabolism All the chemical changes going on in the cells of living organisms.

Metamorphosis A word meaning "transformation", used to refer to the change in form and structure during the development of some animals from the larval to the adult stage. In many insects metamorphosis takes place in the pupa or chrysalis, when the worm-like larva is transformed into an adult, winged insect. (See **Chrysalis**; **Larva**; **Pupa**)

Molar Any of the large, flat cheek teeth in mammals that are used for grinding and chewing food. Large herbivores such as horses and cows have very high, wide molars that can take a lot of wear before they are ground down. An elephant deals with wear in a different way. Each of its teeth is so long, wide and deep that it takes up one whole side of its jaw. As each tooth wears down it is shed and a new one moves down from the gums to replace it.

Moult To shed the skin, fur, feathers or other outer covering of the body. Animals such as snakes, insects and crustaceans shed their skin or **cuticle** as they grow in order to accommodate their larger body. Moulting in birds and mammals is often a seasonal occurrence which prepares them for the heat in summer. It also takes in young animals as they develop their adult plumage or coat.

Musk A substance with a strong, penetrating odour secreted from a gland by certain animals such as the male musk deer, musk rat, badger, etc. The odour is usually released during the breeding season.

Mutant An animal that does not conform in appearance or structure to the rest of its species because of a change, or mutation, in its genes. Most mutations, such as extra horns or toes, or different colouring, are disadvantageous to an animal. These mutations are eventually extinguished through natural selection. But some mutant genes become dominant when, for example, the animal's environment changes. One dramatic example of this is the peppered moth. Normally it is mottled grey to blend in with the lichens on the bark of trees where it rests. Occasionally a mutation takes place that produces a black moth which, easily seen by predators on the grey lichen, has little chance of surviving. But in industrial areas where pollution has killed the lichens on the trees and turned them black, the black mutant moth survives successfully.

New World A term used to describe animals that come from the western hemisphere. Animals native to the eastern hemisphere are described as **Old World**. For example, the New World monkeys of Central and South America have evolved to become noticeably different from their Old World relatives in Europe, Africa and Asia.

Notochord A primitive form of backbone present at some stage in the development of all **chordates**. In adult vertebrates it is replaced by the cartilage or bone that forms the spinal column. The function of the notochord is roughly the same as that of the spine – that is, to support the body and keep it rigid.

Nymph A stage in the development of certain insects such as grasshoppers and dragonflies. A nymph resembles the adult but is usually wingless. A dragonfly nymph with wing buds spends its early life in the water and then climbs up a plant stem into the air. It then sheds its skin and the fully adult dragonfly emerges.

Old World A term used to refer to animal species native to Europe, Asia or Africa to distinguish them from similar species of the **New World** – that is, North, Central and South America.

Operculum Any of a number of flaps or lid-like structures in plants or animals, such as the hard, bony covering that protects the gills of fishes, or the chalky plates that form the "lid" at the top of an acorn barnacle.

Opposable Capable of being applied so as to meet another part. In zoology the term is most often used to refer to the opposable thumb (and big toe) of primates which are capable of grasping and other complex movements.

Ovipositor A long, thin hollow organ at the end of the abdomen of some female insects used for depositing eggs in a suitable place, such as inside plant or animal tissue.

Ovum A Latin word meaning "egg", used to refer to the mature female germ cell of an animal which, if fertilized, develops into a new individual of the same species.

Parapodia Tiny limb-like projections on the bodies of segmented worms such as bristleworms, used for locomotion.

Parthenogenesis Reproduction through the development of an unfertilized ovum as in certain polyzoans and insects. Artificial parthenogenesis is the development of an ovum stimulated by chemical or mechanical means.

Pectoral fin In fishes, either of a pair of fins that lie on either side of the body just behind the head. The pectoral fins correspond to the forelimbs of a higher vertebrate and work with the fish's other fins in swimming, turning and balancing. (See **Anal fin**; **Dorsal fin**; **Pelvic fin**)

Pelvic fin In fishes, either of a pair of fins that lie on either side of the body in the pelvic region. The pelvic fins correspond to the hind limbs of higher vertebrates. (See **Anal fin**; **Dorsal fin**; **Pectoral fin**)

Photosynthesis The process by which green plants "manufacture" food from carbon dioxide and water in the presence of light, and with the help of the chlorophyll in their leaves.

Pigments Any colouring matter in the cells and tissues of plants or animals. One common animal pigment is melanin. This is a dark pigment that is present to a greater degree in, for example, the skin and hair of Negroes, and to a lesser degree in a Caucasian. Most mammals have hair pigmented by melanin. Even haemoglobin in the blood of vertebrates is a pigment, giving the blood its red colour. Another red pigment is cochineal, extracted from a scale insect and used for making dyes.

Placenta The structure that develops inside the uterus of a mammal during **gestation**. It is anchored to the wall of the uterus and is connected to the developing embryo by the **umbilical cord**. It is through the placenta that oxygen and nourishment are passed from the mother to the foetus. Wastes from the foetus pass through the placenta and into the mother's bloodstream. The placenta is discharged from the body shortly after birth.

Polyp Any of a group of sea animals in the phylum Coelenterata, such as the sea anemone and the hydra. They have a mouth fringed with many small tentacles bearing stinging cells, at the top of a tube-like body.

Preen gland An oil gland on the outside of a bird's body near the base of the tail. The gland secretes an oily substance which is squeezed out by the bird's bill as it preens, or cleans itself, and is distributed over the feathers. Water birds such as ducks have well developed preen glands and it is thought that oiling their feathers helps to waterproof them. Not all birds have preen glands.

Prehensile Adapted for seizing or grasping, as the tail of a monkey or the trunk of an elephant.

Primates The order of mammals that include, humans, apes, monkeys, bushbabies, pottos, lemurs and the tarsier. Primates have hands and feet with fingers and toes adapted for grasping, comparatively larger brains than other mammals and nails instead of claws.

Proboscis A tubular organ for sucking, food-gathering or sensing.

Both the elephant's trunk and the tapir's long, flexible snout are kinds of proboscis, as are the organs with similar functions of some insects, worms and molluscs.

Prolegs The short, fleshy limbs attached to the abdomens of certain insect larvae such as caterpillars. They are used for locomotion.

Protein Any of a large group of substances made up of a complex union of amino acids that occur in all animal and plant matter. Proteins are the most important chemical components of all living matter. They play an essential part in the structure and functioning of animals: enzymes, haemoglobin, many hormones, and antibodies are just some of the many different kinds of proteins necessary for life.

Pupa A stage in the development of many insects in which the worm-like **larva** is transformed into the adult form. When it enters the pupal stage, the larva ceases feeding and moving and often hides itself inside a **cocoon**. The pupa "rests" while complete **metamorphosis** takes place, and emerges from the cocoon or pupal case as an adult. The pupa of a butterfly is called a **chrysalis**.

Radula In most molluscs, a ribbon-like structure with rows of small teeth, or scrapers, that tear up food and take it into the mouth.

Respiration In animals, the process of taking in oxygen and releasing carbon dioxide, whether through the skin, or by means of lungs or gills. Respiration continues inside the body as each individual cell is fed with oxygen carried in the bloodstream from the lungs or gills as part of the energy-producing process.

Savanna A grassland, often with just a few, scattered trees, especially in tropical or sub-tropical areas that have seasonal rains. The savanna is a habitat for certain species of animal specially adapted to survive there.

Siphon A tubular organ in some animals used for the intake and output of water. Some burrowing **bivalve** molluscs use their siphons to draw in fresh sea water bearing food and oxygen. Cuttlefishes use their siphons, or funnels, like jets for locomotion. Water is ejected from the siphon with great force, so the animal is propelled along.

Snowline The boundary in altitude above which the temperature is so low all the year round that the snow never melts, as on the tops of high mountains.

Spinneret the organ in spiders and caterpillars with which they spin silky threads for webs or cocoons.

Swim bladder A gas-filled sac inside the body cavity of most bony fishes which gives them buoyancy in the water. Some fishes also use them for breathing. Sharks do not have a swim bladder.

Swimmeret Any of the small appendages on the abdomen of some crustaceans, such as lobsters and crayfish, used for swimming and for carrying eggs.

Thorax In insects, the middle segment of the three main segments — head, thorax, **abdomen** — of the body. In higher vertebrates, the thorax is the chest, the part of the body between the neck and the abdomen, containing the heart and lungs.

Tree line The line above or beyond which trees do not grow, as on high mountains or in polar regions.

Tundra The vast, treeless plains of arctic regions. Most of the tundra is in the Arctic Circle. In winter the tundra is snow-covered. Even in summer the temperature is near freezing and only tough mosses, lichens and dwarfed plants grow. These support animals adapted to the harsh climate.

Umbilical cord A tough, cable-like structure that connects a foetus (at the navel) with the **placenta**. All nutrients and oxygen pass through the umbilical cord to the growing foetus, as does waste from the foetus to the mother's bloodstream. At birth, when the newborn's own circulatory and respiratory systems take over, the umbilical cord is severed. Any remaining portion soon dries up and falls off.

Ungulate A term that means "having hoofs", used to describe the group of hoofed mammals that includes cows, horses, deer, goats, pigs, camels etc.

Valve The shell of a mollusc. In **bivalve** molluscs the shell has two parts, such as that of a mussel or clam. The word valve is also used in anatomy to describe a membraneous fold or structure that permits body fluids to flow in one direction only, such as in the heart or blood vessels. A valve may also open or close a tube or opening.

Vertebrate Any of the group of **chordate** animals with segmented backbones — the opposite of an **invertebrate.** All mammals, fishes, birds, reptiles and amphibians are vertebrates.

Wattle A fleshy, wrinkled piece of skin that hangs from the chin or throat of certain birds, such as the turkey or cockerel, or from some lizards.

ALTERNATIVE NAMES
AND ADDITIONAL CROSS-REFERENCES

A
African Wild Dog *see* Cape Hunting Dog
Amazon *see* Parrot
Andean Bear *see* Spectacled Bear
Apara *see* Armadillo
Armoured Sea-robin *see* Gurnard
Army Worm *see* Noctuid Moth
Arum Frog *see* Reed Frog

B
Bamboo Rat *see* Mole Rat
Banded Ant-Eater *see* Numbat
Barbary Stag *see* Red Deer
Barking Deer *see* Muntjac
Bearded Vulture *see* Lammergeier
Bell Toad *see* Midwife Toad
Bengalese Finch *see* Mannikin
Bezoar *see* Ibex
Bilby *see* Bandicoot
Blackfly *see* Aphid
Black Panther *see* Leopard
Bloody-nosed Beetle *see* Leaf Beetle
Blue bottle *see* Blow-fly
Blue Monkey *see* Guenon
Bobak *see* Marmot
Book Scorpion *see* False Scorpion
Burbot *see* Ling
Butcherbird *see* Shrike

C
Cabezon *see* Sculpin
Cake Urchin *see* Sand Dollar
Camberwell Beauty *see* Vanessid Butterfly
Camel Spider *see* Solifugid
Carpet Shark *see* Wobbegong
Cat-bear *see* Red Panda
Cavie *see* Guinea Pig
Chickadee *see* Tit
Chital *see* Axis Deer
Clownfish *see* Damsel Fish
Cockatiel *see* Cockatoo
Colies *see* Mousebird
Comma *see* Vanessid Butterfly
Crab-eating monkey *see* Macaque
Crawfish *see* Spiny Lobster
Cross Spider *see* Orb Spider
Cutworm *see* Noctuid Moth

D
Dabchick *see* Grebe
Damsel Fly *see* Dragonfly
Demoiselle *see* Damselfish
Desert Rat *see* Jerboa
Diadem Spider *see* Orb Spider

Drill *see* Mandrill
Driver Ant *see* Army Ant
Drone-fly *see* Hoverfly
Dublin Prawn *see* Lobster
Duckbill *see* Platypus
Dugong *see* Sea Cow
Dunnock *see* Accentor
Dustlice *see* Booklice
Dwarf Buffalo *see* Anoa

E
Eared Seal *see* Fur Seal
Eared Seal *see* Sea Lion
Earthcreeper *see* Ovenbird
Echidna *see* Spiny Ant-eater
Edible Snail *see* Roman Snail
Eel-pout *see* Ling
Elk *see* Moose
Elk *see* Red Deer
Euro *see* Kangaroo

F
Feral Pigeon *see* Rock Dove
Ferret *see* Polecat
Finback Whale *see* Rorqual
Firecrest *see* Goldcrest
Fire-fox *see* Red Panda
Fisher *see* Marten
Fish-hawk *see* Osprey
Flea Beetle *see* Leaf Beetle
Flying Gurnard *see* Flying Fish
Fox-cat *see* Red Panda

G
Galago *see* Bushbaby
Galah *see* Cockatoo
Gang-gang *see* Cockatoo
Garfish *see* Needlefish
Gayol *see* Gaur
Gemsbok *see* Oryx
Giraffe-necked gazelle *see* Gerenuk
Glutton *see* Wolverine
Goosander *see* Merganser
Grampus *see* Killer whale
Great Auk *see* Little Auk
Great White Heron *see* Egret
Greenbottle *see* Blow-fly
Greenfly *see* Aphid
Green Monkey *see* Vervet Monkey
Green Plover *see* Lapwing
Greylag Goose *see* Goose
Grizzly Bear *see* Brown Bear
Grosbeak *see* Hawfinch
Gymnosome *see* Sea Butterfly

H
Hairy Hedgehog *see* Gymnure

Hamadryas *see* Baboon
Harvest Spider *see* Harvestman
Hedge-sparrow *see* Accentor
Henfish *see* Lampsucker
Himalayan Raccoon *see* Red Panda
Hog Deer *see* Axis Deer
Honeybear *see* Kinkajou
Horse Mackerel *see* Scad
Horned Rattlesnake *see* Sidewider
Horntail *see* Sawfly
Horseshoe crab *see* King Crab
Hydroid *see* Sea-fir

I
Inchworm *see* Geometer Moth
Indian Antelope *see* Blackbuck

J
Jabiru *see* Stork
Jack *see* Scad
Jaeger *see* Skua
Java Sparrow *see* Mannikin
Jewel Thrush *see* Pitta

K
Katydid *see* Bush-cricket
Kodiak Bear *see* Brown Bear
Kokako *see* Wattlebird

L
Lampern *see* Lamprey
Laughing Jackass *see* Kookaburra
Leatherhead *see* Honeyeater
Leatherjacket *see* Crane-fly
Lechwe *see* Antelope
Legionary Ant *see* Army Ant
Lily-trotter *see* Jacana
Loon *see* Diver
Looper *see* Geometer Moth
Lotus-bird *see* Jacana

M
Manatee *see* Sea Cow
Maneater Shark *see* Great White Shark
Man-o'war Bird *see* Frigatebird
Manta Ray *see* Devil Fish
Marbled White Butterfly *see* Brown Butterfly
Marsupial Anteater *see* Numbat
May-bug *see* Cockchafer
Mealy Bug *see* Scale Insect
Meercat *see* Suricate
Milkweed Butterfly *see* Monarch Butterfly
Miner *see* Ovenbird
Mithan *see* Gaur

Moon-rat *see* Gymnure
Mother Careys Chicken *see* Storm
  Petrel
Mourning Cloak *see* Vanessid
  Butterfly
Mouse-hare *see* Pika
Murre *see* Guillemot
Mustang *see* Horse
Muttonbird *see* Shearwater

N
Ne-ne *see* Hawaiian Goose
Night Monkey *see* Douroucouli

O
O-o-aa *see* Honeyeater
Otter-cat *see* Jaguarundi
Owl Monkey *see* Douroucouli
Owlet Moth *see* Noctuid Moth

P
Painted Lady *see* Vanessid Butterfly
Panther *see* Leopard
Parakeet *see* Parrakeet
Peacock *see* Peafowl
Peacock Butterfly *see* Vanessid
  Butterfly
Peewit *see* Lapwing
Pigeon *see* Dove
Pigeon *see* Rock Dove
Pigeon Hawk *see* Merlin
Plant-lice *see* Aphid
Pollock *see* Coalfish
Possum *see* Phalanger
Prairie Wolf *see* Coyote
Praying Mantis *see* Mantis
Przewalski's Horse *see* Horse
Puku *see* Kob

Q
Quoll *see* Dasyure

R
Rainbow Fish *see* Guppy
Ratel *see* Honey Badger
Red Admiral *see* Vanessid Butterfly
Red-tailed Monkey *see* Guenon

Ribbonfish *see* Oarfish
Rock-borer *see* Piddock
Rock Coney *see* Pika
Rock Rabbit *see* Pika

S
Saithe *see* Coalfish
Salp *see* Sea Squirt
Sand Rat *see* Gerbil
Sardine *see* Pilchard
Sawbill *see* Merganser
Scaly Anteater *see* Pangolin
Scampi *see* Lobster
Scrub Wallaby *see* Pademelon
Sea Biscuit *see* Sand Dollar
Sexton Beetle *see* Burying Beetle
Shag *see* Cormorant
Shaketail *see* Ovenbird
Short-tailed Weasel *see* Stoat
Siamang *see* Gibbon
Siamese Fighting Fish *see* Fighting
  Fish
Sitatunga *see* Nyah
Snowshoe rabbit *see* Hare
Soapfish *see* Grouper
Spanish Fly *see* Blister Beetle
Spice Finch *see* Mannikin
Spinebill *see* Honeyeater
Spotted Cavy *see* Paca
Stink Bug *see* Shield Bug
Stout *see* Horsefly
Sunfish *see* Ocean Sunfish
Sunspider *see* Solifugid

T
Tamandua *see* Anteater
Tatler *see* Sandpiper
Terrapin *see* Tortoises and Turtles
Thecosome *see* Sea Butterfly
Thorny Devil *see* Moloch
Thylacine *see* Tasmanian Wolf
Tickbird *see* Oxpecker
Tiddler *see* Stickleback
Tieke *see* Wattlebird
Titmouse *see* Tit
Tizi *see* Bush-cricket
Torpedo *see* Electric Ray

Tortoise Beetle *see* Leaf Beetle
Tortoiseshell Butterfly *see* Vanessid
  Butterfly
Trader Rat *see* Pack Rat
Tree Fox *see* Grey Fox
Tumblebug *see* Scarab Beetle
Tunnel-web Spider *see* Sheetweb
  Spider
Tunny *see* Tuna
Tur *see* Ibex
Turtle *see* Tortoises and Turtles

W
Walking Stick *see* Stick Insect
Wallaroo *see* Kangaroo
Waller's Gazelle *see* Gerenuk
Wapiti *see* Red Deer
Water Boa *see* Anaconda
Water Buffalo *see* Indian Buffalo
Wels *see* Catfish
Western Native Cat *see* Dasyure
Wheel Animalcule *see* Rotifer
Whistling Duck *see* Tree Duck
Whistling Hare *see* Pika
White curlew *see* Ibis
White Death Spider *see* Crab
  Spider
White Whale *see* Beluga
Whooping Crane *see* Crane
Widow-bird *see* Whydah
Wigeon *see* Duck
Wildebeest *see* Gnu
Wind Scorpion *see* Solifugid
Winkle *see* Periwinkle
Wireworm *see* Click Beetle
Wisent *see* Bison
Wood Rat *see* Pack Rat
Wood Wasp *see* Sawfly
Woodworm *see* Furniture Beetle
Worm Lizards *see* Amphisbaena
Wreckfish *see* Bass

Y
Yellowjacket *see* Wasp

Z
Zebra Antelope *see* Duiker

INDEX

Page numbers in *italics* refer to illustrations.